WILLIAM F. CHRISTOPHER
Holistic Management: Managing What Matters for Company Success

WILLIAM B. ROUSE
People and Organizations: Explorations of Human-Centered Design

HOLISTIC MANAGEMENT

THE WILEY BICENTENNIAL—KNOWLEDGE FOR GENERATIONS

*E*ach generation has its unique needs and aspirations. When Charles Wiley first opened his small printing shop in lower Manhattan in 1807, it was a generation of boundless potential searching for an identity. And we were there, helping to define a new American literary tradition. Over half a century later, in the midst of the Second Industrial Revolution, it was a generation focused on building the future. Once again, we were there, supplying the critical scientific, technical, and engineering knowledge that helped frame the world. Throughout the 20th Century, and into the new millennium, nations began to reach out beyond their own borders and a new international community was born. Wiley was there, expanding its operations around the world to enable a global exchange of ideas, opinions, and know-how.

For 200 years, Wiley has been an integral part of each generation's journey, enabling the flow of information and understanding necessary to meet their needs and fulfill their aspirations. Today, bold new technologies are changing the way we live and learn. Wiley will be there, providing you the must-have knowledge you need to imagine new worlds, new possibilities, and new opportunities.

Generations come and go, but you can always count on Wiley to provide you the knowledge you need, when and where you need it!

WILLIAM J. PESCE
PRESIDENT AND CHIEF EXECUTIVE OFFICER

PETER BOOTH WILEY
CHAIRMAN OF THE BOARD

HOLISTIC MANAGEMENT
Managing What Matters for Company Success

WILLIAM F. CHRISTOPHER

WILEY-INTERSCIENCE
A John Wiley & Sons, Inc., Publication

Published by John Wiley & Sons, Inc., Hoboken, New Jersey
Published simultaneously in Canada

For general information on our other products and services or for technical support, please contact our Customer Care Department within the United States at (800) 762-2974, outside the United States at (317) 572-3993 or fax (317) 572-4002.

Wiley also publishes its books in a variety of electronic formats. Some content that appears in print may not be available in electronic formats. For more information about Wiley products, visit our web site at www.wiley.com.

Wiley Bicentennial logo: Richard J. Pacifico

Library of Congress Cataloging-in-Publication Data:

Christopher, William F.
   Holistic management: managing what matters for company success / by
William F. Christopher.
      p.   cm.
   Includes bibliographical references and index.
   ISBN-13: 978-0-471-74063-6
      1. Organizational effectiveness.   2. Management.   3. Leadership.   4. Industrail
productivity.   I. Title.
   HD58.9.C498 2007
   658.4′012—dc22
                                                                2006050390

When it comes to managing affairs, we characteristically try to deal with that dismantled system—piece by piece—rather that to redesign the totality so that it actually works.
Stafford Beer, *Platform for Change*, John Wiley & Sons, 1975

Objectives are needed in every area where performance and results directly and vitally affect the survival and prosperity of the business.
Peter Drucker, *The Practice of Management*, Harper & Row, 1954

To all those working with the application of system science and cybernetics in the management of business enterprise, and to all those seeking the keys to success and sustainability for their companies.

Contents

Foreword

This challenging and exciting book, written by my mentor Bill Christopher, presents two fundamental management concepts hat will be new for many readers. First, the book presents what we have learned from system science and cybernetics that changes and improves the way we manage the company. Second, the book presents best practices in the key performance areas defined by Peter Drucker that improve the level of organization capability and performance results for any business enterprise.

You will discover in this book the new system science and cybernetics for managing business operations clearly explained in full detail. A chapter for each of the key performance areas gives the reader the basic and fundamental knowledge needed to manage these areas successfully. Both concepts—systems, and key performance areas—will generate in the reader a tremendous synergetic effect . . . for the reader, for the reader's team, and consequently for the company. This outstanding publication will greatly contribute to excellence in developing superior leadership.

From this book we learn key ingredients to simplify and achieve personal targets, with this good work and spirit contributing also to the company goals in the fundamental key performance areas described by Peter Drucker as the areas that determine company success. This book teaches us how to increase the company's greatest asset, the organization's intellectual capability, it's "Collective IQ." The company's people and their capability is the company's greatest value, even if this asset is ignored in the company's balance sheet.

I encourage business people to study this book. They will see that this publication is an essential tool for success whether they run their own business or work at any level of a large corporation.

Throughout his career, Bill Christopher, always positively minded in trying to help people, has been practically involved in difficult, real business problems. Working together with management teams in many different companies, Bill uses the knowledge that's in this book, and his personal business acumen, experience, and common sense. The team uses its practical and specific knowledge of their business. Together, they always find solutions to all problems.

I am only one of many business people who have taken the challenging opportunity to apply the recommendations given in Bill's numerous books written over his career and in seminars, brainstorming, and our meetings. Certainly, my success in my business career is largely due to Bill Christopher and the management fundamentals described in this book. I have continuously applied these fundamentals with my international team to reach business goals and key target account objectives.

The key players in my team of five people of different nationalities and origins, working smartly together with a good attitude and spirit, are Georges Matile and George A. Zarb. This team has been successfully operating for more than 30 years in putting into practice the management concepts and business strategy of Bill Christopher, setting and achieving objectives in the seven key performance areas.

Concrete results sum up as follows: Our team has first been operating with positive results in expanding our core business (automatic equipment for precious metal plating) in all major European countries. Then we created new enterprises in microcomputer technology to expand and diversify from our main business. We made one of the first industrial applications of the Intel 4 bits microprocessor 4004 in 1971, and created a set of microcomputerized nautical instruments for racing sailing boats which prepared the ground for Switzerland to win the America's Cup in 2001. Then we expanded our core business in Asia. We made a first jount-venture in Japan, then built a factory in Singapore, then in Batam (island of Indonesia), then Hong Kong, and then we built a factory with our Hong Kong partner in China. Thanks to Bill Christopher's concepts of management and global business knowledge, when we sold our company in 2003, we had customers in more than 50 countries. Most of our customers, such as Intel, GE Aeronautics, HP, Siemens, Swatch, Rolex, and Patek Philippe, were in high-technology fields. Bill Christopher's ways of making a company globally more successful are also applied today in new companies operating with both present and tomorrow's technologies.

I could mention many successful business enterprises that operate today according to these principles. Two personal examples I would like to mention briefly; the cases of my two sons who are currently applying with success the fundamentals of management described in Bill's book. Each of them is operating in different directions of human activities: one in art, the other in the top-end of business aviation.

Fred, 32 years old, is an artist leading a technological team to develop a new process for painters and sculptors using industrial equipment. This new process will allow painters to produce paintings that can be displayed outdoors year-round, exposed to sand, sea, and snow, over a temperature range of minus 40° to plus 40° Celsius. This art project is using the fundamentals of management described in this book to develop and provide this process to artists worldwide.

My other son, Mike, 37 years old, is Founder and Chairman of Global Jet Concept, a leading European company in the high end of corporate business aviation. His company manages and operates a fleet of more than 50 aircraft from major manufacturers (Airbus, Boeing, Bombardier, Gulfstream, Dassault). Instead of going to university for his advanced education, Mike went straight into practice in luxury service industries, first with Hilton Hotels, Geneva, then Aeroleasing, where he became director of sales and marketing for Europe. After this company was acquired by TAG Aviation, Mike formed Global Jet Concept, receiving from me the fundamentals of business that I learned from Bill Christopher.

Much of what I do now is in the movie and entertainment industry. I find that the management principles described in this book are also very much needed in this Industry.

Consequently I can affirm that this book is unmatchable in its synthesis of new and traditional bases of management. It is useful for everyone: young as well as senior managers operating in the full spectrum of life activities.

For industry professionals planning the future, the contents in this book will be a contributor for reshaping their business models and company activities to meet the evolving needs in the fast-coming, booming Digital Mobile Business (DMB).

After reading Bill Christopher's masterpiece of a book, you will keep changing and challenging all the time. Good answers don't last forever. But what is presented in this book, the fundamentals, endure. Methods, tools, and technologies continuously evolve. Although technological tools available drastically change, the fundamentals of management found in system science and key performance areas will remain.

To conclude, I would like to state that you will learn and discover in this challenging book all the ingredients to become yourself a high achiever and a successful decision-maker. You will also be able to relax away from your working life. Your company and your private life will both benefit.

Thank you, Bill, for all you have done in guiding and helping us lead successfully our multinational corporation. And fruitful reading and pleasant rewards for your readers.

Lausanne, Switzerland   Antoine D. Savary
July, 2006

Preface

This book presents two recently developed knowledge areas that can significantly improve the management and the performance of business enterprise: system science and cybernetics, and the key performance areas that determine company success.

The principles discovered in system science and cybernetics are embedded in Stafford Beer's Viable System Model (VSM) presented in this book. This model and the principles it represents give us a new way to structure and manage the company. The VSM structure and management more realistically describes what the company is and how it works than does the conventional view of the management hierarchy. Stafford Beer was a leading pioneer in the applications of system science and cybernetics in government, business, and other organizations. He developed the VSM to communicate this new understanding of what our organizations are and how they work. This book presents the VSM and its system science and cybernetics and how this new knowledge improves organization capability and performance results. Chapters 1, 2, and 3 discuss system science, the VSM, and their applications in business enterprise.

The prevailing view of company success is the size of the profit number. But not enough is understood about where profit comes from. Profit is not what the company does. Profit is a result from what the company does, if the company does what it does well. What the company does is create and keep customers in ways that enable the achievement of all company goals. In 1954 Peter Drucker wrote in *The Practice of*

Management that eight key performance areas determine success for all companies: market standing, innovation, productivity, physical and financial resources, profitability, manager performance and development, worker performance and attitude, and public responsibility.

For over 40 years I have studied these areas, worked in these areas, and participated in professional societies working in these areas searching for best practices, the newest and best methods and technologies. In the companies I worked for, we included goals in these key performance areas in plans and budgets, and monitored progress with new and different kinds of performance measures.

Instead of accounting measures to measure and improve profitability, we used "management economics" measures, pioneered by Joel Dean, professor at Columbia University. And we used management economics also for the dollar measures in the other key performance areas. Where there were profit problems, the management groups in those businesses were able to improve profitability and achieve desired goals using management economics concepts and measures.

In 1976, working with Stafford Beer in applying the VSM and its system science in the corporation I then worked for was a eureka moment for me. The VSM teaches us how to structure and how to manage the company using the discoveries of system science. Best methods and technologies in the key performance areas teach us how to be successful in all those areas that determine company success, including profitability. The VSM teaches us how to structure and how to manage. Best practices in the key performance areas teach us what to manage, and gives us the needed methods and tools.

This book presents this new, different, superior leadership strategy: the VSM and system science for structuring and managing the company, plus best practices in the key performance areas that determine company success.

The VSM and system science gives a new, realistic way to see and understand what our company is, and how it works, and a new way to manage this viable, immensely complex, purposeful, probabilistic enterprise. The new concepts, the new understanding of what the company is and how it works, derive from more than 50 years of discoveries in this new, integrating science, general system science and cybernetics.

General system science gives us a holistic understanding of science, nature, and our human systems, including the system that is our business enterprise. From system science and cybernetics we learn some fundamental principles for the effective structure and control of business operations. We also learn how to include in structure a capability for change, innovation, and growth. This book is written specifically for business management. The principles and the methods apply equally well for management in government, nonprofits, NGOs, and organizations of all kinds.

System science had its beginnings in the mid-twentieth century. As knowledge in the many disciplines of science accumulated and more and more interrelated, scientists began to search for a more complete understanding at a higher level. They found this understanding in general system theory and cybernetics. Disciplines enable specialization. Specialization loses synthesis. We specialize in the parts and lose an understanding of the whole. The VSM and its system science and cybernetics teach us how to manage the whole to better manage all of the parts.

In recent years, Stafford Beer has applied the VSM and its system science and system thinking in organizations of all kinds, including both government and private sector organizations, and especially corporations. Beer is preeminent among scholars and practitioners of system science and cybernetics applied in business management. His Viable System Model, and the system science and cybernetics embedded in it, enable us to see with new eyes, and manage in new ways, to make our organizations more successful, and more enduring.

In times of turmoil, information on what's happening fits less and less with our models and our prevailing perceptions. Dissonance increases. Then suddenly, and quite unexpected, comes a simplifying revelation, restoring order at a higher level of understanding. Scientific revolutions provide examples. $E = mc^2$ explains more and predicts more than all the accumulated literature of classical mechanics. System thinking and Beer's Viable System Model explains more and enables us to predict more than all the literature of traditional business management. With system thinking and this Viable System Model we understand our company in a new, and different, and simpler, and more realistic way. And we greatly improve company performance.

System thinking and the viable system model give us a holistic view of how everything fits together and how everything works and relates. A system, including a company when understood as a system, is much more than the sum of its parts. A business system exists for a purpose—creating value for customers in ways that enable the company to achieve its other goals, too. This book presents technologies and methods needed to achieve company goals in all the key performance areas that determine company success. The viable system model's structure and management principles make these technologies and methods effective throughout the company to create company success.

Included in this book are advanced (and evolving) methods and technologies for planning and budgeting, creating and keeping customers, quality and productivity, innovation, improving organization capability, sustainability in the company's social and ecological environments, and profitability—all integrated with this new viable systems model and system thinking.

My friendship with Stafford Beer began in November 1976. In the spring of 1976, Paul Rubinyi and I were on the same speaker program at a conference in Cleveland, Ohio, USA. Paul was systems partner for Ernst & Ernst in Montreal, Canada, and in his speech was advocating the VSM and its system science as a new and better way to manage business enterprise. In the work we were each doing, we found much in common. At that time I was director of marketing in a $4 billion manufacturing company, and also had the unique responsibility for working with company businesses that had special problems. Typically these special problems were profit problems, which, of course, were a consequence of what were the real problems. Working with the people in those businesses and using their knowledge of their business operations, we were always able to resolve the problems and improve performance. Solutions were always found in change and improvement in whichever of Drucker's key performance areas were the source of the problem.

Paul had recently engaged Stafford Beer to work with him at Ernst & Ernst. Paul suggested that he could arrange for Stafford to work with management people from my company in using the VSM and its system science to improve company performance. Paul also recommended Stafford's books and I read three of these books, as Paul and I kept in touch over the following weeks. It worked out that a learning session was scheduled with Stafford for three days, in November 1976.

My work with the management groups in company businesses to improve profitability related well with the system science in the Viable System Model. In Drucker's key performance areas we used new and different management methods and technologies. We used new and different performance measures and a new structure of information and feedback, many derived from the existing chart of accounts. We determined the economics of company operations and usually found solutions more in operations improvement, product development, and marketing and sales than in cost reduction. We used management economics measures calculated from the chart of accounts, rather than the traditional accounting measures calculated from the chart of accounts.

By the time of our session with Stafford in 1976, I had worked with dozens of businesses in fourteen countries and had a lot of experience with new and better management practices in Drucker's key performance areas that determine company success.

With this background, my work with Stafford and Paul was a revelation. Here was a way to see a company as a viable, very complex, purposeful, probabilistic system; what it is, how it works. The work I had been doing with new and better management practices in the key performance areas integrates well into the VSM way of structuring and managing the company. The VSM and best practices in the key performance areas that determine company success combine to offer a compelling strategy for company leadership—The VSM and system science plus best practices in the key performance areas. The constant is the VSM and system science. The best practices, the methods and technologies in the key performance areas, continually evolve, while their fundamentals endure.

Over the last 30 years I have been working with the VSM and best practices in the key performance areas, always with success. I did not discover the system science and the new and better methods and technologies in the key performance areas presented in this book. I learned them from others, and in using them over the years developed further what I had learned. Lessons learned are presented in this book.

To understand the VSM and system science, begin by reading the first three chapters of this book. Chapter 1 discusses the idea of "systems" and system thinking, and what general system theory has discovered about the way systems behave that is useful in the structure and management of businesses. Chapter 2 presents Stafford Beer's Viable System Model as a model for all systems, including the viable, very complex, purposeful, probabilistic system that is a modern corporation. We see the corporate VSM and the systems 5, 4, 3, 2, and 1 within the corporate VSM and their functions. We see the recursive nature of company structure with all business units also described by the VSM. We see and understand a new company structure, and new management principles. We see communication channels and the information flow and feedback that moves all actions toward the achievement of company goals. We include the outside environments as part of company structure.

The five case examples in chapter 3 tell the stories of application experience using the VSM to change and improve performance. Chapter 4 introduces seven key performance areas that determine every company's success. Chapters 5 through 11 discuss "best practices" management methods and technologies, and performance measures in these key performance areas:

Chapter 5. The Viable System Model and Planning and Budgeting. This chapter proposes continuous plans and continuous budgets. Continuous planning and budgeting of what matters for company success is now possible using the methods described in this book, and much more effective than annual budgets and the analysis of variances.

Chapter 6. The Viable System Model and Creating and Keeping Customers. The purpose of every company is to create and keep customers, in ways that enable the company to achieve desired goals.

Chapter 7. The Viable System Model and Quality and Productivity. Creating and keeping customers requires quality products and services, and continuous improvement in all that the company does.

Chapter 8. The Viable System Model and Innovation. Innovating the new, different, better creates the company's future, short-range and long-range.

Chapter 9. The Viable System Model and Organization Capability. The company is its people. Their effectiveness in these key performance areas determines company success. The VSM structure and management principles continuously develop organization capability.

Chapter 10. The Viable System Model and Public and Environmental Responsibility. The company must relate successfully to communities, governments, and its environments. The VSM includes these environments and the company's communication links with these environments.

Chapter 11. The Viable System Model and Profitability. Profit results from all the above. Profit pays the costs of creating the company's future, and rewards investors.

Chapters 5 to 11 also explain how the VSM company structure and management methods make the best practices presented in these chapters more effective in achieving desired results in these key performance areas.

This book presents new and useful management knowledge; knowledge that can immensely improve company performance. And this knowledge can be learned and applied quickly. Learning and applying the VSM becomes an experience in rapid knowledge transfer, the new discipline defined as the discovery, learning, and reuse of knowledge, adding to the organization's intellectual capital. I have found that a few days working with management groups can impart a beginning understanding of the VSM and system science. In a week a management group can discover where improvement in the key performance areas is needed and how to go about it.

Among those I'm indebted to for what you read in this book I would especially like to recognize and to thank:

Peter Drucker, for getting me involved in the key performance areas that determine company success, for his many books on management, and for the experience of working with him when he contributed two chapters to my Handbook for Productivity Measurement and Improvement.

Joel Dean, from whom I learned managerial economics at Columbia University. I've used these economics successfully in many profit improvement projects.

John W. Kendrick, for his pioneering work in productivity measurement and the opportunity to work with him in measuring manufacturing plant productivity.

Rensis Likert, University of Michigan, for his pioneering work in participative management, which became a part of my experience in applying the VSM, system thinking, and best management practices.

John Drake and Saul Gellerman, for their work on motivation and our work together in applying this learning in business operations.

Norman Bodek, for first publishing in English the work of the Japanese pioneers in total quality management and the Toyota Production System, for publishing the Christopher and Thor *Handbook for Productivity Measurement and Improvement*, and for the projects we worked on together.

Carl G. Thor, my colleague and co-author in productivity measurement and improvement, for that, and for our recent work on the measuring and management of outcomes.

F. D. "Derm" Barrett, scholar and management authority, for his writings on organization development and innovation, and for his wise counsel.

Theodore Levitt, Harvard University, for his ideas on marketing, innovation, and creating customers; and our collaboration in applying these ideas in the business I worked for.

Howard "Hap" Berrian, for his work on effective salesmanship and the work we did together applying best practices in sales management and sales, and in the training and development of sales and marketing people.

David McClelland, Harvard University, for his pioneering work on achievement motivation and power motivation which we applied in many business operations.

Douglas McGregor, for his work in behavioral science and his "Theory X, Theory Y" concept. The VSM requires the assumptions of Theory Y.

Frederick Herzberg for his work on motivation from the work itself.

And—most of all—Stafford Beer and Paul Rubinyi, who opened to me the door to understanding and using system thinking and Stafford's Viable System Model.

In addition, I would like to express my great appreciation to those business leaders who applied what is described in this book in their companies and created greater business success, especially: René Rochat and Antoine Savary in Switzerland; Gabriel Hevesi in Brazil; Pablo Weinberg in Argentina; Victor Eraña in Mexico; Nicholas de Zubiría in Colombia; Dennis Weimer, John Carder, and Tony Eyles in England; John McLaughlin in Canada; John Halls in Australia; and Frank Hendricks, Jim Simpson, Bill Wetzel, and John Lenahan in the United States.

Think about what you read in this book. It's real. It works.

Walnut Creek, California, USA   Bill Christopher
November 2006
billtmig@astound.net

Contributors List for Chapter 3

Developing a Viable Organization: The Crucial Role of the Meta-System

Markus Schwaninger
Professor of Management
University of St. Gallen
CH-9000 St. Gallen, Switzerland
markus.schwaninger@unisg.ch

How the VSM Helped Transform a Manufacturing Company in Crisis

Patrick Hoverstadt
23 Birchbrook Road
Lymm, Cheshire, WA13 9SA
UK
Patrick@Fractal-consulting.com

The MX Corporation

William F. Christopher
410 Sutcliffe Place
Walnut Creek, CA 94598-3924. USA
billtmig@astound.net

Applying the VSM in the Strategic Management of A Coruña University in Galicia, Spain

José Pérez Ríos, Ph.D.   Xosé L. Martínez Suárez, Ph.D.
Professor of Business Organization
Universidad de Valladolid
Campus Miguel Debiles
47011 Valladolid, Spain
rios@uva.es

Using the VSM to Design a Non-Viable System: The Case of the Social Security System for Teachers in Colombia

Alfonso Reyes A.
Department of Industrial Engineering
Universidad de los Andes
Bogota, Colombia
areyes@uniandes.edu.co

Chapter **1**

From System Science—A New Way to Structure and Manage the Company

Over the post World War II years of the 20th century business success depended mostly on variables business people could get their hands on, understand, and manage reasonably well. "Out there" were opportunities, and the world provided resources to transform into product and service values to develop those opportunities. Environmental antennas were tuned to market needs, technology, and competitive actions, increasingly global. All these provided a flow of information and resources that spurred great economic growth. From 1950 to 2000 world population increased from 2.5 billion to 6.0 billion, up 140%. Over those same 50 years, global economic output (in 2001 dollars) increased from $7 trillion to $46 trillion, up 557% [1]. These trends, and where they are going, change everything.

A TIME FOR CHANGE

Over the later years of the century new and different environmental influences developed; accumulated. What we could control became less and less the key to success, and change "out there" more and more important. In all dimensions, the world changes, kaleidoscopically, and

Holistic Management, by William Christopher
Copyright © 2007 John Wiley & Sons, Inc., Publication

fast. This new world of challenge and change presents both threats, and opportunities. For the timid change is frightening; for the satisfied change is threatening; for the confident change is opportunity.

For the wise, their guide for the times ahead will be system science, cybernetics, and a viable system model (VSM) for organization structure and management. For the turbulent times ahead, the VSM with its system science and cybernetics gives us a new and different view of our company and how it works, and gives us new management principles that greatly improve company performance.

Everything in our experience can be thought of in systems terms. Nothing stands, or happens, on its own, in natural systems, and in the system that is our company. Everything relates and interacts within a system, and in relationships with other systems, and it is the system and these interacting relationships we need to understand and manage. As Stafford Beer wrote [2]:

> It is characteristic of man's way of thinking to contemplate entities rather than systems: to disconnect systems rather than to relate their parts; to record inputs and outputs to systems rather than to measure systemic behaviour itself. When it comes to managing affairs, we characteristically try to deal with the dismantled system—piece by piece—rather than to redesign the totality so that it actually works.

The VSM with its system science and cybernetics gives us a way to understand the totality of our company and how it works, and gives us better ways to structure and manage the system that is our company.

With the VSM and system science we see the company with new eyes, and manage in new ways. Figure 1.1 illustrates a simplified system model of a company. This model will be developed in more detail in Chapter 2. A system model is much different from the typical organization chart. The system model doesn't show people and titles. It shows functions and relationships. It includes the environment outside the company. It includes communication channels and specifies information flow. Stafford Beer, a pioneer in the application of system science and cybernetics in management, developed the system model presented in this book, the Viable System Model (VSM).

SYSTEM SCIENCE AND THE VIABLE SYSTEM MODEL (VSM)

Over the years, the hard sciences and the soft sciences developed in an increasing number of separate disciplines. As we learned more and

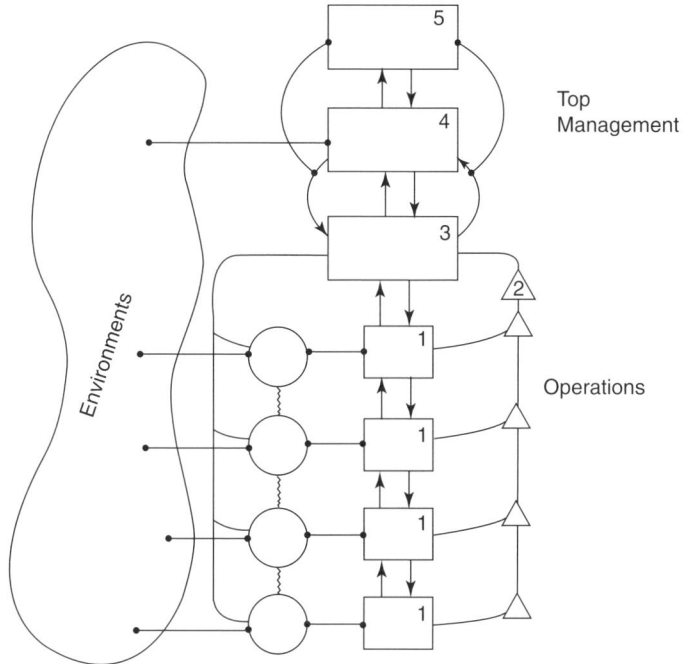

Figure 1.1   A simplified viable system model

more about each, each began to intrude into the realms of others. Physics and chemistry intruded into biology; biology into sociology, and the boundaries of the social sciences blurred. The sciences, whether technical or social, became more and more interrelated. Scientists began to realize that reality can not be understood completely through classification and analysis. Something more was needed. The "something more," a synthesis, was discovered and developed over the years following World War II by Ludwig Von Bertalanffy, Norbert Wiener, Ross Ashby, and others. The work of these pioneering scientists discovered and developed a new science—system science and cybernetics. System science defines what systems are, their characteristics, and how they function and interrelate. Cybernetics, a part of system science, is the science of communication and control in systems. From system science and cybernetics we now have a general systems theory which tells us all that science now knows about how things work, interrelatedly, in nature, and in human society.

Instead of analyzing the parts, system science takes an holistic view. System science gives us an holistic world of holistic parts. Systems science studies the total system and sees systems with holistic parts interacting within the system for a purpose. In a natural system, that purpose is survival. In a system that is a corporation, purpose is survival and something more. Companies are purposeful. They have a purpose more than survival. They have goals they intend to achieve. System science offers management a new view of the company showing more clearly what the company is and how it works. With this new view and understanding, management will manage differently, increasing the capability of the organization to accomplish desired results.

System science has discovered that all systems share common characteristics and behaviors, and these have been identified and described. We now have scientific knowledge of how feedback and communication within the system enables a complex system to interact in ways that will achieve its purpose.

In recent years Stafford Beer, Russell Ackoff, Paul Rubinyi, and others have applied system science to the operation of business enterprise. In systems terms, a business unit, a business group, a company, a corporation are each a viable, very complex, purposeful, probabilistic system. The complex, probabilistic system that is a corporation has the kind of structure and the characteristics discovered by the new system science. But without a knowledge of system science we don't see the structure, and don't understand and make use of some of the characteristics of system behavior that can much improve performance.

System science does not tell us how our company or business unit *should* function. System science tells us how our company or business unit *does* function. And that is different from the views most commonly held by management people today. When we understand how to use system science, we will be able to design and manage the system that is our company or business unit so that it can more effectively achieve its purpose. Stafford Beer developed the viable system model (VSM) to represent and describe the system science and cybernetics needed to manage effectively a business, a corporation, or any other kind of organization.

A simple analogy may help in understanding the value of system science in management. The human body is a very complex system and has functioned in the same way for many thousands of years. But to deal with the health and the pathology of the body, quite different methods have been used by "experts" of different cultures and different times. The physician of ancient Greece, the Mayan priest, the Australian aborigine, the Indian medicine man, and the blood-letting barber were all treating the same system, the human body. But their interventions weren't always helpful. Over more recent years our knowledge of the system that is the human body has increased tremendously. With new knowledge, our treatment of the body's pathology has much improved, and life expectancy has increased by decades. Might we not also expect improvement in our management methods as we increase our understanding of the system that is our business enterprise?

System science gives us new ways to steer the business enterprise to the achievement of its purpose. Seeing with new eyes shows as new ways to manage today's complexities and more successfully achieve desired results. Internal measures and interactions with the environment provide continuing feedback that coordinates all efforts toward the achievement of company purpose. This same feedback provides information for changes in structure when needed to improve performance.

BENEFITS FOR MANAGEMENT

When we use systems science and the VSM to structure and manage our company:

- We learn, adapt to change, and evolve so that we are able to maintain continuing success over time, under changing circumstances
- We are neither centralized nor decentralized; we are both at the same time
- Control is not imposed from a higher level. Control is designed into the structure so that each unit can be self-controlling
- Feedback from the work itself enables self-control
- Measures of progress toward objectives provide on-going guidance toward desired objectives
- Since measures reduce complexity they are developed with great care not to lose information that matters
- Information is available where and when needed for decisions and actions
- Each level does its own planning. There need be no passing of planning documents between levels
- Budgets can be prepared in days or hours, not months
- Recognizing and coping with error is part of learning and continuous improvement
- Each unit succeeds by measures of success developed in that unit in consideration of the purpose of that unit
- Unit successes contribute to the achievement of company goals

System science and system thinking give us a new way to see and understand our company. This new understanding at all levels provides prompt awareness of threats and opportunities, and new ways to manage for improving performance.

The times we work in are filled with change signals. Technology change signals new threats and new ways for creating value. Terrorism signals new threats. Ballooning world populations with many uneducated, unemployed, and poor signal both threats and opportunities. Changes in our ecosphere signal threats, and offer opportunities. How well do prevailing business structures and business practices detect these and other signals, and take actions needed for survival and long-term success?

New successes will be different from the old. Environmental changes—technical, commercial, economic, political, social, and ecological—signal new needs, new opportunities, new threats. New and different information and new inventions will be needed. Structuring the company using system science principles increases awareness of threats and opportunities, and improves the ability for quick response.

In the sciences, in society, in industry, in technology, in our understanding of nature; in all that we do or are aware of, complexity abounds; and grows explosively. How do we find the fundamental simplicities to guide us? Years ago a scientist and corporate executive commented to this author that civilization is a race between complexity and simplification. At that time, in the 1950s, the race seemed challenging, but manageable. But today that race has new dimensions not foreseen in the 1950s: (1) hugely expanding, and conflicting, human populations worldwide, (2) rapid expansion of industrial production to meet ballooning needs, (3) derivative of these first two, threatening changes in the ecosphere that is the home of all life, including ours, and (4) growing social instability. How do we structure and manage our business enterprise for success today and sustainable success through the years ahead?

System science and cybernetics give us a great simplifier for the complexities of management. That's the message of this book—simplifying the complexities of management at a new level of understanding; improving control; improving performance.

ORIGINS OF SYSTEM SCIENCE

System science and system theory developed from the work of pioneering scientists striving for a more complete understanding of the growing complexities in the separate disciplines of science. When complexity grows beyond comprehension, and the new learning no longer fits prevailing conventions, there can suddenly appear new knowledge that simplifies all the complexity at a new level of understanding. System science and general system theory offer that new level of understanding for business management.

The work and writing of Ludwig von Bertalanffy, Robert Rosen, G. J. Klir, W. Ross Ashby, Norbert Wiener, and many others has advanced system science to the point of an established general system theory that we can now apply in many realms, including management. In his book, *General System Theory,* Bertalanffy states that "... systems theory is a broad view which far transcends technological problems and demands, a reorientation that has become necessary in science in general and in the gamut of disciplines from physics and biology to the behavioral and social sciences and to philosophy. It is operative, with varying degrees of success and exactitude, in various realms, and heralds a new world view of considerable impact [3]."

Those not interested in seeing and understanding their company in a new and different way might ignore system science, thinking, "that's just a theory." But a scientific theory is not something to be ignored. In all realms, science studies, analyzes, assembles data, reports findings, proposes hypotheses. Then, from all that's known, comes theory. Scientific theory is the understanding that best fits all that's known about that subject area. All the research, all the facts, all the studies, all the data support the theory. Denying theory is denying the existing knowledge on that subject. Instead of denying system theory, embrace it. Business people who learn about system theory and apply what they learn in structure and operations, will improve the capability and the performance of their organizations.

Stafford Beer's viable system model (VSM), used with a knowledge of the system science and cybernetics embedded in the model offers a new understanding and a new way to structure and manage businesses and other organizations and institutions. But before we can use the model, we need an understanding of the science of systems.

WHAT IS A SYSTEM?

We use the word "system" every day, in ordinary conversation. A computer becomes a computer system; a furnace, a heating system. Manufacturing resource planning (MRP) is a software system, as is customer relationship management (CRM). The software industry seems to have claimed the word "system" as a proprietary attribute of their products. To get a driver's license we "follow the system." Note how often we hear, or see, or use the word, "system." Sometimes the meaning is clear, and specific; sometimes fuzzy. But always it is combining something with something in addition. That's true in system science, too. But in system science we will be specific in how we define "system." In system science, "system" is not the system of everyday conversation.

We can begin with two broad classifications of systems:

Deterministic
Probabilistic

Deterministic systems can be simple, or complex. See Figure 1.2. In a deterministic system we know all the parts, what they do, and their relationships with other parts. When the system fails to work properly, we know how to find and fix the problem. To improve the system we know where improvement would be beneficial, and we know how to go about designing an improved system. A home heating system is a simple, deterministic system. The thermostat is the controller, automatically controlling room temperature to the setting on the thermostat. We used to set the thermostat manually. Now, with digital technology, we program the thermostat for a week for desired temperatures each hour, each day, for both heating and cooling. We can even program remotely.

An automobile is a complex, deterministic system, with the driver-controller and many built-in controllers all activated when the driver drives the car. We know all the parts of the system, what they do, and how they do it. A fleet of cars (company cars, delivery cars) is a more complex system. Each car is a deterministic system, but the fleet management part of the system, how all the elements will perform—cars, drivers, scheduling—is probabilistic.

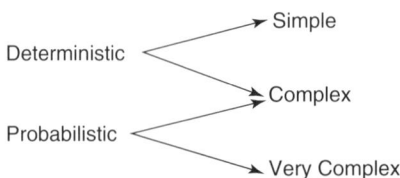

Figure 1.2 Kinds of systems

Probabilistic systems can be complex, or very complex. We know all the parts, but the behavior of the parts will vary, as will the relationships among the parts, and the interrelationships with other systems. Instead of determined, and known, everything is probabilistic. A small business is a very complex, probabilistic system. A large corporation is a very complex, probabilistic system. We will manage both the small business and the large corporation in new ways when we understand them as viable, very complex, purposeful, probabilistic systems. Managed by the principles of system science as expressed in the VSM, our companies will be more capable of achieving desired performance.

If our business or our corporation is a very complex, probabilistic system, what are the parts of that system? Here we come to the recursive nature of systems. Our business, or our corporation, is made up of subordinate systems each with the same complex, probabilistic characteristics as the total business or corporation. And our business or corporation is itself a part of a still larger, more-encompassing system, typically the industry that the company is a part of. And the system that is the industry is a part of a still higher-level system, the economy. What we learn in system science applies in all of these. In this book we deal with the applications of systems science, system thinking, and the VSM in the total company, and the systems at all levels of recursion within the company. All of these can be modeled with the VSM; all have the same system characteristics.

General system theory and system science give us an understanding of these systems and their characteristics. Figure 1.3 illustrates a basic design for any business system.

The business system includes operations (the circle), management of those operations (the square), management systems used by management (the triangle), and the environments outside the business (the amoeboid shape); all interlinked by communications channels. We draw the diagram in this form to show relationships and communications. In actuality business systems is embedded in management; management is embedded in operations; and all three together are embedded in the environment, as shown in Figure 1.4.

Some systems seem quite obvious; they are on the organization chart. The corporation. A business group. A business. A plant. In this book we will define each of these as a system that can be described in a new, different, and better way with the viable system model (VSM).

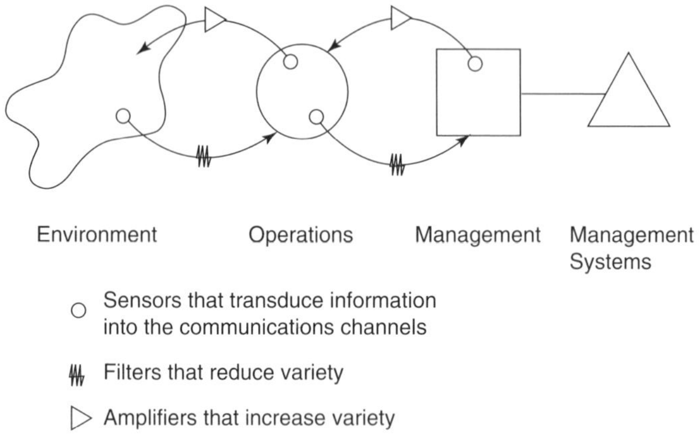
Environment
Operations
Management
Management Systems
Sensors that transduce information into the communications channels
Filters that reduce variety
Amplifiers that increase variety

Figure 1.3 A business system

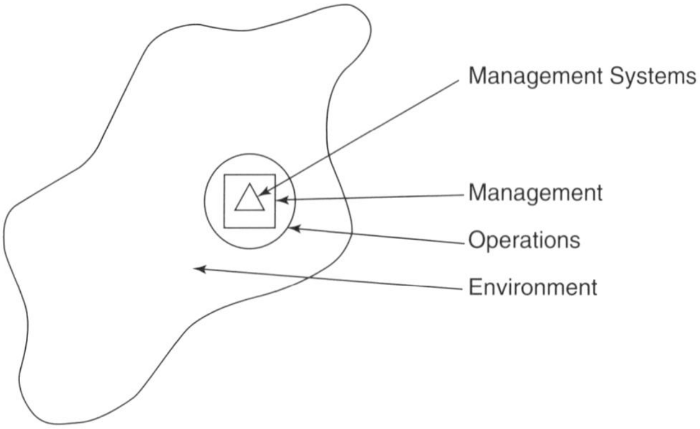
Management Systems
Management
Operations
Environment

Figure 1.4 A business system embedded in the environment

This book describes the business enterprise as a viable, very complex, purposeful, probabilistic system comprised of viable, very complex, purposeful, probabilistic systems:

- Viable: capable of continuing to exist in its environment
- Very complex: so complex in its operations that only the coordinated capabilities of all its members and a carefully designed information structure and information flow can control operations to assure viability and the achievement of performance goals

- Purposeful: capable of achieving desired goals
- Probabilistic: the behavior of the parts of the system are probabilistic and unpredictable, but can be guided toward desired outcomes

Stafford Beer's viable system model and the discoveries of system science give us new concepts of structure and new ways of management. VSM and system thinking give us an order of magnitude simplification of the complexities of management. At a higher level of understanding, we manage more effectively. Performance improves.

CYBERNETICS

Norbert Wiener gave the name "cybernetics" to the science of communication and control in systems. His 1948 book, *Cybernetics: Or Control and Communications in Animal and the Machine,"* describes how information and communications control systems. Beer describes cybernetics as "the science of effective organization [4]." Whatever the system, a deterministic system like a machine, or a complex system like an animal or a human being or a complex, probabilistic system like a corporation, information controls how the system works and what the system does. To enable this control, information becomes an important part of structure. The VSM specifies communication channels and the information flowing in each. In the VSM, information is a part of the structure of the company.

System science has a lot to say about control. When we see the company as a system made up of subordinate systems we begin to get some new ideas about control. Traditionally we have thought of control as imposed on a function or a unit or a company by a higher-level authority. That's a natural impression from the pyramidal organization charts we draw and present as a description of the company. And control from above is an impression many of us get from our experience in our jobs.

When we see the company as a group of interrelated systems and understand what systems are and how they function, our minds open to new ideas. We can see that information is an important part of structure, and that the communication of information can be structured so each system can control itself. So the task of management is less imposing control, and more structuring the system so that it can control itself toward accomplishing desired results.

Another consideration in control is the typical concentration on priorities. Typically, with limitations on resources, executives struggle with priorities. For example, at budget time, executive management may project an ability to fund $XX in new capital expenditures for the year ahead. But proposals come in for $XXXX. This kind of a problem is resolved by priorities. The $XXXX is prioritized down to $XX, often by such financial comparisons as discounted cash flow return on investment, or payback. The VSM and system thinking give us new ways to think about and deal with this kind of situation. Priorities and prioritizing disappear, replaced by different and better decision methods as explained in Chapter 5.

Cybernetics, the science of communication and control in systems, offers three new concepts for management that enable self-organization and self-control: variety, requisite variety, and black boxes.

Variety

In systems science, "variety" is the measure of complexity. Businesses are very complex, probabilistic systems. Complex is obvious. Probabilistic we probably haven't thought much about. A home heating system is not a probabilistic system. We know the parts and we know exactly how they work. If we set the thermostat to seventy-two degrees we get seventy-two degrees. If we get sixty degrees, we know how to fix the system to give us the desired result. In our company we know all the parts, but how they work is a matter of probability. We can put sales revenue of $X in the budget and intend for sales to be $X. We know the parts of the system that produce sales results. But sales will always be some variation of $X. If sales are $X minus 30% we don't immediately know what to do to give us the desired result. Or, if sales are $XX is there new opportunity out there? The VSM and system science offer management methods for discovering and fixing problems before they show up in reports, and for identifying and developing opportunities.

We can put a time line and checkpoints for specified deliverables in a project plan. But when the checkpoints arrive we will likely see differences from the plan. With system science and system thinking we continuously monitor performance and modify the project plan to stay on track toward the project objective. Everything in business is probabilistic. System science helps us follow a heuristic path toward achievement of objectives.

In all elements of the company we are dealing with probabilities. Multiply all these probabilities by all that's going on in the company, each individual in his/her job, each team, each process, each unit, each interaction with customers, everything. The measure of complexity is enormous. Variety, the measure of complexity, is defined as the possible states of the system. Variety can actually be measured in very small parts of small business systems. In Chapter 3, the case example titled "How the VSM Helped Transform a Manufacturing Company in Crisis," the variety in carrying out five production jobs was calculated at 27.5 billion. And that's in one small part of one small business. For a total business, even a small business, the total variety in the total company would be a meaningless number, too huge to comprehend. While variety is not precisely countable, it can be approximated. We can make comparative statements. We can say that the variety in operations is much greater than the variety in management. We can say that the variety in the company's environments is very much greater than the variety in all areas of the company that are dealing with these environments.

Variety, of course, is a word in common usage. There's a variety of choices. People like variety in their work. Which variety of strawberry is the sweetest? The systems definition of variety is completely different from the common usage of the word, variety. In system science, variety is a new word. Variety is a new concept, and a very important concept.

Immediately, we can see that the variety in a corporation is far more than the ten thousand million neurons in the brain of the CEO can comprehend. Nor can this huge variety be matched and comprehended by the ten thousand million neurons in the brains of each of the company executives, combined. The task of management is to lead all this probabilistic complexity, this huge variety, toward the achievement of company goals. System science and the VSM shows us how.

In system science we don't see the CEO and top executives as "running" the company. Instead system science sees the CEO and senior executives as structuring the corporate system and its recursions—the viable systems that are its operating units—so that the company can run itself toward the achievement of company goals. When problems arise, the system itself can usually resolve, or dissolve, the problem. Or, if necessary, higher-level management can change the system so that the system itself can resolve the problem and achieve desired performance results.

Requisite Variety

W. Ross Ashby, one of the pioneers of systems science, formulated the basic law of control, known as "Ashby's Law." Ashby's law states, "Only variety can absorb variety." That's a very precise statement in the language of systems science. Applying this law to business management, it says that all the probabilistic complexity throughout the corporation can be effectively controlled only by an equivalent amount of probabilistic complexity in the controller. In a corporation, how can that happen?

Variety is defined as the possible states of the system. In even a small business the states of the system—the actions behaviors, and results of all the employees, all the machines, all the processes, all the equipment, all of the interactions among all of these, and all of the interactions of all of these in their relationships with people and organizations outside the company, and all the company interactions with all the company's environments becomes a number beyond human comprehension.

We can't put useful numbers on variety. The numbers are too huge. But we can make comparisons. And we know that the variety in operations and in the environment is vastly greater than the variety in management. What attenuation of the variety in operations and what amplification of the variety in the management of operations can establish requisite variety? What attenuation of the vast variety in the environment and what amplification of the variety in the company areas dealing with the environment can establish requisite variety? How can we make the control variety equal to the variety in what is being controlled?

In operations, traditional measures like ROI and ROS are huge attenuators of variety that lose a lot of information needed for wise decisions. Aggregations and averages also lose huge amounts of information needed for decision-making. Measures like sales revenue, cost of goods sold, gross margin, ROI and other aggregated accounting measures too often are used by higher levels of management to make decisions better made at a level where there can be requisite variety. In system management we aim to make decisions at the levels where there can be requisite variety.

How can the huge variety in operations and in the environment be attenuated, and the variety of management be amplified to achieve requisite variety? Great reductions of the variety in operations will be needed. Even greater reductions in the variety in the company's environments will be needed. Eliminating much of the variety loses a lot of information. To avoid losing needed information, we need to go about the attenuation of this variety with care. We need much less variety in operations and in the environments in order to match the variety in management. But we need all the variety that matters.

Management attenuates the huge variety in operations and in the environment first of all by selecting what it is in each of these that matters for the achievement of their business' short-term and long-term goals. This selection of what matters is a responsibility of management through all levels of recursion. The answers will be different. In each business unit there will be differences in what it is that matters in operations. But there will be similarities, too. Selection of what matters will be the responsibility of individuals close to and doing the work. Many individuals will be involved in making these selections.

Selecting what matters in each business' environments determines what to monitor and what to measure. Measures can be qualitative or they can be numbers. In either case, change and trends matter and need to be observed to determine appropriate actions. Attenuating the immense variety in each of the company environments by selecting what matters and by measures of what matters makes requisite variety possible. Possible, but not assured. While variety has been reduced by measures of what matters, there is still a lot of variety to deal with. To match this variety will require amplification of the voice of management. This means that many will be involved, not just a few.

After the selection of what matters, we further attenuate variety in this still very great variety by our selection of measures. At the corporate level and at each level of recursion from recursion 1 to recursion X, measures and trends of measures are designed into the information system. At the corporate level and at each level of recursion, measures are an information resource needed to accomplish desired goals. So the design of measures to provide this information must be carefully done at all levels of recursion. Chapters 5 to 11 Offer suggestions on the design of measures.

A word of warning! What may be out there in the environment and in operations that really matters and is not captured in any measure? With conventional measures, much of the variety that really matters can be lost. Ignorance is the greatest attenuator of all. By ignoring variety that matters, decisions can be made, but not well. Only requisite variety can make wise decisions. All decision-makers need a continuing awareness of Ashby's Law of requisite variety. Effective management makes decisions where there can be requisite variety.

As noted above, the CEO and all corporate executives together are not enough to comprehend the huge variety throughout the corporation. Without knowledge of systems science, many executives today use two methods, typically both at the same time: (1) delegation, and (2) ignoring most of the variety.

Delegation is an improvement. Delegation adds to the variety of the controller. But depending on how the variety in the environments and in operations has been attenuated, may lack requisite variety. Ignoring most of the complexity seems to work, because decisions are made and actions taken, often through reliance on simple measures such as sales billed, ROS, gross margin, or ROI. But how useful are these measures for determining corrective actions? Each problem is a result of many complex interactions involving various functions and many company people and, very often, many people outside the company that company people deal with. Decisions made without requisite variety will likely do more harm than good.

System science and the VSM give us the means to make control decisions throughout the company at locations where there can be requisite variety, locations where the information exists to make good decisions. Requisite variety in the controller is achieved in two ways:

1. By amplifying the variety in the controller through self-control at all levels of recursion and making decisions where the work decided on is done. With many more people throughout the organization doing the controlling, each with their ten thousand million neurons of capability, the variety in the controller greatly increases.
2. By attenuating the variety in operations and in the environment by:
   (a) first, selecting wisely what is important to the successful achievement of organization goals, then
   (b) selecting and monitoring useful measures of what is important.

When operating decisions are made at higher-levels of management lacking requisite variety, the decisions ignore most of the variety needed for wise decisions. Authority does not grant requisite variety.

Corporate management can have requisite variety for defining the company and its boundaries, and for structuring the company to control itself. From monitoring company performance and the company environments, corporate management also can have requisite variety to revise the definition and boundaries, and to make changes in structure as may be appropriate. Corporate management can achieve requisite variety for those decisions. But corporate management can not intervene within lower level operations. They lack requisite variety for decision-making in lower level operations. These operations are black boxes from the perspective of higher-level management.

Black Boxes

Systems are variety generators. A black box is a high-variety operation within a system whose operations cannot be known to higher-level management. Higher-level management lacks requisite variety. Higher-level management can know the purpose of the black box, can know the inputs to the black box, and can know the outputs from the black box. But what goes on inside the black box is unknowable, except in a general way. Higher-level management cannot intervene wisely within the black box, cannot make informed decisions within the black box.

For corporate management, each of the operating businesses in the corporate VSM is a black box. The immense complexity within the operations of a black box can only be managed effectively within the black box. Higher-level management interventions within the black box will more likely hurt than help. Higher-level management has the authority to make such interventions and often does. But higher-level management, while it has the authority, lacks the variety to make wise decisions within the black box. Ashby's Law prevails. And the people within the black box are left to recover from the consequences of interventions from above. See Figure 1.5.

The cybernetics concept of black boxes helps management improve organization performance through indirect management that increases requisite variety where decisions are made. In a corporation, the next level viable systems, its operating units, are black boxes to corporate management. Corporate management does know what goes into the black boxes—resources (people and capital), materials inputs, purpose, and information. Corporate management also knows what comes out of the black boxes—outputs defined by performance measures. But corporate management lacks the requisite variety to comprehend and understand the complexities—the variety—of all the transformation processes within the black boxes. The higher level lacks the requisite variety for control capability. Only the black box itself has control

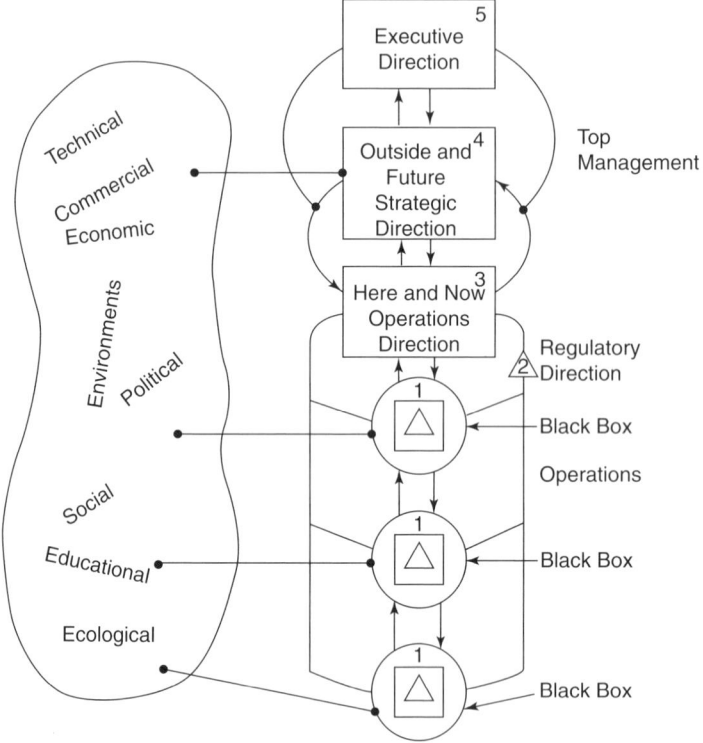

Figure 1.5 Black boxes

capability. Any higher-level management intervention in an operating unit to fix something gone wrong, such as unsatisfactory profitability, will more likely make matters worse, not better. As Stafford Beer stated [5]:

> The major problems arise when matters are not going well—or at least when it is obvious that 'something needs to be done.' Managers, the men themselves, are then expected to take some kind of action. I think it is a major cybernetic conclusion to draw from these remarks that managers generally approach this problem in the wrong way. They usually try to intervene in the equilibrial processes of the self-regulating system—thereby, perhaps, making it fundamentally unstable. The sensible course for the manager is not to try to change the system's internal behavior, which typically results in mammoth oscillation, but to change its structure—so that its natural systemic behavior becomes different. All of this says that management is not so much part of the system managed as it is the system's own designer.

How does higher-level management assure control within the black box? By the design of structure and information flow so the black box can be self-organizing and self-controlling. If the operating system that we are now defining as a black box is unable to produce desired results, the remedial action by higher-level management is not to go into the black box and fix the problem. That would most likely make matters worse. The remedial action that works is to change the system so that it is capable of producing the desired results. Changing the system involves changing people, changing resources, changing information, or some combination of these three. Often, changing information is enough—some different and better management methods, and different and better measures. See chapters 5 through 11 for useful management methods and measures.

Indirect management uses the concepts of the Resource Bargain which defines each business and its boundaries (see chapter 2), requisite variety, black boxes, and self-organization and self-control to assure effective control throughout the company for success today, and for the times ahead.

HOMEOSTATS AND HETEROSTATS

A characteristic of any system, including a system that is a business, is *homeostasis,* a tendency to maintain itself in its present state. Specific elements in the system, or actions of elements in the system, identified as *homeostats*, work to maintain the present state of the system. A good design of the corporate system includes well-designed homeostats. But in business we will call them by different names.

The highest level homeostat in a company is the board of directors, and company top management. One of their key responsibilities is to keep everything on an even keel, and prevent or resolve any serious internal or external conflicts. At the operating level, in most companies, we find homeostats mostly missing, and the function poorly performed. The VSM includes organized homeostats, coordinating operations to prevent internal conflicts and to resolve them when they do happen. See the description of system 2, and the system3/system 4 homeostat, in chapter 2.

Systems, and especially systems that are businesses, also have a characteristic of *heterostasis,* a tendency for change, learning, evolution, creativity, improvement, innovation. Specific elements in the system, identified as *heterostats,* work to change and improve the system.

Heterostats can produce continuous improvement. Heterostats can also produce innovation, rapid change, transformation. The VSM design of the corporate system includes effective heterostats, providing a creative tension between homeostasis and heterostasis that enables the company to do what's right for the present while also discovering the innovations that will create the company's future. Every company needs well-designed heterostats, but in business we call them by different names. See chapter 8.

RECURSION

Stafford Beer uses the term, "recursion," from number theory, a branch of mathematics, to describe a very important attribute of viable systems and the viable system model (VSM). System science says that any viable system is comprised of viable systems and is itself part of a higher-level viable system. There can be many levels of recursion in both directions. While the higher-level recursions and the lower-level recursions will be very different, the viable system model is exactly the same at all levels of recursion. The VSM with its systems science and cybernetics defines a viable system, any viable system. Applied in a company, the concept of recursion provides a vast attenuator of the huge variety in the structure and operations of any large company. The VSM models the corporation. It also models the corporation's business groups, the individual businesses within the groups, and operating units within those businesses. Each can be modeled with the VSM. See Figure 1.6.

Figure 1.6 shows a VSM model of a corporation that has its operations organized into 4 business groups. The figure then shows the first level of recursion, showing the model for corporate group 3, which we see is comprised of 5 companies. For the entire corporation, there will be a total of four VSMs at this level of recursion, a model for each of the Groups. Each of these, of course, will show the number of companies in each of them. Going to the second level of recursion using group 3, Company 2 as an example, we see that company 2 has four profit center businesses. Similarly, at this level of recursion there will also be VSMs for the companies in each of the other groups. Going to the third level of recursion, Figure 1.6 shows that business 4 in company 2 has three plants producing the company's products. Similarly, the third level of recursion will include the VSMs for all the company businesses in all the other companies in all four groups of the corporation. And we could go on to additional levels of recursion.

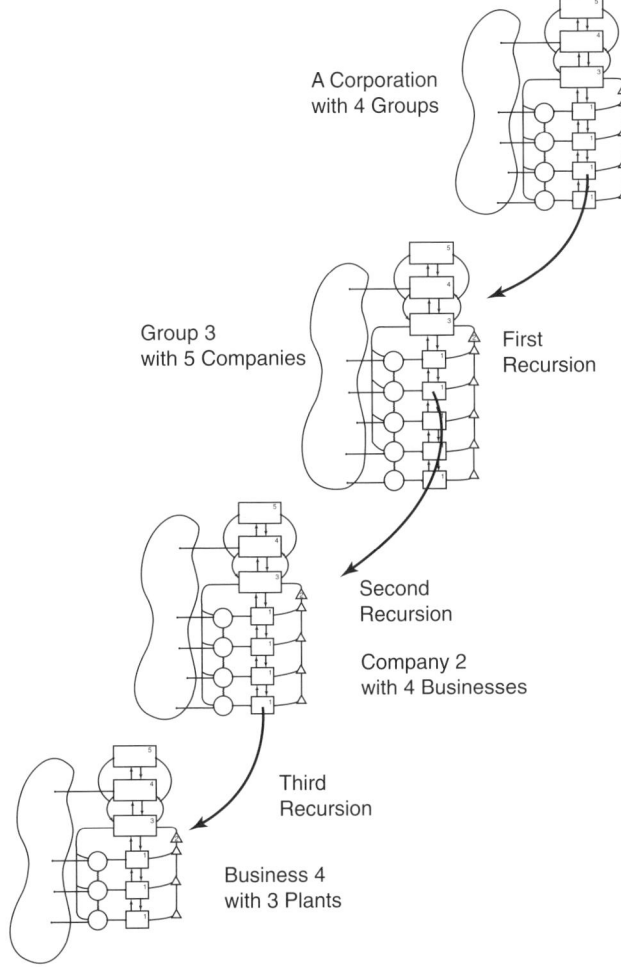

A Corporation
with 4 Groups

Group 3
with 5 Companies

First
Recursion

Second
Recursion

Company 2
with 4 Businesses

Third
Recursion

Business 4
with 3 Plants

Figure 1.6 The VSM models viable systems at all levels of recursion

Typically we look first at the corporate VSM as recursion 0, the system in focus, and the first level of recursion, recursion 1. Or the interest might be at a further level of recursion as the system in focus, and its next level of recursion. Corporate management focuses on recursion 0 and recursion 1. The MX Corporation example in Chapter 3 describes how the VSM was used to improve operations and profitability two recursions from the corporate VSM as the system in focus.

People trained in financial analysis may confuse the idea of recursion with their practice of "drilling down" from a higher level through levels of management to get information from a lower level for their analysis of that level's operations. Recursion is an unrelated and completely different concept. In the VSM and its recursions there is no "drilling down." Lower levels are "black boxes," unknowable to the higher-level. Drilling down can produce additional data, but cannot produce useful information. Using the VSM, companies will rethink their practices of financial analysis and "drilling down" to appraise lower-level operations. The higher-level lacks requisite variety, and such practices result in misleading information, and misguided interventions.

With system thinking and the VSM, for a large corporation, we see not a hierarchy, but a web of inter-relating viable systems. Visualize this web not as a growing cascade descending from the corporate VSM. Instead visualize this web as spreading in all directions and planes, with the corporate VSM among them. For the first level of recursion there may be 3 to 8 VSMs. At the second level of recursion from each of those 3 to 8 there may be 3 to 8 VSMs, bringing the total to something between 13 and 73 VSMs. Stafford Beer in his book, *Brain of the Firm*, compares recursion with a neural network. See Figure 1.7.

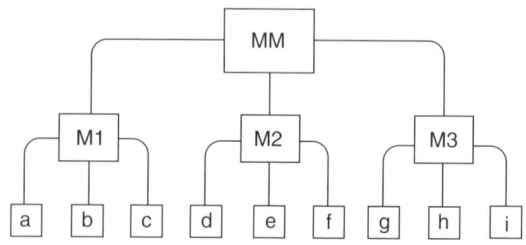

Conventional view of an organization

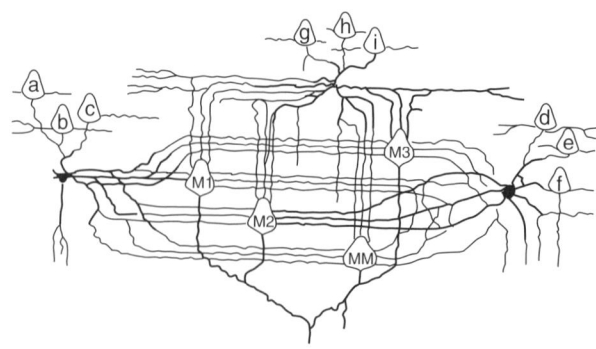

How the organization really works,
showing the same elements

Figure 1.7 A viable business system as a neural network

The first part of Figure 1.7 shows the typical organization chart of a business. The figure shows a corporation with three units at the first level of recursion. At the second level of recursion, each of these three units is also made up of three units. Each of these units could be modeled with the VSM. More typically, in a large corporation the number of units (VSMs) at each level of recursion will be some number from three to eight.

The bottom part of Figure 1.7 shows the same units as they interrelate in a neural network, which Beer says is the way businesses really work when understood as complex, probabilistic systems. He makes a good point. This neural network illustrates a corporation with two levels of recursion totaling 13 units (VSMs). Visualize this neural network with two levels of recursion totaling some 50 units (VSMs). We might be more comfortable visualizing an interconnected web, rather than a neural network. Whether a neural network or an interconnected web, the concept of hierarchy changes.

Visualize a multidimensional, interconnecting web of viable systems, each:

- with the functions and capabilities of a viable business system
- capable of self-organization, and
- capable of self-control.

With this view we can begin to understand how system science and system thinking can give us new ways of managing for success today, and for creating success tomorrow.

Typically we begin with modeling the corporation into the VSM. There's much more involved than transposing the traditional organization chart into a different format. The usual company organization chart identifies executive positions and major units of the corporation. The VSM identifies the corporation's viable systems—its component businesses. The VSM also identifies functions and relationships, establishes communication channels, organizes information flow, and includes all external relationships.

The VSM looks very different from the traditional organization chart, but for all the information it includes is simpler. The company organization chart is a partial view of corporate structure, identifying the major parts of the corporation, and showing who in management reports to who. The VSM shows a different and deeper structure of the corporation, defines the corporation and all of its parts, describes how they work and interrelate, and specifies what they do (their purpose). A system is what it does.

This same VSM model is used at all levels of recursion. The corporate VSM identifies the next recursions of viable systems, the corporation's businesses, or groups of businesses. After developing the corporate model, the next step is to develop the model for its viable system businesses. And this process can be carried out by management groups throughout several levels of recursion. The point, of course, is not to have models, but to discover new guidelines for leaders that will simplify management, and improve performance results.

INFORMATION

In systems science and system thinking, we see how information controls actions, in natural systems and in business systems, too. The human body is a complex system. We run up the stairs (our conscious decision). Messages are sent by the nervous system to leg and arm muscles to move as needed, without any conscious awareness. The autonomous nervous system senses a need for energy and sends a message to the heart to increase circulation. Energy, breathing, respiration, digestion, white corpuscle attack on invading pathogens; unknown to us sensors and information flow within our bodies keep our bodies functioning normally. Our homeostats are working. Similarly homeostats throughout the company keep operations running normally without any conscious awareness by higher-level management. The corporate management responsibility is the design of the corporate system to coordinate and motivate all actions toward the achievement of company purpose. From monitoring performance measures and environmental change, top management can modify structure (resources, people, information) when appropriate so the system itself will perform as desired. The VSM shows us how.

The viable system model includes communication channels, and the specification of the information flowing in these channels. Mapping communication flow in the corporate VSM, and with local managements doing the same at each level of recursion, establishes effective control throughout the company. The appropriate measures at each level of recursion being used by the people at that level, can meet the requisite variety requirements of Ashby's law. Through the wise development of measures, the variety in local management can control the variety in their operations. In today's world, new kinds of measures are needed.

Throughout this book, there is a strong emphasis on measures. Ashby's law and the management need for requisite variety between controller and what is controlled will require simplifications. To simplify, we will need to reduce, or "attenuate," the huge variety in operations, which is both very complex, and probabilistic. We attenuate the complexity through selection of what matters, and well-designed measures of what matters. We take big chunks from that variety and represent those big chunks with specific measures. Those measures can't contain as much information as is contained in the chunks of variety that the measures represent. But if we choose our measures well they can include what is needed for good, practical, and effective decisions and actions where the work is done. Many of these measures will not be the measures we see in our traditional accounting reports. They will not be aggregated measures from periodic reports. See chapters 5 through 11 for useful measures in the key performance areas that determine company success.

TRANSDUCTION

The VSM includes communication channels. And in developing the VSM at each level of recursion system principles specify what information flows in each of these channels. Included will be the measures selected to attenuate variety.

In systems terms, we need "transduction." Wherever information enters a communication channel, what goes into the channel has to be entered into the channel in language or form that can be understood by the receiver. If we have chosen our measures well, the measures will be in a form the receiver will understand. The transducer may receive data; but it will send measures.

In addition to measures, there will be many other kinds of information flowing in the communication channels, as described in chapter 2. In volume, measures will be a small part of the total, but a very important part. For all that goes into the communications channels, the transducers will assure that it will be in language and form that will be understood by the receiver. The transducer will have information needed for a higher-level financial report in the right account numbers and language for the receiver. Information for a compliance report will be in the language required for that report. Information on the performance areas described in chapters 5 through 11 will be measures understandable and useful to the receiver.

SELF-ORGANIZATION

Systems have a capability for self-organization. No central authority organizes the ecosystem of a forest or a saltwater marsh. Like all natural systems, they organize themselves to live in their environment. Bring a group of people together for the purpose of building a playground in a public park, and the group will soon be an organized effort to accomplish that goal. The internet organizes itself.

Self-organization is a characteristic useful to management at all levels of recursion for increasing organization capability. In a corporation, the top executives together with others can develop a viable system model for the total corporation. That requires some learning time, and the collaborative effort of a number of people. But it is not a huge task, if minds open to the principles of system behavior as discovered in system science.

A presentation of system science principles and a first-draft VSM of the company can be completed in a half-day session with top management. But several months will be needed to really understand the VSM, organize all the required functions, determine goals and performance measures, and structure information and communication. All key players in the corporate VSM will be involved in the process. A few months can bring good and very useful results, a big improvement from the conventional organization chart and management methods. But it will not be the optimum. There will be a continuing learning from experience as understanding of the VSM and system thinking grows at all levels of recursion.

Developing the corporate VSM, understanding the functions and the system thinking the model represents, and deciding on goals and measures is self-organization in action. And this will happen at each level of recursion. Over time, many will be involved. The result becomes a system structure for continuously improving organization capability.

The corporate VSM identifies and defines the corporation's subordinate viable systems. Then the management group in each of those viable systems, which will be the businesses comprising the corporation, go through the same kind of self-organizing process to develop a Viable System Model for their operations. Developing the VSM, they learn the system science and system thinking principles they can use in managing business operations. They map the communication channels in the VSM for their business. And they specify the information that will flow in each channel. They will also determine the measures that will help their businesses achieve their objectives. Chapters 5 through 11 offer suggestions.

Then the next level of recursion can go through the same self-organizing process. That's the one-recursion-at-a-time method for gaining the benefits of systems science and system thinking for changing and improving company performance. But companies more confident in system science and system thinking may wish to move faster. These companies can choose to work with more than one level of recursion at a time. They can begin with the corporate VSM and one level of recursion. At the same time elsewhere at other levels of recursion, people can begin learning about and applying system principles and the VSM. Very often, the VSM is first learned and used one or two recursions away from corporate. Lessons learned can then spread wider and higher.

Self-organization, of course, is not a one-time thing. Self-organization is continuous. Systems evolve; and company systems can substantially change over time through internal change, innovation in new products and processes, new ventures, M&A activity, and divestitures. VSM companies become adept at managing for success today in ways that will lead to success over the years ahead.

SELF-CONTROL

Systems also have a capability for self-control. Otherwise they could not continue to exist in their environments. The sun shines (an information signal). Rain falls (an information signal). A seed grows. With many replications, and with many other interactions, the forest continues to exist. No control from a higher authority. The forest, naturally and by the principles discovered in system science, controls itself.

The complex, probabilistic system that is a corporation also has a natural capability for self-control. The company wants to continue to exist in its environment. And it wants something more. The company exists for a purpose. The company wants to continue to exist and continue to achieve its purpose. Unlike a forest, the company system does have a top-level authority. The job of this top level authority is to achieve company purpose over time. But how?

The Board of Directors, the CEO, the senior executives, all collectively, with all their knowledge and experience, immediately confront Ashby's Law. The variety in what needs to be controlled is many orders of magnitude greater that these few people can control. Systems science and the VSM, which identify the problem, also offer a resolution—throughout the company develop measures of what matters, and enlist the capabilities of people throughout the company as controllers. People doing the task control the task. People running the process control the process. Project members control the project. Managers control their functions.

Feedback from the work itself enables people doing the work to control what's happening and achieve desired results. An operator at a machine knows the desired output, and by setting control parameters on the machine, monitoring machine sensors, and by visual, sound, and other perceptions controls the performance of operator and machine to produce the desired output. The supervisor of a process assists operators, checks control parameters, and continuously observes what's happening. Feedback from the work itself enables operators and supervisor to control what's happening to achieve desired results. A salesperson, through customer contacts and customer actions, continuing appraisal of competition, and awareness of company actions and capabilities can achieve a successful level of sales revenue. At all levels, feedback from the work itself controls performance.

Budgets and "control reports" don't control performance. Feedback from the work itself, as the work is being done, controls performance. Companies run on real time. That's why continuous budgets and continuous planning is more useful than budgeting and planning for accounting periods (see chapter 5).

Using the VSM and the system science and cybernetics embedded in the model, decisions are made throughout the company by people who have the requisite variety to make the decisions. The mechanism is not decentralization. The VSM gives us a better way—recursion and information and requisite variety, and self-organization, and self-control as described in this chapter. The design of each viable system model includes the specification of measures needed to coordinate actions and to inform and motivate the achievement of desired results. Information controls performance. Effective information is feedback from the work itself. Sales people get sales and customer feedback, not from reports, but from their customers. People running a process get feedback from measures of process parameters, not from reports. Project feedback informs project members continuously, not periodic reports. The self-controlling business system runs on real time. There are measures of many kinds, as needed for decisions at all levels of recursion.

The VSM and system thinking make system design the number one responsibility of top management at each level of recursion. The responsibility is on-going. Design the system. The VSM is a most useful model for understanding the company as a viable, very complex, purposeful, probabilistic system. Using the model and its system science and cybernetics described in this chapter changes and simplifies the job of top management. Instead of running the company, the job of top management is to continuously design the company to run itself to achieve desired performance.

OVERVIEW: THE ESSENCE OF CHAPTER 1

Chapter 1 describes a number of key concepts from system science essential for effective management in turbulent times. These concepts are used and referred to throughout this book. They are the great simplifiers, fundamentals that make effective management possible in today's turbulent times. It is important to understand these concepts to get full value from the rest of this book. The key concepts, in the order they appear in this chapter:

1. A business is a viable, very complex, purposeful, probabilistic system. We know all the parts of the system but because the system is probabilistic, exactly how the system will perform is unknowable. However, the system's probabilistic behavior can be guided to desired performance results using the principles discovered in system science.

2. The VSM includes in company structure information, and the environments the company operates within. Management manages both the inside and now of company operations, and the outside and future for what's ahead.

3. Cybernetics, a major part of system science, is the science of communication and control in systems. Cybernetics is the science of effective organization, and a part of the system science embedded in the VSM.

4. Variety, in system science is the measure of complexity, and is defined as the possible states of the system. For the viable, very complex, purposeful, probabilistic system that is a corporation or a business, variety becomes numbers incomprehensively huge. Management must deal with the huge variety in operations, and

the very much greater variety in the company's environments. Management can't and doesn't need to comprehend all this variety. But management can comprehend what matters.

The variety in operations can be "attenuated" (reduced) by selecting from all that variety what it is that matters in producing desired performance. And the huge variety in the company's environments can be attenuated to what matters for achieving company purpose. Attenuating the variety in operations and in the environments still leaves great variety, which can be further reduced by wisely selected measures. For effective control, management variety needs to be amplified to be able to deal with this variety. The key to amplifying the variety in management is to greatly increase the number of people doing the managing.

5. Ashby's Law states that only variety can absorb variety. Ashby's law of requisite variety is a fundamental principle of cybernetics. Requisite variety means that to control the variety in operations, the controller must have equivalent variety. And to control variety in the environments that matters to the achievement of company purpose, the controller must have equivalent variety. Requisite variety determines where effective decisions can be made. Within a corporation, requisite variety can be achieved through attenuating the variety in what is controlled as noted in number 4 above and doing this at all levels of recursion for each business unit. To control the reduced variety, the variety in the controller—management—is amplified by the large numbers of decision-makers throughout all levels of recursion.

6. Black Boxes in the VSM are organization units whose internal functions can't be known by anyone outside the black box. Management outside the back box can know the functions inside the black box only in a very general way. To higher level management, each operating unit is a black box. The higher level lacks the requisite variety to intervene within the black box to fix a problem or develop an opportunity. Problems and opportunities can only be dealt with effectively within the black box.

7. Homeostats are those elements in the system that maintain stability and the normal functioning of the system. When some internal or external action disturbs or disrupts the normal functioning, these homeostats act to restore stability. In the VSM, homeostats are designed into the system. Conventional management seldom has organized homeostats. Disruptions are dealt

with on an ad hoc basis, often by decision-makers lacking requisite variety.

8. Heterostats are those elements in the system that create change, learning, evolution, creativity, improvement, innovation. Corporations do have organized heterostats—R&D, strategic planning, project teams, innovation teams, skunk works. System science and the VSM structures effective heterostats at all levels of recursion.

9. Recursion is one of the most powerful concepts in system science and the VSM. The VSM models the total corporation as a viable, very complex, purposeful, probabilistic system characterized by the principles discovered in system science. The idea of recursion shows us that all other business units in the corporation can also be modeled with the VSM with the same system functions and characteristics.

   The Corporate VSM is recursion zero. The first recursion from the corporate VSM is the corporation's main business groups; typically some number from three to eight. Each of these business groups can also be modeled with the VSM. The second recursion, then, is the businesses in each of these groups, each modeled also with the VSM; and so on through as many recursions as may be appropriate. At the corporate level and at all recursions, all can be modeled with the VSM with the same system functions and characteristics. This structure of recursions gives us new methods for effective management.

10. Self-organization is one of the most important characteristics of systems. The system that is the world's oceans organizes itself. A salt marsh organizes itself. A company and its business units, each modeled with the VSM, also have the capability to organize themselves using the principles embedded in the VSM.

11. Self-control is another important characteristic of systems. The world's oceans control themselves. A salt marsh controls itself. And the company and its business units, each modeled with the VSM, also can and do control themselves using the principles embedded in the VSM. Higher-level management, relying on the characteristic and the capability for self-organization and self-control, leads by indirect management as described in the VSM. Indirect management improves control of the present, and motivates the creation of the future.

NOTES

[1] Lester R. Brown, *Plan B, Rescuing a Planet Under Stress and a Civilization in Trouble,* W. W. Norton, New York, NY, 2003, p. 6.

[2] Stafford Beer, *Platform for Change,* John Wiley & Sons, 1965, p. 309.

[3] Ludwig von Bertalanffy, *General System Theory,* George Braziller, New York, NY, 1969, p. vii.

[4] Stafford Beer, *Diagnosing the System for Organizations,* John Wiley & Sons, 1985, p. ix.

[5] Stafford Beer, *Platform for Change,* John Wiley & Sons, 1965, p. 106.

Chapter 2

The Viable System Model (VSM)

If we change the way we look at things, the things we look at change.

Wayne Dyer

Wayne Dyer, a popular psychologist and self-improvement speaker, conducts many seminars on public television. In his seminars he makes this statement, and repeats it, to emphasize the important truth that discovery is often seeing with new eyes.

I experienced this truth in 1976 when I was working with Stafford Beer and Paul Rubinyi in applying the VSM in the $4 billion manufacturing company where I was one of the management group. Working with the VSM, working with the principles of system science, working with cybernetics, we change the way we look at our company. We see the company with new eyes. We have a new, different view and understanding of what our company is and how it works. We see the company in a different structure using different management principles. And we see how the company can become more capable of achieving its goals.

CHANGING HOW WE LOOK AT THE COMPANY

This chapter develops the VSM model, a new and different way for management to see and manage the structure and the operations of the

Holistic Management, by William Christopher
Copyright © 2007 John Wiley & Sons, Inc., Publication

company. The VSM model describes companies and corporations of all kinds, and any of our many other organizations—a government, a non-profit, a university, a charity, a professional society, a political party, and any other. But this book deals specifically with the VSM and system thinking in business enterprise. The VSM presents a new and different management science that gives us a better way to structure and manage the company.

Managers often make decisions with limited data, and much uncertainty. Decisions are made with confidence, but often without the capability for making wise decisions—for two reasons: (1) The decision maker may lack requisite variety. The decision should be made at a lower level of recursion. (2) Managers have models in their heads that guide them in making their decisions. The models they use misrepresent the real situation; they are not viable models. Different managers seldom have the same models in their heads. People build their own models from years of learning and experience. And learning and experience varies.

For the company, and for the business units in the company, this book proposes the system science represented by the viable system model (VSM) as a different and better model for management. The VSM is a system science-based model including all the conditions required for viability—the ability for the company to continue to exist in its environment. With many years of application experience, although not yet widely used, the VSM has proved to be a reliable model of what the company really is and how it really works. The model, and its system science and cybernetics, can be understood and used throughout the company. Best practices in the key performance areas that determine every company's success also can be understood and used throughout the company. Combining the VSM with these key performance areas, management will be different, and better. Company achievement will be greater, and better.

Think about the two key words in the name, Viable System Model: *Viable*, capable of continuing to exist it its environment. *System*, a group of entities doing the system's work and interacting among themselves and with the environments outside the company to accomplish a desired purpose.

The model includes all that's in the company, and all that's outside the company that relates to company viability and the achievement of company purpose.

With this description of the VSM we can begin to envision the company as a viable, very complex, purposeful, probabilistic system.

We naturally expect the company to be viable, capable of continuing to exist in its environment. Even in cases of impending bankruptcy or takeover, the company could be viable. If bankruptcy, it could be restructured to viability. After a takeover it would be a viable business system within a higher-level system. We know something about viability, but not enough. And we need to learn much more about the "system" idea.

CHARACTERISTICS OF A VIABLE SYSTEM

Figure 2.1, a repeat of Figure 1.3 in Chapter 1, diagrams the elements of a viable business system: management, management systems (the systems used by management), operations, and the external environment.

While Figure 2.1 shows four separate elements, these four elements, in reality, are all integrated together as shown in Figure 2.2, a repeat of Figure 1.4 from Chapter 1. Management systems (the triangle) is embedded in management (the square), which is embedded in operations (the circle); and all are embedded in the environment (the amoeboid shape). Showing the four elements separately helps us visualize relationships and the structure of the communications among them.

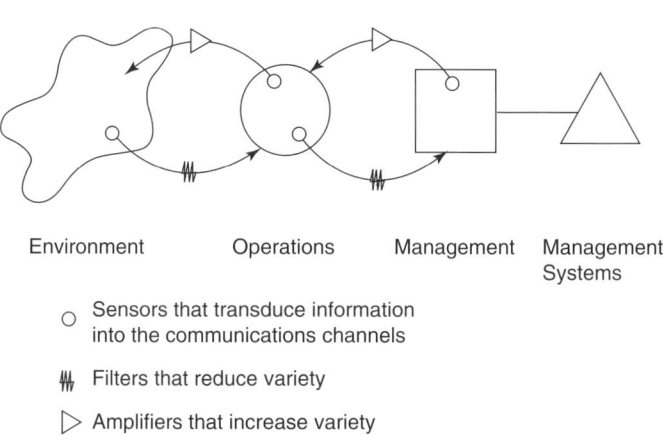

Environment   Operations   Management   Management
                                                        Systems

○   Sensors that transduce information
    into the communications channels

〷   Filters that reduce variety

▷   Amplifiers that increase variety

Figure 2.1   A viable business system

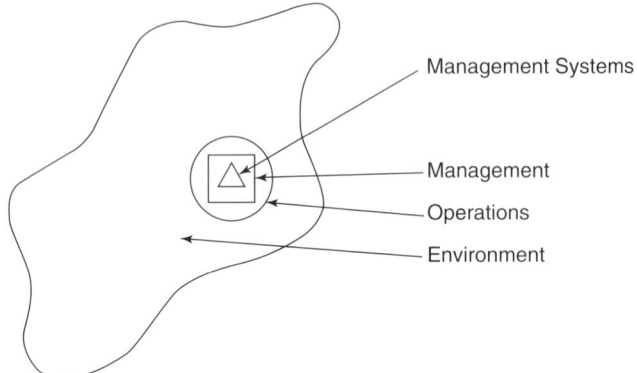

Figure 2.2   A viable business system embedded in the environment

The elements in the viable system are:

- Operations (the circle), which produces the products and services defining the system which is the company or unit we are focusing on as a system. A system is what it does.
- Management (the square), the management of those operations.
- Management Systems, (the triangle), the methods and technologies that are used to organize and operate the enterprise with the aim of achieving company purpose.
- Environment (the amoeboid shape), the external world in which the company or unit works, including the commercial, economic, technical, political, social, educational, and ecological environments.

Arrows in the system diagram, Figure 2.1, indicate the flow of information. Sensors transduce the data into information understandable to the user receiving the information. Filters reduce the vast amount of variety into meaningful information. Management and operations can't know everything that's out there in the environment, but must know all that matters. Management can't know all the variety in operations, but must know all that matters. Amplification makes possible effective communication of information from management to operations, and from management and operations to the environment. Filters and amplifiers, and measures, enable companies to reach the requisite variety needed for effective decisions, and the continuous control of progress toward desired objectives.

These two figures are repeated here for a purpose. Most readers, at this point, are visualizing their companies as shown on the company organization chart. In this chapter, we make a big transition. We leave the company organization chart in the HR department that wants to know where people are and who reports to who. We now want to see the company as visualized in the VSM. We want to see more clearly what the company is, and how it works. These first two figures can be a first step in getting to this new way of seeing and understanding our company.

CONDITIONS NEEDED FOR VIABILITY

The VSM establishes all the conditions needed for system viability. Using the VSM, we begin to understand important viable system characteristics important for business management. We see that our company:

1. Comprises operations and the management of operations
2. Relates to an external environment
3. Has a purpose and a structure to achieve its purpose
4. Is largely self-organizing and self-controlling
5. Is controlled through information flow relating to purpose
6. Provides control information through feedback measures
7. Makes decisions at the level of requisite variety

1. Comprises Operations and the Management of Operations

First there is the total company system, which we can visualize having the above characteristics. Then we come to the next step; defining the viable systems that make up the company system. The words, "comprises operations" gives us the basic guideline. The viable systems create value for customers in the products and services they produce and deliver to customers, satisfying the expectations of their customers with the products and services received. The corporation may have a legal department, but the legal department is not a viable system. The corporation may have an R&D Center, but the R&D Center is not a viable system. The corporation will have operating businesses. These are viable systems.

2. Relates to an External Environment

Viable business systems relate to the external environment in many ways. Customers and prospective customers are out there in the commercial environment, as are competitors and competing technologies. In other environments there are economic conditions, political situations, and social change to deal with. There are scientific discoveries and technological innovations to adopt or relate to. And there is the ecological environment that is the home of all life, including ours. This ecological environment must be preserved and in many cases, because of past practices, remediated.

Figure 2.3 illustrates the company system interacting with the outside environments that its operations relate to. Each of the human, cultural

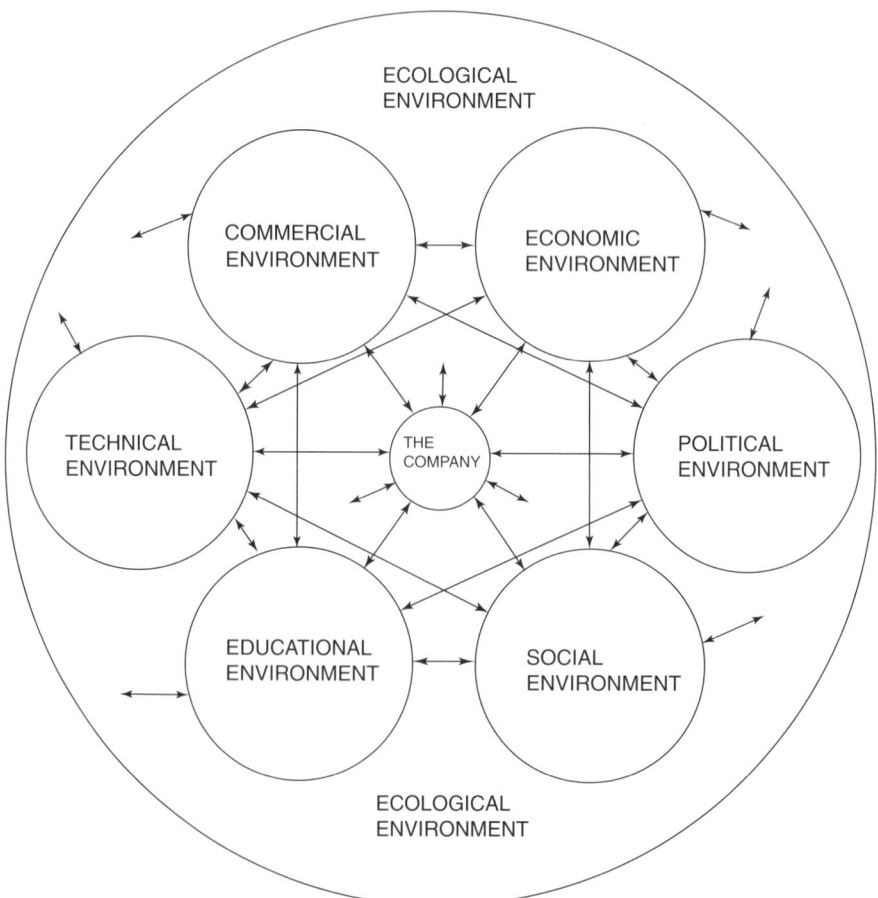

Figure 2.3   The company interacting with its environment

environments interacts with the company, and with all of the other environments. And all of these, and the company, are embedded in and interact with the ecological environment.

3. Has a Purpose and a Structure to Achieve Its Purpose

The first purpose of any system, including business systems, is to maintain viability; to continue to exist in its environment. In natural systems (a wetlands, a forest, the earth) viability is the purpose; to continue to exist. In a corporation, defined as a viable, very complex, purposeful, probabilistic system, viability is in the definition and of course a part of company purpose is to continue to exist. Purposeful is also in the definition. Corporations and all businesses exist to do something, they exist for a purpose. Their purpose, what they all do, is create value for customers. The purpose of a viable business system is to create and keep customers by offering products and service values satisfying and exceeding their expectations. So purpose will be stated in terms of products and services, and markets and customers.

The VSM describes a system structure, communication channels, and the feedback information needed at all decision points. The design of the company system and its network of subordinate systems creates a total system that achieves company purpose. The design of the system determines performance results.

4. Is Largely Self-Organizing and Self-Controlling

Having in mind the concept of variety as the measure of complexity, it is obvious that the ten thousand million neurons in the brain of the CEO is not enough to control the huge variety in all company operations. But it is enough to determine the system structure of the company. Inside the heads of each company employee is another ten thousand million neurons, so there can be ample variety at each decision point throughout the company to direct and control what needs to be done. The design of the system makes it self-organizing and self-controlling. Feedback measures come from the work itself more than from reports, or from managers to subordinates. People at all levels get directly from the work they do the feedback they need to do their jobs and continuously improve. The system becomes self-organizing and self-controlling, to produce desired results.

Higher-level executives can't know all that's going on inside a subordinate level system (see black boxes, Chapter 1). But they can know what's going into that system (resources) and what's coming out (performance results). When performance results are unacceptable, the effective intervention is not to go into that system to fix the problem. The effective intervention is to change the system so that self-organization and self-control will produce desired results.

5. Is Controlled Through Information Flow Relating to Purpose

Information controls performance. The design of the system's information flow and its information channels are described in this chapter. Suggestions for measures needed for self-control are described in the following chapters on key performance areas. Design of the information channels, and the performance measures, determine the effectiveness of the system's self-organization and self-control.

6. Provides Control Information Through Feedback Measures

In a systems sense, feedback is not information from supervisor or manager to subordinate, or from a performance review, or from data in a report. Feedback comes from the work itself. The potter at her potter's wheel gets continuous visual and tactile feedback from the changing shape and feel of the work piece to guide her actions to achieve a desired result. This concept of feedback is illustrated in Figure 2.4.

In Figure 2.4 the sales representative meeting with a customer knows the sales objective for her total sales area and for this customer. Talking with the customer, she learns the customer situation and needs, and information on competitive products and actions. She knows what the customer buys from her firm, her company's standing in relation to other suppliers, and prospects ahead. She learns about any problems that need to be resolved or any dissatisfactions that require corrective action, and works these out. She seeks new sales opportunities. She searches for and finds ways her company's products and services can offer superior value to the customer. She asks for the order. She earns the order, and follows up to assure customer satisfaction. Feedback from doing her job guides her to a desired result. The customer benefits. She achieves her sales objectives.

In processes, work teams, units, and businesses there is continuous feedback from the work itself that helps keep performance results on track toward desired goals. Everyone and every group, in the work they do, knows what goes into their work, their work processes, and the desired results. In a viable system they have feedback measures from the work they do that guides them to the desired result.

Figure 2.4   Feedback from the work itself

Feedback from the work itself, at all the places work is done, provides the information needed to achieve the desired result at each workplace. The combined and coordinated results from all workplaces creates a total performance result. The sales result from one sales area, combined and coordinated with the sales results from other sales areas, produces a sales total. The result from one production process, combined and coordinated with other production processes, produces a production total.

Feedback measures from where the work is done become the performance measures enabling each person and work group to achieve desired results. Performance measures like those described in chapters 5 through 11 provide information that helps decision-makers at all levels achieve their objectives. There's a lot of attenuation of information to get from feedback from the work itself to measures of performance. So we have to design our measures very carefully to assure they can provide useful information on what matters most.

The great amount of attenuation of information between all that happens at all the places work is done in operations, and measures of that performance can provide requisite variety only within the units where the work is done. Whatever those measures, higher-level management cannot have requisite variety within operations. But higher-level management can have requisite variety for decisions in their areas of responsibility as defined by the VSM.

In using performance measures and recognizing the amplification of management variety required, higher-level management will realize they lack requisite variety for intervening in operations where the work is done. They will recognize that the black boxes are real. Only decision-makers in the black boxes can have the requisite variety needed for controlling the transformation processes within the black boxes. Higher-level management lacks the requisite variety to fix problems or develop opportunities inside the black box. But, using the appropriate measures for their areas of responsibility as defined by the VSM, higher-level management can have the requisite variety needed to make changes in the black box itself (resources, information) so the decision-makers in the black box will produce desired results. Only the black box itself can fix problems and develop opportunities for that business unit.

The design of performance measures becomes a key management responsibility. Chapters 5 through 11 offer some guidelines.

7. Makes Decisions at the Level of Requisite Variety

To assure wise decisions we need always to keep in mind Ashby's Law: "Only variety can absorb variety." Ashby's Law says that for effective control the variety of the controller must be equivalent to the variety in what is being controlled. This law, related to management tells us that, for effective control of operations, the variety in management—the square box in Figure 2.1—must equal the variety in operations—the circle. And for decisions on actions to deal with threats or opportunities in the environments—the amoeboid shape—management will need variety equal to the huge variety in the environment. This principle of requisite variety is a key guideline for effective control, and requires the wise attenuation of the variety in operations and the amplification of management variety as described in this book. Only requisite variety can assure wise decisions. Ashby's Law determines where decisions can be made. System science and the VSM give us the means to make control decisions where the information exists to make good decisions. Requisite variety in the controller is achieved by a combination of:

- Relying on the self-control capability of the unit controlled. With many more people at all levels of recursion throughout the organization doing the controlling, each with their ten thousand million neurons of capability, the variety in the controller greatly increases.
- Attenuating the variety in operations and in the environment by:
  - first, selecting wisely what is important in operations and in the environment for the successful achievement of organization goals, then
  - selecting and monitoring useful measures of what is important.

Too often operating decisions are made at higher-levels of management lacking requisite variety, the decisions ignoring much, even most of the variety needed for wise decisions.

THE VIABLE SYSTEM MODEL (VSM)

Figure 2.5 takes the viable system model shown in Figure 2.1 and expands it into a more complete system model, Stafford Beer's viable system model (VSM).

The VSM is made up of five systems, numbered 5, 4, 3, 2, and 1. The model shown in Figure 2.1 is shown four times in Figure 2.5 as system 1s. If Figure 2.5 is the VSM for a corporation, these are the corporation's four businesses. Each of these is a viable system and can also be modeled with the VSM. The four businesses together make the total corporation what it is. A system is what it does. Each of the four businesses produces, delivers, and services their part of the company's products and services, creating and keeping customers. In this chapter we discuss Figure 2.5 as the VSM for a corporation.

A systems principle is that each system is a part of a higher-level system and is itself comprised of lower-level systems. In business enterprise, these systems are business units beginning with the unit that is the total corporation. At the first recursion from the corporate VSM, the four system 1s shown in Figure 2.5 can be modeled, structured, and managed with the VSM. Their VSMs will include their operations system 1s. At the second recursion, each of those system 1s can be modeled, structured, and managed with the VSM, their VSMs including their system 1 operating units. All business units at all levels of recursion—these viable, very complex, purposeful, probabilistic

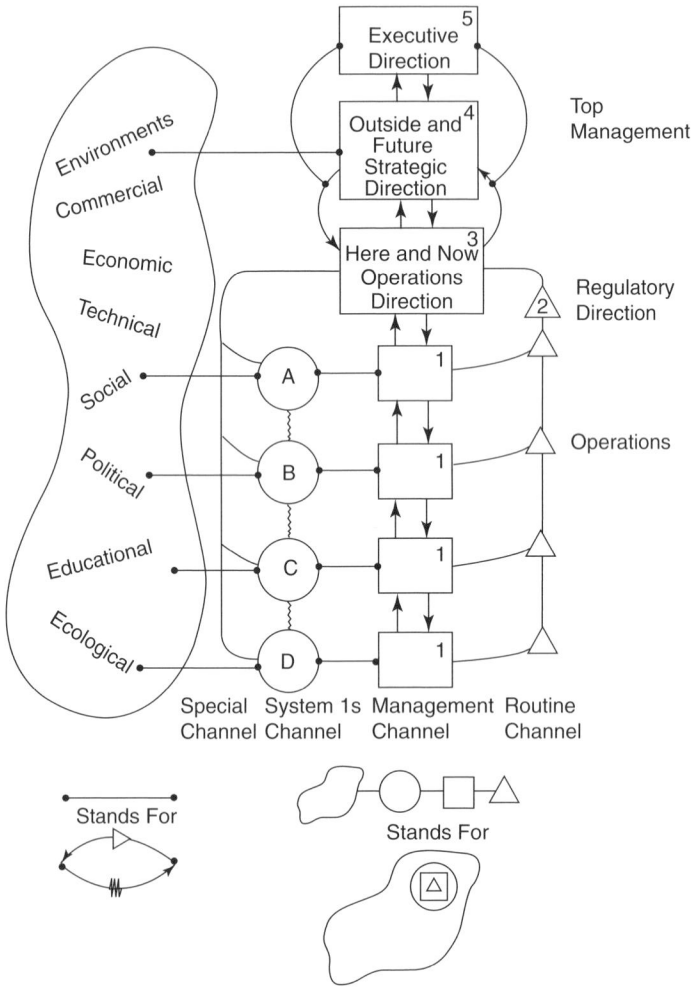

Figure 2.5   Stafford Beer's Viable System Model (VSM)

systems—can be modeled, structured and managed with the VSM. See
Figure 1.6, Chapter 1, for an illustration of recursion.

Figure 1.6 suggests that recursion is linear, recursion 1, recursion 2,
recursion 3, etc. From anywhere in the corporation to the corporate
VSM the connection is linear, one recursion at a time. But from
the corporate VSM through its recursions there are many paths. Each
VSM has several viable system 1s. In Figure 2.5 the corporate VSM
has four viable system 1s, and each of these system 1s modeled
with the VSM would have several viable system 1s. So, instead of

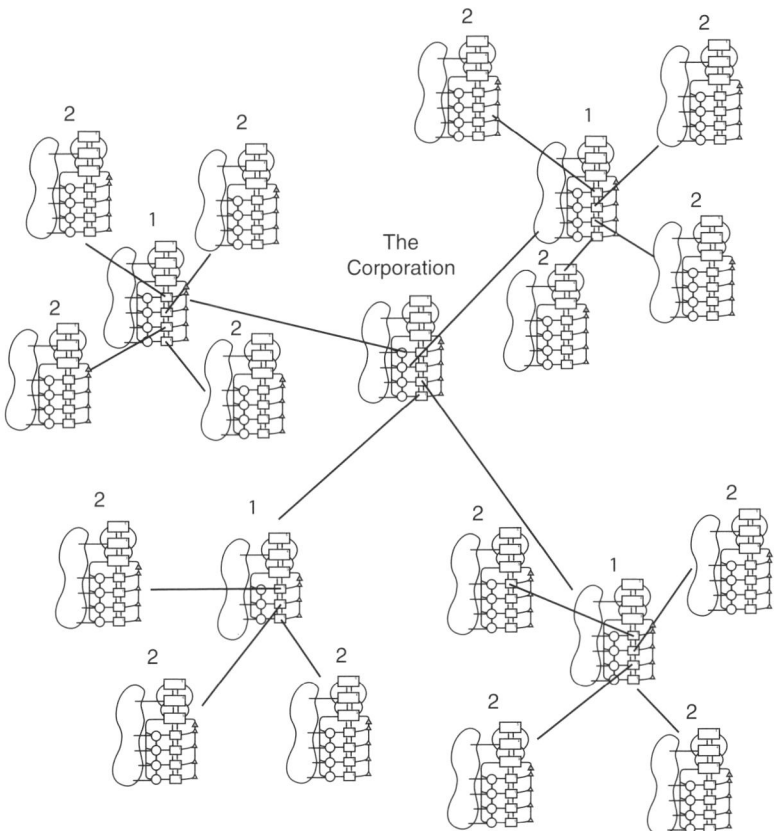

Figure 2.6   Corporate VSM and two recursions

linear, recursions become a multi-dimensional network as visualized in Figure 2.6.

In Figure 2.6, the first recursion VSMs are labeled with a figure 1; the second recursion VSMs with a figure 2. A typical corporate VSM with two recursions would show a more complex network than shown in Figure 2.6. The corporate VSM will likely have more than four viable system 1s. And these VSMs will likely average more than 4 viable system 1s. So, in the typical case of a large corporation, the corporate VSM with two levels of recursion will show a total of more viable businesses than shown in Figure 2.6. Looking at Figure 2.6 we can visualize a multi-dimensional network rather than the two-dimensional hierarchy we are accustomed to seeing in the traditional organization chart. In Figure 2.6, a third recursion would add an additional sixty VSMs.

In applying and working with the VSM at the corporate level we develop the corporate VSM, as the system in focus. The next step, then, is to do the same for the first level of recursion. Best practice is to work with a VSM, the system in focus, and the next level of recursion. So we work with the corporate VSM, the system in focus, and the first recursion from the corporate VSM. Or we could start with one of the corporate systems 1s as the system in focus, and the next recursion from that VSM. Anywhere in the company we would work with a system in focus and the next level of recursion from that system; both modeled with the VSM.

In Figure 2.5 we see additional labels and we see communications channels. The bullets at the origins and destinations of the communications channels indicate that communications flow in both directions, with amplification of management variety, and filtering of operations and environment variety. The four horizontal number 1 "operations" elements are the familiar system model we saw in Figure 2.1. Here they are system 1s in the corporate VSM. Numbers 2, 3, 4, and 5 are the top management functions of the corporate system. They are systems, too, but not viable systems. The total corporation, now modeled with the VSM, is a viable system. In this model, only the system1s are viable systems. They also can be modeled with the VSM.

SYSTEM 1, OPERATIONS

In developing the Viable System Model of the company, defining the system 1s becomes a task for top management that requires a lot of thinking, creativity, and testing. What are the viable system 1s? Defining these viable businesses involves much more than selecting boxes from the traditional organization chart. A viable business system: (1) offers products and services to customers in the marketplace, (2) has an operations structure for providing and marketing those products and services, (3) has the management needed for the above. In short, the viable system 1 has the capability to exist on its own. But it doesn't exist on its own. It is a part of the total company, with many interrelationships that make the company much more than the sum of its parts.

Operating units on the conventional corporate organization chart typically become the system 1 operating units in the VSM. But there may be changes. And almost always there will be clarifications of what these businesses are and their goals. Stafford Beer proposes that system 3, with the direction and approval of system 5, and in collaboration with the management of each System 1 operating unit agree on a Resource Bargain defining the unit as a part of the corporation. System 4 will also be involved in developing each Resource Bargain to provide their consideration of likely future change bringing new threats and new opportunities. The Resource Bargain includes:

- The name of the system 1 operating unit
- A definition of what the unit is and will be in terms of products and services, and markets and customers served
- Prescription of the boundaries for the unit's operations
- The stated purpose of the unit
- A description of resources assigned to and a part of the unit
- Long-term goals and performance measures

The Resource Bargain becomes the operating charter and performance expectations for the system 1 operating unit. Over time, as appropriate, system 3, with information from system 4 and the management of the system 1 and with the approval of system 5, may modify the Resource Bargain.

After agreement on the Resource Bargain, the top management in the business unit will be responsible for the structure and management of the unit. A practical and very useful method for the top management group is the development of a VSM for the unit. The VSM prescribes both structure and management guidelines.

In Figure 2.5 we see four system 1 viable businesses in the viable system model for the company they are part of. We see also the connectivities, through communication channels, with and between systems 2, 3, 4, and 5; with the other system 1s; and with the environment. Instead of a viable system on its own, each system 1 is a viable system that is part of the total enterprise, which is also a viable system. In even a large corporation the number of system 1s will be no more than seven or eight. If there are more than eight system 1s, very likely a whole level of recursion has been overlooked.

Figure 2.5 includes the communication channels that coordinate all functions and units toward continuing survival over time and the on-going achievement of company purpose. After we discuss systems 2, 3, 4, and 5 we will examine in more detail the important work of these communication channels.

SYSTEM 2, COORDINATION

System 2 is represented in Figure 2.5 with a triangle labeled with a 2. The management systems in the system 1s (the triangles) provide information to system 2, as shown in Figure 2.7.

Functions

System 2 is an important regulator, providing four important functions:

1. Coordinating the actions of the system 1s and the interrelations among them, serving as a major homeostat to keep things running smoothly, and to deal with and recover from any disruptions.
2. Budgeting and budgetary control, in collaboration with system 3
3. Transducing information flowing in the Routine Channel from the system 1s to higher-level management, assuring that the information is as needed by systems 3, 4, and 5.
4. Communicating corporate parameters and monitoring compliance.

As described in Chapter 1, "transduction" puts the information in the channel into the language of the receiver. In this case, system 2 ensures that all the information transmitted by the system 1s to higher level

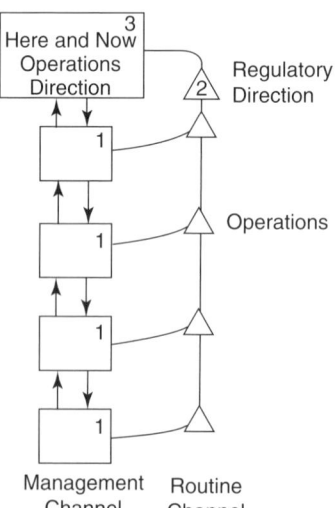

Figure 2.7   System 2

management is information they need, in their language. Included would be information needed for corporate reporting, and any coordination information that would be needed by system 3.

Coordinating the actions of the system 1s requires a facilitator, a tie-breaker, and when needed, an authority. The system 1s may have many relationships among and between themselves. There may be supplier relationships between them. There may be common vendors, and common customers. A technology or method used by one might be useful also for another. While each system 1 has resources and a purpose, each by definition is a viable system capable of living on its own. So they do and should assert themselves in both continuous improvement and innovation—new products, new technologies, new markets, new customers, new processes. This assertiveness should be encouraged. It is good for the system 1 business, and it is good for the corporation.

In their actions there may be conflicting interests among the system 1s. System 2 through its communications channel with the system 1s, anticipates and eliminates such conflicts, and resolves them when they do happen. System 2 is the facilitator, and the tie-breaker in resolving these conflicts. If an authority is needed, there is system 3. System 2 works closely with system 3 and can be considered as embedded in system 3.

Budgets and budgetary control are an important part of inside and now operations, prescribing short-term objectives and coordinating and controlling performance toward those objectives. System 2, embedded in system 3, directs this important responsibility, as facilitator for system 3. System 1 budgets are a collaboration among the top management of each system 1, system 2, and system 3, for approval by system 3.

In the design of the VSM model, the business system triangles in the system 1 diagrams are shown separate from management, represented by the squares. In reality, the triangle representing management systems is embedded in management, the square. Similarly, in company structure the corporate system 2, shown separately, in its structure and function is, in reality, embedded in system 3. System 3, operations direction, can't do its job without system 2.

The functions of system 2 are seldom included in any traditional organization chart. In most organizations these functions are poorly handled, and if at all, on an ad hoc basis. In the VSM, system 2 is an organized function. Using the VSM and system thinking will considerably improve the flow of information, internal coordination, and stability.

Corporate Parameters

An important part of keeping things running smoothly and preventing disruptions, is the system 2 responsibility for assuring system 1 compliance with corporate parameters. Corporate parameters prescribe those matters that need to be done in the same way in all system 1s. The corporate chart of accounts is a key parameter for financial reporting. The corporate policy on ethical behavior is a corporate parameter to be complied with by all company people at all levels of recursion. There will be corporate parameters for compliance reporting (EPA, OSHA, EEOC, etc.). Other parameters include company policy on compensation and benefits, use of the company name and trademarks, and other company policies.

The chart of accounts, standard for the corporation, is an important corporate parameter. All system 1s will be required to report by these accounts. But each business is different, and individual system 1s will be free to use whatever additional accounts are useful to them in their internal management systems. Corporate reporting, however, will be by the corporate chart of accounts. The corporate chart of accounts is an example of an important corporate management function—determination of corporate parameters. Only at the corporate level is there the information and the capability for designing a chart of accounts needed for the total corporation, and practical for each of the very different system 1s. If each system 1 developed its own, unique chart of accounts and reported by its own chart of accounts, the variety would make corporate reporting impossible.

System 2 and corporate parameters help make the VSM much more than the sum of its parts. Corporate parameters, of course, apply also to the higher-level systems, 2, 3, 4, and 5. The responsibility for corporate parameters is a responsibility of system 5; their design an assignment of system 4. Functional groups working primarily in system 3 operations—marketing, human resources, accounting, quality and productivity, and any others—work in system 4 to develop parameters relating to their functions. With approval of system 5 they become corporate parameters and are communicated, monitored, and controlled by system 2. A book could be written on corporate parameters. Here it is enough to suggest a few guidelines:

- Deal only with the essentials
- The fewer parameters, the better.
- The less restrictive, the better
- Allow and encourage local initiative

SYSTEM 3, OPERATIONS DIRECTION

System 3 directs the inside and now—all aspects of current operations to achieve desired results. In the Viable System Model we label system 3 inside and now operations direction. This sounds very much like the typical Chief Operating Officer position shown on many organization charts. But the VSM direction of operations is a different way of directing current operations for desired results. Figure 2.8 illustrates the system 3 part of the VSM.

System 3, mindful of Ashby's Law, views the company's viable system 1s as black boxes. A black box is an entity that has much greater

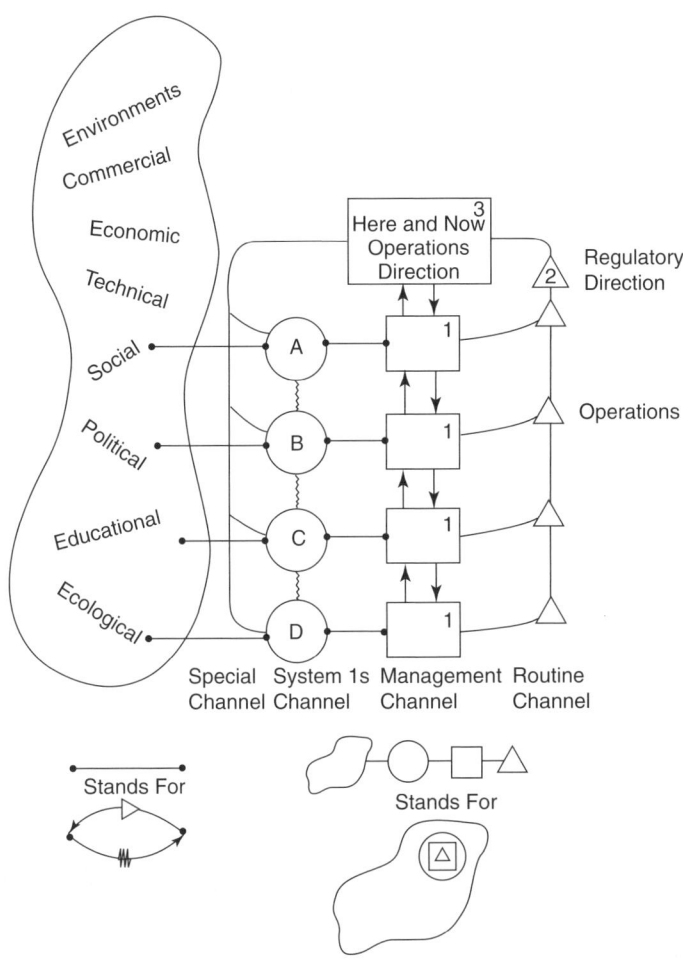

Figure 2.8   System 3

variety that can be known or controlled by the much lower variety in a higher-level system. But to the black boxes themselves, the system 1s, they are not black boxes. They are viable systems that are largely self-organizing and self-controlling, and are quite able to control themselves.

System 3 leaves operating decisions to the System 1s. System 3 lacks the capability and the variety to intercede in lower level operating decisions. But System 3 does know well the system 1's Resource Bargain. So system 3 does know in detail what goes into each system 1, and what comes out. But the processes that go on inside the system 1 black box system 3 knows only in a very general way. System 3 lacks requisite variety. System 3 will recognize when any change in structure may be needed to produce desired operating results. Changes in structure include resources, and, very importantly, information, which in the Viable System Model is an important part of structure. Information controls performance. Changes in information on best management practices, and changes in performance measures can be an important part of any needed changes in the Resource Bargain to improve operating results. With system 5 approval, system 3 makes any appropriate changes in the system 1 resource bargain, when needed.

System 3 Responsibilities

System 3 has the overall responsibility to see that the system 1 operations perform as expected. But system 3 does not have the requisite variety to intervene in system 1 operations. Instead, with the VSM and system thinking, system 3 relies on indirect management and the system 1's capability for self-organization and self-control to achieve desired results.

The responsibilities of system 3 include:

1. Developing each system 1's Resource Bargain. With direction from system 5, system 3 collaborates with each system 1 top management and with system 4 to determine name, definition, boundaries, purpose, resources, goals, and performance measures for each system 1. Put in writing and with approval of system 5, these become the Resource Bargain between the system 1 management and corporate management.

2. Reviewing purpose and determining short-term objectives and performance measures. In collaboration with system 1s managements, system 3 reviews the Resource Bargain and reaches agree-

ment on key short-term objectives and performance measures in the key performance areas that determine business success. For each system 1 these objectives and performance measures become their budget; preferably the continuous budget described in Chapter 5.

3. Providing overall direction of system 1 operations. System 3 provides overall direction of operations much like the Board of Directors provides overall direction of the corporation, or, in part, like a portfolio manager oversees a portfolio of investments. System 3 doesn't run the system 1 operations. System 3 sees that the system 1 operations are successfully managed for desired performance results.

4. Effecting coordination and stability. System 3 collaborates with system 2 to assure coordination and to prevent or resolve any conflicts among the system 1s. System 2 is the regulator; a facilitator, a tie-breaker, and at times needs an authority for decisions resolving conflicts between the system 1s. System 3 is that authority.

5. Making changes in a system 1 Resource Bargain. When required, system 3 using information from system 4 and the system 1 management, and with approval from system 5 makes any needed changes in a system 1 Resource Bargain to improve capability of achieving desired results.

6. Providing overall direction of key management functions. System 3 provides the inside and now functions needed in operations, including: marketing and sales, budgeting, quality and productivity, human resources, engineering, and accounting. In addition to the inside and now, these functions also work at times in system 4 which is responsible for the outside and future of the corporation.

In thinking about the above listing, it's clear that system 3 Operations Direction does not get involved in the operations of the system 1s. But system 3 is responsible for seeing that the system 1s perform within an acceptable range of expectations. The Board of Directors doesn't involve itself in company management and operations, but does see that these perform as expected. System 3 does not involve itself in system 1 management and operations, but does see that they perform as expected. System 3, like the Board, has powerful tools for higher level, indirect control: resources, information design, performance measures, and the Resource Bargain that defines what each system 1 is and what it does.

How System 3 Deals with Problems in Operations

System 3 does not go into a system 1 to fix a problem or develop an opportunity. Although that is what a typical COO in a conventional organization does do and often gets recognition and reward for doing it. The typical COO hasn't heard of Ashby's Law. Typical COOs seldom realize that they lack the capability, the variety, to successfully intervene in system 1 operations. Many, in past assignments, have been operations executives where, in their operations, they could have requisite variety to deal with such matters. Now, as COO and working at a higher level, they have the authority to intervene and feel quite capable of doing so. Actually, in intervening, they ignore most of the system 1 variety—the complexity of the situation—and decree an action. Then they become the judge of the results. Whatever the results, they typically judge these results an improvement over what otherwise would have happened.

One example. An overseas subsidiary of a manufacturing company at mid-year was projecting a loss for the year of $6 million. There was no COO in this company. The subsidiary business reported directly to the corporate CEO. The CEO, ignoring the great variety in that system 1 business, assigned a headquarters finance manager to replace the managing director of the business, with the assignment to cut costs and fix the problem. The new managing director, a finance executive and like the CEO also lacking requisite variety, followed the instructions of the corporate CEO and immediately cut costs. He closed the company headquarters building, moving to lower cost offices. He fired several of the subsidiary's management people, ordered cost reductions in operations and staff departments. Several key people who were not fired, resigned. That year, the subsidiary lost $12 million. The corporate CEO expressed his appreciation for the "tough action" taken, saying: "Think how bad the results would have been if we hadn't taken this tough action!"

A senior professional in corporate planning who had worked with this subsidiary and was familiar with system science and the VSM analyzed this turn-around project. Corporate planning had been monitoring the subsidiary before, during, and after the intervention. The study concluded that, because of the intervention that changed both structure and management methods, the subsidiary had lost about twice as much as it would have lost without the intervention. Over the following years the subsidiary's profitability was millions of dollars less than what could have been achieved if the subsidiary had been supported in its effort to deal with the profit problem. A weaker company, in the following years the subsidiary greatly under-performed in comparison with what could have happened without that intervention. A few years later the subsidiary was sold. If the corporate leadership had been using the VSM and system thinking at the time of the profit problem, they would have acted differently and would have had a flourishing business over the years instead of a smaller, less profitable business. There can be a very high cost when system 3 ignores Ashby's Law, and then judges the result.

System 3 can not successfully intervene inside the system 1s to mandate an action. While system 3 has the authority to intervene, system 3 lacks requisite variety. System 3 has different and more important responsibilities—the six responsibilities listed above:

1. Developing Each System 1's Resource Bargain

The Resource Bargain includes a clear definition of what the system 1 does and its boundaries, its resources, its purpose, its goals, and its performance measures.

Definition and Boundaries   The system 1s are the operations part of the company. The products and services produced, marketed, and serviced by the system 1s are what makes the company what it is. A system is what it does. The system 1s are viable systems, capable of living on their own. But they don't live on their own; they are part of the company which combines them into something more than the sum of the parts. That something more is the responsibility of company management. In the company Viable System Model, company management is the responsibility of the higher-level systems 2, 3, 4, and 5; the company's top management.

A first job of management is determining definition, boundaries, purpose, resources, goals, and performance messures. The VSM and system thinking can be very helpful in creating and launching new business ventures. See chapter 8. In most instances, however, the VSM and system thinking is used in existing businesses to simplify and strengthen management and to improve operating results.

System 3 with guidance and approval from system 5 and in collaboration with system 4 and the management of each system 1 develops each system 1's name, definition, boundaries, purpose, resources, goals, and performance measures. Put in writing and approved by system 3, this becomes the Resource Bargain between corporate management and the system 1 management. Developing a Resource Bargain will include an appraisal of the existing business operations and future prospects. The process may result in the existing businesses becoming the system 1s, but with clearer definitions, boundaries, purpose, resources, goals, and performance measures.

In a highly centralized company operating as one profit-center business, the result might be rearranging operations into three, four, or more system 1s. System 3 with the guidance and approval of system 5, with the help of system 4 on future prospects, and with the collaboration of each system 1's top management develops a clear business definition of what each system 1 business is and what it does, and the boundaries of its operations. Business definition is a major part of the Resource Bargain.

There are no right ways to define the system 1s. There are only different ways; some better than others. The management group in a large plastics products company in Brazil considered their options. In three plants the company produced five product groups, which they marketed in seven markets. To organize their thinking, they prepared a matrix of product groups and markets, and included year-to-date information on key measures in each of the cells of the matrix:

A. Sales revenue (Cr $millions)
B. Contribution margin (Cr $million)
C. Contribution margin (%)
D. Forecast market growth rate (next five years)
E. Competitive position (company position in the market/total number of competitors)

See Figure 2.9.

In Figure 2.9, column totals are product group totals; row totals are market totals. Company totals are in the bottom right cell. The management group reviewed this information carefully, considering possible opportunities for the future:

1. Increasing sales and market share in product/market segments
2. Increasing contribution margins
3. New products in the product groups
4. New product groups
5. New markets

	Product Group 1	Product Group 2	Product Group 3	Product Group 4	Product Group 5	Market Totals
Market A				A. 27.1 B. 17.0 C. 63% D. 20% E. 3/3		A. 27.1 B. 17.0 C. 63% D. 20% E. 3/3
Market B		A. 4.9 B. 3.0 C. 62% D. 35% E. 1/5 +			A. 12.8 B. 7.3 C. 57% D. 13% E. 2/5	A. 17.6 B. 10.3 C. 59% D. 19%
Market C	A. 18.4 B. 9.5 C. 52% D. 20% E. 2/15					A. 18.4 B. 9.5 C. 52% D. 20% E. 2/15
Market D	A. 4.6 B. 2.3 C. 50% D. 5% E. 3/3	A. 9.7 B. 5.0 C. 51% D. 20% E. 2/4	A. 1.8 B. 1.0 C. 56%			A. 16.1 B. 8.2 C. 51% D. 15%
Market E	A. 13.6 B. 7.5 C. 55% D. 10% E. 3/5 +	A. 19.0 B. 10.4 C. 55% D.5% E. 2/3	A. 7.0 B. 4.1 C. 58% D. 15% E. 4/6			A. 39.6 B. 22.1 C. 56% D. 10%
Market F	A. 1.9 B. 1.0 C. 53% D. 10%	A. 32.9 B. 16.4 C. 50%	A. 0.5 B. 0.3 C. 58%			A. 35.3 B. 17.7 C. 50%
Market G	A. 22.7 B. 12.9 C. 57% D. 15% E. 1/3	A. 31.6 B. 16.4 C. 52% D. 15% E. 1/3				A. 54.3 B. 29.3 C. 54% D. 15% E. 1/3
Product Group Totals	A. 61.2 B. 33.2 C. 54% D. 15% E. 2/5 +	A. 98.1 B. 51.2 C. 52% D. 15% E. 1 or 2/8	A. 9.3 B. 5.4 C. 58% D. 10% E. 5/9	A. 27.1 B. 17.0 C. 63% D. 20% E. 3/3	A. 12.8 B. 7.3 C. 57% D. 13% E. 2/5	A. 208.3 B. 114.1 C. 55%

Key: A. Sales volume, Cr $ millions
   B. Contribution margin, Cr $ millions
   C. Contribution margin, percent
   D. Market growth rate, next 5 years
   E. Competitive position

Figure 2.9   Product/market matrix used in defining system 1s Brazil plastics products company

But the main question was: What is the best definition of the system 1 viable business systems? Previously this question had never been asked. The company operated as one profit center business with five product groups, each managed by a product manager. There were no profit measures by product group. There were no contribution margin measures. The contribution margin measures in Figure 2.9 were developed from the company's chart of accounts after a seminar session discussing management economics (See Chapter 11).

The management group had much more information to work with than the data shown in Figure 2.9. The group included product managers and sales managers. Many others in the management group were also involved in customer relations. And there were manufacturing, research, financial, and human relations people who understood well their dimensions of decisions made. The great depth of knowledge in the management group could understand the present, as summarized in the data shown in Figure 2.9, and could visualize potential problems and opportunities ahead. There was requisite variety for wise decisions on business definition.

After their review of present performance summarized in Figure 2.9, and expected future opportunities, the management group decided to structure five market-defined businesses, each headed by a market manager:

1. Market A
2. Related markets B and D
3. Related markets C and E
4. Market F
5. Market G

The company was very strong in its marketing and its customer relationships. They felt their market strength would be enhanced by the market/customer structure. This outside-focused market structure could better serve customers, and also find opportunities for product improvements and for new products.

Management developed a new approach to profit measurement and improvement. Taking an holistic view, they recognized that profit is not created at the product level, or at the customer level. Profit figures for products or for customers can be very misleading because of the way costs are allocated. In reality, it is the total business that generates profit or loss. For profitability targets for both products and markets, the company adopted contribution margin as the measure. The measure is not profit, but contribution first to the payment of fixed costs, and after fixed costs are paid contribution margin is operating income. For the first time the company had information for controlling product costs and contribution margins, fixed costs, and breakeven, as described in Chapter 11. And with the new market/customer structure they had improved capability in achieving sales objectives. With this approach, the company could set contribution margin objectives, and monitor and manage contribution margins by product and product group, and by customer and market. An American manufacturing company going through a similar process to define its system 1s viable systems decided on definitions of four product businesses and one market business.

Paul Rubinyi, a colleague of Stafford Beer, reported the options for a large insurance company in deciding on their system 1 viable business systems. They might choose the traditional division of insurance company operations: actuarial activities, distribution (field offices and agents), investment (investing premium income and maintaining the reserve), and production (the processes for underwriting, policy administration, and claim management. Or, from a different perspective, they could view the operations geographically, with a U.S. unit, a Canada unit, a Caribbean unit, etc. For information on the application of the VSM in this insurance company see figures 2.13, 2.14, 2.15, and text later in this chapter.

A new technology business might be best defined as an area of technology, with products and markets for the most part still to be developed. In defining the company's viable business systems there are always options. It is wise to consider different perspectives with a view toward the future, rather than, with little thought, simply select boxes from the present organization chart.

Purpose With agreement on business definition and boundaries—what the business is and what it does—the next step is a clear statement of purpose. The basic purpose of any business is to create and keep customers. Purpose may be stated in some combination of broad goals in one or more of the key performance areas described in chapters 5 through 11. Purpose might be stated in terms of market position, some level of organization development, some level of quality/productivity, some level of innovation, some basic level of profitability. However stated, purpose needs an emphasis on creating value for customers.

Resources   Achieving purpose requires resources. The system 1s in the corporate VSM are, usually, existing business units more clearly defined. People and capital resources are already in place, and continue. In consideration of purpose, decisions may be needed on some changes in resources in order to achieve purpose. Adjustments in resources are made as appropriate in developing the Resource Bargain. And there will be corporate policies—corporate parameters—on the management of resources and procedures for authorizing changes in the future, as may be appropriate.

Goals and Performance Measures   The Resource Bargain includes only broad, strategic goals, perhaps only one; maybe two or three. Strategic goals might be expressed in terms of market position; number one or two in the business' key markets. The performance measure would then be market position, often a less than reliable or helpful measure since it depends on how the market is defined (how broad, how narrow), and the availability of reliable data. More broadly, and probably better, a strategic goal for market position might be in terms of leadership in the business' key markets or business areas. Performance measures could then include technology leadership, innovation in products, innovation in business methods, sales revenue, reputation, and customer satisfaction.

There might be a strategic goal in terms of profitability, such as performance in the upper 10% of the 20 largest companies in the same industry in percent return on sales. Return on investment measures are less useful measures. See chapter 11. Or there might be strategic goals and performance measures in innovation (chapter 8) or in quality and productivity (Chapter 7).

The Resource Bargain   The Resource Bargain is developed through a collaboration between system 3 and the top management of each system 1, with help from system 4, and guidance and approval from system 5. The Resource Bargain for each system 1 includes, as summarized above:

- Name
- Definition and Boundaries
- Purpose
- Resources
- Strategic Goals and Performance Measures

At each level of recursion the system 3s at that level of recursion develop Resource Bargains with the top managements of their system 1s, with direction and approvals from their system 5s, and help from their system 4s. This process coordinates all company units toward the achievement of company goals. The Resource Bargains don't flow upward to the corporate level for review or approval. Resource Bargains stay at the two levels of recursion that developed them. They help make possible self-organization and self-control where the work is done.

2. Reviewing Purpose and Determining Short-Term Objectives and Performance Measures

System 3 reviews the resource bargain with the management of each of the system 1s to assure understanding and agreement on the definition of the business and its boundaries, and its purpose, resources, goals, and performance measures. Having the Resource Bargain, the next step for each system 1 is to undertake the actions now that will enable the system 1 business to achieve its goals as measured by its performance measures. The Resource Bargain is strategic. But the business operates in real time; this minute, this hour, this shift, this day. In addition to the strategic view, the system 1 needs the on-going kind of plans and budgets, and performance measures that will keep everyone on track toward achieving their contribution to the strategic goals. See Chapter 5.

Purpose All that the system 1 business does relates to the purpose and goals stated in the Resource Bargain. Every viable system has survival as a purpose. The corporation and the corporation's viable system 1s, each a viable, very complex, purposeful, probabilistic system, also have survival as a purpose. That's assumed. Purpose for the corporation, and for each of its system 1s, is something more. Purpose is what they do and for what result, and their intention for the future.

The corporation's purpose could be stated in its Vision, or its strategic plan, or some other document. If not in writing, the corporation's purpose is implied by what it does. A system is what it does. Using the VSM, the corporation will have a clear statement of purpose, its version of a Resources Bargain for the total company. The purpose of each system 1 is a part of its Resource Bargain—the definition of the system 1 business, its purpose, its boundaries, its resources, its goals and performance measures. The Resource Bargain establishes the system 1 as a company business.

Profit might be considered the purpose of the company, and of its system 1 businesses. Profit is an essential requirement. Without profit there is no future. Without profit the business dies. But profit is not the purpose of a corporation, or of its system 1s businesses. Purpose is something about creating value; creating and satisfying customers. Toyota is a very profitable company. Toyota makes cars. To make the best cars possible, Toyota invented new ways to make cars for lower-cost production and higher quality cars. Automotive and other manufacturing companies around the world are now working to apply the methods of the Toyota Production System (TPS), now referred to as lean manufacturing, and lean operations. Toyota is a very profitable company, but Toyota's purpose is not to make a profit. Toyota's purpose is to make the world's best cars at the lowest cost. Creating value for customers earns profit. See Chapter 11. Purpose and strategic goals are the starting point for developing short-term objectives and performance measures.

Objectives   Short-term objectives with dates and performance measures become milestones toward the achievement of purpose. Reviewing the Resource Bargain with each system 1 management group, system 3 works with the group to determine its short-term objectives. For each objective there needs to be the performance measures that will help people doing the work achieve the desired objective. We tend to think of performance measures for the purpose of evaluating performance. But the great value of good measures is to provide information that helps people doing the work accomplish desired results. Good measures are an essential part of achieving objectives. Objectives with performance measures guide today's operations, and also guide the planning to create the business's future. Typically, objectives and performance measures will be developed for some combination of the key performance areas discussed in Chapters 5 through 11.

Performance Measures   In systems, both natural systems and human systems like a corporation, information controls performance. In a corporation, measures are a part of that information. With the clear statement of business definition and boundaries, purpose, and strategic goals and performance measures, each system I management group, with system 3, can develop the short-term objectives and performance measures needed to reach those goals.

An important part of the VSM is the communication channels and the information flowing in them. Included are the key measures that enable those doing the work to achieve desired objectives. Where the work is done, feedback from the work itself—readings from process sensors, visual cues, sound, reactions of others, etc.—help those doing the work achieve the desired result. System 1 operations management gets some feedback from the work they do through their interactions with others. They also see performance measures on the processes they are responsible for which may be real time measures or periodic measures—hour, day, week, month. These measures will be developed as appropriate for their operations. The measures become an important information resource for self-control. In systems terms, they are attenuators of the great complexity (variety) in operations that make self-control possible, and effective.

In each system 1 business there will be performance measures developed for the key performance areas discussed in Chapters 5 through 11—creating and keeping customers, quality and productivity, innovation, organization capability, physical and financial resources, public and environmental responsibility, and profitability. A total of seven to about ten objectives and performance measures in some combination of these seven key performance areas can measure the overall performance of the system 1. These objectives will be an important part of the system 1 budget, and are especially effective when using the continuous budget described in Chapter 5.

Performance measures help those doing the work achieve their objectives. These key measures are used within the system 1, and flow in the management channel to system 3, usually monthly, to inform system 3 on the system 1 performance. In the VSM, all that system 3 really needs to hear from system 1 is the message "I'm OK," if all is on track toward goals. Or, "I'm not OK" and a statement on what's not OK if not on track. There's no need to explain why or to explain any corrective actions being taken. Those are matters for the system 1 to deal with. While "I'm OK" is all that's really needed if things are going well, including the six to ten key performance measures says I'm OK more completely.

The seven to ten key performance area measures are the control part of the communications in the management channel between the systems 1 and system 3. For system 3, these are not measures of the processes within the black boxes that are system 1 operations. They are measures of the outputs, the results, of system 1 operations. They do not give system 3 the variety to intervene in system 1 operations to fix a problem or develop an opportunity. But system 3 does have the variety to determine if changes in structure are needed for desired performance results. Changes in structure can be people, resources, or information. Often information on better management practices or information on better performance measures, produce desired improvement.

Of course, decisions to change structure to improve performance have to be made wisely. Changes based on conventional measures that ignore most of the variety in operations, such as ROI, will usually make matters worse. Profitability is one of seven key performance areas, and results from performance in all the other key performance areas. ROI is an unreliable measure of profitability. Poor ROI may or may not indicate a problem, and provides no information for corrective action, if corrective action is needed. There are better methods. See Chapter 11.

All businesses have a lot of experience in setting objectives—in their budgets, for projects, for financial measures, and more. And all businesses use performance measures. But many conventional measures, in today's world, are neither sufficient nor reliable. With a system view of the company and system thinking, measures typically change from the conventional, and very much improve. Chapters 5 through 11 offer some guidelines on measures.

3. Providing Overall Direction of System 1 Operations

The job of system 3 is not to manage system 1 operations. System 3 lacks requisite variety. The job of system 3 is to ensure that the system 1 operating units achieve results within a range of expectations. System 3 provides overall direction, and support. System 3 uses indirect management, relying on the self-organizing and self-controlling capabilities of the system 1s.

4. Effecting Coordination and Stability

System 2 is the homeostat for maintaining stability in the actions of the system 1s and the interactions among them. To handle this important responsibility, system 2 uses corporate policies, other corporate parameters, and the information flowing between the system 1s and system 2 in the routine information channel. When there are conflicting interests between system 1s, these are usually settled by system 2 acting as mediator or tie-breaker. If an intervention becomes necessary to resolve a dispute, that responsibility will be handled by system 3. So there needs to be good communication between system 2 and system 3. When the system 2 mediation is not able to resolve a conflict, system 3 authority will. While system 2 and system 3 are shown separately in the VSM, we can consider system 2 embedded in system 3.

5. Making Changes in a System 1 Resource Bargain

When there is a need for system 3 to intervene in system 1, system 3 needs to keep Ashby's Law in mind. Only self-control in system 1 can manage and control operations to produce desired results. To system 3, each system 1 is a black box beyond the comprehension of system 3. System 3 can know what goes into the black box, resources and information, and what comes out, measures of performance results. But all the transformation processes within the black box are only controllable by the people and the resources there. System 3 lacks requisite variety.

Many system 3 executives were, in previous assignments, executives in system 1 operations. They feel competent and comfortable in personally intervening within system 1 operations to fix problems. And they do intervene. But such interventions will likely make matters worse, not better.

Instead of intervening in the operations of system 1, the effective form of intervention is to intervene by making changes in the system 1 Resource Bargain so that self-control in the system 1 will deal with the problem situation. Each system 1 Resource Bargain is a responsibility of system 3 with inputs from system 4, and direction from system 5. Changes in the resource bargain can be changes in resources—people and capital resources, or changes in information—purpose, management methods, goals, measures. The simplest and often the most effective interventions are information changes, especially information on better management and operations methods, and more useful performance measures.

6. Providing Overall Direction of Key Management Functions

The system 3 direction of key management functions includes: marketing, budgeting, quality and productivity, human resources, engineering, accounting, and any other function of current operations. While these functions deal primarily with the company's inside and now, they also have some responsibilities for the company's outside and future, a responsibility of system 4. So people in these system 3 functions will at times work in system 4.

Marketing   The VSM models the company, including the outside environment. Company success happens outside the company, out there in the commercial environment. The business of any company is creating and keeping customers. Much has to be done well inside the company to create and keep customers. But the proof is outside the company, in the marketplace. The proof is successfully creating and keeping customers. In each system 1 that's the job of system 1 sales and marketing with guidance and support from system 3, marketing. See Chapter 6.

Budgeting   Conventional budgeting and variance analysis does not fit the needs of businesses today. Using different approaches, budgets can be much more effective in helping organizations achieve desired goals. See the Chapter 5 discussion of continuous budgeting.

Quality and Productivity   In best management practices today, quality and productivity have become different names for essentially the same thing. Both quality and productivity offer technologies for producing and delivering to customers products and services satisfying customers' expectations, without error or waste, and continuously improving the process.

Quality evolved to this definition through concentration on eliminating error and waste, and on customer satisfaction. Productivity evolved to this definition through concentration on the continuous improvement in the production and delivery of products and services without error, without waste, and satisfying customer expectations.

Both quality and productivity have developed disciplines essential for success in all companies today. See Chapter 7.

Human Resources   One of the great values in the VSM and system thinking is using the capabilities of all parts of the company for self-organization and self-control. In all VSM business units self-organization and self-control help provide the requisite variety for effective control of their operations, and for managing their relationships with other systems out there in the environment. Self-organization and self-control develops organization capability, and continuous improvement. So using the VSM and system thinking throughout the company is an important part of the human resources responsibility for training and development.

Many HR responsibilities, including hiring, compensation, health care and other benefits, labor relations, training and development, and regulatory compliance are handled in the system 3 at each level of recursion, following corporate parameters.

Engineering The engineering functions for designing, building, and maintaining company facilities; for developing company products and services; and for engineering and maintaining company manufacturing and business processes is an important system 3 function. This book does not specifically deal with the function of engineering, but does include some relevant comments in Chapter 5 Planning and Budgeting, Chapter 6 Quality and Productivity, Chapter 7 Innovation, and Chapter 11 Profitability.

Accounting Accounting is a major function of System 3. The accounting function is well-structured in existing business organizations. In developing the VSM this function can simply be classified as part of system 3. But a part of their work will be in System 4. Most of finance will be in system 4, some in system 3; accounting will work mostly in system 3, some in system 4.

In using the VSM and system thinking, it is wise to consider if these functions are appropriately organized and working well. Corporate finance and accounting already has strong supervisory relationships with the finance and accounting functions in the system 3s at all levels of recursion. Is wise use made of self-organizing and self-controlling at all levels? Corporate parameters prescribe what is required for corporate finance and accounting, and how it will be done. But in addition to corporate requirements, each lower level business, a viable system, is unique, and its finance and accounting function also will need to contribute specialized services and information for its management. For example, at all levels of recursion, accounting can provide specialized management economics measures very useful for performance improvement. See Chapter 11.

Many finance and accounting departments feel they have too much work and too little time in meeting all reporting deadlines. In developing the VSM think about possible simplifications and improvements in corporate parameters on reporting. For example, in system thinking there is no need for planning and budget documents to flow from lower level recursions to corporate headquarters. Plans and budgets can be simplified by an order of magnitude and be much more effective in guiding performance to desired objectives. There are simpler and more effective ways of measuring costs. See Chapters 5 and 11. In every function, continuous improvement is a requirement; innovation often an opportunity.

SYSTEM 4, STRATEGIC DIRECTION

While system 3 has the responsibility for inside and now, system 4 has the responsibility for outside and future. See Figure 2.10. System 4 includes all the functions needed to get the company from where it is today, to where it intends to be tomorrow. In the VSM, system 4 includes many of the corporate functions typically shown in the company's organization chart reporting to the CEO. But in the VSM we don't show "reporting to." We show functions and communications links. In the VSM, every function is an important part of company success. People in each function collaborate to achieve company purpose and goals. Instead of command and control, the VSM relies

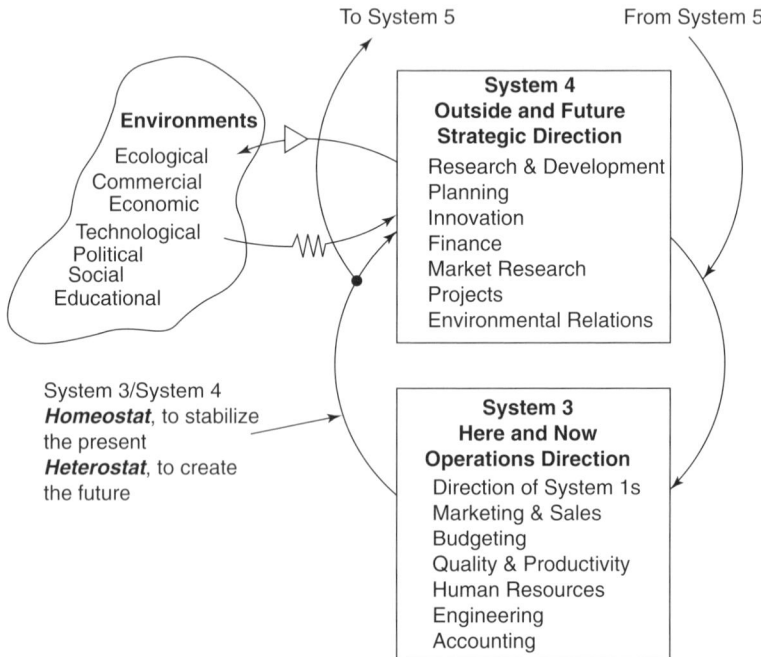

Figure 2.10 System 4 and linkages with system 3

on indirect management, relying on the self-organizing and self-control capabilities of systems at all levels of recursion for effective management. Indirect management relies on the reality that all of us can do more, better, and faster than any one or any few of us.

System 4 has a strong, collaborative linkage with system 3. Just as the future has strong connections with the past, system 4 with responsibility for outside and future maintains strong connections with system 3 with responsibility for inside and now. The functions listed in system 3 in Figure 2.10 are involved with current operations, working to assure that the viable system 1s operate successfully today. But they also want to assure continuing success on into the future, so part of the time they will be working in system 4. Tomorrow emerges from today.

One of the methods for effectively connecting operations today with operations tomorrow is the system 4 responsibility for monitoring the VSM to see that it's working as expected. Monitoring the model is a specific responsibility of corporate planning, but other functions in both system 4 and system 3 will be involved for their areas of expertise. The same is true for the system 4 linkage with the environment. System 4 corporate planning scans the environment in areas of interest and concern to the corporation. So do the system 4 and system 3 functions in their areas of expertise. Constant awareness of the company's inside performance measures and trends, and the selected outside environmental measures and trends helps provide early awareness of threats and opportunities.

These very strong connections between system 4 and system 3 make the system 4/system 3 collaboration a powerful homeostat to keep things running smoothly in the here and now; and a powerful heterostat for change and innovation to create the future. Both are needed. As Ludwig von Bertalanffy states in his book *General System Theory* [1]:

> Concepts and models of equilibrium, homeostasis, adjustment, etc., are suitable for the maintenance of systems, but inadequate for phenomena of change, differentiation, evolution, negentropy, production of improbable states, creativity, building up of tensions, self-realization, emergence, etc.; as indeed Cannon realized when he acknowledged, beside homeostasis, a "heterostasis" including phenomena of the latter nature.

In system science, innovation is a characteristic of viable systems. Innovation is also an essential strategy for on-going business success. The VSM and system thinking help make innovation happen. See Chapter 8.

The Corporate system 4 functions include:

1. Research and Development
2. Strategic planning
3. Innovation
4. Finance
5. Market research
6. Projects
7. Environmental relations

This same list of functions is also the list of functions of the system 4s at lower levels of recursion, for their operating units. At lower levels of recursion there may not be organization units for many of these functions. Instead they may be individual assignments or parts of individual assignments. However structured, the functions are essential at all levels of recursion.

In addition to the functions listed above, people in the system 3 functions of marketing, quality and productivity, human resources, engineering, and finance and accounting, when working on "outside and future" will be working in System 4.

1. Research and Development

Large corporations may have very large R&D organizations, which in the VSM are part of system 4. Also, viable business systems at each level of recursion have an R&D function in their system 4. To create their future, all viable business systems need research for new ideas and new discoveries that can hurt or help their business; to deal with what might hurt, and to develop what can help. Development, in turn, leads to innovation—applying the new idea or discovery in company operations. Innovations in products and services create new values for customers, increase company sales and income, and improve operating results. Innovations in processes, methods, and management practices can also significantly improve performance and reduce costs.

The primary R & D responsibility for corporate system 4 is the research and innovation that will change and improve the corporation. See the 3M example in Chapter 8. Corporate R & D may also do contract research for other company businesses as may be provided for in company policy. At each level of recursion, the system 4s in each of those businesses has the R & D responsibility for the research and innovation needed in those businesses. They may contract some of this research with corporate R & D or with outside sources.

2. Strategic Planning

Strategic planning is a well-organized function in most companies, whatever models they use. Using the VSM, the existing function will be identified as part of system 4. But that would be missing an opportunity. One of the major functions of system 4 is innovation. The VSM and system thinking is a management innovation. And there are often very desirable innovations possible in the methods used in planning. With the VSM and system thinking, planning can be a continuous process. Plans can be much simpler, always up-to-date, and much more helpful in achieving desired performance than periodically-prepared, conventional plans.

Budgets are the short-term, action now, part of the strategic plan. Since budgets deal with the inside and now, budgets and budgetary control become a responsibility of system 2, which is embedded in system 3. With the VSM and system thinking, budgets, like strategic plans, can be continuous, not a once-a-year event for a fiscal year. And a budget can be prepared whenever wanted, in hours or days, not months. For information on continuous planning and budgeting, see Chapter 5.

The strategic planning function also includes responsibility for developing the VSM structure and management methods for the company. Developing the model for the company, and the use of system thinking embedded in the model would become a special project of system 4, and involve all senior managers, and others for their part of the model. After the VSM is developed, the planning function of system 4 will use the communications channels to continuously monitor the model to assure that: (1) the model is functioning as intended, including all systems, communications channels, homeostats, heterostats, and sensors; and that attenuators, and amplifiers are working to provide requisite variety for effective and efficient control, and (2) the system 1s are using effective performance measures and achieving desired performance results.

3. Innovation

Key requirements for on-going company success are continuous improvement in all the company is now doing, and innovating the changes that are right for the company in the pursuit of its purpose.

Innovation opportunities exist for every function and every output. The VSM and system thinking is a management innovation. Innovations that can change and improve performance can be found for all company functions, systems, processes, products, and services. There is always a better way. See chapter 7.

4. Finance

Accounting and some of finance are a part of system 3, operations. The functions of accounting, operations financing, and financial reporting are all a part of system 3, current operations. But finance is also a key part of system 4 which is responsible for the outside and future of the company. Determining and managing the capital structure of the company; evaluating, deciding on, and managing the financial aspects of acquisitions, mergers, and divestitures; and providing the funding needed for creating the company's future are important finance functions in system 4.

5. Market Research

Market research relating to current operations is a part of the marketing function in system 3. But system 4 also needs market research for discovering and evaluating events and trends in the company's environments—technical, commercial, economic, political, social, educational, and ecological—that might become threats or opportunities for the marketing of the company's products and services. Identifying threats is important. Even more important is discovering new market opportunity. Creating the company's future, or the business unit's future, depends on the discovery of market opportunity.

6. Projects

Successful projects change the company and make it better, each project improving performance today, and a step toward the company's future. The company's future will be created through projects. Projects will improve today's operations and help create the future for the business units at all levels of recursion. Projects are a key responsibility of the corporate system 4 for the corporation, and at all levels of recursion the responsibility of the system 4s for those units.

Initiatives to change and improve the company become projects of the company system 4. At all recursion levels, projects to change and improve that unit, that system, are the responsibility of its system 4. Developing the company's use of the VSM is a system 4 function. Every innovation is a project. A new plant is a project. An acquisition or a merger is a very large project. Purchasing and installing new production equipment is a project. In R&D there are research projects. The corporate system 4 project function assures that all company projects are consistent with company purpose and professionally managed. In a large corporation this responsibility often rests with a Corporate Project Office in system 4 for developing standards and methods, project management training, researching project management technologies for best practices, and consulting and mentoring.

7. Environmental Affairs

The environments outside the company are part of the VSM. System 4 in the corporate VSM and the System 4s at all levels of recursion monitor all that's going on in the environment that relates to the achievement of the company's or their unit's purpose. This book discusses seven environments: commercial environment, economic environment, technology environment, political environment, social environment, educational environment, with all of these and the company living in the ecological environment. See Figure 2.3.

In these environments there is huge variety; far, far more than can be matched and comprehended and dealt with by the limited variety in system 4. So the first task of system 4 is to identify just what it is in each of these environments that matters in the achievement of company purpose. However this is done, in each of these chunks of the environment there will not be requisite variety without further attenuation. That attenuation of variety can be accomplished by the wise selection of what to measure and how.

For example, system 4 may conclude that energy cost and availability, and environmental effects will be an increasing constraint on operations and profitability, and may provide opportunities also. So the R&D function will monitor energy technologies, and the human relations function or the government relations function will monitor political and environmental trends for what may become opportunities or threats or constraints for the company.

Designing the reduction of the huge variety in the environment for effective monitoring is a major task of system 4. All the business functions in both system 4 and system 3 will be involved in environmental monitoring for their areas of interest. Involved in environmental monitoring in system 4 will be R & D, strategic planning, and environmental relations. Involved from system 3 will be marketing, human relations, finance and accounting, quality, and productivity. While involved in environmental monitoring, these functions will be working in system 4. However done, system 4 will need to maintain an exploratory monitoring to detect anything out there in the environment that is really important to the company but not included in what is being monitored.

There is also the task of amplification of communication from system 4 to the environment. An important part of this amplification will be: (1) the many individuals involved in environmental monitoring at all levels of recursion, (2) using such methods as well-planned Public Relations involving many company people, news releases, speeches, presentation of technical papers, web pages and other internet techniques, (3) participation in professional societies and the appropriate NGOs, and (4) whatever other methods that can communicate the company's actions and ideas, and also listen.

The ecological environment, now and for the years ahead, will more and more constrain company operations, and more and more offer opportunities. The uncrowded world of 2.5 billion people in 1950 over the following 50 years became a crowded and conflicting world of 6 billion people with population still expanding; fast. The consequences of swelling population and the even more rapidly expanding global economy have brought threats of global warming, water shortages, loss of arable land, pollution, social ills, and threats of pandemics. With world population projected to reach 9 to 10 billion within the next 50 years these and additional threats will grow. The energy, the ideas, the technologies, the products, the services needed to resolve these threats and achieve sustainability offer new and immense opportunities for business enterprise. The system 4 monitoring of the ecological environment will be a key resource for corporate planning.

System 4 Overview

System 4 is the outside and future for the company. System 4 does work that is essential for continued company success into the future, as described above. System 4 monitors the VSM to assure that all is working as desired, and does the environmental scanning, corporate planning, R&D, and innovation to assure the changes needed for creating the desired future for the company. At all levels of recursion, system 4 has the same functions for each of those business units.

SYSTEM 5, EXECUTIVE DIRECTION

System 5 in the corporate VSM is the executive direction and the executive leadership of the corporation. See Figure 2.11. System 3 performs many executive functions in relation to operations. But system 5 as the executive direction of the company is responsible for the company's most important executive decisions—determining company structure and management principles. Structure defines the company, it's purpose, and its boundaries; establishes company goals and performance measures; and provides the needed resources. Management principles determines how the structure will be managed. System 5 also sets the overall character, the ethos, of the company. And system 5 provides the leadership for making the structure, management principles, and character happen. The VSM provides a valuable model for these system 5 responsibilities.

System 5 has the responsibility to see that all the functions of system 5, system 4, system 3, system 2, and the system 1s are structured and functioning. In developing the corporate VSM, system 5 will include the Board of Directors, the CEO, and other offices, executives, and personnel who are a part of the executive direction of the company. Where there is an Office of the Chairman or Office of the President these are part of system 5.

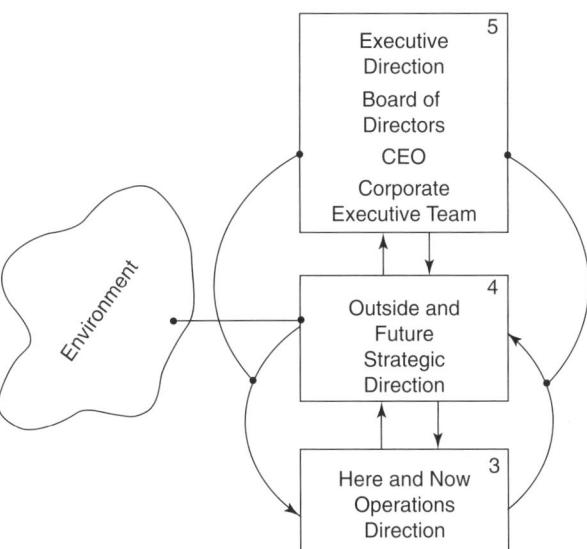

Figure 2.11   System 5 with its communication links

Very important is the system 5 linkage with the system 3/system 4 homeostat. There can be conflicts between the outside and future considerations of system 4 and the inside and now considerations of system 3. System 5 as the company's top homeostat strikes the appropriate balance.

Executives who are members of system 4 or system 3 or the chief executive officers of system 1s may work at times in system 5, the executive direction of the company. Examples would include Board meetings for any of these executives who are members of the Board; attendance at meetings of corporate executives; preparing proposals, or guidelines, or policies, or other corporate parameters for CEO and Board approval; or one-on-one or small group meetings with executive officers. When working on the executive direction of the company, executives, managers, and professionals from other systems will be working in system 5. And the CEO, the chief system 5 executive, will work sometimes in system 4 and sometimes in system 3.

The VSM is a structure of functions, not titles. Every officer, every manager, and everyone else whatever their home (system 1, 2, 3, 4, or 5) in what they are doing in their jobs needs an awareness of when they are working in their home system and when they are working in another system. For someone working in a corporate system 1, the next level of recursion, they will be looking at the VSM structure in their operations and their role in system 1, 2, 3, 4, or 5. The VSM gives us an excellent guide for clarifying what needs to be done, and where. Titles and job assignments follow from that.

Others working with the VSM who are authorities in system science and cybernetics sometimes develop variations in their presentation of the system 3/system 4/system 5 linkages, and other elements in the VSM. While Stafford Beer resisted changes in the model, he also noted that the value of any model lies in its usefulness. Stafford's VSM is a very useful model. But if variations help in explaining the science in the model, these can be helpful, too. Figure 2.12 shows the VSM as it is used by Markus Schwaninger, professor of management at the University of St. Gallen, in Switzerland. In Figure 2.12, systems 3, 4, and 5 and their linkages are visualized differently. This visualization has been used in explaining the system 3, system 4, and system 5 functions and communications in many VSM projects, and helped in resolving the K&K problem that Schwaninger discusses in his case example in Chapter 3. This way of designing the model shows system 4 in close contact with the overall environment. And it presents in a different way the interactions between system 3—the inside and now—and

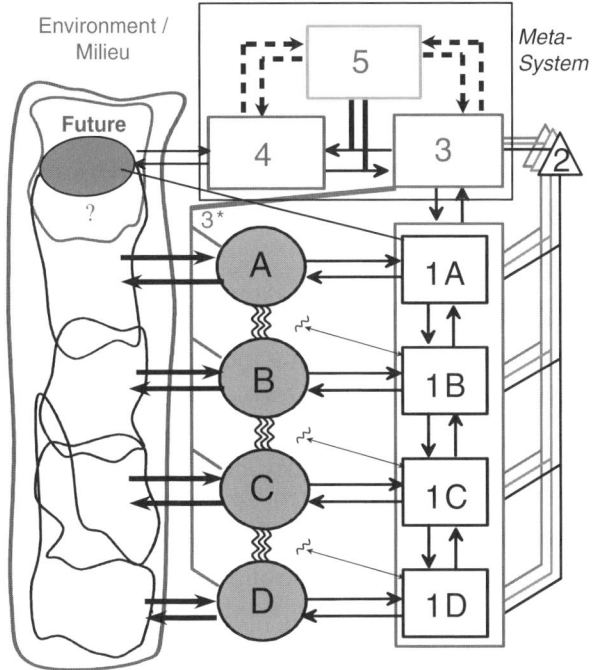

Figure 2.12 Another presentation of the VSM (Source: Markus Schwanninger (2006) Lecture Slides, University of St. Gallen, Switzerland. Used with permission.)

system 4—the outside and future. This presentation may help in understanding the inherent conflict between system 3 and system 4 and the moderating function of system 5. What's right for the future sometimes seems to conflict with what's right for the present. System 5 strikes the right balance. Figure 2.12 also shows the communications linkages between the system 1s and their relevant environments.

The VSM shown and discussed in this book, Figure 2.5, is the basic model as Stafford used it during the 1970s in discussions with clients. In his work, Stafford developed his model further, to visualize additional principles embedded in the model. For Stafford's latest model, see Figure 37 in his book *Diagnosing the System for Organizations.* [2] To grasp all the principles visualized in this model, read (and do the exercises in) the preceeding pages of that book. But all these principles are also part of the simplified model used in this book. To use either the more complete VSM, or the simplified VSM presented in this book, it is important to have a clear understanding of the system science and cybernetics principles embedded in the model.

Responsibilities of System 5

Paul Rubinyi in his book, *Unchaining the Chain of Command,* [3] describes his work with Stafford Beer, and his experiences with the VSM and system thinking in his consulting work. Rubinyi describes 20 functions of system 5 executive leadership. The following listing edits and combines some items to present a shorter listing of the responsibilities of system 5:

1. Designing the enterprise, including defining the company and the operating units, providing resources, and establishing the corporate indicators and information flow centered on these indicators
2. Informing the Board of Directors on the state of the company and the implementation of Board decisions.
3. Establishing and maintaining the corporate top management team, assigning responsibilities and performance measures
4. Appointing key personnel, developing capability, and ensuring succession
5. Developing and adapting the organization for survival and success, including M&A, divestments, R&D, and organization development
6. Providing direction for the company's operations
7. Directing finance and administration functions
8. Identifying, fostering, and utilizing the unique synergies in the resources and capabilities of the total company
9. Providing financial incentive systems for meritorious performance
10. Determining corporate parameters
11. Preserving and developing the core capabilities of the company
12. Determining the company's ethical values, communicating them throughout the company, and establishing an audit system to assure compliance
13. Determining compensation levels for key personnel
14. Entering into contractual obligations on behalf of the total organization
15. Representing and promoting the company to the outside world

In his book, Rubinyi describes his work with an insurance company. In consultation with the top management group, the group reviewed their present operations, then remodeled the company's operations to the Viable System Model (VSM). Figure 2.13 shows the company's organization chart, with numbers in the boxes to use for showing where these functions appear in the VSM. Figure 2.14 shows the company

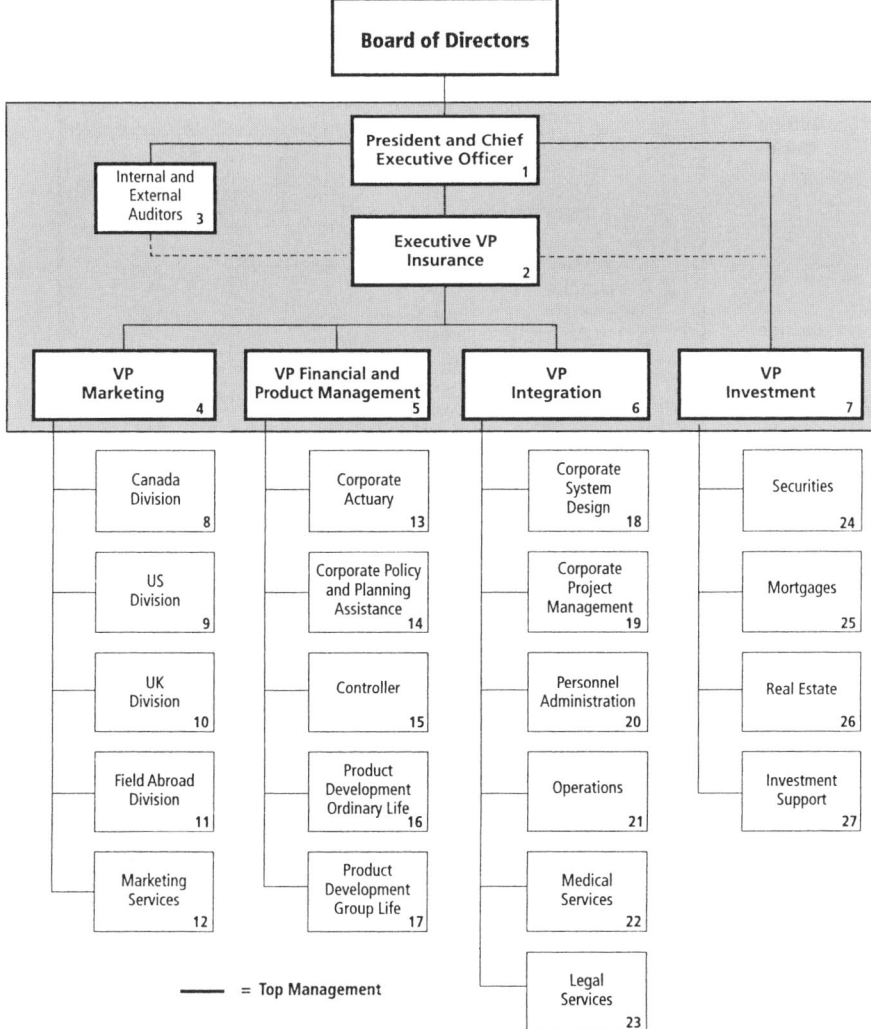

Figure 2.13 Organization chart for a large insurance company (Source: Paul Rubinyi, *Unchaining the Chain of Command*, Crisp Publications, 1998. Used with permission.)

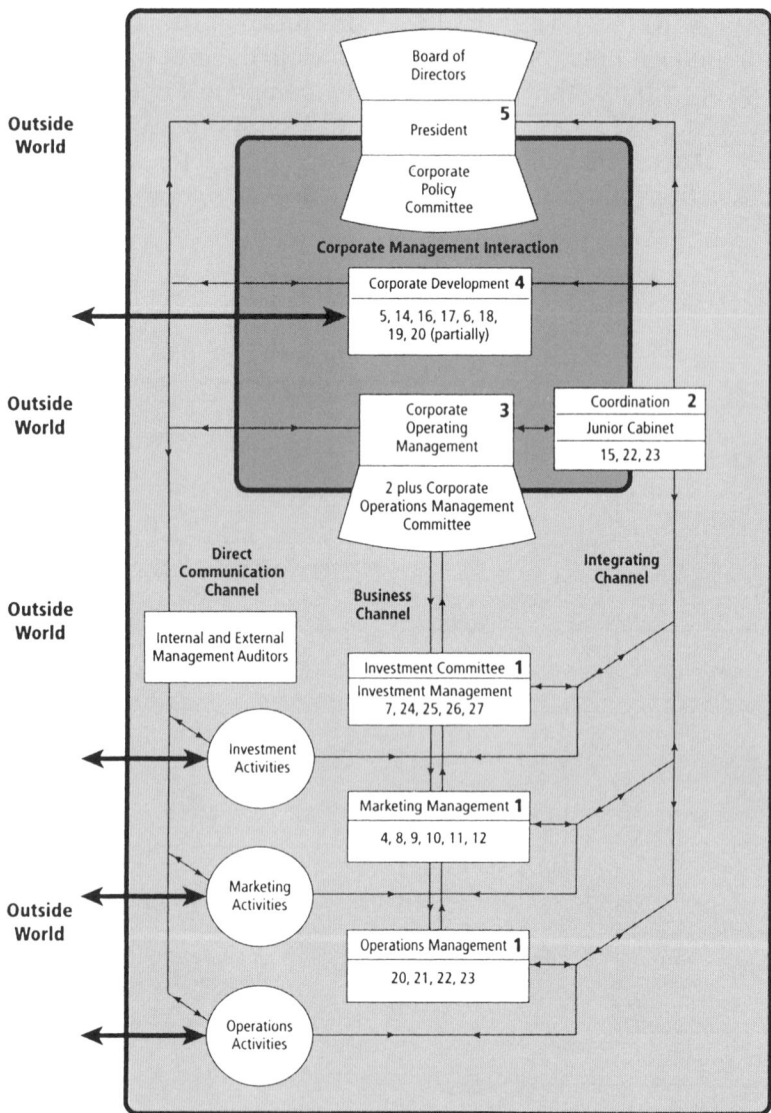

Figure 2.14 VSM for the large insurance company (Source: Paul Rubinyi, *Unchaining the Chain of Command*, Crisp Publications, 1998. Used with permission.)

viewed as a Viable System Model. The numbers shown in Figure 2.13 each fit into one or another of systems 5, 4, 3, 2, or 1 in Figure 2.14.

The management group then goes on to define and assign the top management functions to seven senior officers, as shown in Figure 2.15.

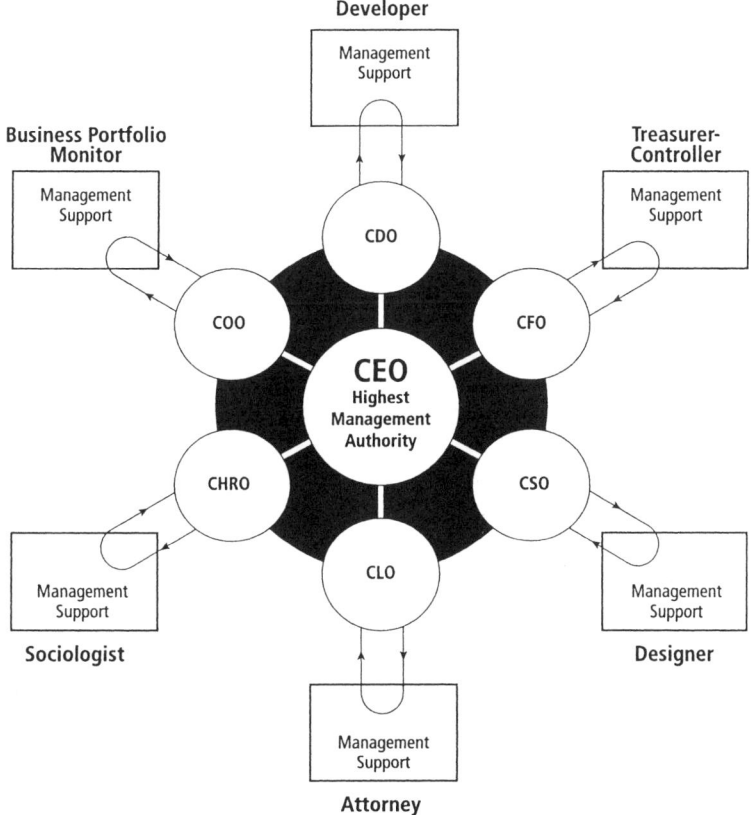

Figure 2.15 Top management leadership for the large insurance company (Source: Paul Rubinyi, *Unchaining the Chain of Command*, Crisp Publications, 1998. Used with permission.)

In Figure 2.15 top management includes seven executive officers:

1. Chief Executive Officer (CEO), the highest executive authority.
2. Chief Operating Officer (COO), the executive for operations heading all system 3 functions, the operations functions required for the here and now.

3. Chief Development Officer (CDO), the executive for all the outside and future system 4 functions, including R & D, corporate strategic planning, corporate projects, and mergers and acquisitions.

4. Chief Financial Officer (CFO), the executive for the traditional CFO responsibilities. Some of these responsibilities are in system 3, the here and now (accounting, audits); some in system 4, the outside and future (financial planning). The CFO is also responsible for the finance and accounting parameters that apply at all levels of recursion.

5. Chief System Officer (CSO), the executive for the system 4 responsibilities for system design, system monitoring, and system support. Ensures that the communication channels are working through all levels of recursion.

6. Chief Human Resource Officer (CHRO), the executive for corporate HR functions and for formulating, communicating, and auditing the HR parameters that apply at all levels of recursion.

7. Chief Legal Officer (CLO), the executive responsible for representing the company on legal matters, for ensuring that the company fulfills its legal responsibilities, and for monitoring changing interpretations and practices and new and prospective legislation and advising the company on any actions needed.

All of these seven executives, in addition to their specific responsibilities in systems 3 and 4, also work with the CEO in system 5 responsibilities.

A System 5 Example

In Chapter 3, the case example titled, "The Crucial Role of the Meta-System," describes the use of the VSM in K&K, a health services company. The VSM helped the company deal with expected changes in the regulatory environment. Examining the company with the view and the understanding of its VSM, it was clear that the company was almost all system 3 and system 1 operating units. Everything was the here and now operations of the company. There was no system 4, outside and future, and system 5 had collapsed into system 3. Everything was today's operations. Establishing a system 4, and reestablishing system 5 as the executive leadership, the company dealt successfully with new regulatory requirements, and grew and prospered over the following years.

Many company managements today, using the VSM, may see their company almost all system 3—successful results this quarter, successful results this year. With no outside-and-future system 4, the system 4 R&D function focuses almost entirely on supporting today's businesses (see Chapter 7 for a description of how 3M handled this kind of situation). With no outside-and future system 4, planning function focuses on the here and now system 1s. With no outside-and-future system 4, system 5 collapses into system 3. Companies where everything is system 3 can have no future. All management systems, 5, 4, 3, and 2 are needed to create continuing success.

System 5 Essential Responsibilities

While system 5 has all the responsibilities listed above from Paul Rubinyi's book, system 5 has four essential responsibilities that pretty well include all the others:

1. Defining the company and determining the company's purpose and goals
2. Structuring the company to achieve its purpose and goals
3. Maintaining stability within the company as the company's highest-level homeostat
4. Creating the company's future as the company's highest level heterostat

The VSM and system thinking helps system 5 accomplish all four of these important responsibilities.

Over the years, company purpose has been defined in various forms: company charter, company purpose and goals, business definition, corporate strategy statements, strategic plan, mission statements, and company vision statements. Whatever the caption, a company needs a clear view of its purpose, broadly understood and agreed on. So it's best to have the company's purpose in writing and broadly communicated. Then all company structure, plans, and operations can relate to and contribute toward this purpose. A clear statement of purpose becomes the first, and a huge attenuator of complexity for management, and a great simplification. So a statement of purpose clearly states the company's unique values offered to customers for creating success today, and on through future years.

A clear statement of purpose and goals coordinates actions on today's problems and opportunities for successful results today and moves the company on toward its long-term goals. With clear purpose and goals, all company people work for success today in ways that create continuing success for the times ahead. Without purpose and goals, we work only for today. With purpose and goals, we work for continuing achievement. So finding purpose and goals is a first task of system 5 executive direction.

For companies without a written statement of purpose, its purpose is implicit in what the company does. But it's implicit to different people in different ways. It's best to develop a written statement of purpose. System 5 could invite executives in systems 2, 3, and 4 to write down their view of company purpose. These statements, authors unidentified, can be the starting point for a dialog to discover and agree on company purpose, and goals.

The essentials of Purpose can be stated simply:

- Business definition: What unique customer values in what products and services will the company produce and market for what markets and customers?
- Goals: For what result?
- Strategy: How will these goals be achieved?

A statement of purpose, even for a large corporation, can be short—less than one page; maybe a page or two—yet be the starting point for continuing success. Goals make the Statement of Purpose specific, and direct all actions toward continuing success. Typically, a company's statement of purpose will include goals in five performance areas in what the company does:

1. Creating and keeping customers: Growing sales revenue; achieving market position
2. Quality and productivity: Continuous improvement in delivering customer satisfaction; increasing output in relation to inputs of labor, materials, energy, and capital; elimination of error and waste
3. Innovation: Developing and marketing new products and services, finding and using different and better methods, discovering and using new and better processes, creating new businesses
4. Profitability: Generating the profit needed for creating the company's future and rewarding investors

5. Environmental relationships and sustainability: Good corporate citizenship, conservation of the natural environment

But a company works with resources as well as for results in what the company does. Achieving company goals requires effective use of the company's human and capital resources. Goals and measures are needed in these two areas also:

6. Organization capability: Developing the capability of the organization to achieve desired goals, continuously motivating high achievement
7. Capital resources: How these resources are brought into the company, and how maintained and managed so that people using this capital achieve the desired goals

Typically, 8 to 10 or 12 goals in some combination of these 7 performance areas can fully specify the company's intended success. But each company is unique. So companies may specify their goals differently from this listing.

Goals make purpose specific. The performance measures monitoring performance toward those goals make the goals real, and important, and motivating for everyone in the organization. Performance measures in the on-line and always current information system are what matter. Goals without measures are destinations without a road map, a target without a way to get there. Good measures motivate. Good measures are the information system that steers the organization toward the achievement of its goals. Good measures don't evaluate performance. Good measures do help people achieve desired results.

A Chemical Company Example

After collaboration, study, and looking ahead, the top management of a chemical company defined its purpose and goals in a document widely communicated: GCX will operate in the broad business areas of industrial chemicals, specialty chemicals, polymers and plastic products, petrochemicals, building materials, fibers and textiles, and services and processes that relate to these. GCK will continuously and systematically study, evaluate, and select new business activities within this scope: (1) where growth prospects are particularly promising, and (2) where it can aim to develop a position of market leadership. Changes in this group of business areas by new ventures, acquisition, or divestiture, may be made as appropriate.

Goals were then set in the following performance areas:

Earnings performance. Increase earnings a minimum of 10% per year, on trend.

Market position. Achieve and maintain a leading market share and profitability position in the specific business areas targeted for concentration of efforts and resources.

Public responsibilities. Conduct operations to meet the company's responsibilities to the general public and the communities in which it operates. On environmental matters, the company will fully comply with applicable law, sensitive to conservation needs.

New business areas. Change the company's business mix to increase growth rate and improve earnings. Creatively search for and find new business areas that have high growth rates and in which the company can achieve leadership.

Competitive abilities. Achieve and maintain unique and superior technological and marketing competence and unsurpassed competitive economics in all targeted business areas.

Facilities. Locate, design, construct, and maintain physical facilities to contemporary standards of competitive efficiency and employee and public safety.

Management. Build a high level of organizational competence to ensure prompt and firm decision-making and implementation through practice of a participative management style receptive to creative contributions of individuals within a framework of clearly-defined delegations of authority.

Motivation. Motivate high performance by making jobs challenging and meaningful in content, and competitively rewarding in compensation, position, and other forms of recognition.

Measures were then developed to monitor performance toward the achievement of these goals. This statement of purpose and goals was developed by managers who had no knowledge or awareness of system science and the VSM. But they knew something about good management. With system science and the VSM they would have revised the statement of purpose a bit to rely on self-organization, self-control, and requisite variety. They would have considerably strengthened their ability to achieve their goals for the company. System science and the VSM provide a framework, a perspective, and new management principles that improve company performance.

THE PURSUIT OF PURPOSE

Companies that have a statement of purpose should review this statement thoughtfully, and continuously. Whenever decisions are made, the statement of purpose should be on the table to assure that decisions made and actions taken are decisions and actions toward the achievement of that purpose. When they are not, it is time to change the decision, or change the statement of purpose.

Often, companies that have a vision statement or a mission statement or a statement of purpose, distribute the document after which it goes into files. Then decisions are based on ROI or discounted cash flow, or payback, or some other criteria. But with the holistic view of system science and the VSM, the first criterion will be pursuit of purpose.

Defining the System 1s

Developing the company statement of purpose and goals is the first task. Then system 3, with direction and approvals from system 5 and with the participation of system 4, and the management group of each system 1, develops each system 1's Resource Bargain. The Resource Bargain becomes the system 1's statement of purpose and goals, and something more. It describes the system 1 as a part of the company:

The name of the system 1 operating unit

Definition of the business

Prescription of the boundaries for the unit's operations

The purpose of the unit

The System 1's resources

Long-term goals, and performance measures

Some methods that can help in defining the system 1s are described earlier in this chapter in the discussion of system 3.

Developing the Resource Bargain for each system 1 will help top management realize the validity of Ashby's law of requisite variety. Ashby's law tells us that for effective control, the variety of the controller must equal the variety in what is being controlled. Developing the resource bargain helps make clear the immense variety in each system 1, and the multiple of that immense variety in the total variety of all the system 1s. While we can not measure this immense variety in numbers, we can make comparisons. And we can see clearly that the variety in corporate management is far, far less than the variety in all or even one of the system 1s. So effective control within the system 1s cannot be imposed from above. The system 1s are black boxes to higher-level management. Effective control relies on each system 1's capability for self-organization and self-control, operating within the boundaries of its Resource Bargain. Indirect management works.

When change in performance results is needed, the Resource Bargain can be modified so that self-organization and self-control can produce the desired results.

Structuring the Company to Achieve Its Purpose and Goals

With purpose and goals clearly established, the next responsibility of system 5 is to assure that the company is structured to achieve those goals. History is the prevue of tomorrow. What do company history and recent trends say about the present condition and the outlook ahead? Are we heading toward our goals? Where are we strong? Where do we need to be stronger? What is the organization's capability of achieving those goals? Company history shows where we are and where we're heading. What we achieve will depend on capability. The VSM and system thinking gives us a way to assure organization capability.

We begin by developing the corporate VSM, as described in this chapter. As we develop the model, we learn about system science (Chapter 1) and the experience of other organizations using system science and the VSM (Chapter 3). Then, as we develop the model we'll more and more understand the company as a viable, very complex, purposeful, probabilistic system. We'll see the company with new eyes as we understand the system science principles in the VSM. In Chapter 1, we listed beneficial characteristics in managing the company as a viable, very complex, purposeful, probabilistic system. As we develop the model, we'll more and more understand and rely on these characteristics:

- We are neither centralized nor decentralized; we are both at the same time
- Control is not imposed from a higher level. Control is designed into the structure so that each unit is self-controlling
- The design of feedback from the work itself enables self-control

- Measures of progress toward objectives provide on-going guidance toward desired objectives
- Since measures reduce complexity they are developed with great care not to lose information that matters
- Information is available where and when needed for decisions and actions
- Each level does its own planning; there need be no passing of planning documents between levels
- Budgets can be prepared in days or hours, not months
- Recognizing and coping with error is part of learning and continuous improvement
- Each unit succeeds by measures of success developed in that unit in consideration of the purpose of that unit
- We learn, adapt to change, and evolve so that we are able to maintain continuing success over time, under changing circumstances

System science says our companies work as described in the first two chapters of this book. The VSM models the company as a viable, very complex purposeful, probabilistic system, helping us understand more realistically what our company is and how it works. We can forget about centralization/decentralization/delegation and with a new understanding achieve better performance results using recursions of the VSM and requisite variety. We use the self-organizing and self-control capability within each unit at all levels of recursion. System science and the VSM gives us an understanding, different from the conventional, of how our company and its parts really work.

Designing the company by the VSM and its recursions doesn't much change the people, or the machines, or the bricks and mortar. But it very much changes how they relate, and how they work. And it very much expands organization capability.

Maintaining Stability within the Company

The corporate system 5 linkage with the system 3/system 4 homeostat makes system 5 the company's highest-level homeostat. With this linkage, system 5 strikes the appropriate balance between the inside and now of system 3 and the outside and future of system 4 to maintain stability while making the changes needed to create the company's future.

There are important homeostats throughout the VSM. There's the system 3/system 4 homeostat monitoring the VSM and maintaining its stability. There's the system 2 homeostat maintaining stability in operations. And there are the system 5, system 3/system 4, and system 2 homeostats in each business unit at all levels of recursion. The VSM is designed to maintain stability.

Conventional organization gives no thought to homeostats or to homeostasis as a function. When frictions, disputes, disruptions happen they are dealt with, if simple, by the people and functions involved. If more serious or complicated they may be resolved by some other ad hoc process. We don't see homeostasis as an assignable responsibility. In the VSM it is.

In recent corporate history, the experiences of Enron, WorldCom, Arthur Andersen, Tyco and many others shows that the system 5 homeostat in some companies is not working.

Creating the Company's Future

Successful companies evolve, change, and are different today from what they were a year ago and five years ago. Their heterostats are working. The corporate system 5 is the company's highest-level heterostat. Heterostats continually evolve, create, change, differentiate, transform what the company is and does to move the company from success today to continuing success over the times ahead. All companies have heterostats, but use different names, such as R&D, strategic planning, projects, innovation teams, M&A; all part of system 4. The VSM puts these heterostats in system 4, and system 4 collaborates with system 5 in creating the company's future. The system 5 linkage with system 3/system 4 supports appropriately the system 3 needs of today and the system 4 opportunities for tomorrow. And in each business unit at all levels of recursion there are also the system 5 and system 4 heterostats for invention and innovation. The VSM is designed for invention and innovation. For more information on innovation, see Chapter 8.

VIABLE SYSTEM TOP MANAGEMENT

In the VSM, systems 2, 3, 4, and 5 in combination provide all the top management functions needed for company success today, and continuing success over the years ahead. See Figure 2.16. The VSM shows

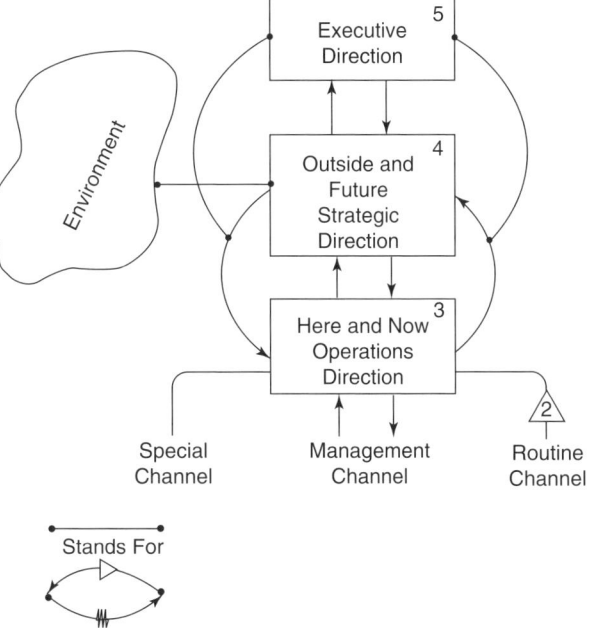

Figure 2.16   Viable system top management

functions, not jobs. Executives and managers will work basically in one of these systems, but may at times work in a different system. The VSM and system thinking help in the design of individual top management jobs.

At all levels of recursion, the top management of each VSM business unit is the unit's systems 2, 3, 4, and 5. At all levels of recursion the system 2, 3, 4, and 5 top managements have the same responsibilities described above for the corporate systems 2, 3, 4, and 5. But they have these responsibilities for their business units as defined in the unit's Resource Bargain.

COMMUNICATION CHANNELS

Figure 2.5 shows a corporate VSM with four communications channels:

Routine communication channel
Management communication channel

System 1s communication channel

Special communications channel, also called the three star (3*) channel

These communications channels connect all the system 1s with each other and with higher-level management. In addition, there are communication links between systems 3, 4, and 5, and with the external environments. Figure 2.5 also shows communications links within the system 1s. These system 1 internal communications links will be shown more completely in the VSM for each system 1. At all levels of recursion, the VSM for each business unit has these four communications channels, the same communications channels between systems 3, 4, and 5, and the same linkages with the environment.

Considerations in the design of the communication channels include variety, capacity, attenuators, amplifiers, and, very importantly, content. With conventional management thinking, all four channels together would need the capacity to handle the total variety in all the system 1s. With conventional management thinking, communication channels are greatly overloaded with information better left at the point of origin. But viewing the system 1s as black boxes, much less information travels in the communication channels. Let's look at each of these four channels.

Routine Communication Channel

This is a very high capacity channel, with communications moving in both directions. Information flowing in the routine channel from the system 1s includes financial statements, required management reports, compliance reporting, information required for other corporate reporting (annual reports, 10 Ks, quarterly reports, company PR, etc.), communications with system 2, matters dealing with corporate parameters, information on conflicting relations between the system 1s, and other routine communication between the system 1 businesses and higher-level management.

Information flowing in the routine channel from higher-level management (systems 2, 3, 4, and 5) to the system 1s includes corporate parameters and instructions relating to them, instructions regarding required reporting, information from system 2 regarding and resolving conflicts between system 1s, and any other routine communication between top management and the system 1s.

With the VSM and system thinking the amount of internal communication can be significantly reduced. For example there is no longer a need to pass planning documents from one level to another. Each level does its own planning and budgeting. So these documents and correspondence and instructions relating to them remain at the system 1/ system 3 levels that developed and monitors them. Information from the planning documents that is related to the Resource Bargain will be communicated in the management channel to systems 3, 4, and 5.

Management Channel

The management communication channel is a low capacity channel, transmitting essential management and leadership information. Flowing in the management channel is information on the Resource Bargain and any changes in it. Both of these will be more a dialog than documents between higher-level management and the system 1 management. Flowing from the system 1s is a continuous stream of information on the system 1 performance on the agreed-upon performance measures toward objectives. If all is on track as desired, the message is basically, "I'm OK, I'm OK." Measures not on track are noted along with comments on actions being taken. Measures better than anticipated are also noted, along with comments on possible new opportunities in that performance area.

Best measures are not comparisons with budget and explanations of variances. Best practices in budgeting eliminate that complex, time-consuming procedure. Much more helpful, and much simpler, are progress measures toward objectives in the seven key performance areas as explained in Chapter 5. With system thinking, budgets will be simplified, continuous, and directly linked with operations, with less data but more information. Real time, continuous budgets, with objectives and measures for the seven key performance areas are simpler than conventional budgets, and more useful. See Chapter 5.

Communications in the management channel are simple, direct, and often conveyed by email, phone calls, or personal visits.

System 1s Communication Channel

The squiggly line between the system 1s is a communication channel between each system 1 and each of the others. This is a medium capacity, high variety channel. The information flowing in this channel includes buy/sell relationships between system 1s, information on common methods or technologies, information relating to customers who buy from both system 1s, mutual purchasing relationships, and information on any other relationships between system 1s.

Special Communication Channel

This is a low capacity high variety channel, also called the three star (3*) channel. In addition to the specified information flowing in the routine channel and the specified information in the management channel, higher-level management may at times need additional, specialized information. This can be provided by audits or by special studies communicated in this special channel. Audits are not only financial. Other kinds of audits might be wanted by top management: capital equipment audits, function or program audits, audits to determine commonality of markets and customers among all company operations, compliance audits, audits of operations support of company strategy, or audits of any area of interest or concern to top management.

In addition any emergency situation that needs to be communicated immediately to top management from operations, or from top management to operations travels in this special communications channel. Emergencies might be a natural disaster, a product liability problem, a security threat, a strike threat or settlement, or any other emergency situation requiring urgent action. And this information will travel by fastest available means, typically phone or internet or both.

Transducers, Amplifiers, and Attenuators

In addition to capacity, variety, and content there are other important elements in the design of the information channels: transducers, amplifiers, and attenuators, as explained in Chapter 1.

Transducers encode the message at point of origin and decode the message at destination. At point of origin the message is encoded into a language that will be generally understood by receivers, such as agreed-upon measures. At the destination point, the message is decoded, if necessary, into the specific language of the receiver.

Amplifiers increase the variety in messages from a low variety system to help achieve requisite variety with a higher variety system. Examples include messages from management to operations, from management to the environment, and from operations to the environment. Methods of amplifying include methods of delivery to many groups and people, group meetings, use of several media, use of many management voices, and continuous repetition in all methods used. But most of all, with the VSM and system thinking management variety is augmented by:

1. relying on self-control at all levels of recursion, which
2. greatly increases the number of management voices, with
3. decisions made at the levels where requisite variety can be achieved.

Attenuators reduce the huge variety in high variety systems to help achieve requisite variety with the lower variety system. Examples include messages from operations to management, from environment to management, and from environment to operations. There is a huge difference in the vast variety in the environments and the variety in management and in operations. At the corporate level, the first attenuation of this vast variety comes from the careful selection of what matters in these environments to the achievement of corporate purpose. Similarly, at each level of recursion, each VSM business unit carefully selects what matters in their environments to the achievement of their purpose. The next step, at the corporate level and at each level of recursion, is finding the most useful measures of what's important.

In each system 1 there is also much more variety in operations than in management. This great variety is attenuated by selecting what is important, and finding useful measures of what is important. These measures become the performance measures for operations. Performance measurement is an area needing innovation and change. As we learn the principles of system science we begin to understand the requirements for managing the huge variety in company operations and in the environments the company operates within. Many conventional and widely used performance measures are simply not adequate for managing this complexity. They ignore much of what really matters in what is being controlled. These first years of a new century must be a time for revolutionary change in performance measurement. And for revolutionary change in where decisions are made. Chapters 5 through 11 describe experience with some new and different kinds of measures.

Attenuation is an extremely important consideration in the design of information systems. The great variety in the environment and in operations must be attenuated into meaningful and useful information. The lower variety receiver of the information must receive all the information that matters. How can the great variety in the environment and the great variety in operations be attenuated without losing needed information? At the corporate level, the answer to that questions lies, first of all, in selecting from that great variety only what matters for the achievement of corporate purpose. The next step, then, is the development of a small number of measures that capture what it is that really matters.

At all levels of recursion the same procedure is followed in each viable, very complex, purposeful probabilistic business system, for that business. Each will be different from what is decided at the corporate level. In total, for the entire corporation, this will be a huge attenuation of the variety in the environments and in operations. And the involvement of so many decision-makers throughout the corporation will be a huge amplification of the variety in management. Requisite variety can be achieved where the decisions are made. Self-organization. Self-control. System principles work.

But there will always remain the probability that something that really does matter will be overlooked in the selection of what matters and in the measures. So system 4 must have an "outlook" function continuously scanning all the environments to discover anything that really matters that was missed.

OVERVIEW: THE ESSENCE OF CHAPTER 2

The VSM and system thinking give us a new way to see and understand what the company is and how it works. When we change the way we look at things, the things we look at change. When we change the way we look at our company by using the VSM and system thinking, our company changes. We understand what the company is and how it works in a new and different way. We see opportunities for different ways of managing for greater success today and success also tomorrow.

System science has discovered common characteristics and behaviors in systems. Our company—a viable, very complex, purposeful, probabilistic system—works like other systems work and we can use these characteristics and behaviors to manage more effectively, and improve company performance.

System science and the VSM give us a framework that improves management in any company, any business, any organization organized for a purpose. The VSM has a lot to say about structure and how the organization works. But the VSM does not tell us what the organization does, what its goals are, or its performance measures. In addition to system science and the VSM we need to use effective technologies and methods in all the key performance areas that determine company success. The management methods we learn from the VSM and system science will be constants, the same tomorrow as today. They show us how to structure and manage the organization for high performance. Effective technologies and methods in the key performance areas for company success will evolve as we find better ways. Chapters 5 through 11 discuss some of the technologies and performance measures proven effective in the world of today. System science and the VSM offer new ways to manage that help us use these technologies and methods, and other best practices throughout the company to continuously Improve performance results.

With the VSM and system thinking we see with new eyes. We file away the traditional organization chart in the HR Department. The traditional organization chart shows units and their executives. It shows who reports to who. The new VSM model of the company shows us much more about the company. The VSM describes the functions and the relationships needed for viability and company success. And through the powerful concept of recursion, the VSM shows the same through all levels of recursion for each and all of the viable system business units. The VSM prescribes the communication channels that keep the company and all of its parts on track toward their goals. The VSM organizes the connectivities and the interrelationships with the environments outside the company. With the VSM we see the company in a new, different, more realistic, and more useful way. Models, including the company organization chart and the VSM, are neither right nor wrong. They are more or less useful. The VSM is proving to be a very useful model for management. The traditional company organization chart shows who reports to who, so it belongs to the HR department. The VSM and system thinking shows what the company is and how it works. So the VSM belongs to all members of the organization.

People working with the VSM begin to see that the VSM really does describe the way their company works, even though the company may not be managed that way. Conventional management sees the company as a hierarchy with the CEO running the company. The VSM sees the company as a network of viable systems. Executive management of the corporate VSM, system 5, designs the company in recursions each capable of self-organization and self-control. Requisite variety determines where decisions are made. The structure of Resource Bargains and communication channels aligns all recursions toward the achievement of company purpose.

The company runs itself. System 3 directs the system 1s. System 4, with its system 3/system 4 linkages monitors the model, maintaining the present while creating the future. And, with its system 4/system 3 connections, system 5 executive direction makes changes in corporate structure and management as appropriate. These same system 3, 4, and 5 functions are a part of each VSM business unit at all levels of recursion, for each of those business units. Control and performance improve.

The VSM, and the system science and cybernetics principles it embodies, is an innovation in management; a new and better way to structure and manage the company. The VSM is a new and better way to structure and manage the company because it more realistically describes what the company is and how it works. The VSM is real. It's practical. It works.

System science is young, originating a bit more that half a century before the publication date of this book. Scientists keep learning more. Practitioners keep adding to our knowledge on application experience. So it's wise for the corporate system 4 to monitor developments in system science for ideas that may be useful to the company, beginning with the books by Stafford Beer and the ideas presented in this book.

It's wise to keep in mind at all times the system science and cybernetics principals summarized at the end of Chapter 1:

1. A business is a viable, very complex, purposeful, probabilistic system. We know all the parts of the system but not how they will work; that's probabilistic. The VSM tells us how to coordinate this probability, and achieve desired goals.

2. The VSM includes in company structure: (1) information, and (2) the environments the company operates within.

3. Cybernetics, a major part of system science, is the science of communication and control in systems, and is embedded in the VSM.

4. Variety is the measure of complexity. Management must deal with the huge variety in operations, and the much greater variety in the company's environments. The VSM instructs us how to do this.

5. Ashby's Law tells us that for wise decisions, the variety in management must be as great as the variety in what is being managed. The VSM shows us how to achieve this requisite variety.

6. Black boxes in the VSM are organization units whose internal functions can't be controlled by anyone outside the black box;

they lack requisite variety. The VSM instructs us on the management of black boxes.

7. Homeostats are those elements in the system that maintain stability and the normal functioning of the system. With the VSM we design homeostats into company structure.
8. Heterostats are those elements in the system that create change, learning, evolution, creativity, improvement, innovation. With the VSM we design heterostats into company structure.
9. Recursion shows us the company, not as a hierarchy, but as a network of systems, each modeled with the VSM. All have the same system characteristics, enabling management to manage in new ways, and manage more effectively.
10. All systems are self-organizing, resolving the problem of decentralization and delegation in a new, different, and more effective way.
11. The company and its business units, each modeled with the VSM are self-controlling. They can and do control themselves toward the achievement of their goals using the principles embedded in the VSM. Self-control improves performance.

NOTES

[1] Ludwig von Bertalanffy, *General System Theory*, Braziller, New York, 1969, p. 23.
[2] Stafford Beer, *Diagnosing the System for Organizations*, Wiley, New York, 1985, p. 136.
[3] Paul Rubinyi, *Unchaining the Chain of Command*, Crisp Publications, Menlo Park, California, 1998.

How the Viable System Model Improves Performance— Reports on Five Applications

This chapter describes how five organizations used the viable system model and the system science and cybernetics embedded in the model to improve the management of their operations and achieve better performance results.

THE FIVE REPORTS

1. In the first report, "Developing a Viable Organization: The Crucial Role of the Meta-System," K&K, a health services firm in Germany, using the VSM changed its thinking about management and restructured top management to deal with the strategic development of the company. Over the following years, the company increased its competitive position, grew, and prospered.

2. In the second report, "How the VSM Helped Transform a Manufacturing Company in Crisis," the UK GRS company confronted a crisis. Its major customer, accounting for more than half of company sales, was moving to stockless production, and would require JIT deliveries from suppliers. They would also reduce the number of their suppliers by two-thirds. What should GRS do? The company

undertook a "total quality" program to improve manufacturing. But complex organization and scheduling problems remained. With the help of a consulting firm using the VSM the complexity problems were resolved, GRS retained its customer and sales to the customer increased.

3. The third report, "The MX Corporation," describes the use of the VSM in a large US manufacturing company. In a work session with Stafford Beer and Paul Rubinyi, the VSM and its system science and cybernetics were explained. Then, working with the company's organization chart, and the knowledge in the heads of the people in the work session, a tentative corporate VSM was developed. In a further session, tentative VSMs were developed for the first recursion from the corporate VSM. The report describes the development of the corporate VSM and the development of the VSM for one of the business units in the first recursion. That business unit included three system 1s and was only marginally profitable because of profitability problems in the largest of its three businesses. Using the management principles in the VSM, and methods and technologies from the key performance areas that determine company success, profitability improved to desired levels.

4. The fourth report, "Applying VSM in the Strategic Management of A Coruña University in Galicia, Spain," describes how the vice-rector of the university used the VSM to develop strategic, tactical, and operating policies. The first step in the process was to clearly define the purpose of the university and its boundaries. Then the VSM was used to model the university and its recursions. All those involved in the achievement of the university's purpose, those inside the university and those outside the university in the political and social environments, participated in the process. The process identified deficiencies in each recursion level for achieving purpose, and developed plans for corrective actions. Where VSM functions were missing or performed poorly, changes in structure were made, or planned. The VSM successfully guided the structuring and management of the vice-rectorship's responsibilities, and defined actions needed to accomplish the desired purpose.

5. The fifth report, "Using the VSM to Design a Non-viable System," shows how the VSM can be used to design a non-viable system that is a part of a higher-level viable system. This report describes the case of the social security system for teachers in Colombia which was not working as intended. How could this system be redesigned to

accomplish its desired goals? Using the VSM, and involving all parties in applying the principles embedded in the VSM, a new and different system was designed that would perform as intended. All parties contributed to the solution, which included changes in the law that regulates the social security system for teachers.

DEVELOPING A VIABLE ORGANIZATION: THE CRUCIAL ROLE OF THE META-SYSTEM (Markus Schwaninger)

The following case is about a health services organization. The author coached a corporate development project with that enterprise. This case was chosen to be reported here because it is one of the few instances in which a systematic follow-up was realized five years after the project. Normally projects of this kind are completed, perhaps written up and then usually forgotten. Here, the successful transformation of the firm will be expounded from the viewpoint of the Viable System Model (VSM), and with a retrospective evaluation. The case will be presented in a focused way, in order to make the crucial aspects understandable. Therefore some simplifications are necessary.

Initial Situation

Kur- und Klinikverwaltung (hereafter termed K&K) is a provider of health services in a well-known resort in southern Germany. At the time of the project it owned a share of 50% of the local bed capacity. The company was constituted by three clinics, a hotel, and a comprehensive bathing and health facility. The resort has a salt spring which provides the strongest brine in the country. Moreover, the little town enjoys a high reputation for the cure of rheumatic and bronchial diseases, as well as psoriasis. Clients are mainly patients financed by public insurance providers.

K&K approached the consulting company of which the author was a member at the time. In a first meeting, the general manager of K&K outlined the situation of the company. It was in good condition, but there was trouble ahead. Changes in the regulatory apparatus of the health sector were due, and this would lead to a crisis of health resorts in general. Eventually, K&K and the consultants agreed on realizing a project to work out a corporate policy and a strategy that would strengthen the viability of the firm.

Organizational Diagnosis

A diagnosis of K&K in terms of the VSM was made. It showed that the "inside and now" (systems 1, 2, 3) was indeed solidly embodied and well functioning. However, there was clear evidence that systems 4 and 5 were weak to non-existent.

The operative management of the overall company—in the sense of a system 3—was essentially provided by two persons, the general manager and his deputy, plus some central staff around them. It appeared to be flawless, working very well and efficiently. However, a management for the long term and the environment at large—in the sense of a system 4—did not exist, except in a rudimentary and informal way. There must have been people who reflected about the "outside and then" of the company, otherwise the general manager would not have perceived the environmental changes and taken the initiative for the consulting project. What the company lacked was an organ that dealt with these issues on a regular basis.

As far as the normative management is concerned, i.e. the ethos of the organization—in the sense of a system five—the situation was different. There was a pertinent body—the supervisory board, which had the task of deciding the ultimate questions of the company: What was its identity? Which were the basic values to which it adhered? What was the corporate purpose and mission? What was the corporate policy?

The board included a set of highly respected persons from the community, including the mayor of the city. These people met on a regular basis. The meetings had a rather formal character. There were few substantive discussions since the operations were under control while strategic development was not a subject that would be raised regularly. As a consequence, no substantial tensions or conflicts between the "inside and now" and the "outside and then" appeared. A system 5 has the role of a moderator between systems 3 and 4. As a system 4 barely existed, there appeared to be no need for a moderating function. The system 5 collapsed into system 3.

The general manager's "hunch" that the firm, even though it was functioning well at the moment, was heading for a crisis, could thus be confirmed on structural grounds.

The Corporate Development Project

A joint corporate development project was set up with two external consultants—the author and one of his colleagues. The main activities of the project were two workshops of three days each, completed within six months. Before and after the workshops additional analytical work had to be done.

The first workshop was about the formation of strategies. For a start, the business units were identified, which was not a trivial exercise. Then, product-market-strategies were elaborated for these businesses. Substantial attention was directed towards the company's overarching capabilities. The second workshop was dedicated to corporate policy, namely the elaboration of a corporate charter (normative management), on one hand. On the other hand, the main implications of the policy and strategy were cast in plans and action programs.

It was possible to assemble an outstanding group of people to cooperate in these workshops:

- All members of the Board, including the mayor of the town
- The general manager, his deputy, and two of his central staff
- The managers of the five sites of the company

It must be noted that the management of a clinic is normally constituted by a medical superintendent and an administrative director. For this reason, the group assembled for the strategy project was an interdisciplinary one with people of medical, commercial-administrative, and technical backgrounds. The workshops included demanding analytical work as well as a weighty decision process. A fundamental insight generated was about the nature of the place: it was not a tourist destination but a health resort.

One important decision was the inclusion of a new syndrome into the portfolio of indications attended to by the K&K facilities. Another decision was for a strong ecological commitment, including a substantial upgrade of the outdoor facilities, necessarily accompanied by a reduction of concrete and asphalt structures ("green in, grey out").

One *astonishing* feature of the project was the extremely fertile collaboration across disciplines. It was especially novel to see medical doctors working at strategic plans and programs, which had nothing to do with the domain of medicine.

In these workshops the systems 4 and 5 of K&K had been formed. Both the members of the strategy team and the board continued that work in the years thereafter. This came out clearly in the follow-up.

Follow-Up

One year later, the resort crisis came as foreseen, but the difference for K&K was that—on the basis of the corporate development project—

it weathered the storm quite well, at least better than most other such resorts.

Five years after the project, a follow-up including multiple interviews and document analysis was made and minutely documented in a book [1]. According to the data, the company prospered in the years after the project. Besides consolidating and expanding its activities, it increased both value potential and operating performance. The value of the company grew vigorously, more exactly, by a factor of 2.5 within five years. In addition, the firm contributed significantly to its municipal environment. It was the strategy project, which had pointed the way for K&K's prosperity in the years thereafter.

However, this evolution was not free of difficulties. During the first three years K&K suffered serious decreases in revenue. Even so, the company adhered to its strategic orientation unswervingly, despite enormous difficulty in staying the course. In spite of temporary operating losses, investment in the development of value potentials continued. This went so far that the corporation realized the largest investments during a period in which, from an operating point of view, it was faring worst. Management was not thrown off course by the slump, nor did they overreact. Without the normative guiding principles and the strategic orientation created beforehand, this perseverance would most probably have been impossible.

The follow-up ascertained a strong learning effect with the managers involved in the project, in the sense of both first- and second-order learning. First-order learning meant that they improved in doing what they already did—run the business efficiently. Second-order learning meant that they became capable of thinking out new strategies and handling them effectively.

Conclusions

In sum, with the new system 4 K&K had formed an organ to deal with the strategic development of the company. But it had also reactivated the Board in its function as the supreme decision unit (system 5). All of this proved to be very effective.

At the outset, there had not been a system 4, and for that reason, whatever there was of a system 5 collapsed into system 3. See Figure 3.1. In other words, a dialog about the future of the company was lacking, with the consequence that there was no role for a system 5, whose main task would be to moderate the interaction between systems 3 and 4.

The new strategy team spoke a language, which was new to the company, the language of the long term. The innovation consisted in

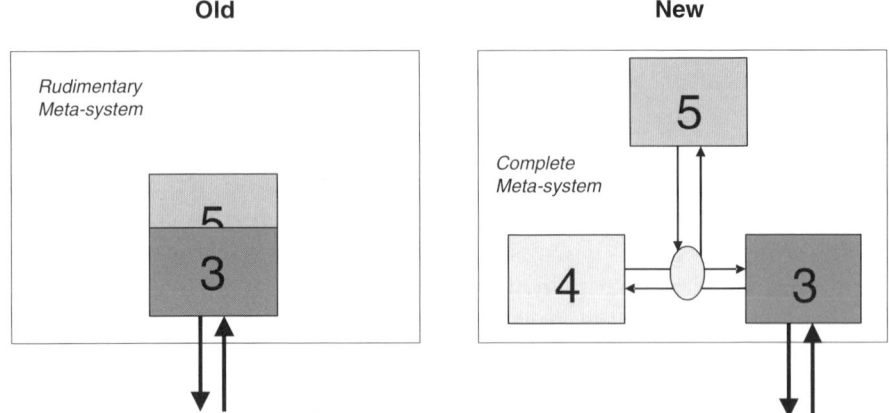

Figure 3.1 Evolution of the Meta-system

the fact that from then on discussions about quarterly results (systems 1, 2, and 3) to were separated from those about strategic development (system 4) of K&K [2]. In cybernetic terms, the system 5 ceased to collapse into system 3. System 5 was activated in the new approach to managing the firm. Now, contrary to the past, both the "inside and now" as well as the "outside and then" were anchored in the organization.

The project reported here was not just a one-off job. On the contrary, the systems 4 and 5 work initiated therein was continued internally over the following years. The resort as a whole and the company continued a solid and healthy development. K&K expanded the saltwater pools, created quiet zones, parks and gardens, and new clinical facilities. An additional indication was taken on in the business portfolio: disturbances of language and voice, with new and unique forms of treatment. The therapy center was expanded and a modern sanatorium for rheumatic indications was added to the extant facilities.

On the grounds of the interviews with the executives of K&K it is reasonable to assume that much of this progress would not have happened without the corporate development project. The corporate development project had triggered crucial decisions and, perhaps more important, it had led to an adequate structure for dealing with the "outside and then" in a systematic fashion. The interdisciplinary strategy team developed requisite variety for dealing with the complex challenges ahead.

To conclude, the K&K case impressively demonstrates the potential value of building up a managerial meta-system with an appropriate structure and sufficient capacity.

NOTES

[1] M. Schwaninger, Anwendung der Integralen Unternehmungsentwicklung. Bern/Stuttgart: Haupt, 1988.
[2] I. Davis, "How to Escape the Short-term Trap," *The McKinsey Quarterly*, 25 April 2005, Member Edition. <www.mckinseyquarterly.com>.

HOW THE VSM HELPED TRANSFORM A MANUFACTURING COMPANY IN CRISIS (Patrick Hoverstadt)

The GRS project is an example of the VSM showing the systemic links between strategic and operational issues. It also illustrates how the VSM and variety analysis can bring out the connections between different operational problems and provide managers with a rigorous language for both the diagnosis of organisational problems and their resolution.

The Company Situation

GRS was a medium-sized engineering company with approximately 200 employees producing pressed and welded automotive subcomponents for several car and truck manufacturers. One major customer accounted for over half of the company's total sales. At the time this project took place, this major customer was initiating a program of transformation for its supplier base. One part of this program was to move toward stockless, just-in-time production (JIT).

JIT can only work if suppliers have the capability to deliver product in exactly the right quantities, to exactly the specified quality, at exactly the right time. Without this supplier capability, the whole production line of this major manufacturer would be brought to a halt for want of a single component not delivered by a supplier. Inevitably then, as part of its change initiative, and to assure meeting the new requirements, the car company was instituting a program to transform the way its suppliers operate. This program involved suppliers in a "total quality" approach to quality management as part of the development of the capability for tighter delivery performance. The program also involved cutting the number of suppliers of pressed components by two-thirds. This left GRS with a set of interconnected strategic and operational challenges.

The Challenges   At the operational level, GRS had the problem of radically improving the standards of its operations. Supplying its major customer on a JIT basis would require it to radically improve its standards for product quality, production scheduling, and accuracy of batch sizes, all of which were woefully inadequate. This set of operational problems, important and significant in their own right, was nested within a set of strategic challenges.

With its most important customer reducing its supplier base by two thirds, GRS was clearly at risk of losing the customer. Losing the customer would have a catastrophic effect, since in a shrinking and highly competitive market, the loss of the most profitable half of its market would almost certainly mean bankruptcy for GRS. Conversely, retention of the customer would demand that GRS grow significantly to fill the gap left by the de-selected firms. The strategic dilemma facing the GRS management was whether to focus on retaining their status as a preferred supplier, or to broaden their customer base to try to reduce the risk. The operational challenge of meeting their customer's demands for higher levels of quality and service played a critical role in the strategic decision-making process. Whichever strategy was pursued with whichever customers, success would depend on being able to meet the higher expectations of a changing market. So improving operational capability was a prerequisite of being able to implement either strategic option successfully.

Complexity and the Problem Set   This group of problems—with a set of operational challenges nested within a set of strategic challenges—will probably look fairly familiar to many business people. If we look at it in terms of complexity or variety, then we can start to see how the VSM relates to solving these sorts of organizational problems.

What we have is a situation of an organization that has been more or less in balance with its stable operating environment for many years. The variety of the organization just about matched that of the environment, so it was able to supply the needs of its markets within the environment, only just, and with much swearing, shouting, and firefighting by managers. Nevertheless, usually the work got done, the goods got delivered somehow, and customers eventually paid their bills. Suddenly, a change elsewhere in the environment disturbed this company's immediate operating environment so that the variety being demanded of the company increased dramatically.

This increase in variety isn't just a metaphorical or notional change in the requisite variety required, much of it can be quantified. So, for example, JIT required more and smaller deliveries, which meant more batches to be put through production, a straight-forward and measurable increase in complexity. Similarly, the new requirements for batch accuracy in terms of numbers of components, quality of components, and timing of delivery were all direct and quantifiable in terms of the complexity and variety of operations that the organization needed to be able to deal with.

The Initial Response   The first response of the company was to undertake a major change initiative using a Deming-based "total quality" program led by an external consultant who specializes in helping companies achieve total quality operations. The implementation plan was based on current best practices and included a significant training program for the directors and management team down to supervisor level. The training was fairly successful in changing both the language and ethos of the company, but was less successful in changing practice in the shop. In particular, it became increasingly clear that the operating structure of the company was making it difficult for production scheduling to handle process-based initiatives. Whenever a process crossed organizational boundaries between departments, change tended to stall.

Analysis and Intervention Using VSM

Analyzing the company's operational base using VSM gave the "unfolding of complexity," shown in Figure 3.2. Operations were organized as three functional departments: light pressing, heavy pressing, and welding; and two "cells," one a specialist assembly cell "ADO" which assembled two large car sub-assemblies from pressings, and the other a department based on new CNC machines.

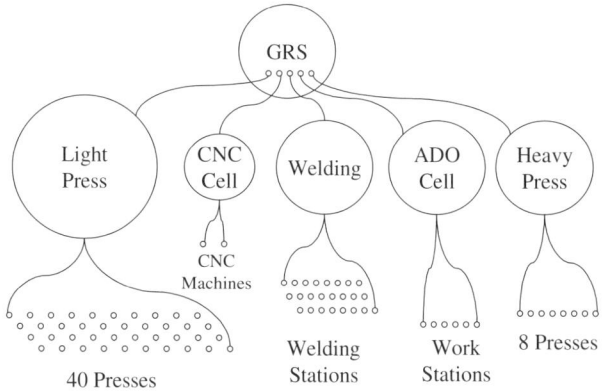

Figure 3.2   Unfolding of complexity: operational structure for GRS at start of project

Unfolding of Complexity   Tracking the workflow through this structure showed complex interactions between these operational departments. Of approximately 2000 different product lines almost all involved work by more than one department. A process flow analysis of workflow between departments for a typical small job needing three pressing operations and two welding operations showed this required no less than 16 interdepartmental information transfers involving six departments.

Coordinating the huge variety of these interactions between departments required a corresponding capacity in the VSM system 2. There was ample evidence that this capacity did not exist. On the floor between the press shop and the welding department, there was a set of wire crates stacked to the roof. These crates were "lost jobs," subcomponents that had been pressed ready for welding into assemblies, but had never been welded up. Some were known to have been there for months, but no records existed to show how long some had been there. This in-process inventory was evidence of very poor coordination between the welding and pressing departments.

Customers calling up to progress-chase their orders were unable to find out where their order was in the process, and would get conflicting information each time they called. This situation showed poor coordination between operational departments, and also created disruption in operations as there were frequent stoppages as the planned production process was altered part way through a batch to "fast-track" another job in response to customer demands on a "who shouts loudest wins" basis. All these were symptoms of persistent breakdowns of system 2 that should have been coordinating production between departments.

Production planning is one of the main components of system 2, intended specifically to smooth operations between departments. But GRS system 2 was unable to cope with the complexity of operations. The instability of the production process was obvious every Friday afternoon. Without fail, one of the senior management team would come into the production control office straight from a heated conversation with a valued customer. The manager would be clutching a piece of paper with the details of the customer's urgent job and insist on the immediate rescheduling of production plans in order to prioritize this particular job. In vain, the planning team would complain that this would wreck the next week's plans and set the scene for a repeat performance the following week.

An unintended emergent property of this persistent failure of system 2 to cope with interdepartmental processes was a culture of blame, which was directed specifically at the production planning team. The blame for the persistent failure of scheduling to deliver accurate quantities on time was put on the schedulers, not on the organizational system they were being asked to cope with. Politically, of course, this had major repercussions, as the planning team's arguments for change were undermined by the perception that they were themselves the problem.

A variety calculation of the complexity that they were trying to deal with soon showed the scale of their problem. For each job requiring pressing operations, a series of decisions were required. Taken in isolation, these were not too difficult, but of course, these were not being taken in isolation as each decision on one job affected the choices available for planning capacity to do other jobs. So the reality facing the schedulers was a need to examine different permutations of jobs going through the system and to prioritize these to optimize overall production. The worst problems were in the light press shop.

In the light press shop, the first stage was to break a "job" down into its component operations each of which was planned and scheduled separately. Immediately, this increased the complexity and fragility of the system and meant that the integrity of the process was only owned by the schedulers, and not by the actual production team. It also of course meant that the production schedule had more things to deal with. The next stage was to prioritize each of these individual operations, then to allocate each of them to one particular press of the 40 in the shop. Once this was done, the press shop team leader would allocate a press operator to each press. Taken altogether, this was a very complicated process. For a group of five fairly typical jobs with two, three, four, four, and six operations respectively, there were no less than 27.5 billion different permutations (the variety) for carrying out these five jobs. Given this scale of complexity, it wasn't really surprising that the production planners frequently failed.

The Alternative Structure

The sort of massive loading on system 2 that was evident in the original structure is very often an indicator that the basic alignment of an organizational structure is wrong. In this case the recommendation was to switch to a multi-functional "cell" based structure, which would combine equipment and personnel from both the press shop and welding shop. This represents a move from a structure split into departments operating different technologies, to one where structure is split by groups of products. See Figure 3.3.

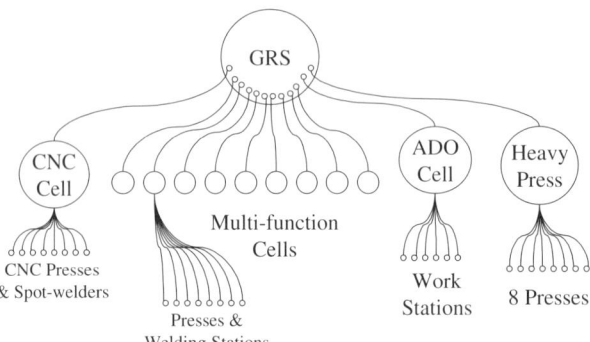

Figure 3.3 Unfolding of complexity: operational structure for GRS after restructuring to cellular manufacturing

In each of the new cells there was the equipment and personnel necessary to do all the operations for a set of products within the company's product range. This involved taking presses and welding plant and putting them together to form a mini-production line that could carry out all the operations needed to complete a set of products. This change is a fairly common solution in the engineering industry, but has been carried out with varying success. In those companies where it was successful it had improved both productivity and response times dramatically. However, in some instances it had had little effect, and had even been blamed for some company failures. Using VSM and variety calculations allowed us to work out the likely impact of this change and assess how well it would address the company's problems.

We repeated the same analysis of workflow and complexity of planning decisions as we had used to evaluate the previous structure. The proposed new structure showed how much more of the complexity of operations management the new structure would absorb. From receipt to completion of order, the job involving three pressing and two welding operations would now involve only three interdepartmental information transfers between two departments instead of 16 transfers between six departments. This change was a significant shortening of the process, giving much greater robustness in the process with much less chance of interruption or misinformation being passed to customers.

Some of the shortening came about because the whole of the actual production process was now contained within a single production cell. Some came about because a reduction in the complexity of production planning allowed a re-engineering of order processing. The analysis of the complexity of decision-making in production planning showed a dramatic change. For the same five jobs, the number of possible permutations had fallen to just 70 from 27.5 billion. For those unfamiliar with variety calculations, this may seem an extraordinary reduction, but in many instances complexity is exponential, so comparisons between very large and relatively speaking very small figures is not uncommon. This reduction meant that the planning process had gone from one that was almost impossible to carry out successfully, to one that was almost trivial.

Outcomes and Conclusions

Using VSM provided a high-level view of the dynamics of the company's problems and of the way that these seemingly disparate problems were related, both causally and in time. The new cell-based structure designed using the VSM proved much more cohesive and a better basis for introducing other technical and commercial changes to address both the operational and strategic challenges. While the structural solution chosen could have been arrived at by other means, what the VSM provided was a rigorous and partially quantified approach that showed why it was likely to be effective in this particular case. The security of this VSM approach contrasts with the risk inherent in adopting such a change plan based purely on copying someone else's solution and hoping that the fundamentals of both organizations are sufficiently similar for the "solution" to work.

THE MX CORPORATION (William F. Christopher)

This report describes how the Viable System Model and its system science, and the key performance areas that determine company success were used in a large manufacturing company.

Company Situation

The MX Corporation is a $4 billion manufacturing corporation comprised of five companies reporting to the CEO. The corporation used the traditional organization chart, shown in a simplified form in Figure 3.4.

One of the corporation's companies is a business with proprietary products, strong market position, and effective new product development programs. The other four have some proprietary products, with

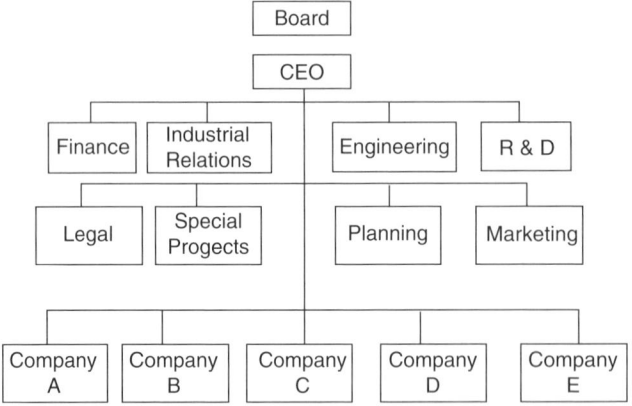

Figure 3.4   Organization chart, MX Corporation

the bulk of their volume in products highly competitive with other well-qualified producers. In profitability the five companies ranged from moderately satisfactory to satisfactory, and corporate headquarters was seeking improvement.

Introducing the Viable System Model (VSM)

Improvement in profitability would require changes. Corporate planning was looking for new and better ways. One of their advisers was Paul Rubinyi, the partner in charge of systems work for a major consulting firm in Montreal. Stafford Beer was working with Paul at that time, and Paul proposed a seminar/learning session with Stafford on the new system science and the VSM. After some exploratory research, the MX Corporation agreed to Paul's proposal, and scheduled a three-day seminar/learning session.

A Three-Day Seminar/Learning Session with Stafford Beer   In a half-day dialog session, Beer explained the Viable System Model (see Figure 2.5), and the system science and cybernetics principles that make this model a valid representation of what the corporation **is** and also of how the corporation **works**. He presented application examples from his consulting experience. There was lengthy discussion on all aspects of the VSM—the system 1s, system 2, system 3, system 4, system 5—and the communications channels.

In following sessions, Beer led the discussion in developing a preliminary draft of the VSM for the MX Corporation. Large-size copies of the corporation's organization chart (Figure 3.4) and the VSM (Figure 2.5) were posted on the wall for reference. Beer pointed out a significant difference in the two charts. The organization chart is a hierarchy of executive positions and the corporation's five companies, from the CEO downward. The VSM is a model of functions that make the MX Corporation what it is, and how the functions interrelate. Additional levels of recursion spread in all directions, more a network than a hierarchy, each business unit at each level of recursion modeled with the VSM.

Working from a large flip chart Beer led a discussion developing the corporate VSM. He began with a sketch of a generalized VSM, as shown in Figure 2.5. As systems 1, 2, 3, 4, and 5 were discussed, the group, referring to the organization chart, decided which MX Corporation people and groups would be a part of each system. These names and groups were posted on the VSM model. Figure 3.5 shows the draft VSM for the MX Corporation, as sketched by Beer during this discussion. Note that the circles representing the system 1 companies vary in size. This was done to indicate the relative size of the five companies, measured in sales revenue. By the end of the discussion, all the corporate functions and the five companies shown in Figure 3.4 were placed in the VSM.

System 1. Defining the system 1s was the next step. Beer explained that each system 1 produces goods and services for customers, achieves a purpose, and reports key performance measures to system 3. The total of what all the system 1s do makes the corporation what it is. A system **is** what it **does**. Each of the corporation's five companies was identified as a system 1. But Beer noted that there is much more involved than just transferring blocks from the organization chart to the VSM. He described his concept of the Resource Bargain. What is the definition of each of these system 1s? What are the boundaries? What is the purpose? What are the resources? What are the goals and the performance measures? It will take some time, and dialog with the system 1 managements to agree on answers to these questions. The Resource Bargain needs to be fully supported by the system 1 management and acceptable to system 3 and system 5 executive management. Good answers to these questions motivate all involved to the achievement of purpose.

System 2. There was lengthy discussion on exactly what system 2 is and what it does. There was no organized system 2 in the MX

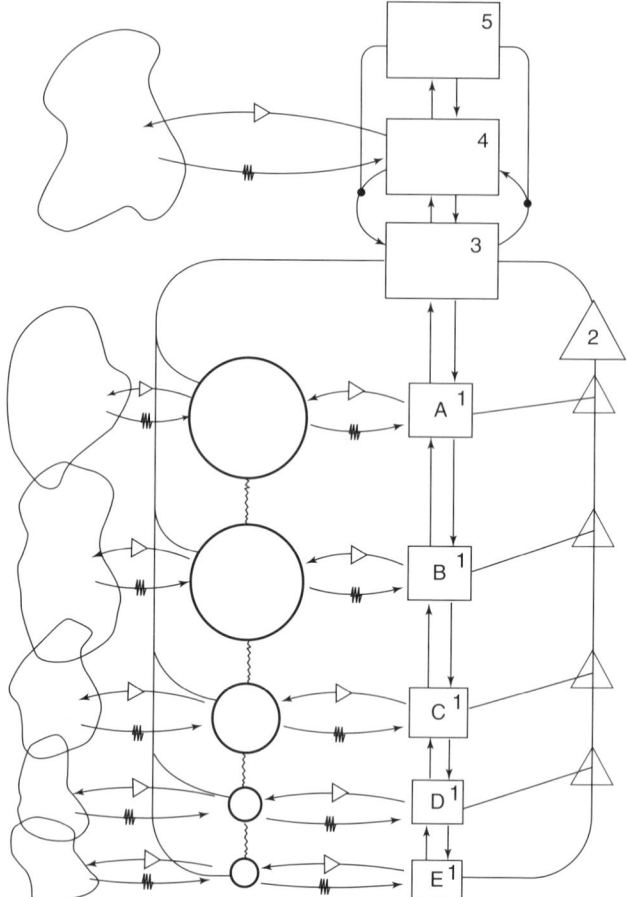

Figure 3.5   MX Corporation VSM

Corporation. The general feeling was that these functions, when performed, were handled on an ad hoc basis with various system 1 and corporate people involved. Further work on system 2 was deferred to a later time.

System 3. Beer explained that system 3 directs the here and now for the corporation. The here and now is the totality of what the system 1s do. A system is what it does. System 3, with the top managements of each of the system 1s, develops the Resource Bargain for each system 1:

- The name of the system 1 operating unit
- A definition of what the operating unit is and will be in terms of products and services, and markets and customers served
- Prescription of the boundaries for the unit's operations
- The purpose of the operating unit
- A description of the resources assigned to and a part of the operating unit
- Long-term goals and performance measures

System 5 provides direction and final approval of the Resource Bargains. In on-going operations, system 3 provides executive direction of the system 1s, monitors system 2, and when needed makes the appropriate changes in the system 1 Resource Bargains. Where system 3 was in the MX Corporation was easy. This function was handled by the CEO.

The here and now also includes other corporate headquarters executive functions: finance and accounting, marketing and sales, industrial relations, engineering. Are these also part of system 3? Most of the work of these four relates to the system 1s, the corporation's five companies. Each of the companies also has these functions in their organizations, and will include them in their VSMs. They carry out these functions in their day-to-day operations. After some discussion, these four functions were placed in system 3. The executives heading these functions, together with the CEO became the system 3 management team. While members of system 3 and working on the here and now, these four functions were also importantly involved in the system 4 responsibility for the outside and future of the corporation. So, part of the time, these four members of system 3 would be working as part of system 4.

There was discussion about the desirability of a chief operating officer as head of system 3, but further consideration was left to later. The VSM models functions, not positions and titles. In the MX Corporation the CEO, system 5, also heads system 3. If a COO is appointed, the four executives heading the system 3 functions of finance and accounting, marketing and sales, industrial relations, and engineering could still report to the CEO. They would work part time in system 5, part time in system 4, and most of the time in system 3 with the COO as the management team directing operations.

System 4. There was long discussion of system 4. Beer described system 4 as responsible for the outside and future of the corporation. System 3 directs the inside and now; system 4 directs the outside and future. Looking at the MX Corporation's organization chart, obvious parts of system 4 would be R&D, corporate planning, and special projects. Legal was also placed in system 4 as probably a better choice than in system 3.

The discussion of system 4, outside and future, considered additional functions:

1. Planning and managing projects, including:
   Mergers and acquisitions
   Divestitures
   Innovations
   Capital expenditures
   Corporate-sponsored technologies, such as:
      VSM and system thinking
      Performance measurement methods
      Six Sigma
2. Monitoring the outside environment
3. Monitoring the VSM
4. Developing corporate parameters

Items 1 and 2 were placed in system 4. A project team would be appointed for each project undertaken. Monitoring the outside environment would be a responsibility of each system 4 executive for that person's area of responsibility.

Items 3 and 4 involve both system 3 and system 4. Responsibilities would be assigned to the appropriate individuals. Beer suggested considering a "management center" or "operations room" for combining systems 2 and 3 and including the communications linkage with system 4. He commented on the close working relationship needed between systems 3 and 4, the two together being the management center for the corporation. The system 3/system4 linkage with system 5 in Figure 3.5, balances the needs of the "outside and future" and the "inside and now." This linkage serves as both a high-level homeostat for maintaining stability, and also a high-level heterostat for the innovation that will create the corporation's future. System 5 provides the appropriate balance.

System 5. The CEO and the Board of Directors became system 5. As shown in the information linkages in the VSM model, system 5 uses advice and counsel from system 4, system 3, system 2, and, when needed, the senior management of the system 1s. Individuals in these other systems, when participating in the work of system 5, temporarily depart from their home systems to wear the hat of system 5.

Beer pointed out that the VSM systems, 1, 2, 3, 4, and 5 represent functions. An individual will usually be assigned in one of these systems, but can work, at times in another system. A CEO in addition to the system 5 functions, may direct a system 4 project. Or, as in the MX Corporation, the system 5 CEO could also be the system 3 executive. With this arrangement, however, system 5 is likely to collapse into system 3, leaving the strategic work of system 5 undone, as happened in K&K, the first example in this chapter.

A system 4 vice president may also be a member of the Board of Directors (system 5). An executive vice president for operations (system 3), may serve on the Board of Directors (system 5), may head up a corporate project (system 4), and may serve on the Board of Directors of a system 1 company, a system 5 function of the system 1 company. When individuals work in more than one system, for effective collaboration it is well for those individuals to recognize where in the VSM they are working and the relationships of that system.

The MX Corporation VSM. The MX Corporation system model, Figure 3.5, shows the four communications channels described in Chapter 2. The model also shows the communications assuring successful collaboration among systems 3, 4, and 5. Communications link all systems together in common purpose.

Preparing the system model of the MX Corporation made no changes in the physical structure of the organization or the number of people or the capital assets of the corporation. There were no "restructuring costs." But there was a huge change in how people thought about their company, what the company really is, how the company really works. They could see how the MX Corporation: (1) with the VSM structure and management principles, (2) with its values specified in corporate parameters, (3) with a shared purpose, and (4) controlled by feedback from the work itself and well-designed performance measures, could be a better way to accomplish desired results.

In the MX Corporation organization chart, and in the company's planning and budgeting, there were no specified connections with external environments. But these connections did come up in relation to various company activities or as required by legislation and regulations. R&D and engineering had contacts in the technological environment. The company maintained a Washington office for information and concerns in the political environment. Marketing and sales, of course, continually interacted with the commercial environment. The VSM requires communication and interaction with all relevant environments, for information and measures on what matters for the achievement of company purpose.

Having the MX Corporation VSM, company executives began to see a new approach to control, which can be called "indirect management." Instead of the traditional concept of the CEO running the corporation and the company presidents running their companies imposing control from above, the VSM and system thinking offer a new and different concept: indirect management. Instead of running the corporation or the company presidents running their companies, the top managements using the VSM structure and management principles design the corporation and its recursions to run themselves. Indirect management structures the system. The system runs itself.

The first job of the Board and top management is to design the system structure, the resources, the purpose, the communications, and the measures that effectively attenuate variety so that requisite variety can empower decision-makers to act in ways that will contribute to the achievement of company purpose. With the VSM structure, this same process can be followed at each level of recursion. Measures attenuate variety. Involving more people at more levels in decision-making amplifies management variety. Done well, the result is requisite variety at all levels where decisions are made, and good decisions.

Company E

Company E, is a manufacturing company, a system 1 in the MX Corporation's VSM. In Company E, margins were declining and profitability was unsatisfactory. There was clear need for profit improvement. Corporate management had sent in cost accountants to cut costs. Costs were cut, but there was no improvement in profitability. The VSM and system thinking offered a new and different approach.

The President of Company E invited a corporate system 3 manager to work with his management team on the VSM and system thinking, and whatever new ideas might improve company performance. A dialog process with company E management and professional people defined purpose and established structure:

Purpose   The company developed a written statement of purpose in terms of the kinds of products and services it would offer, the markets and clients it would serve, and the country markets in which it would operate. This purpose was quantified by objectives in the key performance areas described in this book (Chapters 4 through 11).

Structure

1. VSM. The Company E management group developed the VSM for their company, shown in Figure 3.6. The model included three system 1 business operations. Each of these system 1 profit center businesses developed their own VSM and their key performance area measures and objectives, using many of the key performance area measures explained in this book.

2. System 1 s. The company's three profit-center businesses became the system 1 s, so Company E's people and capital resources remained unchanged. But there was significant change in the information structure in all three businesses.

3. Success Measures

Company E developed success measures for the total company and set specific objectives. Similarly, the three businesses developed objectives and performance measures. Operations variety attenuated by the measures selected, and management variety amplified by spreading decision-making broadly in the organization achieved needed requisite variety. Self-control was built into the system.

4. Communication Channels

Company E redesigned its information system so that key performance measures flowed from the three businesses in the company's business channel, routine information in the routine channel, inter-business communication in the system 1 channel, and special and emergency information in the special channel.

This work was done over several months. All company E employees were involved in the process for their areas of work. Management workshops were the primary method used for developing the VSM and for developing purpose, objectives, and measures; and exploring and testing new management methods. This participative process, system thinking, performance measures, and exploring and using some new and better methods in sales, new product development, and cost man-

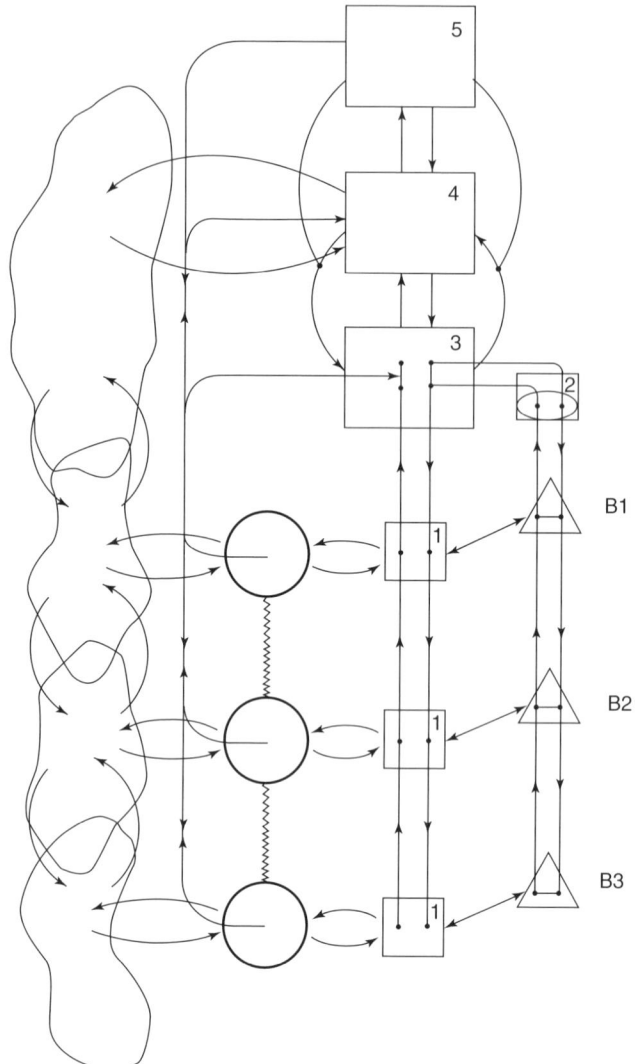

Figure 3.6   Company E VSM

agement, improved attitudes and morale, and began improving operating income.

Company E, Business 2

Business 2 (B2 in Figure 3.6) was Company E's second largest business in sales revenue, but profitability was less than satisfactory, only slightly above breakeven. B2's management, now recognizing its business's own capability—and responsibility—for self-organization and self-control, sought new and better ways for managing profitability. They were using product full costs, an annual budget, and monthly analysis of variances, and targeting cost reduction and sales increase as the route to profitability, without success.

Change to new and better began with a seminar on "management economics" and other best practices in the key performance area of profitability. They eliminated calculations of product profitability, recognizing that profitability is created as a result of all the actions of all parts of Business 2. For product contribution to profitability they calculated contribution margins (sales revenue minus variable costs). They reclassified all fixed costs in the chart of accounts into three groups: people costs, capital costs, and programmed fixed costs. They now saw, for the first time, the total monthly fixed costs for their business. These costs had to be paid each month by the contribution margins earned on sales to reach breakeven. Above breakeven, contribution margin is operating income.

Recognizing the importance of contribution margins to profitability, a small team of sales and accounting people conducted a product line audit following the format explained in Chapter 6. Contribution margins for their products ranged from a little less than zero to 80%, average 34%. Sorting by sales revenue, products were listed by product group, showing for each product: sales revenue, contribution margin dollars, and contribution margin percent. This listing showed clearly where profit contribution was coming from, and where there were problems. Actions were then taken to increase low contribution margins where they could find ways to do this, and to expand sales of the high-contribution products. Changes in mix is often an important part of profit improvement. B2 managers set short-term objectives for improvement in contribution margin percent.

B2 produced calendered film and sheet, and coated fabrics, and marketed its products to other manufacturers for producing their products. B2's products were a major part of their customers' variable costs. Developing new products for specific market requirements was an important and on-going part of B2's business strategy. B2's targets for new products had been set in terms of sales revenue. B2 now added an important new dimension in their new product development projects—contribution margin. New product development projects now had, from the start, objectives for both sales and contribution margin percent. At the time this work was done, average contribution margin on total sales was 34%. Desired target CM% on new products was 50%.

B2's sales people were experts in their business's products and in the applications of these products. They were good, professional sales-people. But their focus had been only on sales revenue. They partici-pated in the product line audits, and in planning corrective actions. They now understood the importance of both sales revenue and con-tribution margin. They undertook contribution margin objectives as well as sales revenue objectives, and sales reporting was changed to include both figures. Sales people recognized their leverages on product contribution margins through pricing, product substitution where appropriate, and sales concentration on high contribution products. Contribution margin maintenance/improvement also became a part of the sales incentive plan.

In their sales planning, sales people used the Pareto 80/20 principle that 80% of sales revenue will come from about 20% of the customers. This 20% became their target accounts and target prospects. For each sales assignment, the salesperson, in consultations with the sales manager, selected the largest customers and the largest prospective customers as the salesperson's target customers. Sales reports listed first the target accounts and prospects, then all the others. Target pros-pects, even if they had not yet purchased anything, were included in the report to maintain awareness of the sales opportunity and encour-age actions to make the sale. Reporting included both sales revenue and contribution margin.

Within a year average contribution margin increased to 43%, sales revenue was up more than 10%, and the company was meeting profit-ability objectives.

APPLYING VSM IN THE STRATEGIC MANAGEMENT OF A CORUÑA UNIVERSITY IN GALICIA, SPAIN
(José Pérez Ríos and Xosé L. Martínez Suárez)

The following case is an example of the use of the viable system model (VSM) at the highest level of management in a highly complex orga-nization, A Coruña University (in Spanish, Universidade Da Coruña (UDC)). UDC is a public university, one of the three universities con-stituting the university system in Galicia, Spain.

In this report we will describe how the top management of UDC used the VSM. The UDC led by its Rector, Dr. José María Barja, undertook to use the VSM first in the area of responsibility of the Vice-

Rector of Infrastructure and Environmental Managing, Dr. Xosé Lois Martinez Suárez. This report shows how the VSM was used both to shape this vice-rectorship's view of the university, and to develop strategic, tactical, and operating policies.

We begin our report with a brief description of the geographic and institution boundaries that provide a background for our case. Then we will describe the circumstances which resulted in the use of the VSM at this particular organization. The VSM helped to diagnose the situation at the starting point and to design the initial and top priority actions. We describe how the VSM was used by the vice-rector to guide both the contacts with the different institutions and companies involved in the initial decisions (mainly strategic) and the formulation of these decisions. Some of the actions undertaken or planned throughout the 19 months from the beginning of this project to the writing of this report are included. We will also show some of the main conclusions from the use of the VSM. We finally complete the report with some conclusions on the value of the VSM, and some comments on the continuing use of the VSM at UDC.

Galicia and A Coruña University

A Coruña University, Vigo University, and Santiago de Compostela University make up the university system in Galicia. Galicia is one of the 17 regions in Spain. Located in the Northwestern Iberian Peninsula, to the North of Portugal, Galicia's population is 2,750,985, in an area of 29,574 square km. The local government has a presidency and 12 consellerias (ministries), including the ministries of education, and town and land planning.

A Coruña University (UDC), founded in 1990, has 24,012 students, 1,326 teachers and 769 staff personnel. Its annual budget is 92 million Euros. The university's campuses are located in the cities of A Coruña and Ferrol. A Coruña campus has its core in the Elviña-A Zapateira campus. Nine teaching buildings are located there, where 14 degrees related to education, sociology, economy, law, civil engineering, philology, science, and architecture are taught.

The Ferrol Campus is located in the city of Ferrol, 60 km away from A Coruña. It has four teaching buildings, where eight degrees are taught.

The Viable System Model and the UDC

The connection between UDC and the VSM dates back to the professional relationship between the current UDC vice-rector, Xosé Lois

Martinez Suárez (Ph.D. in Architecture, and Urban Planning professor), and José Pérez Ríos, (Ph.D. in Engineering, and Business Organization Professor). The interest of Dr. Martínez Suárez in the potential of the systemic approach in general and particularly the VSM for urban planning, and the specialization of Dr. Pérez Ríos in these areas, resulted in a cooperation between them. The designation of Dr. Martínez Suárez as the new infrastructure and environmental managing vice-rector in January, 2004, made feasible the use of these approaches at UDC.

The VSM application started by defining the purpose of the UDC, and the geographic frame in which it will operate. The identification of the proper recursion levels made possible the study and design of the right policies in each of them.

Purpose of the UDC   The application of the VSM began by making clear the purpose of the UDC. To define purpose we used the definition and functions set by the University Act 6/2001 (LOU) for Spain's universities, the Act 11/1989 on University System Planning in Galicia (LOSUG), and the UDC charter. The nature and part of UDC's purposes are stated as follows:

1. A Coruña University is a public, legal, and autonomous entity with their own resources, providing the public service regarding university education by means of research, teaching, and study.
2. The University functions in the service of society are the following:
   a. Creation, development, transmission, and critique of science, technique, and culture.
   b. Training both for professional activities requiring the use of scientific knowledge and methods, and for artistic creation.
   c. The diffusion, valuation, and transfer of knowledge in the service of culture, quality of life, and economic development.
   d. Knowledge and culture diffusion through university extension to society and through-life training.

Environment of the UDC   Once we had defined the purpose of the UDC (our system in focus), we identified the relevant environment—the geographic and institutional boundaries involved. The geographic boundary was defined as the A Coruña-Ferrol urban region. This region has an estimated population of 650,000, a quarter of the total population of Galicia, and is one of Galicia's most dynamic areas. The importance of setting this boundary (later identified as recursion level 1) instead of limiting ourselves to the cities of A Coruña and Ferrol proved to be of great significance for the achievement of UDC's aims.

Some of the potential students in this geographical area live away from the cities of A Coruña and Ferrol. A car would be their only means to reach the university. Those not having a car would need to move to one of these cities to attend the university. Accessibility was one of the key issues.

Other aspects such as the University's cultural, social, and economic integration in the urban region, can only be approached by considering this recursion level (recursion level 2).

Recursion Levels Due to the environmental size and complexity (variety) of the A Coruña-Ferrol urban region, we unfolded this variety into the following five recursion levels:

R-0. The entire region of Galicia, Spain
R-1. A Coruña-Ferrol urban region (A Coruña University)
R-2. A Coruña urban area and Ferrol urban area
R-3. A Coruña campus and Ferrol campus
R-4. UDC's centers, buildings, and facilities

Among the criteria of possible use in determining the recursions (urban-planning, academic, legislative, administrative, etc.) we mainly used the urban-planning criterion.

At each level of recursion the system 1 subsystems were defined as follows: [1]

R-0. Three system 1 subsystems: A Coruña University, Vigo University, and Santiago de Compostela University
R-1. In A Coruña University, two system 1 subsystems: A Coruña urban area and Ferrol urban area
R-2. In A Coruña urban area, five system 1 subsystems: Elviña-A Zapateira, A Coruña's central campus, Riazor, Oza, A Maestranza, and Bastiagueiro
R-3. In A Coruña's central campus, buildings and public areas with specific functions
R-4. Several system 1 subsystems. Each public building and facility is a system 1 subsystem

For each recursion level we determined: (1) purpose of that system, derived from the purpose of the UDC, and the system's boundaries, and (2) the system's system 1 subsystems and their interactions with related activities in their environment. These activities included, among others, the town-planning legislation, the administration structures capable of making decisions at that level, those public or private enterprises with the capability to facilitate or impede the purpose of the system at this recursion level, and any of the above relating to the UDC.

With the problem structured into five levels of recursion, we then developed information on the starting situation in each of these rercursions from an institutional, town-planning, and ground and buildings use point of view. From this information we developed a proposal for needed first actions. The proposal included 17 actions on town-planning and 17 more on architecture. In the meantime, the UDC drew up a report on the Galicia Town and Land Planning Guideline Memorandum proposal, drafted by the regional government. This UDC report, titled, "The UDC and Town and Land Planning," presents the view of the UDC on the relationship between the university and the society regarding land use. The VSM was used in the structuring of the report.

The concrete actions defined so far relate to urban planning. We defined actions needed at each recursion level as shown in Figure 3.7. Actions are listed as URB 1, URB 2, etc. Several of these actions are in progress. In Figure 3.7 we can see the environment, the applicable legislation (mainly urban development at this stage), the organs and institutions involved that have decision-making and execution capability, and some of the actions undertaken by the UDC.

We cannot get into the details of the actions, decisions, and interactions with the involved stakeholders at each recursion level, but we can show two examples of the important impact that some of them have on the society UDC serves. These examples are two actions at two different recursion levels, for improving accessibility to the University Campus.

Recursion Level 1, Action URB 1: Territorial Accessibility   This is one of the main actions included in the memorandum "The Campus as a Model and Reference of Sustained Town Planning." The memorandum was drafted by the current university board to show its view of the university. In the memorandum they state the need for developing a university transport plan at an urban region level. This plan is now being developed, and it involves different public administrations (towns, cities, province, region) as well as public transport companies (urban

Recursion level	Environment	Relevant Aspects	Applicable Legislation	Institutions/ Organs Involved	Actions
0	Galicia. Territorial Scale 1	- Social Function of the Universities. - Relationship with the Urban Policy. - University Housing Policy.	1. Act 10/1995 on Town and Land Planning of Galicia. 2. Ground/Building Act of Galicia (December 2002). 3. Act 11/1989 on Galicia University System Planning. 4. University Act 6/2001 5. UDC Charter.	- Government of Galicia. -Ministries: Education, Territorial Policy, Housing, Environment and sustained development. - Universities: A Coruña.; Santiago de Compostela; Vigo.	- Contribution of the UDC to the Town-Planning Guidelines in Galicia (in progress) - URB 16. (Campus Elviña) University Residential Area
1	Urban Region A Coruña Ferrol Territorial Scale 2.	- Accessibility. - Range (Number of Potential Students). - Visibility of the UDC in the Cities, Small Towns and Villages. - Economic and Social Development of the Urban Region. - Connection with the Business Network.		- RENFE. (Spain's Railway System) - Cities: A Coruña; Ferrol and all the rest in the Urban Region. - UDC. - Government of Galicia. (For transport systems)	- URB 1. Territorial Accessibility: shire Public Transport Suburban Trains, and coach network. - URB 12.Parking Lots - Parking Lots at Railway Stations. - URB 13. Bus, Train Station Campus Elviña. - URB 15. Research Area. Creation of new enterprises.
2	a) Urban A Coruña. b) Urban Ferrol.	- Accessibility. - Integration University/City. - Cohesion University/City. - Structuring of Public Equipments and Urban Services with the University.	Urban Master plan of A Coruña (1995). Urban Master plan of Ferrol.	- City of A Coruña. - UDC. - City of Ferrol.	- URB 2. Enlargement of Urban Coaches network. - URB 17. Bicycle lane pedestrian Path from the city-centre to the campus.

Figure 3.7   Actions and relevant aspects at each recursion level

| 3 | a) Campus A Coruña | - Adaptation to the European Union Directives on Universities Degrees.
 - Urban Attraction.
 - Urban and Architectonic Referent (Model of Sustained Development). | - Urban Plan for Elviña-A Zapateira Campus (1991) and its modification in 2002.
 - Environment Plan. | - UDC
 - City of A Coruña. | - URB 11. Campus Center
 - URB 10. Area 30. Elviña Campus coach.
 - URB 8. Redesign of Zapateira Square.
 - URB 9. Scientific-Technological Park. Botanical Park.
 - URB 16. University Residential Area (Campus Elviña). |
| 4 | Single Buildings. | - Functionality.
 - Comfort and Environment Managing.
 - Optimizing spaces. | | - UDC
 - Institution Board | Actions at each particular centre. |

Figure 3.7   *Continued*

coaches, trains) both public and private. The actions needed are reasonable in cost since the railway line, A Coruña-Ferrol, is already established. The railway connects both cities and also many smaller towns between them. The change needed is to establish timetables and stops appropriate for potential students in the area. This change, and adequate parking at the intermediate stations, will allow UDC students in this area access to the university at a low cost.

The current alternatives for students living in the area to get to the university are commuting by private car, renting an apartment in A Coruña or Ferrol, or living in a university residence in the cities of A Coruña or Ferrol. Among the benefits is greater use of public transport, less private transport requiring less parking space at the campus, and allowing a larger number of students in the area to attend the university.

Recursion Level 2, Action URB 2: Enlargement of Urban Coaches Network, and URB 17: 3.5 km Bicycle Lane from the City Center to the Campus The effect of action URB 2 is to turn a great part of the suburban areas into commuting distance for students by providing low-cost public transport. Since the coach line goes across the city, the districts crossed become an easy commute for students. More young people in aging urban areas increases economic, social, and cultural activity, strengthens the cohesion of the people in A Coruña, and reverses the disintegration effects of past town-planning policies. Increasing the city's area of interest for the students increases housing supply, potentially reducing its cost.

URB 17. 3.5 km bicycle lane from the city center to the campus. Like URB 2, this bicycle lane provides another option to commuting by private car, which means less parking space needed at the campus.

These two actions, and the possibility of having a railway stop at the campus, not only have social, urban, and integration effects, but are also an important alternative to commuting by private car.

We have shown two examples that improve access to the university, and also have positive impact on society. These actions relate to transportation. But the effects are more than improving access to the university. The changes also result in more students attending the university, sustained development, more available apartment rentals at lower cost, and revitalized urban areas.

These kinds of multiplying effects can also result from the other URB actions. They are generated both from connections between the system 1 components (the "squiggly lines" mentioned by Beer), and their environments in the different recursion levels.

Lack of space keeps us from reporting the results of our work in the functions of system 2, system 3, system 3*, system 4, and system 5 at each of the recursion levels. However, we must mention the gap between the different institutions and the UDC in some of the systems in which the presence of UDC in these systems is imperative (e.g., system 4 and system 5 at recursion level 2 in urban area A Coruña).

In applying the VSM in the UDC project, we used specialized software to facilitate the VSM application process in all its stages: creation of the recursion structure; defining the system 1 s in each level of recursion; constructing the VSM map for each level of recursion; providing required information on each VSM element including system 1, system 2, system 3, system 3*, system 4, and system 5; environments; homeostats; transducers; and information channels. We used VSMod® software [2, 3], which is specifically created to facilitate VSM applications. In Figure 3.8 we show one of the screens created with VSMod® for the A Coruña project.

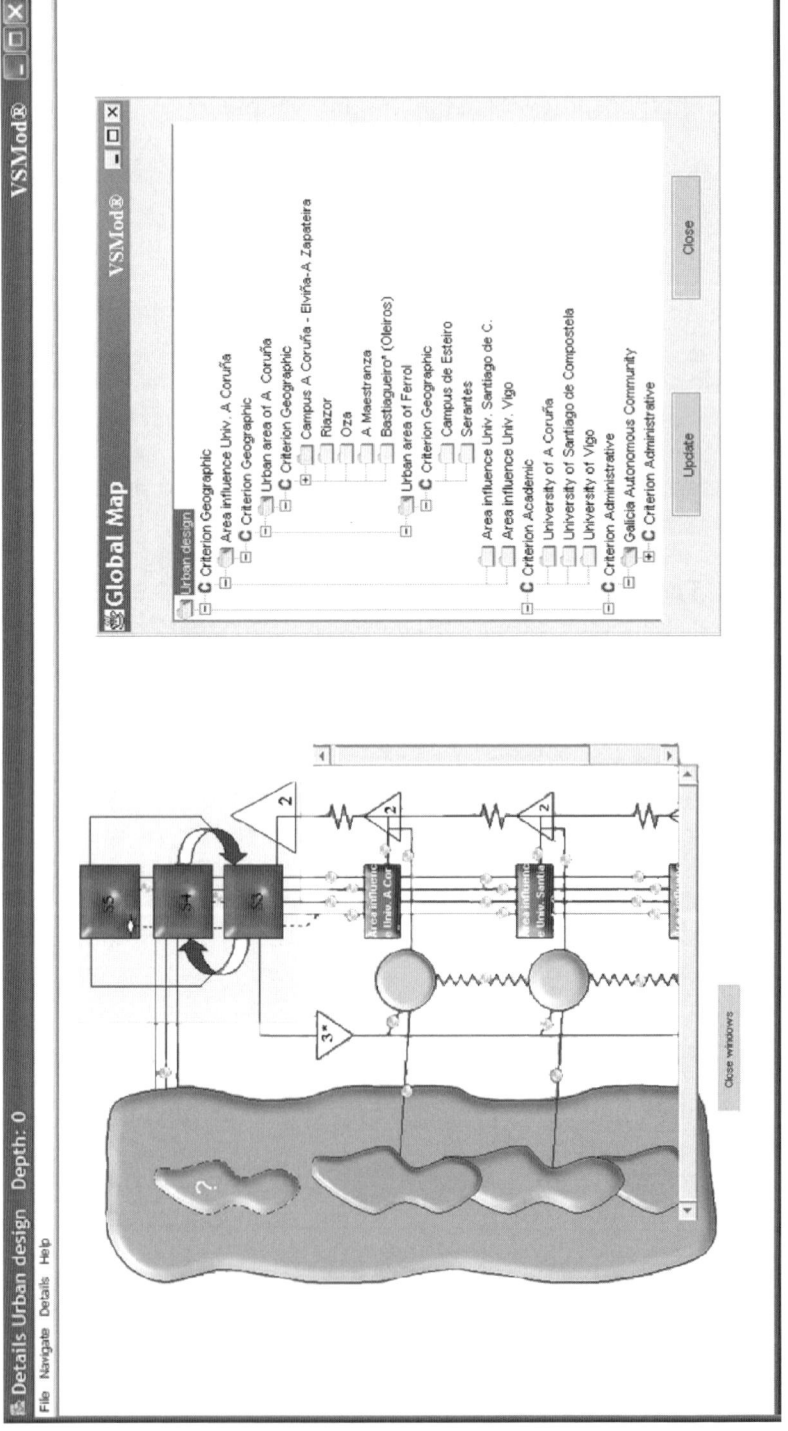

Figure 3.8 VSM chart (RO) and global map

Results

One of the most important effects of the VSM application in the UDC was increasing the vice-rectorship's confidence level in the potential of the VSM for turning their aims for the University into reality. The results achieved included:

1. Identification of the deficiencies in each recursion level for achieving the UDC's purpose.
2. Identification of the necessary UDC contacts at each recursion level to assure needed dialog.
3. Acknowledgement of lack of adequate organizing structures to deal with the problems in a number of recursion levels, particularly level 1 (urban region).
4. Confirmation of the wrong design of, or even the lack of, some of the systems (system 2, system 3, system 3*, system 4, and system 5) necessary for system viability at several recursion levels.

With regard to concrete actions, we described three of those listed in Figure 3.7. UDC is also acting on the others and will undertake additional actions to be determined. Among these, UDC will plan to improve some of the current buildings and provide new ones with facilities needed which will make the UDC a sustainability and an aesthetic resource for A Coruña and Galicia.

The infrastructure and environmental managing vice-rectorship plans to continue using the capability of the VSM to increase the area served by the UDC, to design UDC's urban actions, to design the structure and functions of UDC, and to help assure that A Coruña University at each level of recursion will achieve its purpose.

Conclusion

In this case, we have seen how the VSM served as a guide for designing the structure and management of the UDC Infrastructure and Environmental Vice-Rectorship's responsibilities, and for defining the actions needed.

We have shown how the VSM was used to diagnose the starting point and to design the intervention plan that turns this view into reality. We describe the process of complexity unfolding and we also show some of the actions identified for its execution at each recursion level.

We have mentioned the usefulness of the VSMod® software to facilitate the VSM application and the storage of the information generated throughout its application.

We finally describe some of the results achieved, or about to be achieved, as a consequence of the VSM application in A Coruña University. The project also increased the vice-rector's confidence in the usefulness of the VSM in his area of responsibility. From this experience the vice-rector, and the university, are likely to continue using the VSM.

NOTES

[1] Beer, Stafford, *Diagnosing the System for Organizations*. Wiley, New York, 1985, p. 56.

[2] José Pérez Ríos, "VSMod: A software tool for the application of the Viable System Model," *47th Annual Conference of the International Society for the Systems Sciences (ISSS)*, Heraklion, Crete, Greece, 2003.

[3] José Pérez Ríos, "Information and Communication Technologies for Viable Organizations." *WOSC 13th International Congress of Cybernetics and Systems*, Maribor, Sovenia, 2005.

USING THE VSM TO DESIGN A NON-VIABLE SYSTEM: THE CASE OF THE SOCIAL SECURITY SYSTEM FOR TEACHERS IN COLOMBIA (Alfonso Reyes A.)

Since its early presentation in his most popular books, Stafford Beer's VSM was intended to be a very practical tool for managers. Stafford himself was well known as a very insightful trouble-shooter of organizational issues. Many examples of applications of the model can be found in the literature ranging from small companies through medium and large public and private organizations.

In all this variety of applications the system discussed, the system-in-focus, is a viable system. The VSM is a Viable System Model, that is, a model for any viable system. However, many organizational systems we deal with are not and should not be viable. This is the case, for instance, of an R&D department of a company and the library in a university. These two are important to support the primary activities of the organization they are part of, but they are not business units by themselves. It is precisely in these cases where the question that triggers this case example arises. Is it possible to use the VSM to design a non-viable system? In our specific case, how can we use it? But before going any further let us clarify the point about viability.

On the Use of the VSM

According to Beer a viable system is able to maintain its existence in its environment. This implies that a viable system should be autonomous but not independent. An organization is autonomous if it has the capacity to *create, regulate,* and *produce* its own primary activities, that is, those activities that realize its mission. Stafford himself pointed out that a viable system, while autonomous, cannot survive independently from its environment. Indeed, it has to develop a capacity to adapt to unexpected changes in its environment. But how can we characterize in operational terms a system that is not viable?

In the public sector the Ministry (or in some countries called the Secretary) of Education is an instance of an institution that is not viable. It does not exist on its own. It usually creates and regulates the primary issues related to the educational system of a country (e.g., what should be the minimum standards in mathematics in public schools, what requisites educational organizations should comply with, and so on). However, the Ministry does not deliver the courses itself; this is usually the job of public schools and universities. The same can be said for public institutions in charge of the regulation of other public goods such as infrastructure, health, justice, and social security, to mention the most common. It is apparent that none of these institutions are viable in themselves because none of them actually produce the goods they regulate. However, their design is important for the viability of the bigger system they are part of. The design of a social security system for teachers is a good example. How, then, can we use the VSM to diagnose and re-design these kinds of systems?

Public teachers in Colombia are part of the payroll of the Ministry of Education. Their social security (i.e., health care and professional risk services) was the responsibility of the National Social Security Institute. Services provided were usually of a very low quality, users did not have the chance to choose other institutions to get these services, and corrupted practices were generally denounced by the public.

In December 1993, the Congress passed a law to redesign the social security system in the country. However, the general design proposed was not well received by the teachers union and they decided to continue with the previous system. Ten years later the system collapsed and the Ministry of Education hired a consultancy to design a social security system for teachers (SSST).[1] This project was carried out during the fall of 2004.

Defining the System in Focus

To begin with it is important to stress a methodological point. The VSM is a model, that is, a tool useful to design or to diagnose a system. Beer was an excellent practitioner in the use of the VSM but he did not explain how to use the model in specific terms. He tried to do so in his last book of the trilogy. However, he never developed a formal method for using the model. During the 1980s Espejo developed such a method that he called Viplan.[2] This was the method we used to design the SSST.

Viplan starts by establishing the organization's identity, that is, the purpose of the organization as articulated by its stakeholders. Four types of stakeholders are identified: those carrying out the work, those providing the organization with resources, the beneficiaries and others affected by the organization's activities, and those managing the organization. Other participants are also identified, particularly those external to the organization but with an influence on it.

The second step of the method is to work out the organization's primary activities needed to develop its identity. This is done by using different structural models to represent how the organization actually groups its activities. These models can be based on technology, customer-suppliers, geography, or time.

Primary activities are autonomous units producing the organization's products or services. These activities can be decomposed in other subsumed primary activities and regulatory functions needed to give them cohesion. Mapping how the organization distributes this functional capacity along primary activities at different structural levels is the third stage of the method. Finally, it is possible to map this functional distribution into the VSM and use viability criteria in diagnosing or designing a system.

Following Viplan, the starting point to design the SSST was to produce a structured name for the system-in-focus. In short, the SSST

---

[1] This consultancy was carried out by the Centro de Gestión Hospitalaria in Bogotá, Colombia. <http://www.cgh.org.co/>
[2] A tutorial and some other documents related to Viplan can be downloaded from <www.Syncho.com>

is a system that offers health services and professional risk services for the teachers working in public schools across the country with the purpose of increasing their quality of life. It is clear that this is not a viable system in itself but part of a regulatory one of the primary educational system of the country. So in order to use the VSM in designing a non-viable system it is necessary to identify the minimum viable system that contains the system-in-focus. In this case, the minimum viable system that contains the SSST is the Colombian primary educational system. Figure 3.9 shows a schematic VSM for the Colombian primary education system.

Using this model as a reference, we may locate our system-in-focus (the SSST) as one of the regulatory systems of the VSM. In other words, the SSST is part of the cybernetic loop connecting systems 3, 2, 1 and 3* at every level of recursion of the primary educational system (i.e., the gray zones in the model). In Viplan jargon this is called an instance of a cohesion mechanism of the system. This mechanism takes care of the social security issue for teachers working in public schools in every region of the country.

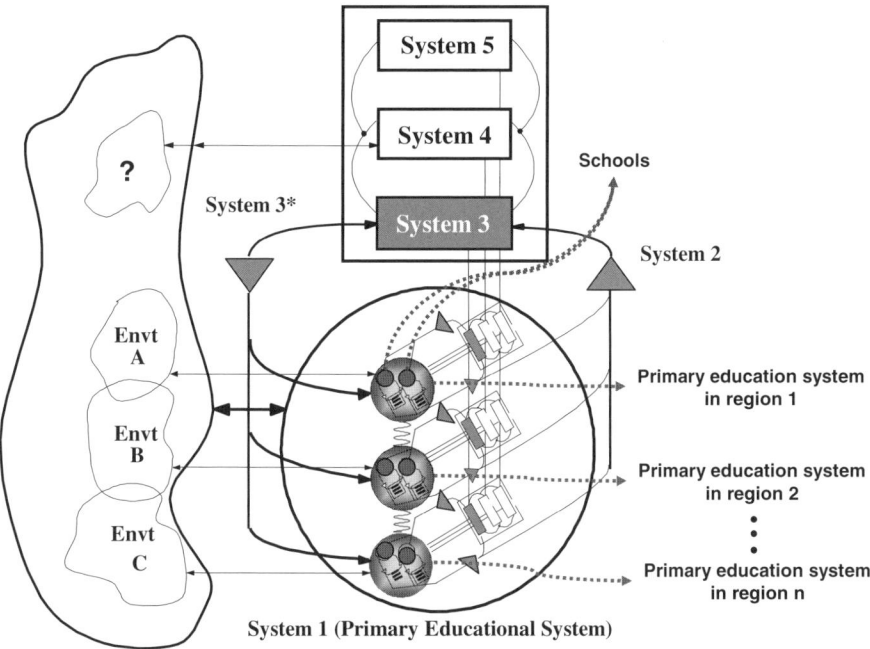

Figure 3.9 A schematic VSM for the primary education system in Colombia

Designing the SSST

The design of such mechanism consists of identifying the institutional actors needed to carry out its purpose as well as their relations. Using Viplan we identified the following institutional actors for the SSST: (1) the teachers affiliated to the National Foundation of Social Services in Teaching (NFSST), (2) the Ministry of Education, (3) the Ministry of Finance, (4) private contractors who may provide the services of the system, (5) the General Council, an external entity defining the legal and regulatory context for the operation of the system, and (6) the Regional Committees that will act as local controllers.

Next, we identified two main primary activities of the SSST: (1) offering health services and (2) offering professional risk services. It was decided that both services should be offered by a third party (private contractors) that will, in turn, make use of a network of health institutions (hospitals, health centers, and so on). Figure 3.10 illustrates the unfolding of complexity of the primary activities of the SSST.

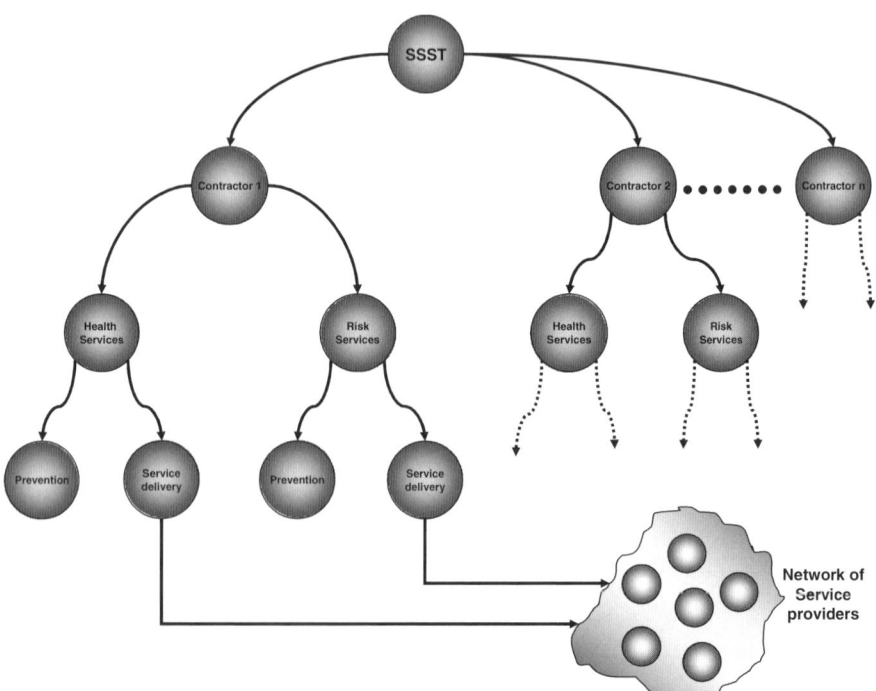

Figure 3.10 Unfolding of complexity for the SSST

The next step in designing a general structure for the SSST was to identify the relations that would articulate the role of each institutional actor with the others. It is important to see that from the way these relations are performed in time some structural patterns may emerge and be perceived by observers of the system. Some of these emerging properties will be desirable and some will not. Inefficiency, bad quality, and corruption are among those non-desirable emergent properties of any public system. Therefore, it made sense for the design of the system to start by identifying a set of desirable properties we would like to observe. In the case of the SSST, five characteristics were established:

1. Fairness. The SSST should provide equal quality services to all affiliates.
2. Integral protection. The SSST should offer health services to its beneficiaries in all its phases (prevention, diagnosing, and treatment).
3. Free choice. The SSST should allow the existence of several service providers and should allow its members to choose freely among them.
4. Coordination. The SSST should promote the coordination of different institutional actors at all levels.
5. Quality. The SSST should have control mechanisms that assure high quality of the services offered.

By taking into account these desirable characteristics it was possible to define the articulation among the different institutional actors of the system. Figure 3.11 makes explicit these relations.

In methodological terms this articulation was established by analyzing the relations of each institutional actor to all other actors regarding the need to fulfil these characteristics. In other words, we specified a network of relations by building a matrix. If we take apart each institutional actor, we have a set of tables specifying these relations. For instance the relations from the point of view of the users of the SSST are described in Table 3.1.

In a similar way Table 3.2 shows the relations from the point of view of the Regional Committees.

In the same way we built a table for each one of the institutional actors. These relations defined the basis of the organizational structure for the SSST. It is quite possible to break down this analysis to further levels of detail. However, this will be far beyond the scope of this report.

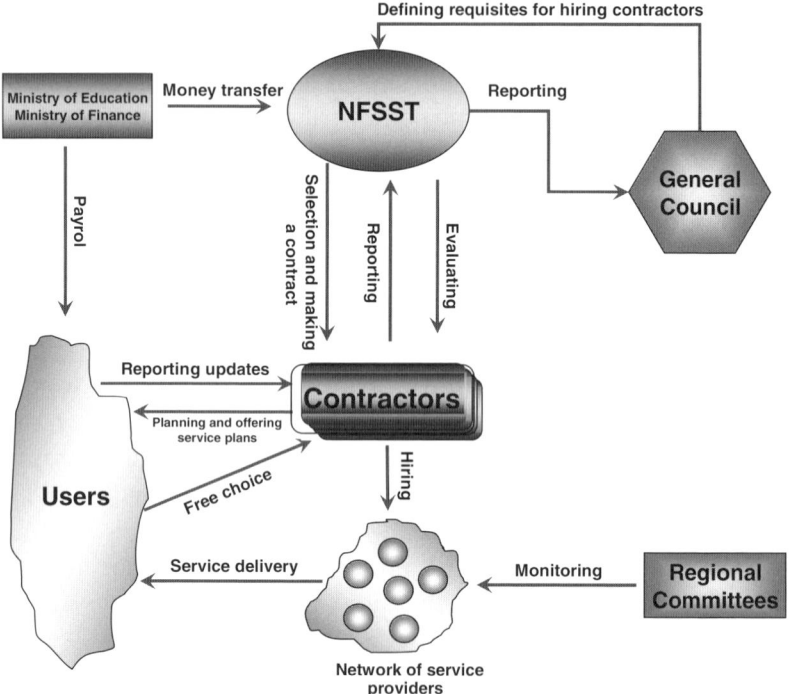

Figure 3.11 Articulating relations among institutional actors for the SSST

TABLE 3.1 Articulating Relations from the Point of View of the Users of the SSST

Articulating Relation	Actor Receptor	Description	Preconditions
Free choice of contractor	Contractor	Teachers make a free choice of contractors according to the quality of services they offer	A public information system tracing the effectiveness of the SSST
Registering	Contractor	Teachers register with the best contractor	Rules of the registering process
Updating	Contractor	Teachers report updates about them and their families	An efficient mechanism to keep up to date the record of benefits for users

TABLE 3.2 Articulating Relations from the Point of View of the Users of the Regional Committees

Articulating Relation	Actor Receptor	Description	Preconditions
Monitoring	Contractors and network of service providers	Regional committees monitor the work of local contractors	• Regional committees develop effective mechanisms to monitor and audit the work of local contractors • Contractors register basic information used in monitoring
Regional survey about perception of services	Users	Regional committees carry out an annual survey about user's perception of services received	• Regional committees guarantee funds to contract the survey • Regional committees define parameters to carry out the survey

Project Results

This report shows that the VSM can be used to study organizational systems that are not viable. Many institutions in the public sector belong to this category of non-autonomous systems. This is also the case for many sub-systems within a viable organization (as a library in a university, the R&D department of a company, or a social security system for teachers in the primary educational system of a country).

In order to use the VSM in these situations it is necessary to distinguish between two relevant systems: on the one hand, the system-in-focus (e.g., the SSST, which is not viable) and, on the other hand, the minimum viable system that contains it (e.g., the primary educational system). Once this distinction is made and a VSM for the inclusive system is built, it is important to see what role the system-in-focus plays within that viable system. In the case of the SSST we saw that this system is part of the cohesion mechanism for the primary educational system of the country (i.e., a relationship among systems 1, 2, 3 and 3* at every level of recursion). The problem then is to design such a regulatory mechanism for the inclusive system (e.g., the primary educational system).

To carry out such a design we showed that the use of a method is needed to organize observations and desirable properties in order to identify institutional actors, their roles and the relations among them. Viplan was presented as a useful method in this regard, a method that guides the practical use of the VSM.

This proposed design for the SSST was discussed with actors at different levels of the government in Colombia, and finally, it was used as the basis to adjust the law that regulates the social security system for teachers in the country. We believe that the use of the VSM as a hermeneutical tool rather than an objective representation of the structure of a system "out there" was a key factor to reach the level of consensus in the discussions that took place during the project.

Acknowledgments

I would like to thank the Centro de Gestión Hospitalaria (CGH) for inviting me to participate in the project for the design of the SSST. In particular, I would like to stress the valuable contributions of Carmen Elisa Nuñez and Sergio Luengas Amaya, senior researchers of the CGH, during the project. I would like to thank also Raul Espejo for several suggestions on the use of Viplan; its final use and interpretation is, of course, my own responsibility. Many thanks also to the Department of Industrial Engineering at Universidad de los Andes for all its support during the development of this paper.

Chapter **4**

Key Performance Areas That Determine Company Success

This chapter is the author's introduction to this book's discussion in the following chapters of the key performance areas that determine every company's success. Peter Drucker described these areas more than 50 years ago [1]. At that time Drucker lamented the lack of useful methods, technologies, and measures in these areas. Since that time, we have made great progress in methods, technologies, and measures, but much of what we have learned is not yet widely used in business management. The system science described in the first three chapters of this book will help companies use these methods, technologies, and measures to improve their performance in all seven of these key performance areas, including profitability. We begin this chapter with a few comments on profitability and management economics.

PROFITABILITY

We are into a time of change for our measures of company success. The most accepted measure of company success is the size of the profit number, and its trend; trend firmly upward preferred. Key measures widely used include sales revenue, net profit, earnings per share, return on investment, return on sales, return on equity . . . with management looking at these numbers, and aiming for rising stock price. What is not seen in any of the profit numbers is:

1. All that the company does in its operations that produces this profit number and the trends and changes in the key measures of those operations, and
2. The consequences of financial transactions that affect the profit number.

The company, like all systems, is what it does. Profit (or loss) results from everything the company does. Operating income is a key profit-ability number; the income from what the company does.

Making the expected profit numbers is always a management goal. But the profit number is not something that can be managed directly, except by misuse of financial transactions. Profit is a result from all the company does. What companies can manage and do manage is all those things the company does in its operations that result in operating income. Operating income is a key measure for profitability and trends in profitability. The profit number comes from operating income plus or minus other transactions that add to or subtract from profit. These transactions need to be well-managed, too, and clearly reported.

In recent years we have had too many examples of companies making the profit numbers by financial management, noted but not comprehended in financial statement footnotes—Enron, WorldCom, Adelphia, Tyco, Parmalat, HealthSouth among them. Real profit numbers come from good management of company operations, every-thing the company does.

The Financial Accounting Standards Board (FASB) has a challeng-ing task in specifying the accounting standards that all companies follow in their financial reporting. The objective is realistic financial reporting, and comparability from one company to another. The hundred thou-sand pages specifying accounting standards do specify good practices. But in all this complexity, financial experts can find justification for transactions that improve the numbers but depart from the Board's intention for transparency and real numbers.

Creativity in the finance department to enhance revenue and improve reported profitability whatever the reality is deceptive, and harmful to corporate health. To survive, grow, and prosper, companies must be profitable in their operations. That's where profitability comes from. A reliable statement of operating income should be a requirement in financial reporting, such as Standard & Poor's proposal on "core earnings." Another idea might be a two-part income statement as suggested in Chapter 11. Part A would be the statement of operating income. Part B would be everything else, plus or minus, that affects profitability, resulting in the reported profit figure. Everything would be transparent, in one statement.

Still, ill-intentioned people, or even well-intentioned people striving to "make the numbers" might find ways to depart from reality and brighten the numbers through various kinds of financial transactions. To encourage broad-scale improvement in the way people behave, companies could prepare and require "standards of conduct" for their members. Many companies have such standards, not always with 100% compliance. With the VSM, standards of conduct become a corporate parameter to be complied with by everyone, at all levels of recursion. It is always on the table, continuously taught and discussed, and periodically audited for compliance. The standards of conduct become "the way we do things around here."

MANAGEMENT ECONOMICS

Financial reporting is one dimension. Economic information for decision support is another and different dimension. Business managers have been trained to use accounting measures designed for financial reporting for use also in making decisions. Accounting measures commonly used for decision-support include: budget objectives expressed in accounting terms and variances from these objectives; product full costs; gross margins; cost of goods sold; sales, general, and administrative expenses; return on investment; return on sales; return on equity; discounted cash flow rate of return; cost allocations, and others. In the view of management economics—the economics of the firm and its transactions—using accounting measures for decision-support can be misleading, and can result in bad decisions. Management economics offers a better way; much simpler and much more reliable measures of the real situation. See Chapters 5 and 11.

KEY PERFORMANCE AREAS THAT DETERMINE COMPANY SUCCESS

Whether measured by accounting measures or management economics measures, profitability is a key performance area that results from what the company does in all its operations, in all seven of the key performance areas described in this book. A system is what it does. What the company does, and what all companies do, is create and keep customers. Companies start with an idea of creating value for customers. Henry Ford had an idea a hundred years ago—build a car that everyone can buy. Ford's Model T put America on wheels. Larry Page and Sergey Brin ten years ago had an idea—organize the world's information and make it universally accessible and useful. Seven years after start-up, Google was turning over more than 200 million searches a day, searching among 4 billion Web documents. Making an idea a successful business, and continuing that success over the years depends on a small number of key performance areas that determine every company's continuing success.

The idea of key performance areas, and the identification of what those key areas are, was first explained by Peter Drucker in his book, *The Practice of Management*, in 1954 [1]. In that book, Drucker wrote:

> To emphasize only profit, for instance, misdirects managers to the point where they may endanger the survival of the business. To obtain profit today they tend to undermine the future. They may push the most easily saleable product lines and slight those that are the market of tomorrow. They tend to short-change research, promotion and other postponable investments. Above all, they shy away from any capital expenditures that may increase the invested capital base against which profits are measured; and the result is dangerous obsolescence of equipment. In other words, they are directed into the worst practices of management.

He goes on to say that profitability objectives are important, but also important are objectives in all eight of the key performance areas that determine company success:

1. Market standing
2. Innovation
3. Productivity
4. Physical and financial resources
5. Profitability
6. Manager performance and development
7. Worker performance and attitude
8. Public responsibility

These eight key performance areas determine success for all companies, whatever the kind of company, whatever it's size. Drucker explains:

> At first sight it might seem that different businesses would have entirely different key areas—so different as to make impossible any general theory. It is indeed true that different key areas require different emphasis in different businesses—and different emphasis at different stages of development of each business. But the areas are the same, whatever the business, whatever the economic conditions, whatever the business's size or stage of growth.

Writing in *The Practice of Management* (1954), Peter Drucker was confident in identifying the key performance areas that determine company success. But at that time performance measures in these areas did not exist:

> We have adequate concepts only for measuring market standing. For something as obvious as profitability we have only a rubber yardstick, and we have no real tools at all to determine how much profitability is necessary. In respect to innovation and, even more, to productivity, we hardly know more than what ought to be done. And in the other areas— including physical and financial resources—we are reduced to statements of intention rather than goals and measurements for their attainment.

> For the subject is brand new. It is one of the most active frontiers of thought, research and invention in American business today. Company after company is working on the definition of the key areas, on thinking through what should be measured and on fashioning the tools of measurement.

Over the last 50 years we have made some progress in measurement. But most of this progress has produced accounting measures for evaluating performance. More recently "scorecard" measures have included measures in addition to the accounting measures. And this whole area of measurement is still evolving, with a focus on evaluating performance.

Evaluating performance is important. But much more important are measures that help people while they are doing the work accomplish desired results. These are the measures emphasized by the management principles in the VSM, beginning with feedback from the work itself. Feedback from the work itself guides the person doing the work toward the desired result. The most useful performance measures in each of the key performance areas guide decisions and help all those doing the work accomplish desired results. Examples of this kind of measurement are described in the following chapters. The important area of measures to help people achieve goals gets little attention. Looking back, measures can evaluate past performance, Looking ahead, measures can also help people achieve their goals. Measures that help companies create the future, the future beginning today, create much greater value than measures evaluating the past. We do need to understand the past. But the management job is to create the future, beginning now.

The VSM and the system science concepts of "variety" explain the need for what I call "achievement reporting," measures that help people achieve goals. To manage the great variety in operations, and the much, much greater variety in the company's environments, this variety must be greatly reduced (attenuated). How? First, by selecting what matters for the achievement of company purpose. Second, by developing useful measures of what matters. This new, different, better kind of measurement—to guide and coordinate work toward goal achievement—is still at the frontier of discovery and development as it was 50 years ago. This book presents some of what we know now.

I read *The Practice of Management* soon after it was published. At the time I was market research manager in a General Electric subsidiary company. I had joined the company after receiving an MS degree from the Columbia School of Business following five years of service in the US Army Air Corps. What I read about the key performance areas made sense to me, and I determined to learn all I could about all of these areas. I joined and participated in professional societies representing these areas. I read their journals. I read the books of the leading thinkers and contributors, especially those with new and better ideas. I cite a number of these in my Preface to this book.

Over the years I worked with many of these pioneers in applying their ideas in the companies I worked for. The more I learned and the more I experienced, the more I realized the validity of Peter Drucker's key performance areas. Over the years I discovered useful goals and useful performance measures in each of these areas, all of this expanding into a growing resource of best practices and best performance measures in the key performance areas. Over some 50 years I have worked with the evolving best methods and technologies in the key performance areas in more than a hundred businesses in 16 countries, always with success.

In the 1970s I worked with Stafford Beer and Paul Rubinyi in applying the VSM in the corporation I then worked for. Over the last 30 years I have used both Peter Drucker's key performance areas, and Stafford Beer's VSM and its system science and cybernetics. The key performance areas give us information on what needs to be managed well. The VSM gives us a better way to structure and manage the company, improving the company's capability for success in the key performance areas.

Over the years, the captions I use for Drucker's key performance areas have evolved, to relate more clearly to today's circumstances. The territory covered remains the same, but somewhat broader. And my listing of the key performance areas is now seven, combining Drucker's manager and worker areas into one—organization capability. The seven key performance areas, as I now use them in comparison with Peter Drucker's key performance areas:

Key Performance Areas for Today	Peter Drucker's Key Performance Areas
1. Creating and keeping customers	1. Market position
2. Quality and productivity	3. Productivity
3. Innovation	2. Innovation
4. Physical and financial resources	4. Physical and financial resources
5. Organization capability	6. Manager performance and development
	7. Worker performance and attitude
6. Public and environmental responsibility	8. Public responsibility
7. Profitability	5. Profitability

There is a logic to listing the seven key performance areas for today in this order. The first three deal with what the company does. First of all, successful companies create customers and keep them. That's the company purpose. To create customers the company produces products and services that offer satisfying values to customers. All the technologies of quality are focused on assuring those values. Productivity assures continuous improvement in company operations, to produce and deliver those values at favorable costs. Innovation assures that the company finds and does the right new things—new products and services, new processes, new management methods—needed to create the company's future.

Numbers 4 and 5 are the company's human and capital resources needed for accomplishing desired results in all the key performance areas. Number 6 deals with the company's responsibilities in the public sector, the company's relationships in its environments, the threats and opportunities in the ecological environment, and sustainability. Number 7, profitability, is a result from all the previous six. Commenting briefly on each of these seven:

1. Creating and Keeping Customers

Creating and keeping customers, part of the system 3 here and now of business operations, is what companies are organized to do. The purpose of every company is to create and keep customers. Peter Drucker expressed this idea in his term, market position, which is a measure of success in creating and keeping customers. Competitive position is another expression of this same measure, such as "In this product line, my company is number 2 of 8 competitors." In today's global economy customers are created in many countries and areas, and market position is usually measured by country or area.

Number 1 on our list has to be creating and keeping customers. That's what companies do. A system *is* what it *does*. Successful companies are better than their peers in creating and keeping customers. To create and keep customers, companies need to perform well in all the other key performance areas. For information on creating and keeping customers, and how the VSM and its system science and cybernetics, improves results in this key performance area, see Chapter 6.

2. Quality and Productivity

Key performance area number 2 is quality and productivity. Along with creating and keeping customers, quality and productivity are part of the system 3 here and now of business operations. Peter Drucker listed only productivity, and I began working in the technologies of productivity measurement and improvement. Productivity is defined as the relation of outputs to the inputs used in the production of those outputs, the level of this measure, and the trend of this measure over time. The outputs are the products and services produced and delivered to customers. The inputs are the hours of labor, consumption of capital, the components and materials used, and units of energy used to produce the outputs. Productivity improvement creates benefits at all levels:

1. Personal   Self-fulfillment and rising real income
2. Company   Profitability and survival
3. Industry   Lower costs and prices
4. National   Economic growth and debt reduction

Then came the quality revolution. The quality revolution over the years following World War II moved from inspect and reject, to statistical quality control (SQC), to quality control (QC), to total quality control (TQC), to total quality management (TQM), to all the technologies of the Toyota production system (TPS), to lean manufacturing, to the present lean operations. As the quality revolution progressed it became clearer and clearer that quality and productivity, properly defined, become one and the same thing.

When we define output as products and services delivered to customers and satisfying their needs and expectations without error or waste and continuously improving, then productivity equals quality, and quality equals productivity. We have measures for productivity. We have measures for quality. Collectively these measures help us continuously increase the outputs of products and services satisfying customer expectations in relation to inputs used. Chapter 7 discusses best practices in quality and productivity, and the value of the VSM and its system science and cybernetics in continuously improving quality and productivity performance.

3. Innovation

The third key performance area is Innovation. Innovation is part of the outside and future of business operations. Innovation changes the company from what it is to what it will be for success in the times ahead. The VSM and its system science and cybernetics very much strengthens a company's capability for innovation. The VSM designs "heterostats," centers for change and innovation, throughout the enterprise, at all levels of recursion.

Innovation begins with a new idea, a discovery, an invention. Innovation applies the idea, the discovery, the invention to create value for customers and users. For the company, small innovations improve competitiveness. Big innovations change the company. Really big innovations can change the industry, and change the market. Innovations in the company's environments can change the world. Innovation creates the future in all its dimensions. Chapter 8 discusses best practices in innovation, and how the VSM and its system science and cybernetics improves the company's capability for innovation.

4. Organization Capability

Organization capability is what makes possible the desired performance in all the key performance areas that determine company success. Organization capability needs to be world-class in all the key performance areas described in this book. And then the organization's capability must continue to improve as the standard for world-class grows higher. Over the last half century pioneers in expanding organization capability discovered new ideas that are now essential for business success:

> Douglas McGregor and his "Theory Y" concept, discovered through his work in behavioral science
>
> Frederick Herzberg and his work on the structure of jobs to provide motivation from the work itself
>
> Rensis Likert and his pioneering work on participative management
>
> David McClelland and his work on achievement motivation and on power motivation

Many conventionally managed companies worked to apply these new discoveries but without much success. There was still too much "Theory X" in the commercial environment; still too much hierarchy, too much command and control. A new structure was needed. That new structure is now here, described in the VSM and its system science and cybernetics. The VSM not only allows space for these new ideas on the human side of enterprise. The VSM needs them, and requires them. The VSM asks for and develops the full potential of all members of the enterprise. Chapter 9 describes how the VSM helps expand organization capability.

5. Physical and Financial Resources

This book does not have a chapter specifically on this key performance area. But it does offer some important ideas and methods. Chapter 5 discusses some different measures for budgeting capital costs, and a different and better method for evaluating new capital investments. Chapter 7 describes a method for measuring capital productivity.

The management of finances we leave to FASB, the SEC, and Sarbanes-Oxley.

6. Public and Environmental Responsibility

This key performance area includes the company's relations with and responsibilities to the seven environments described in this book:

- Six cultural environments
- The natural environment, the earth's ecosphere

The cultural environments:

1. Commercial environment
2. Technical environment
3. Economic environment
4. Political environment
5. Social environment
6. Educational environment

The natural environment:

7. The ecosphere and its biosphere which support all life on earth.

The company's six cultural environments and the company are all embedded in this natural environment and depend on it for their viability.

Companies have created great successes at the leading edge of changes in the first three cultural environments, commercial, technical, and economic. Companies, less innovational, less adaptive, can be hurt or killed by changes in any of these three environments. Changes in the three other culture-created environments, political, social, and educational can be opportunities, or threats.

All of the cultural environments and the company, too, live in the natural environment:

- The earth's ecosphere now threatened with global warming, melting polar ice caps, rising sea levels, changing weather
- The earth's biosphere which supports all life on earth, now threatened by pollution, declining water tables, loss of arable land, and extinction of species

These threats have developed since World War II, resulting from the increase in world population from 2.5 billion people to 6.0 billion, and a seven times growth in the world's economic output. Companies individually and collectively now need to find what they can do to reduce these growing threats, and to achieve sustainability.

The VSM includes communication channels with all seven of these environments to inform the company on both threats and opportunities. The VSM also includes a structure to deal with the threats, and to develop the opportunities that are right for the company.

Chapter 10 discusses best practices in relationships with and responsibilities to all these environments. Chapter 10 also describes how the VSM structure and information flow enables the company to deal successfully with changes in these environments.

7. Profitability

How well the company performs in the other key performance areas determines company profitability. Chapter 11 offers some management economics measures that can help company people working in the key performance areas change and improve their ways of working to improve profitability. These measures give everyone a better understanding of costs and an understanding of value created. People make wiser decisions. The MX Corporation example in chapter 3 cites one example. The VSM with its system science and cybernetics, and the best methods and technologies in all of the key performance areas give us the best way to achieve profitability objectives. See Chapter 11.

OVERVIEW: THE ESSENCE OF CHAPTER 4

The VSM with its system science and cybernetics gives us a new and different way to structure the company, and new and different principles for managing the company.

For company success we need to manage well the seven key performance areas described in this book. The VSM gives us the information we need on *how* to manage. Best practices in the key performance areas gives us the information we need on *what* to manage. High performance in these key performance areas, with goals and the right kinds of measures, creates profitability. The seven key performance areas:

1. Creating and Keeping Customers. The purpose of every company is to create and keep customers. Chapter 6.
2. Quality and Productivity. Creating and keeping customers requires quality products and services, and continuous improvement in all that the company does. Chapter 7.
3. Innovation. Innovating the new, different, better creates the company's future, short-range and long-range. Chapter 8.
4. Organization Capability. The company **is** its people. Their effectiveness in these key performance areas determines company success. Chapter 9.
5. Physical and Financial Resources. These are the "tools" company people need to achieve company goals. Chapters 5 and 11.
6. Public and Environmental Responsibility. The company must relate successfully to communities, governments, and its environments. Chapter 10.
7. Profitability. Profit results from all the above. Profits pay the costs of creating the company's future, and reward investors. Chapter 11.

The VSM with its system science and cybernetics helps companies succeed in all these key performance areas.

NOTE

[1] Peter F. Drucker, *The Practice of Management*, Harper & Row, New York, 1954.

Chapter 5

The Viable System Model and Planning and Budgeting

In the 1940s and 50s, corporate planning was simple, and done by executive management. Then planning became a professional function, planning departments appeared, and corporate planning evolved to the complex and the very complex. Recently, the desire is back toward the simple. With the VSM, and the key performance areas that determine every company's success, plans can be simple, include all that matters, and effectively guide company operations.

A BRIEF HISTORY OF PLANNING

In the 1940s, after World War II, a manufacturing company was working to convert from war production to consumer products. From war production and one customer, the US government, the company needed to again make consumer products and develop the customers and the distribution to market the products. The president of the company announced, "It's hectic around here now, but we'll get all this behind us soon, and get back to normal." The company did get through the conversion to consumer products, but the "normal" disappeared into continuing, and now accelerating change.

Holistic Management, by William Christopher
Copyright © 2007 John Wiley & Sons, Inc., Publication

At that time as companies were reorganizing from their war production and war services back to commercial operations, the planning was day-to-day. How should we plan the conversion from wartime operations to commercial sales, production, and services, in a free and unpredictable economy? World War I was followed by recession. What would happen this time?

Plans then were pretty much, "We'll do $XX in sales and $X in profit this year. Next year our aim is X% more. Better than last year by X% was a typical budget plan. Then forward-looking companies, General Electric among them, began developing new and better ways to plan, and to budget operations for the fiscal year. They defined their businesses, and set long term goals. They developed plans and budgets from both a market orientation and a financial orientation. The focus was on creating customers, and competitive advantage. They set budget objectives for sales revenue, costs, prices, new business, changes in resources, and profit.

From this start in the late 1940s, over the following years corporate planning and budgeting evolved into the professional disciplines of planning and budgeting, and the continuing development of technologies and methods. Plan and budgets grew from the simple to the complex to the very complex. In the 1960s, one large capital goods manufacturer developed a "Plan for Planning" that, diagrammed in a flow chart, covered a wall six by ten feet. As corporate planning groups grew in size, so did the plans, from "business plans," to "long range plans," to "strategic plans," and variations of and supplements to these.

As plans grew more and more complex, simpler forms—but not replacements—appeared. Companies developed "mission statements:"

Who we are
What we do
Our purpose
Specific goals

And the essence of strategic plans and mission statements was captured in "vision statements:"

A hospital supply company: "We will be the leading single-source of products and services which help hospitals achieve cost-effective, high-quality health care."

An early cell-phone company: "We will provide an automatic call delivery system, connecting people to people, not to places."

A luxury hotel company: "For every guest, a warm welcome, anticipate guest needs, and a fond farewell, from Ladies and Gentlemen
serving Ladies and Gentlemen."

An automotive and miniature lighting company: "Sustain a leadership position in automotive and miniature lighting by providing
the highest quality light sources and lighting systems at competitive prices."

A major hotel chain: "Grow a worldwide lodging business using total
quality management principles to continuously improve prefer-
ence and profitability. Our commitment is that every guest leaves
satisfied."

Among the most famous vision statements were these, though they
were not called vision statements:

Henry Ford (1908): "Produce a car that everyone can buy."

NASA (1960): "Put a man on the moon and bring him back, by the
end of the decade."

Google (1998): "Organize the world's information and make it universally accessible and useful."

Vision Statements encapsulate strategic goals. Both Henry Ford and
NASA accomplished their goals. Ford built the first Model T automobile in 1908 and the last one in 1927. Over that time, 15 million were
sold, Ford was the largest automaker in the country, and America was
on wheels. In one of the great engineering achievements of our times,
NASA engineers learned how to design and build the equipment
and train the astronauts for flight to the moon. On July 26, 1969, Neil
Armstrong and Buzz Aldrin stepped off the lunar module, *Eagle*, onto
the surface of the moon. After 21 hours on the lunar landscape they
piloted the lunar module back to the command module, *Columbia*,
orbiting the moon and returned safely to earth. While the achievement
of the Google goal is more difficult to measure, seven years after start-
up the company was handling 200 million searches a day among 4
billion on-line documents.

Vision statements were not constructed by planning groups from
studies, analyses, and projections. They were created by leaders, looking
ahead. Vision set a direction into the future, saying to everyone, "This
is what we are all about." Vision stated the company's drive and direction—the essence of the company's competitive advantage, to be
created and grown.

From the evolution of business planning, long-range-planning, strategic planning, mission statements, and vision statements, what's best for the world of today? System thinking and the VSM can help.

The Products Group of a large oil company wanted to improve their strategic planning. The corporate planning group had a structured procedure they went through each year to produce the corporation's strategic plan. When finally approved, the strategic plan was a series of loose-leaf binders filling about two feet of shelf space. And that's about what happened. When finished, it went on the shelf. The plan did not direct company actions to create their future. There was no connection to operations except when individual managers and executives who learned something from their participation in the process took some actions they might not have taken otherwise. With system thinking and the VSM, that shelf of binders could be replaced by a few pages, with other sets of a few pages at many locations throughout the company for those businesses, all solidly linked to operations.

THE VSM FRAMEWORK FOR PLANNING

Thinking of company plans, let's begin with the basic viable system model that we first saw in Chapter 2. This is a system science model for a viable, very complex, purposeful, probabilistic system, a new way to model and understand the corporation. Each of the four system 1s in the corporate model shown in Figure 5.1 can also be modeled with this viable system model, as can each of the system 1 businesses throughout the company at all levels of recursion.

Figure 5.1 is the viable system model of the entire corporation, in this example with four system 1 operating businesses. In the first recursion of the corporate model, each of the four system 1s in Figure 5.1 could be modeled with this same viable system model. These businesses might have four, or three, or six system 1 operating units. For all recursions there will be the same system model for every system 1 operating unit with its system 1s which might be as few as three on as many as eight. Figure 5.2 (shown in Chapter 2 as Figure 2.6) shows the corporate VSM in Figure 5.1 with two levels of recursion; each system 1 modeled with the VSM.

In the first recursion from the corporate VSM in Figure 5.2, each of the corporations four system 1 businesses is modeled with the VSM

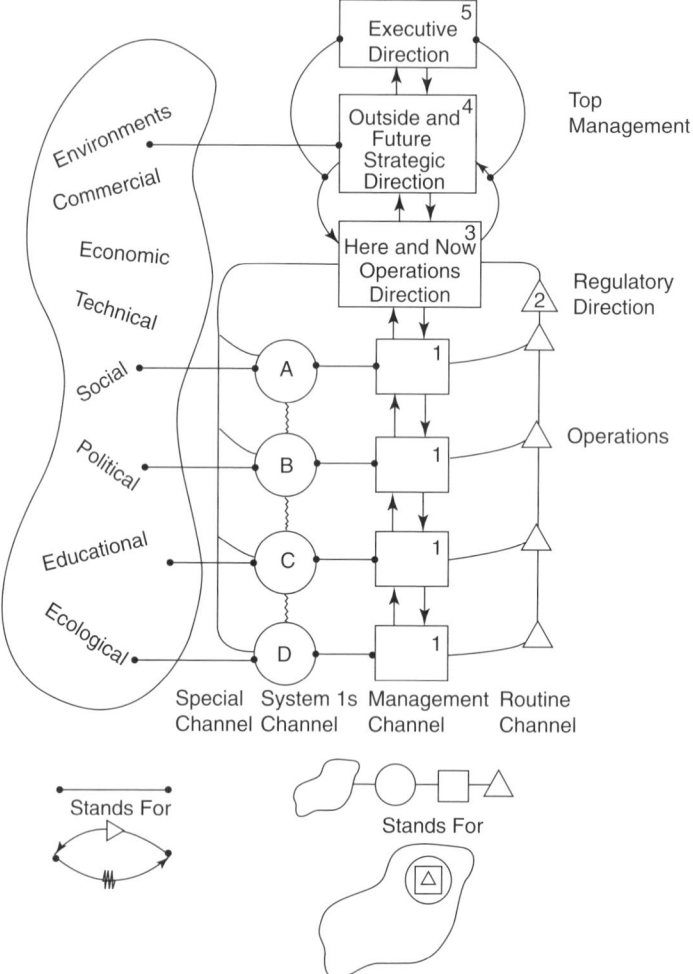

Figure 5.1 The Viable System Model

labeled with the number 1. The first, second, and third system 1 in the corporate VSM each have four system 1s. The fourth corporate system 1 has three system 1s. In the second recursion from the corporate VSM, each of the first recursion system 1s is modeled with the VSM, labeled with the number 2. And the recursions continue. With the VSM we depart from hierarchy to a web of interconnected systems. Let's consider Figures 5.1 and 5.2 as the VSM framework for corporate planning.

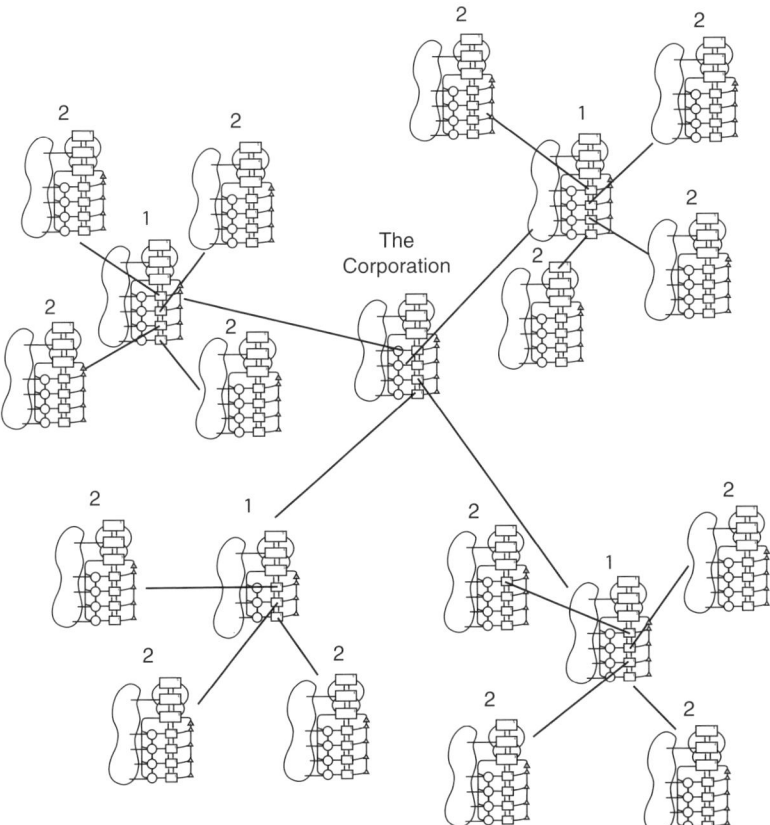

Figure 5.2   Corporate VSM with two recursions

THE CORPORATE PLAN

In Chapter 2 a company is defined as a viable, very complex, purposeful, probabilistic system. "Purposeful" in the definition makes the corporate system different from a natural system. The purpose of a natural system is viability, to continue to exist in its environment. The purpose of a company is more than survival. The purpose of a company is to create customers, to achieve goals. A company is purposeful. It exists to do something. That "something" is defined in the corporate plan.

At the direction of system 5 executive management, system 4 corporate planning, collaborating with system 3, develops the corporate plan. The corporate plan and the goals specified in the plan are the purposive part of the company system for the times ahead. The corporate budget and objectives, discussed later, is the purposive part of the company system for the fiscal year.

Directing and working with the system 4 corporate planning function, system 5 executive leadership leads the development of the corporate plan, or business model, or strategic plan, or vision, or whatever the format is. System 4 provides information and puts the plan together. System 3 and management of the system 1 business units will be involved, and contribute their specialized knowledge on the here and now. System 5 executive leadership determines the planning format, and approves and communicates the final plan. Then the plan can be continually maintained so that planning is continuous, as described later in this chapter.

A good approach for preparing the plan is brief answers to eight basic questions:

1. What is the company's purpose?
2. What are and will be the company's products and services and operating boundaries?
3. Who are and will be our customers?
4. What is and will be important to our customers?
5. What are our goals, and measures of success in the key performance areas?
   Creating and keeping customers
   Quality and productivity
   Innovation
   Organization capability
   Physical and financial resources
   Public and environmental responsibility
   Profitability
6. What are our strategies for achieving our goals?
7. What are our standards of behavior?
8. How will we relate to the world around us—our environments?

Conventional plans are primarily financial—sales revenue, costs, prices, and profitability. This kind of information will be included in the answer to question 5 but in a much simpler and more useful way, as discussed later in this chapter and in Chapter 11. A corporate plan that summarizes the company's answers to the eight questions listed above—even for a very large company—can be a few pages, not a shelf of loose-leaf binders.

The corporate plan deals only with the answers to these eight questions for the total corporation. Each of the system 1 business units at all levels of recursion can follow a similar procedure, developing their plans for their businesses. Their plans don't flow up to the corporate level. They stay at the levels that developed them—the VSM business and the system 3 in the next higher level of recursion.

Throughout the corporation, statements responding to the first six questions will be unique for each VSM business unit. The corporate answer to question 7 will become a corporate parameter on the standards of behavior to be followed by everyone in the company. There will need to be processes to assure that the standards of behavior prevail throughout the company. With broad and continuous communication, and audits at irregular intervals corporate leadership can assure that the corporate standards of behavior is more than words; it is prevailing company behavior with no exceptions.

Statements responding to question 8 will differ among the VSM business units for the cultural environments—commercial, technical, economic, social, political, and educational. For the ecological environment, relationships can best be specified in a corporate parameter applying in all company businesses.

Measures

The company decisions on key performance area measures of success will be an important part of achieving success. Keep in mind Ashby's Law described in Chapter 1: Only variety can absorb variety. In system science, "variety" is the measure of complexity. There is huge variety (complexity) in company operations. There is much greater variety in the environments affecting company operations—commercial, technical, economic, social, political, educational, and ecological. Management can only direct and control this immense variety by:

1. Greatly cutting down (attenuating) the amount of the variety by careful selection of what matters
2. Representing what matters by carefully developed measures.

With operations and environment variety attenuated by selection of and measures of what matters, and management variety amplified through self-organization and self-control, there can be requisite variety where decisions are made.

For measures of success we tend to think of profit in relation to some other measure: ROI, ROE, ROS, EPS. These are measures calculated by generally accepted accounting practices producing specific numbers. If not restrained by corporate standards of behavior, however, the measures of profit, sales, and investment can be improved by changes in assumptions, classifications, and selective or special kinds of financial transactions. Profit, sales, and investment, calculated by economic methods rather than accounting methods will be different, and more useful for managing the enterprise. With the VSM and system thinking accounting measures are used for financial reporting, but decision makers at all levels will use economics measures for managing operations. See Chapter 11.

From the viewpoint of company planning and operations management ROI, ROE, ROS, and EPS kinds of measures are less than helpful for two reasons:

1. ROX measures are derivative from something else. The something else is the seven key performance areas that determine every company's success. These need to be the focus of corporate planning, and
2. ROX numbers are not actionable. They give us no clue on actions needed for improvement. The most useful measures for management track performance, and guide us to the achievement of desired objectives.

Key Performance Areas

Profitability derives from company performance in the key performance areas that determine every company's success:

1. Creating and keeping customers
2. quality and productivity
3. Innovation
4. Organization capability
5. Physical and financial resources
6. Public and environmental responsibility
7. Profitability

Peter Drucker, in his 1954 pioneering book, *The Practice of Management*, stated the importance of objectives and measures in eight key performance areas [1]:

Objectives are needed in every area where performance and results directly and vitally affect the survival and prosperity of the business. These are the areas which are affected by every management decision and which therefore have to be considered in every management decision. They decide what it means concretely to manage the business. They spell out what results the business must aim at and what is needed to work effectively toward these targets.

There are eight areas in which objectives of performance and results have to be set: market standing; innovation; productivity; physical and financial resources; profitability; manager performance and development; worker performance and attitude; public responsibility.

The previous list of seven key performance areas is Professor Drucker's list modified just a bit and combining two of his eight into one in consideration of new developments over the last half-century. This book emphasizes objectives and measures in these seven key performance areas along with information on how the VSM and system thinking helps people at all levels manage each of these seven areas for successful company results. Commenting on these seven key performance areas:

1. Creating and Keeping Customers   Company success is created in the marketplace. All that the company does focuses on what is needed to create and keep customers. Sales revenue and the contribution of those sales to profitability are the measures of that success.

All companies closely monitor sales revenue, and analyze sales revenue in many ways. Few companies monitor the contribution of sales revenue to profitability. Many companies monitor measures of market position, and often aim for being first or second in the market place. But there are many ways to define market, and more than one way to calculate or estimate position. In today's huge, segmented in many dimensions, and rapidly evolving markets there are better guides than being first or second in market position.

At all levels of recursion, in each viable, very complex, purposeful, probabilistic business, the VSM and system thinking will help the business find and use best practices for creating and keeping customers. For information on creating and keeping customers, see Chapter 6.

2. Quality and Productivity   Peter Drucker in his books describes productivity as a first task of management. In all the company is doing, it must continuously do better and better, continuously improving results in relation to resources used. Then came the quality revolution pioneered by W. Edwards Deming and the Japanese who learned statistical quality control from Deming. The Japanese then went on to create the still developing quality evolution from inspect and reject quality control (QC), to statistical quality control (SQC), total quality control (TQC), total quality management (TQM), the Toyota Production System (TPS), agile manufacturing, lean manufacturing, and lean operations, with the evolution continuing.

Over this evolution, productivity and quality have become old names for the same new technology: producing and delivering defect-free products to customers, with products and after-sales service and all customer relationships satisfying their expectations, and doing this without error and without waste, and continuously improving.

While the technology and measures of productivity and quality will be key to operations success, these same technologies and measures apply also in the management of corporate processes. Referring to the corporate VSM, leaders in systems 5, 4, 3, and 2 can establish quality and productivity measures for the work they do, and monitor the measures for continuous improvement.

Quality and productivity measures improve performance in the workplace, where the work is done. Statistical process control (SPC) measures keep production within specifications. Mistake-proofing (Poke-Yoke) eliminates errors. Kaizen involves everyone in continuous improvement. Input-output measures provide baselines for improvement (output per unit of input, output per hour, etc.) In the years following World War II, Japan used these measures to transform their industry to world-class leadership. The best of these quality and productivity measures, now included in "Lean," are an essential part of operations management today. Using the VSM, information on the use of quality and productivity technologies will be shared on the System 1s communication channel, and communicated throughout the company on the special communication channel.

But how can we measure the productivity and quality of a total system 1 business? Quality and productivity measures are difficult to calculate for a total business, and of little use in controlling and improving performance. Aggregation loses information. Quality and productivity measures help operations management control and continuously improve production processes, and can help all management control and continuously improve management processes. But what is a useful quality and productivity measure for the total company and for each profit center VSM business in the company?

Each VSM business creates value for customers. Creating value for customers is the source of company revenue and the beginning point for company profitability. So it's wise to measure and continuously monitor how successfully each profit-center system 1 business creates value for customers. A useful measure for the company's efficiency and success in creating value for customers is economic productivity ($P). Economic productivity is a productivity measure. It measures the company's productivity in creating value for customers. This makes it also a measure of the quality of management performance. Economic productivity is a measure useful for every P&L business at all levels of recursion. For information on economic productivity measures, see Chapter 7.

Quality and productivity measures and improvement are essential where the work is done, as the work is done. Most of the work of the corporation is done in operations in the system 1 viable business systems. Quality and productivity measures will be used in these operations, and continuous improvement achieved.

But there is also corporate work done at the corporate level, in systems 2, 3, 4, and 5, and in the systems 2, 3, 4, and 5 at all levels of recursion. Quality and productivity measures are useful for the continuous improvement of this work, including the work done in:

- Planning
- Budgeting
- Research and development
- Engineering
- Marketing and sales
- Finance and accounting
- Project management
- Monitoring the VSM
- All other units and functions

Measures will include cycle time, error reduction, waste reduction, throughput, customer satisfaction, process improvement, and the appropriate measures of outputs in relation to inputs. For more information on quality and productivity, see Chapter 7.

3. Innovation For continuing success in creating and keeping customers, and achieving the company's goals for the future, companies and each VSM business unit need to do two things well in their operations:

- Quality and productivity. Use best practices to meet today's requirements, and continuously improve in all areas of operations.
- Innovation. Anticipate customer needs and values, find and develop the new products and services, and adopt the new processes and practices needed to achieve company purpose and goals. Innovation creates the company's future, beginning now.

Quality and productivity creates success today. Quality and productivity plus innovation creates success over time. Today's leaders and managers recognize that tomorrow morning is the beginning of the future. There's great emphasis now on innovation as the key to success. That's good. But there are six other key performance areas, too. All seven key performance areas determine company success. For information on how the VSM and system thinking helps us create and manage innovation. See Chapter 8.

4. Organization Capability   Under this heading we include all the company's training and development programs, and much more. The "much more" is greatly aided by the VSM and system thinking. A major part of the VSM and an important lesson from system science is the self-organizing and self-controlling characteristics of systems. Systems work that way. The VSM helps us recognize and use that natural capability, at all levels of recursion.

Operations become black boxes to higher-level management which is constrained by Ashby's Law from any capability to control what goes on inside the black box. But what goes on inside the black box is capably controlled by its own self-organizing and self-controlling ability. System science gives us a new perspective on what decentralization, delegation, empowerment, involvement, and participation have been striving for. Those words were the hierarchy trying to make more effective use of all the organization's people. As we have seen, the VSM changes the hierarchy to a network of systems. The hierarchy diffuses. The VSM structure and management principles make everyone a part of management for their area of responsibility. Managing by the structure and the principles of the VSM and system thinking makes effective use of all the organization's people. Organization capability increases.

HR departments deal primarily with administrative kinds of matters, including wage and salary administration; labor negotiations and contract administration; health insurance, pension plans, vacation plans, and other benefits; performance review policies and administration;

recruitment; training programs; community relations; and maintaining the appropriate records on all of these. For many years HR professionals have had an awareness that they could do something more. They advanced the ideas of participation, participative management, involvement, job enrichment and others to more involve the knowledge and the capabilities of all employees in their part of company operations. Frederick Herzberg in his 1966 seminal book, *Work and the Nature of Man*, [2] pointed out that all the administrative responsibilities of the HR department, which he called *hygiene requirements*, can satisfy or dissatisfy employees, but they have no effect on motivating job performance. From his research, he found that motivation comes from the work itself. He proposed an additional role for HR: finding ways to organize work to meet the motivator needs of employees. That's one of the things the VSM does. It organizes work to meet the motivator needs of all employees.

More fully using the capabilities of all employees significantly increases organization capability, but more is needed. Each individual's capabilities for doing their kind of work can also continually improve. Continuing education and learning raises the organization's collective IQ, increasing organization capability. College and university courses, in-company training programs, seminars, on-the-job learning and experience, company sponsored learning/doing projects such as six sigma, kaizen, and lean operations, reading and internet learning, and other learning and development can make careers both doing and learning. Success in the other key performance areas depends on organization capability. For more information on organization capability see Chapter 9.

5. Physical and Financial Resources   To achieve their purpose and their specific goals, companies employ two kinds of resources: people, and capital resources—equipment, buildings, land, and financial resources. Equipment, buildings, and land are fixed costs of operations in the calculation of the operations income statement. These fixed costs need to be managed. But there are better ways to manage them than the commonly used budget practices. See Chapter 11.

The use of equipment, buildings, and land needs to be managed both day-to-day and strategically:

- Day-to-day in current operations, by the principles of total productive maintenance (TPM), one of the disciplines in lean operations.

- Strategically, over time, by monitoring the environments as specified by the VSM, and making the changes needed to assure that the company has the right technologies, capabilities, and resources for on-going success.

Capital budgeting is usually a difficult and complicated procedure, with decisions typically made on the basis of ROI or some other profit kind of measure. Sounds logical. But the first criteria should be pursuit of purpose, how the investment moves the company toward its goals.

In one corporation at budget time, top management determined that the maximum amount of new capital investment they could finance in the coming year would be about $300 million. But proposals from operations totaled more than $600 million. All offered discounted cash flow rates of return higher than the company threshold for consideration. How to resolve? By ROI? Or? Evaluating the proposals in relation to the company's purpose and goals determined that about $300 million could comfortably support all that really mattered to the continuing success of the company. Sorting by purpose will be more effective and more profitable than sorting by prospective ROI. Achieving purpose is what matters. Prospective ROIs may or may not happen, and the project may or may not be related to purpose.

Financial resources are managed by the finance and accounting function. These resources can be used for acquisition of equipment, buildings, and land; for investment; and for other needs in the pursuit of company purpose and goals. The effects of these actions are typically reported in footnotes to the income statement. They might better be reported as part of the income statement itself. See Chapter 11.

6. Public and Environmental Responsibility   Companies in their operations relate to important environments they live in and work in:

> The cultural environments that are created by and for humanity:
> - The commercial environment of customers, prospective customers, competitors, suppliers, transactions, and applicable laws and regulations.
> - The technical environment, the international arena of technology that we contribute to and learn from.
> - The economic environment of general business conditions.
> - The political environment of laws and regulations and the processes for creating and changing them.

- The social environment including:

  The communities in which the company operates

  The broader public everywhere in relation to the company's products and services and the consequences of their use, recycle, or disposal

  Prevailing norms and behaviors.

- The educational environment of school systems, colleges and universities, and life-long learning.

The natural environment that all the cultural environments and our company live in:

- The ecosphere

At all levels of recursion, each VSM business unit needs to specify its relationships with these environments, define the responsibilities for environmental relationships, set goals for each of the environments, and establish appropriate measures.

The need for conservation of the ecological environment, and remediation of damage already done makes environmental responsibility a major management concern. Growing populations, expanding production to satisfy rapidly growing demand, consumption of natural resources, after use disposal; all impact the ecosphere. What is our company's environmental responsibility? What should be our goals? Our measures? See Chapter 10.

7. Profitability   A business is a viable system. All viable systems, by definition, are systems capable of continuing to exist in their environment. For a company to continue to exist in its environment requires profitability. A definition to think about:

Profitability = The Cost of the Future

Consider the company's long-range plan and company goals. These goals will require innovation and change to the new, different, better. How much new investment will be needed for additional people, new equipment and facilities, new research, new business development internally and by M&A, new requirements for conservation of the environment and for dealing with social problems arising from rapidly growing and conflicting populations? The company's future has a high cost. Profitability pays that cost. Without the needed profitability, the company can have no future.

Profitability is not the purpose of the company. The purpose of the company is to create value for customers in the company's products and services, and to create and keep customers in a way that satisfies all requirements. One of those requirements is profitability. Profitability pays the company's costs for creating its future. Profitability pays a return for investors. Profitability helps keep the company viable.

With the VSM and system thinking, best practices on measuring and monitoring profitability will be communicated throughout the company on the special communication channel. See Chapter 11.

PROJECTS

Projects are an organized way to develop and implement new products, services, and processes; changes in plans or strategy; changes in the company infrastructure; and changes in organization structure. At the corporate level and at all levels of recursion, strategic projects—the outside and future—are a responsibility of system 4; operations projects—the inside and now—are a responsibility of system 3.

Strategic projects would include such projects as a major new product or new product line, a merger, learning and adopting the VSM, a new and different primary strategy. Developing and commercializing a new technology would be a strategic project with many subordinate projects. Operations projects would include such projects as purchasing and installing new production equipment, a sales campaign, an annual meeting of shareholders, a product redesign and improvement, learning and adopting a *kaizen* suggestion system. Projects:

- Begin with a statement of purpose and a time line.
- Are usually conducted by a cross-functional team.
- Are planned and implemented in stages. See Figure 5.3.
- Specify results to be accomplished at each stage. Stages 5 and 6 in Figure 5.3 will have several sub-stages.
- Are reviewed at each checkpoint, and revised, terminated, or expanded as appropriate.
- Are managed using best practices in project management.

Except for major innovation projects, stages 1 through 4 will be completed quickly by the project team. Stage 5, development, and stage 6,

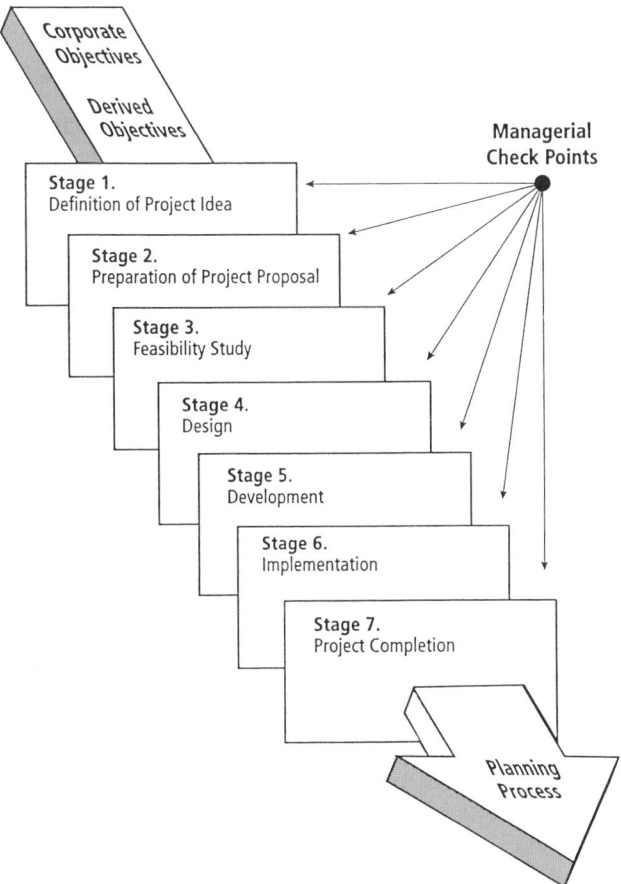

Figure 5.3 Project stages. (Source: Paul Rubinyi, *Unchaining the Chain of Command*, 1998. Used with permission.)

implementation, determine project success and will take more time and work. Each of these two stages will have several benchmark dates, with deliverables, that are also managerial checkpoints for review and any appropriate replanning of the project.

Large companies maintain a Project Office to inform and assist project teams in all the above. The key person for project success is the project manager who must have the knowledge of the subject area, the leadership ability, the enthusiasm, and the commitment to make the project succeed.

GOALS AND MEASURES

Each business, of course, is a special situation and will differ in the measures best for them in each of the seven key performance areas. And companies may add an additional performance area especially important for them. But usually any unique performance area will fit within one of these seven.

A good total number of objectives and performance measures is one to three in a key performance area. Figure 5.4 lists the goals and measures used by one business that set goals in each of the seven key performance areas.

Figure 5.4 shows goals and measures for the total business. With experience in using the measures there may be a desire to improve the measurement system by adding additional goals and measures. It's better to improve the measurement system by simplifying it. Would any of these measures be more appropriate at a lower level? Can any be dropped because other measure(s) adequately cover that area? Are there any measures really not useful in improving performance? Can any of the measures be simplified and improved?

In Figure 5.4, goal 2(c) originally was to improve total productivity 5% per year. (See Chapter 7 for information on calculating total productivity.) The measure of total productivity is very difficult to calculate for a profit-center business, and is of little value in improving performance. So the measure was changed to economic productivity. This measure is easy to calculate and monitor, and is very helpful in improving performance. Economic productivity measures the company's efficiency in creating value for customers, the starting point for earning profitability. Measures of total productivity are much more useful at lower levels of recursion where the work is done. For goal 5(a) management might teach and promote total productive maintenance (TPM), leave the goals and measurement to operations. Item 6 goals and measures would benefit from more thought on what matters most, and measurable goals.

For the corporate plan, and for the plans in each of the profit-center business units, a total of 7 to 10 goals in some combination of the seven key performance areas can fully specify successful performance. In Figure 5.4, for example, the selection might be: 1(a), 2(c), 3(a), 3(b), 4(b), 5(c), 7(a), 7(c), and a measurable goal for item 6, such as zero harmful emissions in five years, with a goal for each of the five years.

While the form of a corporate plan can be what is best for each specific company, system science and the VSM gives us a new fundamental, much different from typical practice. The corporate plan is

Goals	Measures

1. Creating and Keeping Customers

(a) Double sales revenue (constant dollars) within eight years

(b) Be a market leader in each strategic business

(c) In each strategic business create a competitive advantage that will win the major share of target client business

(a) 12-month moving total from three years ago showing also annual totals in constant dollars and the 8-years target ahead

(b) Quarterly estimate of market position in relation to top six competitors

(c) Quarterly review of competitive position in key target accounts

2. Quality and Productivity

(a) Increase value added per dollar of payroll expense by 5% a year

(b) Reduce cost of poor quality by 19% per year

(c) Increase economic productivity every year

(a) 3-month moving average of value added per dollar of payroll expense

(b) Quarterly measures

(c) Quarterly time series data and chart:

$$\frac{VA}{L + K + PFC}$$

3. Innovation

(a) Create new products that will amount to 25% or more of sales revenue within five years

(b) Find new technology and methods to improve processes and reduce costs by $8.5 million per year

(a) Sales revenue from products and services new within the last five years—dollars and percent of sales—charted in time series

(b) Cost changes from process improvements reported monthly and cumulatively,year-to-date

4. Organization Capability

(a) Receive and implement 5 suggestions per employee per year within two years, with a steadily rising trend thereafter

(b) Provide at least 40 hours of learning for all employees each year

(a) 12-month moving average: Number of suggestions and number of implemented suggestions, left scale; Number of implemented suggestions per employee. right scale

(b) Quarterly and year-to-date report on learning hours by employee group

5. Physical and Financial Resources

(a) Establish and maintain a system of total productive maintenance in all operations

(b) Find and invest in new process technology that will keep operations world class

(c) Improve capital productivity 2 1/2 % per year on trend

(a) Monthly plant reports on unscheduled off-lines

(b) Annual technology audit

(c) Quarterly time series of the index of capital productivity from base year = 100; capital productivity = O/K

6. Public and Environmental Responsibility

(a) Fully comply with all regulatory requirements

(b) Openly communicate with the media and with other outside constituencies

(c) Support employee participation in community affairs

(d) Manage all company actions to conserve the environment

(a) Annual audit

(b) Annual audit

(c) Annual audit

(d) Annual audit

Figure 5.4   Examples of goals and measures

7. Profitability

(a) Grow net income 8% per year, on trend

(b) Maintain profitability in the top quartile of 12 major competitors

(c) Invest new capital assets in support of company plan, with about half in new technology

(a) 12-month moving total of net income from three years ago showing the annual 8% goals for eight years ahead

(b) Quarterly report on the 12 major competitors listed in rank order by return on sales and showing also total sales revenue and net profit

(c) Include company plan screen in RFEs; monitor: Quarterly and annual totals, total investment and investment in new technology

Figure 5.4 *Continued*

developed by corporate leadership for the corporation. It is not a total from lower level plans. It is not directly linked to lower level plans. It is not the model for lower level plans. There is no directive to lower level units on how to develop their business plans. The corporate plan is a plan for where the company is going, and how. Key points in the corporate plan, however, are communicated within the corporate VSM, and with the top managements at all levels of recursion. This will not be a bulky document.

A useful plan can be the answers to the eight basic questions proposed earlier in this chapter:

1. What is the company's purpose?
2. What are and will be the company's products and services and operating boundaries?
3. Who are and will be our customers?
4. What is and will be important to our customers?
5. What are our goals, and measures of success in seven key performance areas:

   Creating and keeping customers

   Quality and productivity

   Innovation

   Organization capability

   Physical and financial resources

   Public and environmental responsibility, and

   Profitability
6. What are our strategies for achieving our goals?
7. What are our standards of behavior?
8. How will we relate to the world around us—our environments?

Finding the best answers to these questions requires a lot of both practical thinking, and creative thinking by many people. But when determined and committed to, the plan doesn't require a lot of words. A few pages, two to four or five should be enough. It's important for everyone in the company to have an understanding of their company, its aspirations, its standards of performance, and its goals and measures of success. The company plan, broadly communicated, helps develop this understanding. The corporate plan, now a brief document, should be on the table and in everyone's awareness whenever corporate decisions are made. Every decision is a step toward the achievement of the company plan.

Similarly, each VSM business unit at all levels of recursion will have their plan on the table and in everyone's awareness whenever decisions are made. Having this kind of a plan always in everyone's awareness sharpens the focus on what matters.

Plans in all the viable business systems at all levels of recursion can be developed, reviewed, monitored, and adjusted on whatever schedule is appropriate for that business. The method summarized above can be recommended but not required. There will be variations as appropriate for each VSM business. The most appropriate format is whatever is best for that business. There will be commonalities required by corporate parameters. For example, all VSM businesses in their plans will include the same standards of behavior as the corporate plan, plus any additional standards that may uniquely apply in that business. And the plans of all VSM businesses will include the relationships with the ecological environment as specified in the corporate plan, plus whatever in addition may be appropriate for the business. Standards of behavior and environmental relationships are corporate parameters to be followed by everyone in the company.

Using the VSM, planning documents are communicated only between the system 1s and system 3. Plans are not forwarded up the chain of command to corporate headquarters. The corporate plan is not a total of the company's system 1 plans. The corporate plan is something different, and more.

In each business, plans are developed by the people in that business working with the people in system 3. With effective collaboration with system 3 people in developing the plan, the final approval by the system 3 executive is routine. Throughout the corporation, each system 1's link with system 3 coordinates all plans and actions toward the achievement of corporate purpose and goals.

Using the VSM and system thinking, the most appropriate schedule for all plans is continuous.

PRIORITIZING

Corporate headquarters and company businesses at all levels of recursion are continually having to "prioritize." Their "to do" lists are longer than their "can do" capabilities. The requests for capital expenditures add up to more than can be financed. Several research programs look promising for commercialization. With new media and methods available for communicating the company message there are attractive new options for advertising and publicity. In the needs of the system 3 here and now and the system 4 outside and future there is continuing conflict for resources. Companies deal with these kinds of situations by prioritizing.

Prioritizing, however, has nothing to say about how to prioritize. The "how" is left to judgment, and typically judgment relies on some kind of an accounting measure, such as discounted cash flow rate of return, or ROI, or payback. Much better, and most profitable over time, is to use purpose and goals as the judgment criteria. What is needed to reach our goals and achieve our purpose? And whatever is needed, how is it best planned over time? Important decisions are often what to do and when to do it. The plan, as summarized above, will always be the best guide and should be on the table whenever decisions are made.

CONTINUOUS PLANNING

Companies typically prepare their business plans on an annual cycle, a revised, or new, or up-dated plan every twelve months for each new fiscal year. We are programmed to relate planning and budgeting and anything else important to the fiscal year. But the company doesn't run by sequential twelve-month periods. The company runs continuously. And companies are managed continuously, at the corporate level and at all levels of recursion. Company operations are heuristic, finding and making their way day by day, always aiming to achieve desired results. For each VSM business at all levels of recursion the results desired are specified in their objectives for the key performance areas. Measures monitor performance and help operators, supervisors, and managers make changes and adjustments as appropriate, always aiming toward the objectives and to adjust objectives when appropriate. Planning is preparation for managing. So the best planning is continuous planning.

To plan continuously, we need to simplify the plan. The plan does not have to be "all we know about everything" condensed down to two feet of shelf space filled with loose-leaf binders. All of this information is continuously changing, and by the time it gets into the binders and on the shelf it is becoming obsolete. No wonder such corporate plans don't relate to operations. With system thinking and the VSM, in all VSM business units at all levels of recursion those doing the work and making decisions get information continuously in six ways, and use it continuously:

1. Feedback from the work itself
2. The performance measures in the key performance areas relating to their work
3. The continuous monitoring of their operations
4. The continuous monitoring of what matters for their business in the commercial, technical, economic, social, political, educational, and ecological environments
5. The system 4s monitoring of their VSMs
6. Continuous learning in the subject areas of their work

The people at the corporate level and at all levels of recursion continuously receive this information for their VSM business unit. And they use this information to achieve the objectives agreed on in their plan, and to change the plan when appropriate.

With the VSM and system thinking each viable business system, which can be dozens or even hundreds, does its own planning. The system 1s develop their plans in consultation with, and the approval of system 3. There is no need for passing planning documents to higher levels. As described in Chapter 2, each viable system operation is quite capable of self-organization and self-control. And that begins with planning their operations and their goals.

The management in all businesses knows the corporate plan, which is widely communicated. And since each system 1 business plan is coordinated with system 3, alignment and support is created throughout the company for the achievement of company goals. There is no need to distribute planning documents beyond the units where they originate. There is no need for the corporate plan for sales revenue, operating income, or any other measure to be the total of the plan numbers from subordinate units.

In the VSM, we define the corporation, and each business unit as a system, comprising operations, management of those operations, management systems which organize information in relation to purpose, and the environments that the business unit operates within. Communication channels carry information. Sensors at origins and destinations sense and transduce what's communicated. Filters reduce the variety of the vast amount of information into what's meaningful for the achievement of business goals. Operations management can't know everything that's out there in the environment, but must know all that matters. Operations management can't know everything about operations, but must know all that matters. Filters selecting what matters, and the appropriate measures greatly attenuate the variety in what is managed. Involvement of many decision-makers throughout the company at all levels of recursion greatly amplify management to achieve requisite variety. Each VSM business plans, organizes manages, and controls itself.

As described in Chapter 2, determining what matters, and the measures of what matters become the major attenuators filtering and reducing the variety (complexity) in what needs to be managed and controlled. Involving people throughout the company in making and implementing management decisions becomes the major amplification of management variety. Through reducing variety and expanding the voice of management the goal of "requisite variety" can be achieved throughout the company, at all levels of recursion, where decisions are made. For sound decisions, decision-makers need to have available variety equivalent to the variety in what is being managed. That can happen only when wise selection of what matters and wise measures of what matters attenuates variety in operations and in the environment, and management is amplified by many people making decisions where the work is done. For good decisions, the variety of the controller needs to match the variety of what is being controlled.

Review again Figure 5.2 showing only two levels of recursion. The corporate VSM has four system 1s. At the next level of recursion three of these four also have four system 1s, and one has three system 1s. More typical would be three to eight system 1s in a VSM business. More than eight would probably mean that a level of recursion is missing.

Visualize Figure 5.2 with more VSMs in the first and second recursions, plus additional recursions. In all these many VSMs there is continuous attenuation of variety in operations, and in information from the environments. There is expanding amplification of the variety in management. Self-organization and self-control works. Operations are black boxes to high-level management. Black boxes can and do run themselves.

Developing a corporate plan for the total company is a responsibility of the planning function in system 4, directed by the system 5 executive leadership, as described above. Then the system 4s throughout the company at all levels of recursion, directed by their system 5s can develop plans for their businesses. Knowing the plan for the next higher system and the corporate plan, all will be appropriately coordinated.

In the VSM structure, the system 4 at the corporate level and the system 4s at all levels of recursion:

1. Continuously monitor the relevant environments:
   Commercial environment
   Technical environment
   Economic environment
   Social environment
   Political environment
   Educational environment
   Ecological environment
2. Continuously monitor the VSM in which they are the System 4, to assure:
   All functions are working as expected
   Performance in the key performance is on track toward goals
3. With direction from system 5, continuously plans the company's future.

Monitoring the relevant environments requires observation and measures of what it is in those environments that relates to the achievement of plans and budget objectives. The first huge filtering of environmental information comes in defining what to monitor in each environment. The next filtering is in the selection of measures, which can be qualitative or quantitative. And for amplifying on the management side to achieve requisite variety, at the corporate level and in each business unit at all levels of recursion, the monitoring of the environments and the decision-making will be done by a number of people. At the corporate level the responsibilities might be:

For the commercial environment: Marketing, working in system 4
For the economic environment: System 4 corporate economist
For the technical environment: System 4 corporate R&D, and corporate engineering

For the political environment: All top management
For the social environment: HR, working in system 4
For the educational environment: HR, working in system 4
For the ecological environment: All top management

In each of the system responsibilities, monitoring will be done by individuals most familiar with and involved in that environment. For example, in system 4 the marketing monitoring of the commercial environment will include all salespeople. Corporate planning will coordinate the monitoring effort, and maintain an information resource. At all levels of recursion there can be similar assignments of responsibility. At all levels, the monitoring of the environment will identify: (1) new business opportunities, and (2) threats to the achievement of business goals.

For monitoring the VSM there will be similar assignments of responsibility. Monitoring the VSM includes:

All functions working as needed to achieve plan goals:
  Homeostats
  Heterostats
  Monitoring of operations
  Monitoring of environments
Performance on trend toward goals

The Resource Bargain establishing each viable business system includes business definition, boundaries, purpose, resources, and goals. That's the starting point for the units to develop their own business plans and performance measures. In considering performance measures, the following performance areas and the relationships among them, can help in designing a small number of measures that capture what matters most:

Creating and keeping customers
Quality and productivity
Innovation
Organization capability
Physical and financial resources
Public and environmental responsibility

Profitability:
   Sales revenue
   Operating income
   Fixed costs:
      People costs
      Capital costs
      Programmed fixed costs
   Contribution margin

See Chapters 6 through 11 for information and measures on each of the above.

With the continuing flow of information, why plan once a year? When plans are binders-full, once a year may seem enough. But when plans are a few pages with a small number of goals and measures, continuous planning is better. The few pages in the corporate plan does not mean the corporation lacks information. The corporate plan is concerned only with what matters for the total corporation. It leaves out a lot of data that doesn't provide useful information. In each VSM business at all levels of recursion, the plan, too, is concerned only with what matters for that business, omitting useless data. All the plans throughout the company add up to a huge amount of control information, needed and useful for self-organization and self-control. The corporation, in total, operates information-rich. The information resides where the work is done.

In each VSM business, those doing the work and managing the work know the progress toward goals through feedback from the work itself, and the performance measures. Their monitoring of their environments reveals threats and opportunities. They can judge when desirable changes should be made in goals, or in their performance measures. They can judge when any new and different goals should be established. But why once a year? Continuously is better. No longer measuring and explaining variances from plan, business units will always be measuring progress toward goals and continuously acting in ways to achieve those goals.

BUDGETS AND BUDGETARY CONTROL

In Chapter 2 we defined a company and each of its businesses as a viable, very complex, purposful, probabilistic system. Planning defines the purposeful part of this definition. Planning sets goals and prescribes measures. Budgeting is the purposive part of this definition for a fiscal year. Budgeting sets goals and measures for a fiscal year.

In the early days of budgeting and planning, after World War II, budgets were simple, worked out with wooden pencils on yellow pads of paper with the aid of mechanical calculating machines. Preparing a budget was not a big project. It could be done easily in a week or two. The early long-range plans took longer, and typically ended with "hockey stick" projections for sales and income in future years, slow in the early years, then rapid growth.

Good ideas, simple at the start, tend to grow in complexity as they are continuously improved. In 20 years, instead of preparing budgets in a month, companies were beginning to make them in July, and often not having the final until a month or more into the new fiscal year starting January 1. With the VSM and system thinking companies can get back to simplicity, and at the same time improve effectiveness, with continuous planning and continuous budgeting. Budgets can be prepared in December for a fiscal year starting January 1, or whenever needed. And the budgets will be rich in information, and directly tied to operations.

The system 4s develop longer-range plans collaboratively and continuously, as explained earlier in this chapter. These plans, always current, and the continuous monitoring of both operations and the environment, provide information for budgets. The system 1 managements, communicating with system 2, develop the budgets for their business units. System 2, embedded in system 3, provides the guidance that keeps system 1 budgets coordinated with company purpose, and provides system 1 budget information to system 3 which approves the system 1 budgets. This book proposes that these budgets, like the plans, be continuous. Budgeting only what matters most for system 1 success and using well-selected measures, budgets can be simple enough for continuous budgeting, with information flowing continuously in the system 1, system 3/system 2 business channel. Budgeting is continuous, communication is continuous, acceptance is continuous, with changes made as appropriate.

Businesses have become accustomed to preparing budgets for a fiscal year, coinciding with required financial reporting. Then the budget numbers are distributed by month so that with each monthly closing actual can be compared with budget, and the variances analyzed. All this sounds so logical, that few people have realized that, in the language of "lean" it is waste and unproductive in managing performance.

Although companies go through this kind of budget procedure, they don't actually manage operations this way. They make decisions and take actions each moment, each hour, and each day in relation to the actualities at that time. And over the fiscal year those actualities more and more differ from the budget.

Variances, of course, can always be explained. Costs were higher or lower by $X. Volume was higher or lower by $X. Selling prices were higher or lower by $X. Cost of goods sold, gross margins, absorption of fixed costs, special situations, financial transactions ... many influences will be different from what was expected in the budget numbers. But why analyze variances? How does that help continuously improve operations? The budget is an algorithm. But life, and business, is heuristic, a moving picture, constant change, each day developing from what went before, and interventions coming from many directions.

Companies manage their operations as things develop, always with an eye on their goals, and working to make whatever changes and adjustments are needed. So the company's experience and actions will always vary from a fiscal year budget. Why not change the budget? Make it heuristic, continuously changing. In conventional budgeting we make nods in this direction by monthly forecasting key budget measures, and even at times during the fiscal year revising the budget. Why not do the obvious—make the budget continuous:

- Focus on objectives
- Continuously monitor progress toward objectives
- Continuously take actions as appropriate:
  (a) to exploit strengths
  (b) to shore up weaknesses
  (c) to change the budget whenever appropriate

Conventional fiscal year budgets have also proved ineffective in managing costs. Using conventional budgets, we absorb fixed costs by manufacturing products whether the products go to customers or go to the warehouse as an asset. But in "lean" operations, inventory is a waste to be reduced, not an asset. And in real life terms we don't absorb fixed costs, we pay them every month in cash from the contribution margin earned from sales to customers. Better ways to budget and manage costs are discussed in Chapter 11.

Continuously?

Continuously sounds like a radical, and impractical idea. But as discussed earlier in this chapter, continuous planning works better than annually preparing long-range or strategic plans. For budgets with their focus on managing the here and now, continuous budgeting is especially effective.

Companies are accustomed to constructing budgets for a fiscal year, measuring variances monthly, analyzing the variances, revising forecasts, and at midyear starting the process all over again. Budgets are used for performance measurement, but can not be used for managing operations. A company is a very complex, probabilistic system that can not be managed by the algorithm prescribed in the conventional budget. Company performance for a year ahead, with continuous changes in operations in continuously changing environments, can't be prescribed in an algorithm. All decision-makers have to manage by the heuristics of on-going experience, continuously acting to achieve desired results. That's the way companies work. That's the way systems work. And that's the way a continuous budget for the company works, providing the information decision-makers need for continuously acting to achieve desired results.

Conventional plans and budgets are algorithms, precise projections for a very probabilistic future period. But future performance is heuristic, a continuously moving picture. The VSM and system thinking enables us to match plans and budgets to an evolving future. Continuously.

Readouts from the plans, always current and always available on computer screens, provide the information needed to monitor performance, and to revise plans and budgets if appropriate. Performance measures included in the budget will be continuously monitored. The budgets will be much shorter in length and fewer in measures than conventional budgets, a few pages instead of a binder full. But in a few pages the budgets will include more information useful to management. And the continuous measures will help managers at all levels achieve desired results. System thinking greatly simplifies the work of planning and budgeting, and more effectively guides operations to the achievement of budget objectives.

Monitoring will continuously inform, and decisions will continuously act to steer performance toward the achievement of plan and budget objectives. And, if appropriate, continuously change the budget. Why wait to the end of the year and then report "Here we were up 12%.

There we were down 17%. Etc. Etc. Better at all times to have all functions of the organization on track to achieve the best performance they are capable of, and to know what that is.

Measures of Success

The key to budgets that help companies achieve desired results is the selection of measures of success. Success is what the company intends to achieve in the budget period. We tend to think Budgets = Expenses, what we will spend in each of the accounting classifications. In our VSM businesses, we first think Budget = Deeds, what we will accomplish in each of the seven key performance areas.

A budget that says what the company intends to achieve needs to be clear on exactly what that is, and what measures will be used to help company people get there. Instead of financial or scorecard measures of what the company did, the budget will specify measures that can help company people achieve their objectives in the seven key performance areas.

Performance measures will not be variances from a fiscal year budget. Performance measures will be those few measures showing company progress toward budget objectives, and helpful to decision makers in achieving those objectives. System science is a science of relationships. So some of the measures will be measures of relationships. For example, a manufacturing company that has traditionally budgeted product selling prices, and purchasing costs for materials, instead will budget the relationship between product selling prices and variable costs. Budgeting a target for one number, contribution margin percent, instead of hundreds of cost and selling price numbers, is a great simplification and provides much more useful information for decision makers. Figure 5.5 lists some examples of useful budget measures.

Continuous budget measures show trends and changes in trends toward objectives. Measures of variance from plan motivate people to conform to an algorithm that departs further and further from reality as the year progresses. It is much better to know the reality, and act day-by-day to achieve objectives within the constraints and the opportunities in that reality. The kinds of measures shown in Figure 5.5 can help.

Sales Revenue Measures   For measures having seasonal variation, which is typical of sales revenue, a 12-month moving total is a useful measure. The data can be reported, or, better, the data can be charted.

Objectives	Budget Objective	Measures
1. Creating and Keeping Customers		
(a) Sales Revenue	$X	12-month moving total, plus monthly variance from year ago
	Units	12-month moving total, plus monthly variance from year ago
(b) Competitive Position	A Leader	x of y competitors
	X%	Share of market, time series chart
2. Quality and Productivity		
(a) Economic Productivity	% Improvement	3-month moving average
(b) Other output/input	% Improvement	3-month moving average
(c) Cost of Poor Quality	% Improvement	3-month moving average
3. Innovation		
(a) New product contribution margin $	$X	12-month moving total, plus monthly variance from year ago
(b) New product contribution margin %	%	3-month moving average
4. Organization Capability		
(a) Value created per compensation $	$X	$\dfrac{\text{Value Added}}{\text{Compensation \$}}$ 4-quarter moving average
(b) Collective IQ	Improvement	Appraisal. See Chapter 9
5. Physical and Financial Resources		
(a) Investment in and maintenance of physical assets	$	Actual $ plus annual audit of adequacy for achieving business goals
(b) Relation of new investment to business purpose and goals	Relates	Include relation to purpose and and goals in RFEs

Figure 5.5   Typical key performance area budget objectives and measures. For plotting moving totals and moving averages, it is best to plot each total or average at the mid-point. A 12-month moving total ending December 31 would be plotted at June 30, the mid-point of the 12 months. A 3-month moving average for January, February, March would be plotted at February

**6. Public and Environmental
   Responsibility**

(a) Reduction in environmental impact	% and Units	Measures for each impact
(b) Company reputation	Ranking	Opinion surveys

7. Profitability

(a) Profit/Loss from operations	$X	12-month moving total, plus Monthly variance from year ago
(b) Plus/Minus from financial actions	$X	12-month moving total
(c) Contribution Margin $	$X	12-month moving total
(d) Contribution Margin %	%	3-month moving average
(e) Total Fixed Costs	$X	3-month moving average
People Costs	$X	3-month moving average
Capital Costs	$X	3-month moving average
Programmed Fixed Costs	$X	3-month moving average

Figure 5.5 *Continued*

Data would look like Figure 5.6. The fiscal year for this business is January 1 to December 31. Fiscal year 12-month totals are indicated by an asterisk, centered at June 30. The chart would look like Figure 5.7. Fiscal year 12-month totals are indicated by a small circle with a dot. Fiscal year totals are centered, plotted at June 30. After the 12-month total for year 1 is plotted at June 30, 12-month totals are plotted monthly, showing trends and changes in trends.

We are accustomed to thinking of annual totals, the annual totals being the totals for each fiscal year. But for managing and controlling operations any 12-month period is equally important; January 1 to December 31, April 1 to May 31, October 16 to October 15, or any other. Since financial data are available from month-end closings, 12-month totals represent fiscal months.

Figure 5.7 shows business cycles, trend, and changes from whatever cause. It does not show the two additional measures that determine the operating income resulting from those sales. The president of a Brazilian company added to this chart 12-month moving totals for contribution margin and fixed costs. The difference between the 12-month moving totals for contribution margin and fixed costs is operating income.

	Sales Revenue	Monthly Variance from Year Ago	12-Month Moving Total, Centered
Year 1			
Jan	10,992		
Feb	11,748		
Mar	14,765		
Apr	12,595		
May	13,103		
Jun	12,707		149,780*
Jul	12,304		150,656
Aug	10,446		152,410
Sep	12,238		152,103
Oct	13,836		153,760
Nov	12,602		155,761
Dec	12,444		157,310
Year 2			
Jan	11,868	876	156,808
Feb	13,502	1,754	159,410
Mar	14,458	(307)	161,376
Apr	14,252	1,657	162,960
May	15,104	2,001	164,381
Jun	14,256	1,549	163,570*
Jul	11,802	(502)	164,415
Aug	13,048	2.602	162,970
Sep	14,204	1,966	161,667
Oct	14,186	1,584	159,460
Nov	15,257	1,421	158,928
Dec	11,633	(811)	158,117

* 12-month moving totals, plotted at mid-point

Figure 5.6   Sales revenue, data format

While 12-month totals show trends and changes in trends, they are not early indicators of business cycle changes, changes in the trend, or changes uniquely affecting the company. We can add this sensitivity to our data and to our chart by measures of monthly differences plus or minus from the same month, year ago. Figure 5.8 shows Figure 5.7 including this sensitivity measure.

Figure 5.8 shows a rising trend from the end of year 1 to the end of year 2, with an increase of 9% for the year. At this point, financial reports showed no indication that sales might not continue to increase, and the company budgeted and expected an increase in sales for year 3. By the end of year 2, however, the chart of monthly change from year ago was suggesting possible decline, and by the end of Q1 the decline is definite,

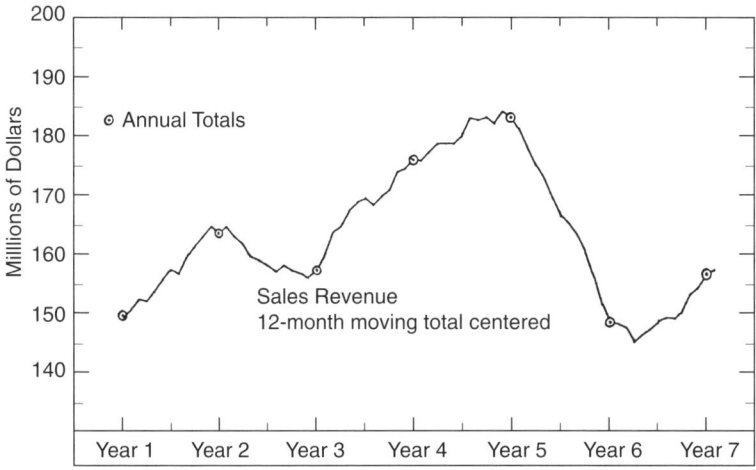

Figure 5.7   Sales revenue, 12-month moving total

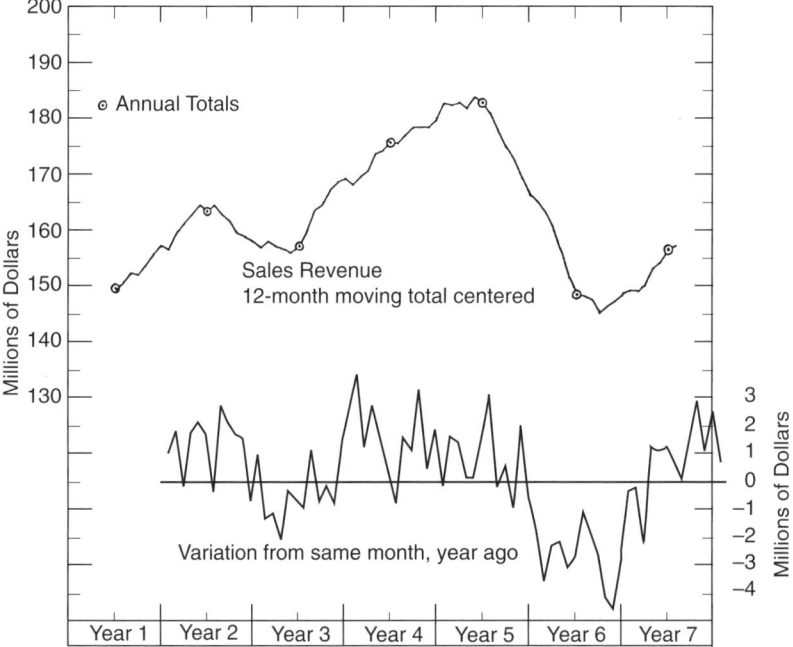

Figure 5.8   Figure 5.7 plus monthly variance from a year ago

while it is not yet clear in the 12-month moving total. And in the conventional financial reporting no decline was yet even suggested.

At the end of year 3, sales had declined and there was no indication of change visible in the financial reporting. Nor was there indication of change in the 12-month moving total. But the chart of monthly change from year ago clearly indicates improvement underway. The upward trend continued through year 4 for an increase in sales revenue of 12%. The early warning of the downturn between year 5 and year 6 and the recovery between year 6 and year 7 is even clearer. Instead of plotting monthly variances from year ago as in Figure 5.8, this curve could be smoothed by plotting 3-month moving averages.

The data and charts shown in Figures 5.6, 5.7, and 5.8 show the results of all that's going on—what's happening in the economy, customer situations, competitive actions, the company's new product programs, marketing promotions, sales programs, etc. All these influences need to be considered in appraising what the charts are saying. The charts are a good way to begin an appraisal each month of the current situation and to plan appropriate actions.

For measures with little or no seasonal variation, monthly data can be useful. To moderate variations in the monthly data, 3-month moving averages smooth the chart line. 3-month moving averages are usually more useful than monthly figures. As noted in Figure 5.5, several series can be usefully monitored with 3-month moving averages.

Fixed Cost Measures   Total fixed costs need to be conspicuously in view, continuously. Yet few profit-center businesses or companies even know what their total fixed costs are. Fixed costs appear in many different categories, but not as a total. That's not required for financial reporting. But this total and its three components—people costs, capital costs, and programmed fixed costs—are very important for management. A 3-month moving average is a good way to track total fixed costs, and each of its three major components. See Figure 5.9.

Fixed costs are poorly managed in many companies, probably in most companies. The traditional method for budgeting and controlling fixed costs virtually assures that fixed costs won't be managed well. In the chart of accounts there are many line items for elements of fixed costs, with these line items in the budgets for several different departments and units, and some allocated out to other units. But there is no total anywhere, and no information on the trend of that total. At budget time, managers present convincing cases for "more" in many of the fixed cost line items. When business is good, and cash available, more goes into the budget. Additions accumulate year by year, and often total fixed costs increase much faster than justified by sales revenue and contribution margin.

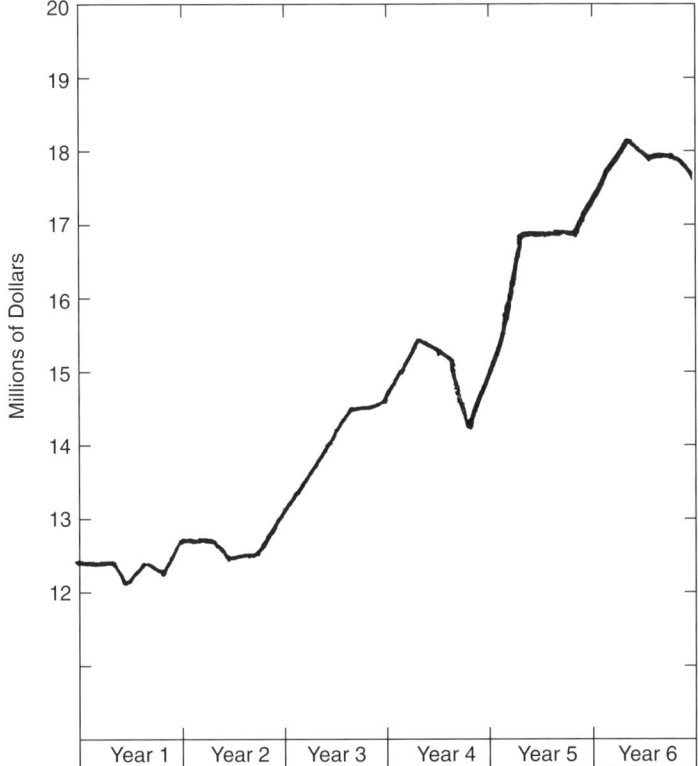

Figure 5.9 Total fixed costs, 3-month moving average

For each VSM profit-center business it's wise to monitor total fixed costs, and the trend. A good way to monitor fixed costs is to assign the line items into three categories:

1. People costs. All wages, salaries, benefits, incentive compensation, employment taxes (workman's comp, social security, etc.), and any other compensation costs
2. Capital costs. More than accounting depreciation and maintenance, capital costs include all the items shown in Chapter 11, Figure 11.2
3. Programmed fixed costs. The line item accounts in sales, general, and administrative costs that are not in the first two categories

The trend shown in figure 5.9 is typical. In their budgetary control processes and financial reports total fixed costs are never seen.

Companies don't know what their total fixed costs are. With traditional budgetary control, fixed costs often rise faster than economically justified. When business slows, there can be a sharp drop in profitability.

Figure 5.9 was part of a profit improvement project at the end of year 5 and beginning of year 6. Management had never before seen this information. There had been no awareness of the trend of fixed costs. All the pieces had never been put together, and control by the traditional budget process had left the total uncontrolled. But management was aware of weakening profitability. Now they were aware also of the trend of fixed costs, the trend of each of the three categories of fixed costs, and the changes in the line items in each of these. They began, immediately, during year 6 to manage fixed costs primarily in relation to the trend of fixed costs and the anticipated trend in contribution margin.

This work was not an intervention by corporate headquarters. In system terms, the work and the following corrective actions were undertaken by the management two recursions away from corporate. The general manager had invited a corporate manager knowledgeable in new and different business practices to work with them on resolving their profit problem. When they learned about management economics and its concepts and measures, they understood clearly what their profit problem was, and how to deal with it.

The mismanagement of fixed costs is a common problem. In one large food company total fixed costs, numbers not previously seen or known, for five years had increased at an average rate of 15% per year, all well-controlled in relation to budget. But sales had grown an average of 5% per year. The contribution margin dollars needed to pay fixed costs were shrinking in relation to the fixed costs. If the company had been monitoring contribution margins and fixed costs as suggested in the listing in Figure 5.5, management would have decided how to deal with this situation when it began to develop, five years earlier. For more information on the measurement and management of fixed costs, see Chapter 11.

More on Measures   In Figure 5.5, the first Organization Capability measure is a partial measure of economic productivity, described in Chapter 7. For additional objectives and measures for organization capability, see Chapter 9. For additional information on environmental objectives and measures, see Chapter 10.

Using the VSM and its system science and cybernetics, progress measures like those presented in Figure 5.5 help companies budget and manage continuously. For company measures, companies will want to see not only numbers, but the trend of those numbers toward budget objectives and long-term goals. Charts of moving totals and moving averages are helpful for evaluating trends. The measures listed in Figure 5.5 are good and very useful measures of success. They include financial measures. But they also include measures of the other key performance areas that determine what the profit figures will be. They show where there may be opportunity. They show where change and improvement is needed. For additional information on these, and other measures, refer to Chapters 6 through 11.

Measures stay where they are made and used. They are not aggregated upward to higher-level management. However, totals such as sales revenue and operating income that are needed for corporate reporting are aggregated upward. But nothing more than what's needed for corporate reporting. With conventional accounting methods, more flows up. Then corporate people such as financial analysts "drill down" to seek more information. But "drilling down" cannot penetrate black boxes. Drilling down can find the source of data, but cannot achieve requisite variety. The result is misinformation, bad decisions at higher levels, and less-than-helpful higher-level interventions. Operations are black boxes to higher-level management. They lack requisite variety.

PREDICTIVE CONTROL

An early pioneer in operations research (OR), Dr. George Kozmetsky, a founder of Teledyne and then director of the IC^2 Institute at the University of Texas, anticipated and worked toward the capability of "predictive control." Management at that time, working from financial reports of past performance were more involved in fixing the past than in creating the future. Now, with computers, they could do better. Computers can be information machines. Computers can help us understand the past and monitor the present. If we could design an information structure for predictive control we could better recover from past mistakes, deal more effectively with today's problems and opportunities, and see ahead more clearly to do today what will build tomorrow's successes. The VSM and system thinking provides the information that enables predictive control, as visualized in Figure 5.10.

There is a VSM structure of information channels and information flow in each VSM business at all levels of recursion, all interconnected. And management is many people. Self-organization and self-control at

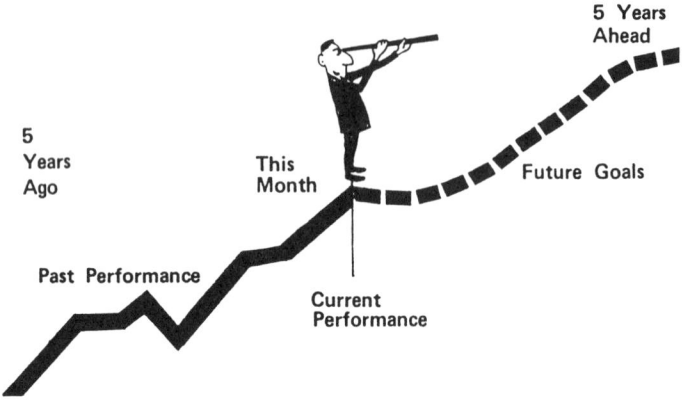

Figure 5.10 Predictive control

all levels of recursion amplifies the voice of management and makes requisite variety possible. With the VSM information structure and system thinking the company can have at hundreds or thousand of decision points:

- Understanding of the past
- Awareness of the present
- Indications for the future

The company can operate by predictive control in all operations.

Developing the Measures

Businesses are different in their own unique ways. The measures described above are useful measures. The seven key performance areas are important in all companies. But for a specific business other measures may also be needed, some of the above less needed. The aim, always:

- Measure what matters most
- Plan continuously
- Budget continuously
- Measure continuously
- Monitor trends toward objectives
- Manage continuously, looking ahead

The chart of accounts will include data needed for many of the measures needed. But we will put the numbers together differently to get the measures listed in Figure 5.5 and other special measures. For example, three key measures determining profitability are sales revenue, contribution margin, and fixed costs. As noted above, total fixed costs are unknown in many companies, and poorly managed in the traditional budget process. Contribution margins are seldom measured, and they are not included in plans and budgets. But these, and many of the other measures needed, can easily be calculated from the chart of accounts.

Few companies have goals and measures for contribution margins, or for fixed costs, even though they have the data needed. And how many companies include in their budgets goals and measures for creating and keeping customers, quality and productivity, innovation, organization capability, physical and financial resources, and public and environmental responsibility? And how many companies measure and monitor trends toward objectives? Generally accepted accounting principles have been carefully crafted for financial reporting. Fine. We also need measures carefully crafted for management. Using these measures, management decisions will be made better and more promptly, and more effective actions taken at many levels, where requisite variety can be achieved.

Many leaders in finance and accounting began to recognize that management needs something more than and different from the traditional accounting measures. Their work created the new discipline of management accounting. Management accounting gave us scorecard measures in other areas of performance, in addition to the financial. A fine contribution. With experience showing the value of scorecard measures, these measures were then deployed to lower levels.

But scorecard measures are looking at what happened, evaluating past performance. To create future performance we need measures of what has happened up to now, and looking ahead providing guidance toward desired goals. With system science and the VSM, and best practices in the key performance areas we add important, new dimensions:

1. The great capabilities in self-organization and self-control at all levels of recursion
2. A design for the requisite variety needed for effective decisions and control by amplifying the voice of management and attenuating variety in operations and in the environments
3. Planing, budgeting, and measuring continuously using measures enabling predictive control

These measures come from several sources: the chart of accounts, management economics and other best management practices, the technologies in each of the key performance areas, feedback from the work itself, the relevant environments, and the VSM experience. For additional information on measures, see Chapters 6 through 11.

Feedback controls performance, in a natural system and in a company system, too. The conventional budget is a snapshot, an algorithm, for the year ahead. How real is that? Not very, as future variance reports will clearly show. The system budget is a moving picture, continuous, and changing with changing circumstance. Each system budget includes objectives and the measures for monitoring and directing performance. The objectives don't change unless there is a compelling reason to change them. Actions change continuously, to move performance toward the objectives. Instead of variances and explanations of the variances, the continuous budget reports progress toward goals in the key performance areas that determine every company's success.

Communication

With system science and system thinking we see our company as a network of systems, as shown in Figure 5.2. In each of the company's VSM business systems there is a system 4 responsible for planning, and a system 2 responsible for budgeting, and each has other functions, too, as explained in Chapter 2. And in the VSM there are communication channels:

1. The routine communication channel for the routine information passing between the system 1s and higher-level management.
2. The management communication channel communicating information between higher-level management and the system 1s on the Resource Bargain and on key performance area measures.
3. The system 1s communication channel for communication among the system 1 business units in each VSM.
4. The special communication channel for communicating information on new and better business practices, for emergencies, and for special studies, audits, etc.

Best practices in the seven key performance areas give us the information and the measures that control performance toward the achievement of plan and budget objectives. Plan and budget documents stay at the levels that created them—the system 1 and the systems 2 and 3.

There is no need to pass these documents on to higher levels. Each system controls itself. The corporate system, described by its VSM, controls itself, beginning with its continuous long-range or strategic plan and its continuous budget. And each of the viable system 1s in the corporate VSM controls itself, beginning with its Resource Bargain which is the starting point for its continuous plan, and its continuous budget and performance measures. And so on, throughout all levels of recursion.

Information that needs to be communicated from system 1 to systems 2 and 3 includes:

Information	Channel
A small number of key performance area measures	Business
Information needed for higher-level and corporate reporting, and information needed for coordination with other company systems	Routine
Any significant, or emergency occurrences	Special

A major change from the conventional is that with system thinking and system management there is no longer a need for lengthy, monthly management reports explaining budget variances along with a great variety of financial data and commentary. All this can be replaced by an operating income statement as described in Chapter 11, and one or two pages reporting progress toward desired goals in a few key performance measures, such as:

1. Creating and keeping customers (Chapter 6)
   Sales revenue
   Sales to Target customers and Target prospects
2. Quality and productivity (Chapter 7)
   Economic productivity
3. Innovation (Chapter 8)
   New product sales revenue
   New process dollar benefit
4. Organization capability (Chapter 9)
   Value added per compensation dollar
   Changes in competitive position
5. Physical and financial resources (Chapters 7, 11)
   Adequacy for achieving goals

6. Public and environmental responsibility (Chapter 10)
   Measures as appropriate
7. Profitability (Chapter 11)
   Contribution margin
   Fixed costs
   Operating income

Plans and budgets simplify to pages instead of binders full of pages because they include fewer measures, but include all that matters. Some of the new measures replace many old numbers, even hundreds or more, with a single number that includes more useful information than the old numbers. Some examples:

1. The continuous budget does not budget a huge array of financial numbers. It budgets fiscal year objectives in measures of success in the seven key performance areas, such as those measures listed above. In a few pages, company people agree on their goals for what the company will do, and have measures that will help them achieve the goals. And the budget can be continuous, with readouts for the fiscal year whenever wanted.

2. Many companies budget costs and prices, which is hundreds or thousands of numbers that are not very manageable. In the simpler budget they can budget one measure, the relationship between costs and prices, which is what matters. That relationship is contribution margin, dollars and percent, which is very manageable. See Chapter 6, "Diagnosing Sales Revenue," and Figure 6.3.

3. The continuous budget, does not budget headcount, it budgets people costs. Employment costs are what matters. "Headcount" is a word that should disappear from the vocabulary of business. The word is demeaning to the company's people, and is not helpful in budgeting or expense control. In management economics, "people costs" is one of the three categories of fixed costs, a huge simplification in budgeting fixed costs. See Chapter 11, "Management Economics."

4. With fewer measures, monthly reporting is much simpler. Monthly reporting can almost be eliminated because the current information on all the measures that matter are always available. All that needs to be reported is special situations. Budgets and any budget reporting is communicated within the system 1s, and between the system 1s and systems 2 and 3.

The following chapters describe how each of the seven key performance areas can be measured, included in plans and budgets, and monitored. Each integrates into, and benefits from, the VSM structure and management principles. Plans and budgets simplify, performance improves.

Chapter 11 discusses profit, fixed costs, and margins. But one important point on margins needs to be mentioned here in regard to budgets. Systems is all about relationships. And budgeting relationships can often reduce the work in preparing the budget by more than an order of magnitude, and at the same time produce more useful information. A manufacturing company typically budgets selling prices, and costs of purchases used in manufacturing their products. This is a huge effort, and produces results differing from what actual experience will prove to be. And a great deal of time and effort will be spent in measuring and analyzing variances. Why budget hundreds of product selling prices, and hundreds of costs for purchased materials, all unpredictable and largely unmanageable? Why analyze variances? All this work provides employment, but very little useful information.

To manage profitability in a manufacturing business, what matters is not all these individual prices and costs, but the relationship between them. And we can budget the relationship between prices and costs with one measure: contribution margin percent. Contribution margin percent measures the relationship between direct (variable) input costs and selling prices. In a manufacturing business the average contribution margin needed to achieve profit objectives might be 46%, a real number that can be decided on as a budget objective. Then costs, and selling prices, and mix, and transactions can be monitored and managed to achieve that objective. This very simple procedure is a huge simplification in budgeting and budgetary control, and much more effective in achieving desired performance.

In a service business where there may be no, or very few, variable input costs, the contribution margin is 100%, or close to that. The contribution margin is sales revenue and the budget target for sales revenue is fixed costs plus $XX. In a service business, the relationship of fixed costs to revenue is the relationship to monitor and to manage. For more information on these measures, see Chapter 11.

Monthly measures for key performance areas will not be actual in comparison with a budget figure for the month, but actual in relation to progress toward the budget objective. Budget measures are trends and changes in trends toward objectives. Operating people take actions as appropriate to expand favorable trends, and to make changes to adjust for the unfavorable. When corrective action is needed, good measures provide also information on the leverages for improvement. The continuously monitored budget includes key performance area goals, and the measures enabling decision makers to take the appropriate actions to achieve those goals to the best of the organization's capability.

OVERVIEW: THE ESSENCE OF CHAPTER 5

The VSM and its system science and cybernetics give managers new and better ways to structure and manage the company. This better way includes information and communications, and relationships with the outside environments, as important parts of company structure. This better way offers a new principle for decision-making—requisite variety. This better way, combined with best practices in the key performance areas, enables more effective planning and budgeting of company operations.

Management begins with planning, defining what the company is and will be, its boundaries, its purpose, its resources, its goals. The budget is the short-term plan for the fiscal year. Plans and budgets can be prepared and continuously maintained by each business unit at all levels of recursion, beginning with their Resource Bargains.

In the 1940s, after World War II, company plans were brief—convert to peacetime production and each year do better than the year before. For a fiscal year beginning January 1, budgets were made in December. The budget was simple—this year's sales revenue and this year's income plus X%.

Then progressive companies thought it would be better to aim for a desired future in their plans, and for specific achievements in their annual budgets. Corporate planning departments appeared, plans and budgets became volumes instead of pages, and by the 1960s annual planning and budgeting cycles were beginning in mid-summer for fiscal years beginning January 1.

In planning and budgeting, it's time now to get back to pages instead of volumes, with more useful information than in those big volumes, and with plans and budgets directly tied to company operations. With plans and budgets only a few pages, and with the information flow provided in VSM operations, companies can delete the annual cycle and plan and budget continuously.

The company plan can be its answers to eight questions:

1. What is the company's purpose?
2. What are and will be the company's products and services and operating boundaries?
3. Who are and will be our customers?
4. What is and will be important to our customers?
5. What are our goals, and measures of success in seven key performance areas?

   Creating and keeping customers

   Quality and productivity

   Innovation

   Organization capability

   Physical and financial resources

   Public and environmental responsibility

   Profitability
6. What are our strategies for achieving our goals?
7. What are our standards of behavior?
8. How will we relate to the world around us—our environments?

These questions are not easy to answer and will involve many people in finding the answers. But when found, the answers can be presented in a few pages. These few pages need to be "on the table" whenever decisions are made. All decisions support the plan.

Budgets are the company's, and each business unit's short-term plan. They are not about what the company and the business units will spend. Budgets are about what the company and the business units will do. Budgets are about achieving objectives in the seven key performance areas that determine every company's success:

1. Creating and keeping customers
2. Quality and productivity
3. Innovation
4. Organization capability
5. Physical and financial resources
6. Public and environmental responsibility
7. Profitability

Well-determined, 7 to 10 goals and performance measures in some combination of these seven key performance areas can fully specify company and business unit success.

With the VSM structure and management principles, and best practices in the key performance areas, management in all VSM business units can plan and budget continuously. The fiscal year is for financial reporting, not for managing. Managing is continuous, hour-by-hour, day-by-day, month-by-month. Managers can't, and don't, manage to a fiscal year budget. Algorithms for a year always differ from what we find as the year progresses. Trying to adjust to the algorithm of a budget limits achievement. With short but more meaningful budgets, and with the information system provided by the VSM, plans and budgets, like management itself, can be continuous.

NOTES

[1] Peter F. Drucker, *The Practice of Management*, Harper & Row, New York 1954, p. 63.
[2] Frederick Herzberg, *Work and the Nature of Man*, World Publishing Company, 1966.

Chapter 6

The Viable System Model and Creating and Keeping Customers

The purpose of any business is to create and keep customers, and to do this in ways that will enable the company to achieve its other business goals, too. Other business goals will be the company goals in each of the key performance areas. The primary responsibility for creating and keeping customers usually is assigned to marketing and sales. It should be assigned to the entire company. All that's done in the company contributes to the task of creating and keeping customers, directly, or indirectly through the achievement of related goals. How can all company actions be coordinated and motivated to achieve success in creating and keeping customers? The viable system model (VSM) and system thinking can help.

To achieve the company's purpose of creating and keeping customers at a targeted level of sales revenue and profitability requires excellence in all functions. Excellence in the management principles in the VSM. Excellence in finding and using best practices in all of the key performance areas. Excellence in using the VSM communication channels internally for managing operations. Excellence in using the VSM communication channels externally for creating and keeping customers, and for dealing with the constraints and the threats, and discovering the opportunities in environmental change. Excellence in attenuating the variety in operations and in the environments. Excellence in amplifying the variety in management. Excellence requires finding and using best methods and technologies in all the key performance areas described in this book.

This chapter deals with best practices in the system 3 sales and marketing functions for creating and keeping customers, and the valuable assists from the VSM and its system science and cybernetics in doing this.

HOW THE VSM AND SYSTEM THINKING HELPS

In this book, a company is defined as a viable, very complex, purposeful, probabilistic system, which can be modeled with the VSM. Like other systems, a company is structured and works as described in system science and cybernetics. How system science provides a new and better way to structure and manage the company is described in Chapters 1 and 2. With the VSM structure and management principles we can more effectively develop the company's capability to create and keep customers in ways that will enable the company to achieve its other business goals, too.

Important characteristics of systems as described in system science and the VSM help us learn, understand, and apply best practices in all functions:

1. Recursion. Every company is a very complex, purposeful, probabilistic system that is made up of some number of subordinate-level very complex, purposeful, probabilistic systems that in turn are made up of their own subordinate-level very complex, purposeful, probabilistic systems, and so on throughout the company. At all levels of recursion, each business unit can be modeled with the VSM.

2. Self-organization and self-control. This is a characteristic of systems at all levels of recursion. In a corporation, this principle enables decision-making throughout the company, where there can be requisite variety.

3. Requisite variety. Variety in systems terms in the measure of complexity, and a company and each of its parts are immensely complex systems. Effective control of this immense variety requires equivalent variety in the controller. The system science in the VSM describes how this "requisite variety" can be achieved to help assure good decisions.

4. Black boxes. Lower level operations, system 1s, are black boxes to higher-level management. They can only be managed effectively within the black box.

5. Homeostasis. A characteristic of all systems is its capability of maintaining the present state. Homeostats prevent disturbances and disruptions, and deal with them when they occur to recover to normal functioning.

6. Heterostasis. Systems also have a capability for discovery, innovation, learning, evolving, even transforming in response to environmental change or opportunity.

7. Information. The VSM includes information as a part of structure, provides information channels, and defines the kind of information that flows in each.

8. Environment. As part of company structure, the VSM includes relationships and information flow with the relevant environments: commercial, technical, economic, political, social, educational, and ecological.

A company using all these system characteristics will find, teach, and communicate best practices in all the key performance areas enabling each VSM business unit to create and keep customers.

MARKETING

The purpose of any company is to create and keep customers. That is a direct assignment for sales, which is a part of the marketing function. Creating and keeping customers is also a direct assignment for marketing to see that creating and keeping customers can happen, and will. And creating and keeping customers is an indirect assignment for all others in the company. It takes the work of everyone in the company doing their jobs well to create and keep customers.

Three Key Questions

For marketing and sales, the key questions are:

1. Who are and who will be our customers?
2. What are and what will be our products and services?
3. What do and what will our customers value?

For the total corporation the first two questions are answered in the definition of the corporation in whatever way the corporation is defined—in a Vision statement, a Mission, or a strategic or business plan. At the corporate level the answer to these two questions and to question 3 will be very general, since the corporation is presenting its intentions for the total of all its businesses. At each level of recursion, the answer to the first two questions is answered in each business unit's Resource Bargain, specifying:

- The name of the system 1 business unit
- A definition of what the business unit is and will be in terms of products and services, and markets and customers served
- Prescription of the boundaries for the unit's operations
- The purpose of the business unit
- A description of the resources assigned to and a part of the business unit
- Long term goals and performance measures

In a company modeled with the VSM, at each level of recursion each of the system 1 businesses is established by its Resource Bargain. This Resource Bargain provides only a very general answer to the first two questions. Both of these questions and question three will be answered in detail by the system 3 marketing function in each of the businesses, in collaboration with system 4.

1. Who are and who will be our customers? This is not an easy question to answer. Customers include users, distributors, agents, intermediaries, recyclers, disposers, and whoever else owns, deals with, or is affected by the product, its use, and its final disposition. There may also be a geographic dimension to this question—local, regional, national, countries, areas, global. How this question is answered is an important strategic decision. The answer determines where the business is going.

2. What are and what will be our products and services? This is a question of boundaries—how narrow, how broad. A general rule for a good definition of boundaries: narrow enough to give direction to the company's efforts; broad enough to provide opportunity for growth. When Telechron changed its boundaries from electric clocks to clocks and timing devices it changed the company, changed the market, and created new values for consumers. (See Market Position, later in this chapter.)

A maker of pens might define the company boundary as pens. Very directional. The opportunity for innovation is new, different, better pens. Or the company might define its boundary as writing instruments. Much broader. The opportunity for innovation is new, different, better ways of getting words on paper or other media. Or the company might define its boundary as communication technologies, which is so broad that it is meaningless. Good boundaries are narrow enough to give direction, broad enough to provide opportunity.

3. What do and what will our customers value? There are many possible answers to this question, such as some combination of the following:

- Reliability—of the product, of the company
- Sales relationships
- Information resource
- Problem solving
- Technical service support
- Prompt response from salesperson
- Prompt response from service person
- Price
- Cost—price plus in-use costs
- On-time delivery
- In-spec delivery
- New product development
- Product design
- Cost reduction from using the product
- Revenue increase from using the product

Each customer and prospect will probably value several of the values on this list, and very likely others not on this list. But among those values, a small number will be much more important than the others. Marketing must understand which values are most important, and for these values how, in the eyes of the customer, their company compares with competitors. The aim will be to find unique ways to make their company superior in the values most important to customers.

Marketing, collaborating with other functions as appropriate will aim to understand value as perceived by the customer. From this information, the company will strive to innovate the new, different, better ways of providing those values. Successful companies achieve and maintain superiority in offering the values most important to customers. But customer value becomes a moving target. Tomorrow will be different from today. For the company a moving target of the values most important to customers demands continuing observation, research, and innovation. But marketing will always stay focused on customers and prospects in the area of operations specified in the Resource Bargain. The Resource Bargain can be changed, of course, whenever a change is appropriate.

Marketing, working in system 4 and collaborating with other system 4 functions, answers these three key questions in detail: (1) Who are and who will be our customers? (2) What are and what will be our products and services? (3) What do and what will our customers value? For marketing, the answers to these questions enable the formulation of effective strategy. For marketing, and other system 3 and system 4 functions, these answers are an information resource for determining needed actions.

The purpose of every business is to create and keep customers. Every business creates customers whether the company is modeled with the VSM or not. But companies that use the VSM and system thinking do it better.

Competitive Position

In their business plans, businesses at all levels of recursion will find their answers to an important additional question: What is our competitive position? Everyone in the company having contact with customers needs to be continuously probing this question and acting to strengthen the company's competitive position. The check-list shown in Figure 6.1 was used in one company by their sales people to understand what customers value and the company's competitive position.

For a product/market business, sales people would list under the heading "List of Values" all the things a customer would consider in the purchase decision. In the next four columns, sales-people would rank their company in comparison with their company's three major competitors. In the next step, the sales-person would sit in the chair of the buyer, go down the listing of values and rankings and put a red circle around the number 1 rankings for those values the salesperson believes are most important to the customer. Compiling these check-lists from several salespeople provides information that helps sales-people plan their sales calls, and helps sales management, marketing, product development, value engineers, and other company people identify opportunities for change and improvement.

Product/Market Business Segment: _____

What is value to the customer?

List of Values	Co.	C1	C2	C3
1				
2				
3				
4				
5				
6				
7				
8				
9				
10				
11				
12				
13				
14				
15				
16				
17				
18				

Evaluation

Directions for this evaluation:

1. Under "List of Values" list what is important to customers in making their purchase decisions. This list can best be prepared by consolidating and editing the listings of several salespeople.

2. List the three major competitors in this product/market business:

C1:_____

C2:_____

C3:_____

3. Evaluation:

Step 1. For each customer value listed, rank from 1 to 4 your company (Co.) and each of the three major competitors (C1, C2, C3)—1, best; 2, second best; 3, third best; 4, weakest.

Step 2. Now think of yourself as a typical major customer in this product/market business. Go down the listing of values and ratings and put a circle around the 1 ratings for those values most important to you as a customer.

Step 3. Appraise company position and take actions as appropriate.

Figure 6.1 Competitive position

Market Position

Market position usually parallels competitive position. Competitive position measures the company against competitors in customer values. Market position measures results in the marketplace. We strive for favorable competitive position in order to a achieve market position. If competitive position is good, and market position less than good, we either have our measures wrong, or our marketing and sales are less than professional.

Many large corporations aim for a position of market leadership, number 1 or number 2 in market share in their strategic businesses. In a globalizing world, global market share may be impossible to measure. Even in an advanced industrial country with good statistical data, market share will vary depending on how the market is defined. If market share is defined in terms of product or product group, such as automobiles, numbers will likely be available. If the market is defined by function including all products and technologies providing a specific function, market share numbers get fuzzy.

The definition of market position can limit or motivate company performance. Here's a long-ago, but useful example. In the 1950s, Telechron was a small subsidiary of General Electric. Telechron made electric clocks. Electric clocks at that time were all handsome, traditionally-designed clocks that people put on the mantle above the fireplace or in other conspicuous locations in their homes. Telechron clocks were run by synchronous electric motors, a proprietary technology. When the clock's electric cord was plugged into an outlet, the clock started. With all other electric clocks, when they were plugged in they didn't start running. The user had to go through a complicated and uncertain procedure to start the clock running. With not infrequent power outages at that time, Telechron had a significant product advantage, and they dominated the market for electric clocks.

At that time Ralph Cordiner, then executive vice president of General Electric, scheduled annual budget review meetings at the locations of the various GE operations. In his review meeting with Telechron, the Telechron president proudly claimed that Telechron had more than 95% of the electric clock market. Mr. Cordiner asked a different question, "What percent of the clock market do you have?" Telechron top managers conferred a bit, then responded that they did not know exactly, but it was certainly less than 3%. All alarm clocks were wind-up clocks. All wall clocks were wind-up clocks. All households had wind-up alarm clocks and wind-up wall clocks. Many fewer households had electric mantle clocks. That meeting changed Telechron. They were no longer in the electric clock business. They were in the business of clocks and timing devices. By the 1960s, electric alarm clocks were waking people up; then clock radios. Telechron sales boomed. Market share over 95%, or under 3%. How companies define their market makes a difference.

Thirty years later, Jack Welch, chairman and CEO of General Electric, required as a goal for all the company's strategic businesses that they be number 1 or number two in market position. GE aimed to be number 1 in all its businesses; number 2 OK, on the way to number 1. After a few years, it became apparent that business managers were defining their markets narrow enough to make them number 1 or number 2. Mr. Welsh, desiring more innovation of new, different, better, and expanding sales revenue, changed the requirement: Define your market so you have less than 10% of the market. Jack still wanted high ratings in competitive position, GE products and services better than competitors, but wanted GE businesses to find new opportunities for growth. With the new requirement, innovation boomed; new business happened. The general rule works: Define the market narrow enough to give direction, broad enough to offer opportunity for growth.

The company that used the checklist shown in Figure 6.1 to measure competitive position, used a similar checklist for estimating market position. The company manufactured specialty chemicals sold to manufacturing companies. Market sales data were not available for calculating market share. But market share can be estimated. The company aimed to be at or near the top in market share, and to be a leader in the customer values offered in their products and services. The checklist shown in Figure 6.2 helped them estimate both leadership and market position.

The checklist shown in Figure 6.2 is used for estimating market position for major products or product groups. Usually, competitors sales revenue information is not available and can only be estimated. In the first step salespeople compare each competitor with their company on each of the values that customers consider in buying these products. Second, a comparison is made on company resources. Third is the estimated market position for each. Salespeople have many sources of information for making these estimates. Every salesperson has the experience of many customer contacts. They have experienced competitive situations. They know what competitors are doing. Other customer contact people will have information, too. And company

Product Group:_____

	Competitors							
	1	2	3	4	5	6	7	8
Customer Values:								
Product Benefits Product Quality Sales Representation								
Information Resource On-time, In-spec Delivery Technical Service								
New Product Development Price, Terms Reduction in Total Costs								
Revenue Increase								
Company Resources								
Proprietary Position Raw Material Position Manufacturing Cost								
Market Position								

My Company _____
Competitors (Rate in Columns)

Instructions:
1. List competitors along the top of the matrix
2. List any additional customer values down the left of the matrix
3. Compare each competitor with your company on each of the values, using the following ratings:
    + Better than your company
    0 Equal to your company
    – Not as good as your company
4. For estimated market position in this product group, rank your company and competitors by actual or estimated sales revenue in this product group, from highest to lowest: 1, highest, 2, 3, 4, 5, 6, 7, 8, lowest.

Figure 6.2   Checklist for Market Position

technical, purchasing, and manufacturing people will have information for comparing company resources.

For market position, salespeople know their company's sales revenue for these products and have a pretty good idea whether each competitor is bigger or smaller, and by how much. Comparisons can be useful when numbers are not available. At a sales meeting, a group of sales people, some eight to fifteen, can each work through this checklist. After the results are summarized, how many 1s, 2s, 3s, 4s, 5s, etc. for each company, a dialog discussion will result in a useful rank order of market position.

A leading market position requires a strong competitive position in product and service values offered. And it requires more. Market leadership adds the dimension of company resources and capabilities to assure continuing leadership in providing customer values. Market leaders need to be among the best in all the key performance areas that determine company success.

Diagnosing Sales Revenue

The top line in the income statement is sales revenue. But how much information is in that number? Not very much. Aggregates—and total sales revenue is a huge aggregate—lose information. And the figure for total sales revenue loses a lot of information marketing management needs. All revenues are not the same. There are pricing differences. There are mix differences. There are always significant contribution margin differences. Sales revenue C might be much better for the company than sales revenue K. In most companies there are no measures identifying these differences, and they are left unmanaged. But they can be measured and they can be managed. With these measures, marketing and sales people can manage these differences to improve the profitability of sales transactions, and usually with this new information also increase total sales revenue.

Management Economics   To manage the differences in sales revenue, the company needs the measures of management economics, which are readily available from the company's chart of accounts. Management economics measures help marketing and sales people create and keep customers in ways that will enable the company to achieve all of its business goals.

Joel Dean, professor of economics at Columbia University, pioneered in applying the discipline of economics in the management of business operations. His book, *Managerial Economics* is a classic [1]. Today's version of the economics pioneered by Joel Dean, in this book referred to as "management economics," provide information for decision-makers that much improves the effectiveness of their decisions.

The concepts and measures of management economics are different from accounting concepts and measures. Accounting concepts and measures are designed for financial reporting. Management economics concepts and measures are designed for managing the business. The two are different, but they both use the same chart of accounts. Companies need both. For a discussion of management economics see Chapter 11. Here we are concerned with the management economics measures that help marketing and sales people both increase total sales revenue, and improve the profitability of the sales revenue.

In management, numbers rule. And most of the numbers are accounting numbers. Accounting measures standardized and useful for financial reporting when used for managing business operations can be less than useful. Marketing and sales management people need economics measures. Marketing and sales people need to know the economics of what happened yesterday. And they need to know more. Their job is to make good things happen tomorrow.

For decisions that will make good things happen, management economics will help. One important measure of sales transactions, in addition to sales revenue, is the management economics measure of value created for customers. Marketing and sales people need this measure to mange their contribution to company profitability. Measures of value created, and other management accounting measures can be found from the company's chart of accounts. But they are seldom calculated because they are not required for financial reporting. So decision-markers use accounting numbers such as gross margin, cost of goods sold, or product standard costs to guide their decisions. These are exact figures, but they contain very little, if any, information for making good things happen.

Management economics begins with concepts. Companies combine people and capital for a purpose—to create and keep customers in ways that will enable the company to achieve the rest of its business goals, too. The cost of employing the company's people, the costs of capital, and programmed fixed costs are fixed costs of the business month after month, whether sales revenue is thousands or millions of dollars a month. To create customers, company people use the company's capital resources to develop, produce, and deliver the products and services offered by the company.

Company people also purchase the materials, components, and energy needed to produce and deliver the company's products and services. These purchases are the company's variable costs. The value that the company creates for customers is the difference between the variable costs that go into the production of the products and services provided by the company and the price paid by the customer. Sales revenue minus variable costs that went into those sales is the value created by the company, for customers. The term for the value created for customers is value added. For more information on value added, see Chapter 11.

Contribution Margin   For an individual product, value added is the difference between the variable costs incurred to make the product, and its selling price. The management economics name for this difference is "contribution margin." This is a meaningful name, since contribution margin is the amount the sale of the product contributes to the payment of the company's fixed costs. After the company's total contribution margin pays all fixed costs, the additional contribution margin is operating income.

So contribution margin numbers should be extremely important numbers for sales and marketing people. But sales and marketing people, and management generally, have no knowledge of contribution margins, and concentrate on sales revenue numbers. To improve the bottom line of the income statement (profit) they strive to increase the top line (sales revenue). That top line is a huge mix of contribution margins that can be managed.

Calculating the product contribution margins for a manufacturing company will likely find a range in contribution margin percents from close to or even below zero to over 70%. And this will be information previously unknown. In a manufacturing business, average contribution margin usually will be over 30% but less than 60%. In a virtual manufacturing company contracting out all or most of its manufacturing, variable costs are higher, contribution percents lower. In some service businesses with few variable costs, contribution margins can approach 100%.

The top line in the income statement is an all-inclusive total. And, like all totals, it loses a lot of information needed for making wise decisions. Total sales includes a mixture of product sales and transactions with a range of contribution margins. Sales revenue needs to be managed by a different metric than volume alone. We need to manage contribution margins. To begin, we need to know what the contribution margins are. Figure 6.3 outlines a procedure for auditing product sales and contribution margins.

The marketing and sales contribution to improving company profitability begins with an understanding of contribution margins by

Prepared by _____ Date _____	Sales (add 000)						
	Units	$	CM$	CM%	AV SP/Unit	Current SP/Unit	Action
Period:_____	___	___	___	___	___	___	_____
Product Line _____							
Market Growth Rate (1) _____							
Competitive Position (2) _____							
P1:	___	___	___	___	___	___	_____
P2:	___	___	___	___	___	___	_____
P3:	___	___	___	___	___	___	_____
P4:	___	___	___	___	___	___	_____
P5:	___	___	___	___	___	___	_____
P6:	___	___	___	___	___	___	_____
P7:	___	___	___	___	___	___	_____
P8:	___	___	___	___	___	___	_____
P9:	___	___	___	___	___	___	_____
P10:	___	___	___	___	___	___	_____
P11:	___	___	___	___	___	___	_____
P12:	___	___	___	___	___	___	_____
P13:	___	___	___	___	___	___	_____
P14:	___	___	___	___	___	___	_____

(1) Indicate: High–growth over 8% per year   Low–growth less than 3% per year
                       Medium–growth of 3% to 8% per year   Neg. –negative growth rate
     Note: all growth rates are in real terms–units or deflated dollars.
(2) Indicate Company position among all competitors.   Example: 2/10 = Company is number
     2 of 10 competitors in sales volume for this product line.
Key: CM - Contribution Margin
          SP - Selling Price

Figure 6.3   Product line audit

product and by transaction. A good place to begin is a product line
audit. Figure 6.3 summarises contribution margin information for individual products in a product group or product line. Begin by listing the
products on the left side of the form. Fourteen products can be listed
on this page. Then, in the columns, list the information for each product.
For the recent x-month period (minimum, 3 months, maximum
12 months):

1. Column 1. List unit sales for each product for the period
2. Column 2. List dollar sales for each product for the period
3. Column 3. List the total contribution margin dollars for each
   product for the period (total sales revenue minus the total variable costs—the purchased inputs that went into the production of
   the product)

4. Column 4. Calculate the average contribution margin percent for each product (contribution margin dollars divided by sales revenue)
5. Column 5. Calculate the average selling price per unit (column 2 divided by column 1)
6. Column 6. List the current price for each product, and note comparisons with column 5. Have there been price changes during the period? Are sales made at varying discounts from the list price?
7. Column 7. Review the information and note any actions needed.

Note: The information for column 3 is best prepared on a separate spreadsheet.

Total contribution margin dollars are the funds available to pay the fixed costs of the business. After all fixed costs are paid, all additional contribution margin dollars are operating income. Sales and marketing, working with other functions, can find ways to increase contribution margin dollars:

- Increase sales revenue with the same product mix
- Improve mix by selling more of the high-contribution margin products
- Find opportunities to substitute a high contribution margin percent product in place of a low contribution margin percent product
- Improve the contribution margin percent for low contribution margin percent products, by:

  Reducing the cost of inputs (purchased variable costs)

  Reformulating or redesigning products to reduce variable costs, or to increase selling price, or both

  Increasing price
- Develop and market new products, with high contribution margin percents.

With data on product sales revenue, contribution margin, and contribution margin percent, company people will make wise decisions for profit improvement. They will know the contribution margin of transactions. They will find opportunities for improvement in contribution margin dollars by increasing sales revenue, especially sales revenue in high contribution margin products. And they will find opportunities also for increasing contribution margin dollars at the present sales rate, by:

- Reducing variable cost
- Increasing price
- Improving mix
- Developing high contribution margin new products

"Value analysis" technologies can help product engineers, manufacturing engineers, and value engineers reduce variable cost, and develop high contribution margin new products. Market and competitive intelligence will help marketing and sales people make wise decisions on increasing price and improving mix.

With information on variable costs and contribution margins by product, marketing and sales people can include both sales revenue and contribution margin in sales objectives, and both can be included in sales incentive compensation plans. Sales people can learn and be involved with the economics of their business. Professional sales people create and keep customers by helping them improve their operations and their profitability by using the products and services offered by the salesperson's company. With their knowledge and involvement in their company's economics, professional sales people can also help improve their own company's profitability. Marketing and sales people can become, also, business people.

Two Contribution Margin Examples

1. Read the MX Corporation example in Chapter 3. The company lost money each year for more than three years. There were cost reduction programs, but no improvement in profitability. Morale sagged. Sales revenue stagnated. Then the management group, including all marketing and sales people, learned about management economics, and about the marketing and sales methods described in this chapter. With this new understanding they saw how their company could become profitable. Read their story. In six months they reached breakeven, and were soon achieving desired profitability.

2. A subsidiary company manufactured, sold, and serviced specialty chemicals for electroplating. Sales revenue totaled $180 million, but margins were well below what corporate headquarters considered acceptable. Aggregates and averages lose a lot of information. The subsidiary's biggest dollar volume product was potassium gold cyanide. Gold, whether in coins, bars, or in solution is bought

and sold at the market price. There is no margin in gold, unless you buy today and sell next month when the price is higher. But the price might be lower. More than half the subsidiary's sales revenue was gold. There were really two parts to their business: a specialty chemicals business heavy in technical service, and gold. The company bought gold on the day an order was placed, and later billed the customer at that price. They chose not to speculate in gold. The subsidiary's income statement was changed to show operations in gold, and operations in the specialty chemical and technical service business. Gold was break-even. But the specialty chemical and technical service business had margins and operating income much higher than the corporate goal.

Gold is an extreme example. But most companies have a significant opportunity in their management of mix.

Pricing

Companies might like to make pricing an accounting function. Calculate the full cost of the product, add a desired margin, and that's the price. The problem is that there's a market out there with a collective wisdom of what is the right price. If the accounting price is too high, sales will be limited. If the accounting price is too low, the company is losing an opportunity for improved profitability. Best practice considers cost as a measure of the profitability of a pricing decision. Best practice:

1. *Find a simpler, faster, better way to measure product contribution to profitability than traditional product costing methods.* While product cost does not determine price, cost does determine the profitability of the pricing decision. And to determine the profitability of the pricing decision, the company needs a true understanding of costs and the relationships between product costs and profitability. Traditional accounting procedures for product costing, gross margins, and cost of goods sold do not give us this understanding. Accounting methods were designed as a standard for all companies for their financial reporting. The aim is to have valid and comparable financial reporting for all companies. Today, with globalization, accounting standards continue evolving toward harmonization of national and international standards. But whatever the status of financial reporting standards, management decisions require additional and different information.

For understanding the profitability of pricing decisions, knowledge of management economics and the economics of business transactions is essential. See Chapter 11.

2. *Find ways to estimate an appropriate market price.* There is no accounting kind of calculation for market price. Best practices include better ways of learning market and competitive information, and better ways of reasoning from this information and from cost data to determine what a good price will be.

For most viable businesses, at all levels of recursion, sales people and other customer contact people, are the best source for market information. They know customer needs and expectations. They know competitive offerings. They can participate in the pricing decision process through dialog. Dialog no longer requires travel to headquarters. It can be done on the company web. Companies can find their own innovative ways to learn from the market. Management economics will give decision-makers an understanding of product cost. Such technologies as value analysis and target costing can help companies achieve costs that make the right price profitable. The relation between product costs and selling prices needs to be continuously managed to assure desired profitability. See Chapter 11.

3. *Change the whole concept of "price."* Instead of pricing the product, price and sell what the product does for the customer.

Instead of pricing products, companies can sometimes price the value the customer receives from the product. A company offering conversion coatings for rolls of sheet metal produced and sold the coatings. Their technical service people worked with clients on their coating lines to assure effective use of the coatings. What the customer wanted was not containers of conversion coatings. What the customer wanted was square feet of metal coated to specifications. The company changed their pricing from dollars per unit of product to dollars per thousand square feet of coated metal. This change involved company service people in collaboration with target clients, gave customers an exact cost for the product they were producing, and eliminated price competition in dollars per unit of product. Innovations in pricing can bring competitive advantage to both the company and the customer.

Distribution

With innovations in ocean, ground, and air transport; with the increasing variety in the ways customers can purchase products and services—

directly from the producer; from distributors; from specialty stores, minimarts, superstores, malls; mail order; and the fastest growing of all, the internet—there's great opportunity for innovation in distribution. Today's largest computer maker, Dell Computer, began with an innovation in distribution—direct sales to the customer. This distribution innovation and continuous innovation in products and service made a small start-up an industry leader.

Advertising, Sales Promotion, and Publicity

There is the one-on-one way of reaching customers and prospects through sales people and other customer contact people. Then there are the advertising, publicity, and sales promotion ways of reaching customers and prospects by the thousands and the millions. In traditional advertising, publicity, and sales promotion there is great opportunity for innovation. There are and will be new kinds of agencies, new kinds of media, new kinds of experts. Increasingly important is the internet, offering a fast-evolving number of ways for reaching customers and prospects. What are the opportunities for communications direct to your company's customers and prospects through links from search engines, clickable banners, blog messages, on-line publications, your own company's web site(s), and all else that's happening, and will happen, on the internet? Fast-growing broadband, open-source software, declining costs of hardware, plus a lot of creative genius inventing and developing new services continuously transforms the internet. Continuously, there will be new ways to communicate with customers and prospects. In advertising, publicity, and sales promotion continuously search for, and use whatever is new and better.

While the techniques and technologies of advertising, publicity, and sales promotion continually evolve, fundamental best practices remain, including:

- Set specific objectives. Measure.
- Integrate advertising, publicity, and sales promotion with sales to achieve sales revenue targets. Measure.
- Maintain flexibility in budgeting to increase/decrease as appropriate. Continuous budgets work better than fixed budgets for a fiscal year.
- Continuously improve.
- Continuously innovate.

Customer Service

Keeping customers requires many contacts, many relationships, many services. Customer services include sales support services; order service; delivery service; after sales technical, business, and support services; and any services relating to recycle and disposal. There are many customer contacts and customer services before, during, and after the sale. Creating and satisfying customers requires professional sales and marketing people, and a lot more. Many company people will be involved. Figure 6.4 shows one company's view of company/target customer relationships.

There can be many company/target customer relationships. Company people and their counterparts in the customer organization will talk and deal with matters of mutual concern. Discussions may involve others than the direct counterparts. Sales people will deal with purchasing, and also with others involved in the purchase decision or the use of the product. Creating and keeping key customers is best assured through collaborative relationships among key people in both organizations.

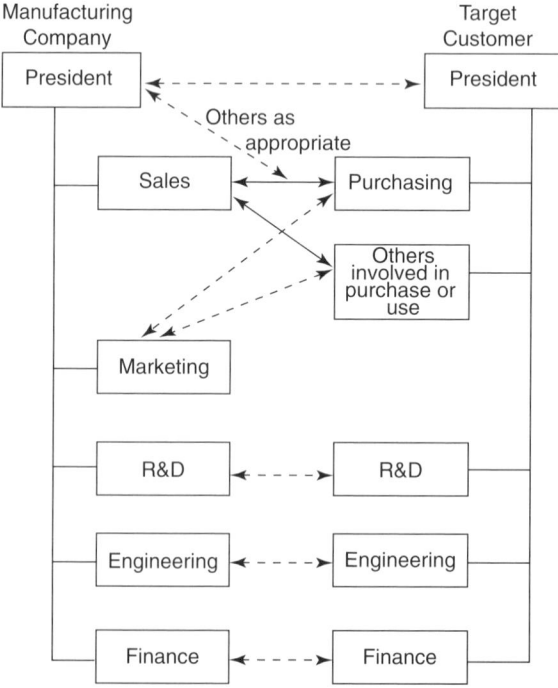

Figure 6.4   Target customer relationships, manufacturing company

One of the important concepts from the disciplines of quality is the simple, yet profound statement, "There is always a better way." Finding and innovating the better ways got successful companies to where they are. Finding and innovating better ways will determine the successful companies of tomorrow.

For customer services, as for all other company functions, innovation springs from a questioning attitude in the minds of those involved in doing the work:

- Why do we do this? Ask why five times in response to answers to get to a true understanding.
- How can we do it better? faster? lower cost?
- How can we strengthen relationships?
- What something different can we do that will be better for the customer?
- What new customer service might help us create and maintain customers?

People doing the work are a good resource for change and improvement. Kaizen is a technology for involving this resource. See Chapter 8.

SALES

Marketing, participating with other functions in the company, formulates and develops the customer values that enable the company to create and keep customers. Many people in the company will be involved in creating and keeping customers. But the point people in finding and creating customers, developing relationships, and continuously managing company-customer relationships are the company's professional salespeople. Professional salespeople combine consultative selling skills with a professional discipline for managing their part of the company— their sales assignment or territory. In managing their sales assignments, professional salespeople are guided by 14 principles:

1. Focus on the sales assignment, or territory
2. Manage the sales assignment as a business
3. Concentrate on target customers and target prospects
4. Develop action plans for target customers and target prospects
5. Schedule calls

6. Maximize selling time with customers and prospects
7. Prepare each sales call
8. See the right people
9. "Counsel with" more than "sell to"
10. Communicate—ask questions, and LISTEN
11. Establish relationships
12. For each customer and prospect develop proposals good for them and good for the company
13. Get the order
14. Follow up and assure customer satisfaction and delight

1. Focus on the Sales Assignment, or Territory

Sales assignments, or sales territories, can be specified in a number of ways. Some of the most common are:

- Geographic area
- Products or product lines
- New products
- New customers
- Market or Industry
- Specific assigned customers
- Channel of distribution
- Maintenance selling
- A combination of two or more of the above

An assignment may be geographic—selling all company products in a specified geographic area. Or the assignment might be specified products or product lines to specified markets or industries, or to specially assigned customers. Sometimes sales assignments are by channel of distribution where the salesperson has the responsibility for selling products to and through a distribution channel.

In some sales assignments the sales job is maintaining and increasing business at existing customers. In a new venture or major new product development, the sales assignment might be developing new sales with new customers. There can be specialized assignments in any of the methods listed above, or any combination of these methods. The kind of sales assignment best for any company or business will depend on the company or business objectives and strategy. A company or business might have several kinds of sales assignments.

2. Manage the Sales Assignment as a Business

Once the sales assignment has been made, the professional salesperson looks at the assignment as a business. For professional salespeople their assignment is their part of the company. They are responsible for making this assigned area successful. Their resources are their company's products and services, their professional selling skills, and the support of other company people. Success is measured by the achievement of sales revenue objectives, contribution margin objectives, and any other sales program objectives.

To achieve these objectives, the professional salesperson first of all develops information on the customers and prospects included in the assigned area, and information on competition. This information identifies the most important sales opportunities, which become the target customers and target prospects, the 20% that can account for 80% of sales.

3. Concentrate on Target Customers and Target Prospects

For each of these target customers and target prospects, and for the total sales assignment, professional salespeople will have specific targets for sales revenue and will be monitoring and managing these sales continuously. For companies including their salespeople in the business management of their sales assignments, professional salespeople will also have objectives for contribution margin. Professional salespeople continuously monitor sales revenue and contribution margin and take actions as appropriate to keep performance on track toward objectives. They also continuously advise sales and marketing management of any changes indicating problems or new opportunities.

4. Develop Action Plans for Target Customers and Target Prospects

With objectives clearly in view, the professional salesperson develops a plan for each target customer and target prospect that can achieve the objectives. The plan will include needed information about the customer or prospect, the sales objective(s), and an action plan.

- Company name, address, and contact numbers
- People involved in the purchase decision, phone numbers and email addresses, and any relevant personal information

- People involved in using the product after purchase, with contact information
- Information about the customer or prospect and their usage of company products
- Competitors selling to the customer or prospect and their strengths and weaknesses
- Company sales history with the customer
- Sales goal
- Sales strategy
- Action plan to achieve the goal

For some customers the customer sales plan may be in the professional salesperson's head. But for target customers and target prospects it's wise to have a plan in writing, for four reasons:

1. Writing the plan helps to think it through, and results in a better plan.
2. A written plan can be reviewed with the sales manager and with others who will be involved. The minds of all who will be involved will produce a better plan.
3. A written plan improves communication and understanding, and coordinates company actions.
4. The plan is not a one-time thing; it is continuous. It evolves with experience to help the salesperson and the others involved achieve the sales goals.

For more information on sales planning, see the sales planning section of this chapter.

5. Schedule Calls

Professional salespeople schedule sales calls carefully to maximize selling time face-to-face with customers and prospects, and to match selling time with sales opportunity. They arrange their monthly schedules and daily itineraries to concentrate on target customers and target prospects, the 20% that will provide 80% of sales revenue. Their daily itineraries enable them to spend most of their time face-to-face with customers.

6. Maximize Selling Time with Customers and Prospects

There are many demands on a salesperson's time, including: planning and scheduling, traveling, waiting, talking on the phone, reporting, attending meetings, coordinating, paperwork. These activities can take most of a salesperson's time. Professional salespeople find ways of spending one-third to one-half or more of their working time face-to-face with customers or prospects. Some ways for increasing selling time with customers and prospects:

- Plan itinerary with alternatives
- Make appointments
- Know intermediaries
- Use telephone and email
- Know best time to call
- Always have something the customer needs
- Use lunch, breakfast, dinner
- Maintain continuing contact

Professional salespeople plan their itineraries very carefully, with alternatives. They know when to make appointments, and they use appointments to assure seeing the right people. They know well such intermediaries as receptionists and assistants, who help the salesperson see the right person. They use lunch or other meals to improve personal relationships. They maintain contact between sales calls by telephone, emails, service reports, news items of interest to the customer, relevant company literature, and other means.

7. Prepare Each Sales Call

The professional salesperson prepares carefully for each sales call. This preparation is a thinking process, a way of thinking through each call before the call is made. Professional salespeople review the situation, everything that is going on at the customer location relating to the sales and use of company products and services, and the competition. They review progress toward achieving the sales goal, and determine a specific sales objective for the call, and a plan of action to achieve that objective. Sales call objectives include:

  *Get an order
  Present product or process information
  *Get product approval
  *Set up trial
  Solve a technical problem
  Train customer people
  Clarify a misunderstanding
  Improve personal relations
  *Schedule meeting for demonstration or special presentation
  Inform customer of price change
  *Get customer acceptance of price change
  *Collect overdue account
  Make proposal
  *Schedule visit to company facilities
  Get information on customer situation, needs, production or expan-
     sion plans, organization change, etc.
  Demonstrate cost reduction possibilities
  Find additional sales opportunity
  Obtain market intelligence
  Obtain competitive information

Some of these objectives are marked with an asterisk. These are objectives that require action by the customer. The other objectives are things the salesperson can do. The professional salesperson will have a high proportion of sales call objectives that require action by the customer. A strong commercial relationship requires actions by both parties.

8. See the Right People

For industrial sales the right person might be any or several of the following:

  *Purchasing Agent
  *Purchasing manager, director, or VP
  Plant manager
  Production manager
  *General manager

*President
*Marketing or sales manager
*Controller
 Plant engineer
 Product engineer
 Quality control manager
 Laboratory manager
 Warehouse manager
 Foreman

The professional salesperson knows each customer well enough to determine who is involved in the purchase decision, and who are the final decision-makers. In the listing above some titles are marked with an asterisk. These are people with management responsibilities. Their interests are financial, and quality, and reliability. The others on the listing have technical responsibilities. They are interested in product information, process information, and problem solving. The professional salesperson helps in both areas.

Professional salespeople sell much more than product features, services offered, and company reliability. Professional sales people sell, primarily, how these features, services, and the company's reliability can improve the customer's operations and the customer's profitability. Operations and profitability can be improved by reducing the cost of inputs to the customer's production process, or increasing the value of the outputs. Professional salespeople learn the customer's present situation, and discuss with the customer how their company's products and services can be used to improve operations and profitability. The opportunity might be in improving productivity, reducing rejects, eliminating waste, increasing yield or process output, reducing downtime, or improving the quality of the customer's product. Professional salespeople shift the discussion of price to a discussion of total costs incurred, and value received.

9. "Counsel with" More Than "Sell To"

Professional salespeople counsel with more than sell to their customers and prospects. They help customers with their business and technical problems, and become, in a real way, helpers and advisors to their customers. When a sale is made, it's a transaction beneficial both to the customer and to the salesperson's company.

Professional salespeople know that a sales call is a process aiming to accomplish a specific result. There is a pre-call part of the process, a sales call part of the process, and a post-call part of the process. Much of the pre-call work is done by marketing and other parts of the company in developing products and services that can provide a superior customer value to customers and prospects. The professional salesperson works out how the product and service values offered by the company can satisfy the specific needs of each customer and prospect. Professional salespeople act very much like brokers between the capabilities of their company and the needs of the customer or prospect. Instead of "selling to," the professional salesperson more "counsels with" customers and prospects. A counseling relationship, however, is a relationship that has to be earned. To earn this relationship, professional salespeople follow a consultative selling process, illustrated in Figure 6.5.

The consultative selling process is summarized by four key letters:

$$R \times R \times S \times S$$

The first "R" stands for "reveal customer needs." This is a discovery process requiring excellence in the selling skills of questioning and listening, all with an attitude of helpfulness.

The second "R" stands for "reduce perceptual differences." There are differences in perception and understanding between the salesperson and the people the salesperson meets with who work for the customer or prospect. Professional salespeople have a thorough knowledge

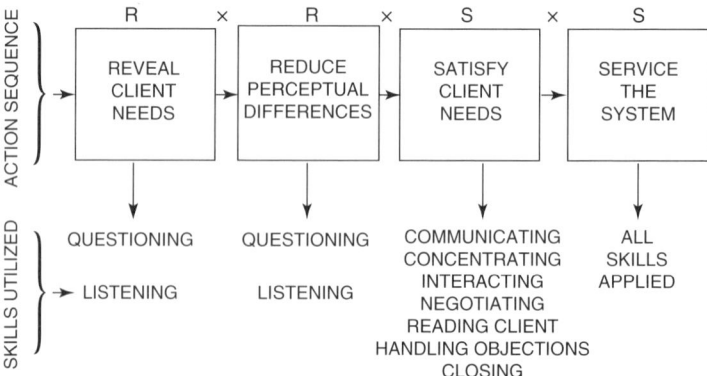

Figure 6.5 The consultative selling process (Source: Howard A. Berrian, Berrian Associates, used with permission.)

of the capabilities of their company and its products and services. They have only limited knowledge of the customer or prospect situation. The people working for the customer or prospect know well their situation, but have limited perceptions or understanding of the products, services, and capabilities of the salesperson's company. The objective here is to reduce these perceptual differences so that an agreement can be reached that is good for both parties. The selling skills needed to reduce perceptual differences are questioning and listening to learn and understand the customer situation.

The first "S" stands for "satisfy customer needs." With the information and understanding from the first two parts of the consultative selling process, revealing customer needs and reducing perceptual differences, the professional salesperson can then offer the products and services that will best satisfy the customer's needs. This solution, and agreement, will result from a dialog process between the customer and the professional salesperson. The selling skills needed during this dialog are: communicating, concentrating, interacting, negotiating, "reading" the customer, handling objections, and closing. Questioning and listening will also be a part of this dialog.

The second "S" stands for "service the system." This is the art of keeping and satisfying the customer, maintaining and strengthening relationships, and seeing that all goes well in the customer's experience with the salesperson's company and products. In servicing the system, all selling skills are used.

The consultative selling process will guide every sales call. For prospects, several consultative sales calls will usually be needed to earn the first order. For existing customers each sales call will include some combination of all four parts of the process. The professional salesperson makes each sales call an important event in the consultative selling process. Figure 6.6 shows a form one company used as a checklist for a sales call.

Just as an airline pilot, however experienced, uses a checklist for each flight, professional salespeople can use a checklist for each sales call. Figure 6.6 illustrates how a day's sales calls might be planned. Depending on the business, the number of sales calls per day might be few, or many. Each call will use the consultative selling process as appropriate, $R \times R \times S \times S$. The form shown in Figure 6.6 was not a form for reporting a day's calls. It was a form used by salespeople however they wished. It is a checklist for what goes into making a quality (successful) sales call, including precall, call, and postcall. It is a reminder of requirements for a quality call, and a method for self-appraisal.

Date _____ Today's Plan _____ Number of Calls _____

Quality Call Checklist

Precall	**Call**	**Post Call**
Review profile and call record.	See target contacts.	Report via SALESNET.
Set call objective.	Listen:	Update call records for continuation selling.
Sales aids ready.	Learn situation.	Take follow-up actions as needed.
Anticipate problems and opportunities.	Get competitive information.	Debrief. Did the call achieve the following:
Plan contacts:	Present information to achieve call objective.	Call objective?
Who?	Use sales aids.	Learn the situation?
For what purpose?	Get customer commitment (order, action).	Satisfy customer expectations?
	Support company image.	Support company image?

	1 Customer or Prospect	2 Precall Q OR Ø	3 Call FTF time	4 Q or Ø	5 Post Call Q or Ø	6 Total Q or Ø	7 Notes
1							
2							
3							
4							
5							
6							
7							
8							
9							
10							

Definitions:

  Q — an overall quality rating

  Ø — an overall non-quality rating

  FTF time — time face-to-face with the right customer/prospect people

  Company image — customer-driven, market-oriented, fast-growing producer and marketer of quality products and reliable service; an organization of quality people; and a great place to work

Figure 6.6 Quality call checklist and self-appraisal

While it is important to have a purpose, an objective, for each sales call, that purpose is likely to expand or change during the course of the call. There may be a problem to deal with. The salesperson may discover new or additional opportunities. There may be some new situation to deal with. There may be a competitive threat. However the sales call situation develops, the sales call objective for the professional salesperson will be a positive outcome, beneficial to both parties. The best positive outcomes are actions by the customer that further the relationship, such as an order, an evaluation of a new product, agreement on a new application, scheduling a seminar or training session.

10. Communicate—Ask Questions, and LISTEN

Instead of "selling," professional salespeople help customers make sound buying decisions, good for the customer and good for the salesperson's company.

Professional salespeople listen even more than they talk. They talk to give information, to ask questions, and to propose an action or ask for an order. They listen to understand the customer situation, to find opportunity, and to get market and competitive information. Questioning is the beginning point for listening. Professional salespeople ask questions to:

- Learn customer needs
- Learn about the customer's experiences with their company's products and services
- Learn about any planned or likely changes ahead
- Get reaction to a proposal
- Understand customer satisfaction/dissatisfaction
- Get information on a problem
- Learn more about the customer
- Strengthen relations by learning more about the other person
- Learn customer's impressions of the salesperson's company
- Learn customer's future plans
- Get competitive information
- Learn about the customer's customers and what's important to them

Professional salespeople listen to understand the customer situation so they can "stand in the shoes of the customer" to help the customer make sound purchasing decisions. Here are some basic rules for questioning:

1. Don't ask "skinny" questions. Skinny questions are those that can be answered with a yes or a no. Skinny questions begin with the words are, is, can, would, will, or do.

2. Always ask "fat" questions. Fat questions ask for an in-depth response that will provide needed information. Fat questions begin with the words what, why, when, where, who, and how.

3. Ask questions in a friendly, conversational tone, avoiding any feeling of interrogation or putting the customer on the spot.

4. Listen to the complete answer; don't interrupt. There is temptation to listen only long enough to jump back into the conversation. But we only learn while we are listening, not while we are talking. Professional salespeople listen in a friendly, interested way to the whole answer.

5. Ask another fat question. To really understand, asking more than one fat question helps. Fat questions bring out all the information needed for making purchasing decisions. A professional salesperson can often ask questions and listen up to the point of asking for the order.

6. Restate. To be sure of understanding the customer, professional salespeople often restate their understanding of what the customer has said. This may bring additional comment from the customer, helping to achieve real understanding.

In addition to talking and listening skills, professional salespeople also use sales aids such as samples, videos, computer screen displays or projections, and relevant sales literature.

11. Establish Relationships

Strong relationships develop from working together on problems and helping the customer achieve desired business objectives. Consultative selling helps both the customer and the company and develops strong relationships that create and keep customers.

12. For Each Customer and Prospect Develop Proposals Good for Them and Good for the Company

Through consultative selling and questioning and listening, professional salespeople understand the customer situation. They also know the competitive situation, and they know well their company's products and service capabilities. With this knowledge they can offer attractive proposals and negotiate agreements good for both parties. Through consultative selling, professional salespeople earn the order, expect the order, ask for the order, and get the order.

13. Get the Order

Of course, many times when professional salespeople ask for the order, the answer is "no." But for professional salespeople, "no" is only "no for now," a temporary roadblock on the road to success. They re-earn the order, re-expect the order, and re-ask for the order until the answer is "yes." Sometimes, with continuing negotiation, professional sales-people get from "no" to "yes" in the same sales call. Whether the answer is "no" or "yes" the consultative selling process continues. See Figure 6.7.

14. Follow-up and Assure Customer Satisfaction and Delight

Getting the order is a key event, but the consultative selling process continues. Professional salespeople follow up to assure that the customer is completely satisfied, even delighted, with their company's products and services. To the extent needed, professional salespeople bring people from their company together with the appropriate people in the customer organization to assure continuing satisfaction and delight. For professional salespeople the order must result in continuing sales. With the consultative selling process, professional salespeople are not only making sales. They are creating and keeping customers.

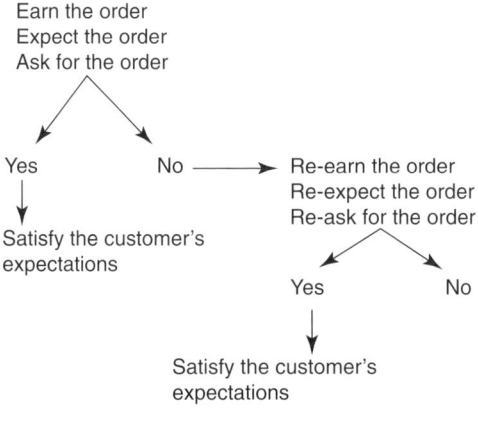

Figure 6.7 Get the order

SALES PLANNING

In practice, sales planning ranges from very little to overly complex and detailed. Whatever the practice, emphasis needs to be on two fundamentals: (1) identifying where the business is—customers and prospects—in each sales territory and sales assignment, and understanding the competitive situation; and (2) knowing how to make the sale. Customer sales planning plus consultative selling skills give salespeople a discipline for both of these fundamentals.

Customer sales planning can be organized into a five-step process:

1. Analysis of sales territory or sales assignment
2. Selection of target customers and target prospects
3. Preparing customer sales plans for target customers and target prospects
4. Implementation of customer sales plans
5. Measurement

1. Analysis of Sales Territory or Sales Assignment

The sales territory examination lists all customers and prospects in the territory. Present customers are known, and many prospects are also known, but probably not all. So this will be an evolving listing, with key information for each customer and prospect. An industrial products company used the format shown in Figure 6.8 for sales territory analysis. Whatever the format, the information needed for a sales territory analysis includes:

- Customer and prospect names, addresses, and contact numbers
- The key people to contact
- Kind of business and what they buy
- Past sales and goals for the future
- Major competitors
- Any appropriate comments

The sales territory analysis becomes a continuing, evolving information resource, built from the salesperson's experience and inputs from other company people from their customer contacts. Each customer and prospect can be set up as a file on the salesperson's laptop, with the following information:

Sales Territory_____
Salesperson_____

Customers and Prospects	Key People	Products Purchased	Sales			Major Competitors	Comments
			Last Year	This Year est.	Next Year Potential		

Figure 6.8   Sales territory analysis

- Company name, address, and contact numbers
- People involved in the purchase decision, phone numbers and email addresses, and any relevant personal information
- Information about the customer or prospect and its usage of company products
- Competitors
- Sales history with the customer
- Record of sales calls and other contacts
- Sales goal

In the sales territory analysis, actual sales, and the salesperson's evaluation of customer or prospect potential, show where the greatest sales opportunities are.

2. Selection of Target Customers and Target Prospects

From the sales territory analysis the salesperson can select the target accounts and target prospects, the few that will account for most of the sales. These will be the customers and prospects to concentrate on.

In each sales territory and sales assignment the salesperson knows existing customers. What is the opportunity for additional sales to existing customers? Which are the target customers? Apply the Pareto principle: about 20% of the customers will produce 80% of the sales revenue. The 20% are the target customers. There are prospective new customers out there, too. Who are they? All customers and prospects need satisfying sales relationships. However, success with target customers and target prospects will produce most of the sales revenue. So professional salespeople concentrate on them. They also maintain relationships and sales with other customers, and work to develop other prospects into customers.

A marketing director from US corporate headquarters was conducting a sales training session for the sales force of a subsidiary in Australia. In discussing opportunities for increasing sales with target customers and target prospects, a sales representative whose sales assignment included automotive customers was reporting on his target customers. A good report: sales were growing. Then a Q & A. Who is the largest automotive manufacturer in Australia? British Leyland. Why isn't British Leyland on your target customer list? I don't call on them. Why don't you call on them? They don't buy anything from us. Why don't they buy anything from us? That question was a eureka moment for the sales representative. He excused himself from the meeting, telephoned British Leyland and scheduled an appointment. Five months later, British Leyland was a customer. The target customer idea, the target prospect idea, the 14 principles, and consultative selling help the professional sales person create and keep target customers, and change target prospects into customers.

An industrial products company in Colombia was losing money. After several years of moderate, but acceptable, profitability the company began losing money. The management group went through a process of defining their business as described in this book, and defining also their businesses at the next level of recursion. They reengineered their distribution system. Sales people attended training sessions on sales planning, target accounts and target prospects, finding sales opportunities, and consultative selling. They changed their method of sales reporting to show sales to target customers, sales to all others, variances from year ago, and sales targets for the year. They also monitored 12-month moving totals for total company sales, and total sales for each of the first recursion businesses. Figure 6.9 shows the format used by a first recursion business for reporting total sales.

Division Industrial
Clientes Especiales
Ventas Netas (000)

Resumen
Mes   Zona

Clientes		Mes.Act. Este Año	Mes.Act. Año Pasado	Var. %	Acumul. Este Año	Acumul. Año Pasado	Var. %	Target. para Este Año
District 1	37	1.868.0	676.6	176	6.133.8	2.533.8	142	24.100.0
Clientes KTA	7	1.491.7	373.4	299	4.915.6	1.660.7	196	20.100.0
Otros	30	376.3	303.2	24	1.218.0	873.1	40	4.000.0
District 2	48	1.531.2	821.6	86	4.250.0	1.980.2	114	19.180.0
Clientes KTA	9	960.7	394.2	144	1.885.2	1.070.5	76	13.700.0
Otros	39	570.5	427.4	33	2.364.8	909.7	159	5.480.0
District 3	13	1.234.9	188.3	556	2.929.0	1.972.8	48	8.530.0
Clientes KTA	3	1.179.6	145.3	712	2.696.1	1.776.7	52	7.030.0
Otros	10	55.3	43.0	28	232.9	196.1	19	1.500.0
District 4	30	983.6	198.7	395	1.738.6	1.008.7	72	15.795.0
Clientes KTA	5	589.6	32.8	NS	673.4	533.1	26	11.700.0
Otros	25	394.0	165.9	137	1.065.2	475.6	124	4.095.0
District 5	8	114.6	54.6	109	276.6	101.7	174	1.800.0
Clientes KTA	3	103.0	35.3	191	255.9	57.4	346	1.500.0
Otros	5	11.6	19.3	(40)	20.7	44.3	(53)	300.0
District 6	7	76.9	97.9	(22)	200.8	127.3	58	1.073.0
Clientes KTA	3	69.6	12.7	448	188.1	12.7	NS	873.0
Otros	4	7.3	85.2	(92)	12.7	114.6	(89)	200.0
Total	143	5.809.2	2.037.7	185	15.528.8	7.724.5	100	70.478.0
	30	4.394.2	993.7	342	10.614.3	5.111.1	108	54.903.0
	113	1.415.0	1.044.0	36	4.914.3	2.613.4	88	15.575.0

Figure 6.9 Division sales report

Figure 6.9 shows the monthly sales report for the total Division. At the bottom of the report, totals are shown for all 143 customers, for the 30 target customers, and for the 113 other customers. For the current year, sales to the 30 target customers were expected to be 78% of total sales, another example of the Pareto 80/20 principle.

There were also sales reports for each sales district. Sales reports for each district included the names and data for each target customer, the names and data for each of the "all other" customers, and the names (without any data of course) of target prospects, and of all other prospects, too. In this way salespeople were continuously informed on customer sales, and reminded also of prospects. The district sales reports listed:

- Sales for each target account with data as shown in Figure 6.9
- Totals for target customer sales
- The names of target prospects. When first sales are made to a target prospect, the salesperson decides if the company stays on the target customer list because of expected sales, or moves to the "all other" customer list.
- Following the list of target customers and prospects, all other customers are listed, with data as shown in Figure 6.9
- Totals for "All Other" customer sales
- Other prospects are listed by name after the all other list of customers

The sales objective was to increase sales with present customers, and create new customers from the target prospects. The combination of customers and prospects represents the salesperson's assessment of sales opportunity, worked out in collaboration with the sales manager. Including both customers and prospects in the sales reporting each month is a continuing reminder of the sales objective. A goal of continuous improvement is measured and monitored by year-ago comparisons. Time series charts as described in Chapter 5 show trends and changes in trends in total division sales revenue, district sales revenue, target customer sales revenue, and all other sales revenue. Reports are maintained in the company information system and available on the salesperson's laptop.

Figure 6.10 shows the result. After slipping to a significant loss in the first half of the year, with the actions summarized above the company

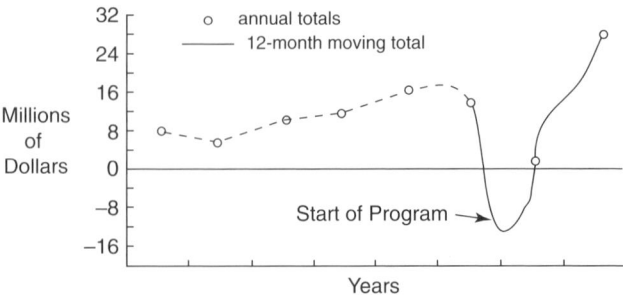

Figure 6.10   Industrial products company, Colombia, net income

recovered to break-even by year-end and went on to achieve highest ever profitability.

Continuously satisfying, even delighting, target customers is usually the greatest opportunity for increasing sales revenue. Figure 6.11 illustrates the format used by salespeople in a plastics materials company in the United States for monitoring their relationships with their target customers.

3. Preparing Customer Sales Plans for Target Customers and Target Prospects

Professional salespeople will usually have written customer sales plans for each of their target customers and each of their target prospects. A customer sales plan includes the following kind of information:

- Company name, address, phone and fax numbers, and email addresses.
- Information on type of business, size, their products and services, and markets served
- Key people to contact, with titles, direct phone numbers and email addresses; their responsibilities in the purchase and use of the salesperson's products and services; and any other relevant comments
- Products and services purchased
- Competition at the customer, share of business, strengths, weaknesses
- Sales history with the customer, dollars and products/services
- Sales objective for the current year, and estimated future potential
- Action plan to achieve the objective and the potential, including what will be done, by who, completed by when

The customer sales plan is not a one-time thing at budget time. It is a living document, the data continuously updated, the action plan continuously evolving from experience.

4. Implementation of Customer Sales Plans

The professional salesperson implements each customer sales plan as the plan is being developed, and as the plan is continuouly updated. There is never a final plan, but there is always a current plan. For the professional salesperson, the continuous customer sales plan works for

Salesperson's Guide for Managing Target Customer Relationship

Customer:_____   Salesperson:_____

	Sales History $ (000)	% of Customer Business	Major Products and Pounds Purchased
20__			
20__			
20__			
This Year Target			

Call Record:

   Date   Contacts and Results

SALES SUMMARY

	2 Yrs Ago	Yr Ago	This Yr	PROBLEMS, SITUATION CHANGES, ACHIEVEMENTS
Jan. lbs.				
$				
Feb. lbs.				
$				
Mar. lbs.				
$				
1st Qtr. lbs.				
$				
AvSP				
Apr. lbs.				
$				
May. lbs.				
$				
June. lbs.				

Figure 6.11   Salesperson's guide for managing target customer relationship

the salesperson like the continuous budget described in Chapter 5 works for the company. Both help achieve desired goals.

5. Measurement

We tend to think of measurement as the way to evaluate performance. Measures can be and are used for evaluating performance. But a high-achieving enterprise develops measures that help those doing the work accomplish desired results. For salespeople, desired results most often are sales revenue in relation to the objective or quota. But that's a measure about the past. It doesn't help the salesperson accomplish the objective. What helps the salesperson accomplish the objective is continuous feedback from each customer's actions; on-going dialog, learning, and training; and the company's sales reporting.

For the company's sales reporting, the territory sales reports described in the text commenting on Figure 6.9 provide a good model. This kind of information monthly, plus what the salesperson knows continuously from sales calls, customer actions, and competitive actions helps the salesperson act in ways most likely to accomplish the desired result. Feedback from the work itself guides performance. And that feedback is continuous.

Companies budget and report business operations by fiscal months and fiscal years because that's the cycle for financial reporting. But they manage their businesses minute-by-minute, hour-by-hour, day-by-day, month-by-month, continuously. The fiscal year often influences people to make decisions just to get better numbers into the fiscal year. Whatever those decisions add to the fiscal year will become subtractions later on. Business operates continuously, not as a series of 12-month totals. From an operations view, the numbers for any 12-month period, ending April 30 or August 31 or any other month and date, are the equal of the numbers for the 12-month fiscal year—except for the motivation to "make the numbers" for the fiscal twelve months. The continuous budget described in Chapter 5 helps the company manage continuously. Continuous sales planning helps professional salespeople manage their sales assignment continuously.

Professional salespeople will have objectives for more than sales revenue. Their objectives might include objectives for some combination of:

· Sales revenue
· Contribution margin percent

- Contribution margin dollars
- New product sales
- New customers
- Sales growth from target customers
- New product ideas
- Competitive intelligence

With the wise selection of measures, continuous reporting of the measures along with the continuous feedback from sales calls, customer actions, and competitors' actions help the salesperson act in ways that will achieve desired sales revenue.

Higher-level management sees sales revenue. It's an important number, the top line on the Income Statement. But that number contains very little information. It is an aggregate of transactions, products sold, problems solved, problems not solved, old customers, new customers, competitive gains, competitive losses, new product development, market conditions, competitive actions, changing customer situations, technology change, and many other considerations and actions. All this cannot be known by higher-level managers. In the VSM structure all this is inside the black box of operations, unknowable to managers in higher-level systems. They lack requisite variety. But inside the black box all this must be known, and is. Inside the black box the voice of management is greatly augmented by the voices and the situation knowledge of all those in sales, customer service, technical support, and sales management. Higher-level managers must recognize that they are managing black boxes, but cannot manage inside a black box.

SALES ORGANIZATION STRUCTURE

There is no right way to structure a sales organization. There is no wrong way, either. There are different ways, some better than others. Companies are different, too. The art is to find a good way to structure a sales organization that will create and keep customers and achieve desired sales revenue. With the VSM and system thinking, sales is a part of system 3 at each level of recursion. It is there in system 3 along with all the other functions of inside and now operations needed for sales support. Good sales structure begins with answers to two questions:

1. *Who are the customers and prospects?* Customers and prospects might include end-user companies or individuals, distributors, retailers, agents, intermediaries, recyclers, disposers, and whoever else owns, deals with, or is affected by the product, its use, and its final disposition. In defining customers and prospects we should keep in mind the Pareto principle that about 80% of sales revenue will come from 20% of the customers. So the location of target customers and target prospects is an important consideration. An industrial company may want target customers to be only minutes or same-day hours away from a call or a visit by a sales or technical service engineer in response to a customer need.

2. *Where are the customers and prospects?* There is also the geographic dimension to consider in structuring the sales organization. Where are the customers and prospects by locality, by region, by country, by area, and globally.

Defining and agreeing on who the customers are and will be, and where the customers and prospects are and will be are important strategic decisions for every business. At each level of recursion the Resource Bargain for each business in defining boundaries will include the definition of who and where their customers and prospects are and will be.

With a clear understanding of who and where the customers are and will be, decisions can be made on sales assignments. Sales assignments, or sales territories, can be specified in a number of ways. Some of the ways of making sales assignments are by geographic area, by products or product lines, by market or Industry, by specific assigned customers, by channel of distribution, maintenance selling (maintaining existing relationships), development selling (developing new customers or developing sales of new products, services, or systems), or a combination of two or more of the above. With decisions made on sales assignments, an effective sales organization can then be structured.

With the VSM and system thinking, structure includes the outside environments that are the source of constraints, threats, and opportunities. VSM structure also includes information channels providing the information needed to deal with the constraints and threats, and to discover the opportunities. The information channels also communicate the internal information that informs, coordinates, and motivates actions toward the achievement of goals.

For sales and customer contact people, the environment includes especially the commercial environment of customers, prospects, and competitors; and the technological environment including new discoveries and innovations potentially threats or opportunities for the company. A responsibility of all customer contact people is to bring relevant information from these environments into the company for both system 3, the inside and now operations, and system 4, the outside and future.

CONTINUOUS LEARNING

As described in Chapter 1, two of the important characteristics of system behavior are: (1) homeostasis, the capability of maintaining order and stability and not regressing from what has been achieved, and (2) heterostasis, the capability for continuous learning, improvement, change, and innovation. In the viable, very complex, purposeful, probabilistic system that is a corporation there are both of these capabilities. To maintain and strengthen these capabilities, and especially to enhance the capability of heterostasis, all company people need to continually learn. System 5 executives, systems 4, 3, and 2 executives, managers and professionals, and system 1 supervisors and operators all need careers of learning along with their careers of doing their jobs.

Some observers feel that today, in many companies, training and learning for sales professionals is not what it needs to be. The purpose of business is to create and keep customers. Creating and keeping customers results from building relationships, people working with people to create value for both parties. Professional salespeople are the leaders in building these relationships. Other company people, too, are an important part of building these relationships, as illustrated in Figure 6.4. Customer Relationship Management (CRM) software can be a part of the information resource. But only people—professional sales people and other company people involved in building customer relationships—can create and keep customers.

Effective sales training will deal with selling skills, and more. Effective sales training will deal with all sales responsibilities:

- Territory (or assignment) sales planning
- Customer sales planning
- Market intelligence (competitive intelligence, technological intelligence)
- Building target customer relationships and sales revenue

- Finding and developing prospects into customers
- Product features
- Customer benefits
- Selling skills, the 14 principles including:
  Consultative selling
  Questioning and listening
- New product sales programs
- Transaction economics
- Distributor and dealer sales support
- Sales events (trade shows, sales meetings, and sales contests and awards)
- Order service
- Technical service
- Credit and collections
- Handling customer complaints

Also sales training will include a thorough orientation in all other parts of the company, and building relationships with the people involved in any part of creating and keeping customers.

There's more to sales than selling. There's more to selling than selling skills. A successful sale is not an event. It is a relationship. Instead of buyer and seller, it's more client and counsel. Professional salespeople use the consultative selling process. Professional salespeople help their clients while they help their company. They act, in effect, as brokers between the needs of the customer and the products and capabilities of their company, bringing the two together to the benefit of both.

To reach and maintain a high level of professional selling, sales people continuously learn best practices in all the subject areas listed above, in training sessions, through coaching, and through on-the-job experience and guidance from their managers and peers.

SALES COMPENSATION

Compensation for salespeople typically includes work on some kind of an incentive compensation plan. The aim is to motivate and reward high performance. Examples include: commission only, some combination of salary and commission, salary plus annual or periodic incentive, salary plus bonus for group or individual performance, base salary plus incentive related to achievement of sales goals. Most often, incentive is related to achieving goals, targets, or quotas for sales revenue.

There's no right way to compensate sales people, except for the generalization that applies to everyone: pay them for what they do. And that begins with the job assignment. The purpose of the company is to create and keep customers. Excellent performance in all the jobs in the company is needed to create and keep customers. Sales people, working with others in the company, have the responsibility to apply all company resources in creating and keeping customers. Incentives can help.

Effective sales incentives relate to achievement of objectives. Objectives for a sales assignment might include specific targets in one or more of the following:

- Sales revenue
- Contribution margin
- Increasing sales to present customers
- Increasing share-of-business with key target customers
- Creating new customers
- New product sales
- Obtaining competitive intelligence
- Obtaining market intelligence
- Obtaining technology intelligence
- Maintaining or increasing profitability
- New product ideas

Sales revenue of $XX is an important objective. But other objectives are important, too. Some combination from the above list, or other considerations, can be designed into an incentive compensation plan to encourage, and reward, achievement of desired results. There's great opportunity for innovation in discovering an effective compensation plan for each sales organization, and each sales assignment. As sales incentive plans are being developed, management economics methods can be used to estimate probable costs of the plan, and contributions to profitability.

Continuous planning and continuous measurement offer a unique advantage for managing incentive compensation. Unexpected influences that reduce or increase sales revenue or other target, such as unexpected business cycle changes or an emergency event of some kind, can be pretty much eliminated so that incentive payments can be based on real achievement.

One innovation in incentive compensation that has been effective in some organizations is an incentive plan that includes achievement of profitability objectives. See the section titled "Diagnosing Sales Revenue" earlier in this chapter. Salespeople can learn and be involved in the economics of their business. They can help the company improve profitability by understanding and growing contribution margin as well as sales revenue. Contribution margin might be the measure used in the incentive plan. Or a "sales margin" figure might be used. Sales margin would be the contribution margin for the sales assignment minus the fixed costs incurred in that assignment (salesperson's compensation plus salesperson's expenses).

INNOVATION

Chapter 8 deals specifically with innovation and the VSM. But a few comments are important here since innovation that brings greater value to the customer is an important part of creating and keeping customers. Some areas of innovation for creating and keeping customers:

- Products
- Services
- Sales planning
- Customer service
- Pricing
- Distribution
- Advertising and sales promotion
- Sales organization structure
- Sales training
- Sales compensation
- Goals and performance measure

Innovation is not invention. It is not discovering something new. Innovation is making something new happen to change and improve a previous condition. With the VSM and system thinking, the technologies for successful innovation in creating and keeping customers will be circulating throughout all levels of recursion on the special information channel.

Usually we think of innovation as product innovation. Product innovation is important, and essential for creating the company's future. But there is opportunity also for innovation in sales and marketing in all the areas listed above. Innovation in these areas, too, can create competitive advantage. A distribution innovation—selling computers direct to customers—no distributors, no retailers, no company stores, and continuing innovations in products, processes, and services, made Dell number one in computer sales and profitability.

In the most successful companies, sales and marketing people are innovators in all the areas listed above. There is always a better way. For more information on innovation, see Chapter 8.

GOALS AND MEASURES

At each level of recursion, all the business units—each a viable, very complex, purposeful, probabilistic, system—aim to achieve the goals agreed on in consultation with system 3. Broad goals, the purpose of the business, are defined in the Resource Bargain. More detailed goals are agreed on in the business' plans and budgets. This book advocates goals in seven key performance areas:

1. Creating and keeping customers (Chapter 6)
2. Quality and productivity (Chapter 7)
3. Innovation (Chapter 8)
4. Organization capability (Chapter 9)
5. Physical and financial resources (Chapters 5 and 11)
6. Public and environmental responsibility (Chapter 10)
7. Profitability (Chapter 11)

At all levels of recursion, in all organization units, members can determine which of these seven key performance areas are important to their success, and any other areas that may apply specifically to them. While all seven of these key performance areas are important for the business, for the units within the business only one or a few may be important. In each unit, having identified their key performance areas, they can then set goals, and performance measures that can help them achieve those goals. The aim is not a lot of goals and measures. The aim is to find the few measures that when achieved will mean good performance in all areas. We need to be good in all that matters, but we must be good in the few that matter most.

An advertising unit providing advertising, publicity, and sales promotion support for the company's marketing and sales programs might select from the above listing quality and productivity, creating and keeping customers, and innovation as key performance areas for them. In the performance area of creating and keeping customers they might include a goal for sales leads, or sales leads that turn into sales and satisfied customers.

For quality and productivity they might choose a goal of collaborating with marketing and sales to communicate the company's competitive advantage to customers and prospects at decreasing cost per $K of sales revenue. They might set goals for reducing cycle times in their work processes, and fast response to requests from customers and from salespeople.

For sales support, advertising goals might relate to specific marketing and sales initiatives such as the introduction of new products, increasing sales through a specific distribution channel, or any other initiative. Sales revenue goals will be set for these initiatives, and advertising will collaborate with marketing and sales on the advertising, publicity, and sales promotion that will help achieve the sales revenue goals. Marketing, sales, and advertising/publicity/sales promotion all have the same sales revenue goal. The advertising group, collaborating with marketing and sales, will monitor sales revenue performance, collaborate with marketing and sales, and make changes as appropriate to achieve the goal. Goal achievement is a collective success.

Digital technology, ubiquitous broadband, the internet, everyone connected, offer great opportunity for innovation in advertising, publicity, and sales promotion. There are many ways to talk with and learn from customers and prospects, to target market segments, to stimulate people-to-people comments on company products and services, to deal with the world out there. That world is continually changing. Out there in the commercial environment, competition is changing, markets are changing, industry structure is changing. and globalization is changing almost everything. In the technological environment, technology affecting the marketability of products and the technologies for communication are changing. And there is continuing change also in the economic environment, political environment, social environment, and ecological environment that offer opportunities and impose constraints. Successful response requires innovation, finding better ways in all marketing and sales functions and making them happen.

In all functions and all units, well-designed performance measures help people doing the work accomplish their goals. The measures identify what matters most. Some provide needed information. Some track performance in relation to short-term objectives and long-term goals. They don't measure against budget numbers. They measure progress toward goals using the methods described in Chapter 5. The VSM and system thinking help by relying on the self-organizing and self-control capabilities through all levels of recursion that put responsibility where the work is done. Self-control works much better than imposed control. Self-control by many achieves requisite variety and sound decisions. Imposed control by few does not. Self-control at all levels of recursion greatly expands company capability for creating and keeping customers.

OVERVIEW: THE ESSENCE OF CHAPTER 6

The purpose of every company is to create and keep customers in ways that will enable the company to achieve other goals, too. Without customers, there is no business. To create and keep customers begins with the company's answer to three questions: Who are and who will be our customers? What are and what will be our products and services? What do and what will our customers value? The company's answers to these questions targets desired customers and enables the company to create superior values in its products and services.

Several principles in the VSM and system science help companies create and maintain customers:

- Recursion defines where the work is done
- Self-organization and self-control expands capability
- Requisite variety assures wise decisions
- Black boxes themselves produce desired results
- Homeostats maintain the system
- Heterostats innovate the future
- Communication channels provide information when and where needed
- Communication channels to and from the company's environments provide awareness of threats, and information on opportunities for change and innovation

For information on these principles, review Chapters 1 and 2.

How successful the company is in creating superior values for customers in its products and services is judged by the marketplace. Companies can appraise how they are doing by analyzing their competitive position, as explained in this chapter.

Sales revenue is the number measuring success in creating and keeping customers. But like all aggregates, the number for sales revenue loses a lot of information. There are many stories in sales revenue—new customers gained, customers lost, new business, new ventures, economic conditions, competitive actions, price changes, lost business, high margin sales, low margin sales, market changes, customer satisfaction/dissatisfaction, new products and services, special situations, and other stories, too. Sales revenue doesn't tell these stories to higher-level management. But at all levels of recursion the sales and marketing people doing the work and making or not making the sales do know these stories. Only these people have the requisite variety needed to take appropriate actions.

One story, however, the marketing and sales people usually do not know—the value created in the sales transaction. Which are the low contribution sales; which are the high? What is the average? What should be the target? Contribution margin is selling price minus variable costs. A product audit can easily calculate contribution margins by products. Salespeople can also be business people, producing both desired sales revenue and the contribution margin dollars needed to produce desired operating income.

Professional salespeople manage their sales assignment as a business and use a consultative selling process to achieve both sales revenue and contribution margin objectives. The fundamentals for the work of the professional salesperson can be summarized in the fourteen principles described in this chapter. These are the principles that create and keep customers in ways that enable the company to achieve its goals:

1. Focus on the sales assignment, or territory
2. Manage the sales assignment as a business
3. Concentrate on target customers and target prospects
4. Develop action plans for target customers and target prospects
5. Schedule calls
6. Maximize selling time with customers and prospects
7. Prepare each sales call
8. See the right people

9. "Counsel with" more than "sell to"
10. Communicate—ask questions, and LISTEN
11. Establish relationships
12. For each customer and prospect develop proposals good for them and good for the company
13. Get the order
14. Follow up and assure customer satisfaction and delight

All professionals at all levels in the company need careers of learning along with their careers of doing their jobs. Circumstances change, knowledge expands, jobs evolve. Continuous learning keeps everyone competent. Professional salespeople need continuous learning in all aspects of their sales responsibility. And they need to keep up-to-date on their own company operations and people.

Sales compensation typically includes incentives, usually for the achievement of sales revenue objectives. Objectives for contribution margin dollars and other sales goals can also be a part of an incentive compensation plan.

Innovation is a key performance area for the work of marketing and sales in creating and keeping customers. All marketing and all sales functions are areas for innovation to create competitive advantage.

Continuous learning from the actions of customers and from other experience, the information in measures of the key performance areas, and the performance measures in company reporting help marketing and professional salespeople accomplish their objectives. The purpose of measures is not to evaluate performance. The real and very important purpose of measures is to help people accomplish desired results.

NOTE

[1] Joel Dean, *Managerial Economics,* Prentice-Hall, New York, 1951.

Chapter 7

The Viable System Model and Quality and Productivity

This chapter deals with best practices in quality and productivity, and how the VSM and system thinking improve (1) training in the disciplines of quality and productivity throughout the company, and (2) measurement and improvement in quality and productivity.

THE NEW QUALITY TECHNOLOGIES

After World War II, the Japanese learned statistical quality control from W. Edwards Deming, Joseph M. Juran, and others. Applying these methods and developing additional quality technologies, Japanese manufacturers became world leaders in quality products and low-cost production. Yasuhiro Monden, Taiichi Ohno, Shigeo Shingo, Genichi Taguchi, Kaoru Ishikawa, Noriaki Kano, Masaaki Imai, Seiichi Nakajima, Ryuji Fukuda, and Hiroyuki Hirano were among the Japanese pioneers who developed the new quality technologies and disciplines.

In the 1970s and 80s, Norman Bodek, the president of Productivity Press, recognized the need for bringing the Japanese Quality technologies to the West. Productivity Press began translating and publishing

Holistic Management, by William Christopher
Copyright © 2007 John Wiley & Sons, Inc., Publication

the work of the Japanese pioneers. He brought Shigeo Shingo and Ryuji Fukuda to the United States for seminars and to consult with American companies. He organized missions to Japan for American company managers to visit top Japanese manufacturing plants. The Japanese had visited American manufacturing plants after World War II to learn from us. Now, Americans and other Westerners are visiting Japanese plants to learn from them. Other publishers also began publishing quality technologies from Japan. Quality technologies and disciplines became world-wide requirements for business success, with the evolution of these technologies and disciplines continuing, world-wide.

Beginning with the work of Deming and Juran in Japan, over the latter part of the twentieth century till now, quality has evolved from inspection and rejection, (QC) to statistical quality control (SQC), to total quality control (TQC), to total quality management (TQM), to the Toyota production system (TPS), to lean manufacturing, to lean operations, to whatever comes next. Each of these is the short name for a significant advance in quality technology. And these advances continue.

THE QUALITY/PRODUCTIVITY CONNECTION

As quality technologies have advanced, quality and productivity shared more and more in common. The quality technologies improve also productivity. If we focus on quality, we improve also productivity.

Quality is what the customer says it is. A six-thousand dollar watch can be a quality product. A thirty-dollar watch can also be a quality product, and keep time accurately. Quality is many things—how well the product or service performs its basic function, but also it's design, reliability, comfort, freedom from defects, color, size, weight, durability, availability, easy-care, cost, capacity, a happy experience, and whatever else matters to the customer. Producing and delivering quality products requires error-free operations, elimination of waste, flexibility, and lean operations throughout the entire process.

Productivity, properly defined for the world of today is company products and services delivered to customers without error and without waste and satisfying customers' needs and expectations, and continuous improvement in this process. Quality is defined as company products and services delivered to customers without error and without waste and satisfying customers' needs and expectations, and continuous improvement in this process. So:

Productivity = Quality, and

Quality = Productivity

At the company level, productivity and quality are the same. Where the work is done, however, the measures for each are different. Quality measures and methods assure the production of quality products, without error and without waste—products that will satisfy customer needs and expectations. The measure of success is an absolute—a quality product.

Productivity measures also are absolutes—products per shift, pieces per hour, parts per unit of raw material. But the significance of the measure is not the absolute measure, but how each measure compares with previous measures. The productivity goal is continuous improvement. So we measure trends and changes in trends, always aiming toward the next improvement target. Quality technologies help us make those improvements. Reducing cycle time. Eliminating error and waste. Increasing yield. Increasing output per unit of input. Quality = Productivity.

For benchmark comparisons in productivity performance, an absolute measure can be useful. Benchmark comparisons, other factors being equivalent, show how our performance compares with the performance of peers. And we need to be as good, or better. If we are as good or better, fine. We proceed with continuous improvement. If we are significantly below, we need more than continuous improvement. We need innovation to different and better ways, beginning with the ideas we get from the benchmark study.

The technologies and disciplines of quality are thoroughly reported in the literature, and beyond the scope of this book. What this book can add is not new information about quality, but new information on how the VSM and system thinking help companies use these quality technologies and disciplines successfully.

QUALITY

Information on the technologies of quality is readily available in courses and seminars at colleges, universities, community colleges, and from quality consulting firms. These sources can also provide specialized consulting assistance. Membership in the American Society for Quality (ASQ) will also provide information on the technologies of quality, and available seminars and training programs.

Information on all the technologies of quality are available in books and published articles. Read the books of the Japanese pioneers mentioned above. Their books have been translated and published in English. Check the ASQ book service for books on quality technologies written by leading authorities. Look in the business section of your local book store; check the listings of online book sellers. Search the web. As of this writing (2005), Google offers millions of references:

Subjects	References
For Quality Management	
Lean operations	1,350 K
Lean manufacturing	2,050 K
Toyota production system (TPS)	845 K
Total quality management (TQM)	34,100 K
Total quality control (TQC)	27,800 K
For Quality Technologies and Methods	
Cost of poor quality	104,000 K
Statistical quality control (SQC)	11,500 K
Six sigma	4,410 K
Total productive maintenance (TPM)	2,850 K
Kaizen	671 K
Stockless production	3 K
Just-in-Time (JIT)	620 K
Poke-Yoke (mistake-proofing)	37 K

All aspect of quality are readily available, in print. But probably none of these will have anything to say about system models and the system thinking that derives from system science, and how these strengthen quality programs. That's what this book offers.

The Idea of Systems

First of all we have to understand the principles of system science and cybernetics that apply in all systems, including the viable, very complex, purposeful, probabilistic system—today's business enterprise. System science is new knowledge. Over recent years, with ever-expanding research and discovery, knowledge in all disciplines began to intrude into other disciplines also. Physics helped explain and develop chemistry. Both physics and chemistry were needed in the biosciences. The hard sciences and the soft sciences are interrelated. Everything was relating to everything else. Over the last half-century scientists studied these interrelationships to discover guiding principles. And we now have a new, holistic system science. Review Chapter 1 for a summary of system science principles that offer a new understanding for management. Review Chapter 2 for a new and better way to structure and manage the enterprise using system science principles. Two principles from system science that help us measure and improve quality and productivity are the principles of recursion, and the system characteristics of self-organization and self-control. These two ideas change the way we think about management initiatives, and the way we implement them.

Recursion

Chapter 1 explains the idea of recursion. Every system is composed of subordinate-level systems and is itself a part of a higher-level system. The corporate viable, very complex, purposeful, probabilistic system is composed of lower-level systems, which are also composed of lower-level systems. And each of these systems, at all levels, can be modeled with the same viable system model. That's the idea of recursion. Chapter 2 develops the Viable System Model (VSM) as a useful model for the structure and management of a company. Chapter 3 presents examples.

A large corporation can be modeled with the VSM. At the first level of recursion, each of the corporation's system 1 business units, typically business groups, can also be modeled with the VSM. And at the second level of recursion each of the system 1 business units in the business groups can be modeled with the VSM. Recursions can be continued to the level of plants, departments, processes, and work groups. Recursion changes our view of the corporation from a hierarchy to something more like a network. Figure 7.1 illustrates this view of the corporation. It shows the VSM for a corporation, with three levels of recursion.

Figure 7.1 may look like a hierarchy. But it only shows recursions from Group 3 of the corporation's four groups. Visualize showing also the recursions from Groups 1, 2, and 4 in all directions from the corporate VSM. The further recursions in all directions from the companies, and businesses, and plants in all of these recursions will be a very large network. The expanded network may seem flat, two dimensional,

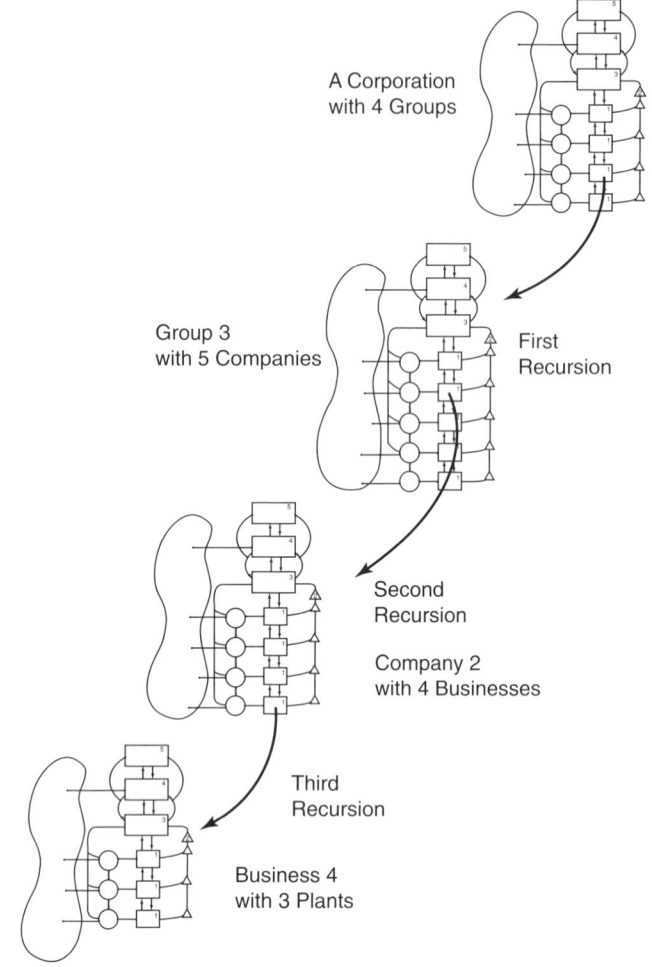

A Corporation
with 4 Groups

Group 3
with 5 Companies

First
Recursion

Second
Recursion

Company 2
with 4 Businesses

Third
Recursion

Business 4
with 3 Plants

Figure 7.1.   A corporate VSM showing three levels of recursion

being on a one-plane piece of paper. Visualize, however, the levels of recursion going in all directions. The network is a multi-axis network, more like a neural network.

Any business unit in this multi-axis network can trace a direct line of recursions to the corporate VSM. And the four information channels and their content tie together all the systems in this direct line. Looking more broadly, from the corporate perspective, there are similar direct lines between the corporate VSM and any VSM unit in the company. The direct lines are communication channels. The communication channels carry information. Information controls performance.

Jack Welch, the former chairman of the General Electric Company, chose "six sigma" as the company quality strategy. Thinking of GE in a VSM structure, six sigma information flowed throughout the company on the special communication channel, in all directions. Within each VSM, six sigma information is shared among the operating units on the system 1 communication channel. Those who use the VSM and system thinking have found that companies function as described by the VSM, whatever our present understanding may be. The principles of system science, the VSM, and system thinking are working in our companies whether or not we understand these principles. Knowing about the VSM we can use these principles more effectively. We can see that GE's corporate system 3 used the special communication channel and the system 1 communication channels very successfully in implementing six sigma.

For a quality initiative like six sigma everyone becomes involved. They will need training in six sigma technologies, and the disciplines in their use. In addition to the information flowing in the special communication channel, company people need both classroom training and "hands-on" experience. GE maintains excellent training and development courses at all levels from on-site to their management school at Crotonville, NY. Training and learning is an ongoing part of six sigma.

But it's not just the communication channels and the training and the "hands-on" experience that makes corporate initiatives effective in company operations. There must also be an organization capability.

Self-Organization and Self-Control

Using the VSM and system thinking, every profit-and-loss business in the company begins with its Resource Bargain, which includes business definition, boundaries, purpose, resources, and goals. The Resource Bargain is the business charter for the business unit, saying what it is and where it's going, and providing the resources to do it.

The Resource Bargain is not a corporate directive. It is more a venture agreement worked out between the top management of the business unit (systems 3, 4, and 5 of the business unit) and the system 3 management of the next higher level of recursion. With the Resource Bargain agreed on, the success of the business unit depends on the capability of the unit for self-organization and self-control.

The VSM and system thinking doesn't change the company. It changes the way we understand the company. It gives us new and better insights on what the company is and how it works. One of the important principles in system science is that viable systems are largely self-organizing and self-controlling. Typically, the people in any business unit have the intelligence and the experience to achieve successful operating results. When results are not satisfactory, or when results are good but better results are desired, often the quickest and most effective action is to discover and learn different and better methods. GE is a high-performance, high-quality company. The six sigma initiative was not undertaken to fix a problem. It was undertaken to make good performance better. The people in each business made the improvements. Six sigma gave them technology and methods to do it.

A study by the author of this book of 10 businesses that were having profit problems, found that the people in all of these businesses were capable enough, and had industry and company experience enough, to resolve the problems, but needed better methods to work with. They were well informed in conventional methods of cost accounting and profit measurement. They were not well informed in the methods and measures in all of the key performance areas, especially the methods and measures discussed in Chapter 6 (for improving sales revenue) and Chapter 11 for improving profitability. When they learned about these different and more useful methods, profitability improved.

Conventional methods for profit improvement say, "Cut costs!" Cutting cost $X = profit improvement $X. This sounds logical, but it doesn't work out that way. Very complex, probabilistic systems don't run on cause and effect. They run on intervention and consequences. There are many complex interrelationships. Cutting cost $X has various consequences throughout the organization, most of these never known. We can measure costs cut. But we can't measure profit improved, and we can't measure, or even recognize, most of the consequences. Many cost reduction programs reduce profit rather than improve profit.

Eliminate unprofitable products and transactions? Sounds logical. But two cautions: (1) The conventional methods for calculating the profitability of products and transactions produce precise figures completely unreliable for decision-making in a complex, probabilistic system. They are based on assumptions that don't match the characteristics of complex, probabilistic systems. (2) Few businesses succeed more by doing less.

A profit problem is not a financial problem. It's a system problem. The business, a complex, probabilistic system, creates and keeps customers. A requirement is to create and keep customers in ways that result in desired profitability. If that doesn't happen, system changes are needed. They are not financial changes, or changes induced from financial measures. They are operations changes. Creating and keeping customers. Quality and productivity. Innovation. Organization capability. Physical and financial resources. Change in some combination of these key performance areas will become the resolution.

When the people in these 10 businesses learned different and better ways of managing their operations to create and satisfy customers with profitable results, company profitability improved. The people in these companies had the capability. They only needed to learn some different and better methods. Different and better methods can be provided by management initiatives, communicated on the special communication channel and supported by training programs. In the 10 companies mentioned above, different and better methods and measures enabled management to resolve system problems that showed up as profit problems. For more information on profit problems, see Chapter 11.

The VSM and system thinking relies on the self-organizing and self-controlling capabilities of all the VSM business units at all levels of recursion throughout the company. Each of these VSM business units is a "black box" to higher-level management. Higher-level management has the requisite variety to design the system of black boxes so that each can control itself. Higher-level management can sponsor improvement initiatives, as GE did with six sigma; as was done in the 10 businesses referred to above. Only by relying on the self-organization and self-control capability of each VSM unit in the company can there be effective control and successful results throughout the company.

PRODUCTIVITY

The ways system science helps companies improve quality will also help companies improve productivity. In discussing quality this book refers readers to other sources for information on quality technologies. There's a huge amount of knowledge on the quality technologies, all well documented in publications authored by leading authorities. Successful companies target quality and productivity for continuous improvement.

Government statistics give us data on the productivity of industries, industry sectors, and the national economy. Information on the technologies for measuring and improving productivity on the shop floor is well-known and widely practiced. For other areas of company operations, methods for productivity measurement and improvement are less known, and less practiced. So in this book we will present some of the basics, and some management-level measures. The basics begin with the simple formula:

$$\text{Productivity} = \frac{\text{Output}}{\text{Inputs}}$$

Productivity: The efficiency of producing and delivering the company's products and services to customers

Outputs: Products and services produced by the company and delivered to customers satisfying their expectations

Inputs: The resources used to produce the outputs

Productivity improvement: Increase in the output/input ratio

In operations, at the plant level, many productivity measures are used, measuring a physical output in relation to a physical input. Examples include defect-free parts per labor hour, assemblies per shift, parts per hundred pounds of raw material, labor hours per engine assembly. Whenever we can measure both the output and the input in physical terms, we have good productivity measures that can be monitored for change and improvement. Continuous improvement does not come from working harder. Continuous improvement comes from improving the way work is done. And everyone can be involved in improving their work processes. Useful methods described in Chapter 8 include kaizen, function analysis system technique (FAST), TRIZ, the various methods of creative thinking, and of course, the methods of industrial engineering.

For producing products companies have productivity measures, and quality measures, at all stages of production. But in other areas of company operations companies usually do not have and do not use quality and productivity measures. For producing a budget, where is the productivity measure . . . or the quality measure? What is the productivity or quality measure for an appropriation request, an engineering project, a new plant, a sales campaign? Wherever in the company work is done, quality and productivity measures can help improve performance. For monthly closings and financial statements we do have a quality standard—zero defects, now reinforced by Sarbanes-Oxley. Productivity and quality goals and measures can help improve performance in all areas of company operations.

Understanding the company as a very complex, probabilistic system to create customers, we don't count output at the end of the assembly line. We count output at the end of the delivery line—output sold and delivered to customers and satisfying their needs and expectations. Company output rather than production line output is what counts. A viable, very complex, purposeful, probabilistic business system exists to produce an output that will successfully create and keep customers.

At the company level, productivity = quality. Within the company, in operations, we have different measures for each. Within the company we use quality technologies to improve productivity. At the company level productivity measures, in dollar terms, can be used to monitor operations performance and relationships that determine profitability and changes in profitability.

TOTAL PRODUCTIVITY

For total productivity measures we expand the basic formula to:

$$P = \frac{O}{L + K + M + E + PFC}$$

P = Productivity
O = Output satisfying customer needs and expectations
L = Labor input, all employment costs
K = Capital input that produced the output
M = Materials input used to produce the output
E = Energy input used to produce the output
PFC = Programmed fixed costs

The term "programmed fixed costs" is an accounting term for fixed costs that are not employment costs or capital costs. Programed fixed costs are costs decided on (programmed) by many people in the course of doing their work, and include such costs as travel expenses, telephone, office supplies, contract research, memberships, entertainment, consulting services, and postage and delivery services. These are the fixed costs in the accounting category of sales, general, and administrative costs that are not employment and capital costs.

The measure "total productivity" measures total output and the total of all inputs. Using this formula, we need a unit of measure that can be applied to all the outputs, and to each of the inputs. The only common measure for all of them is the monitory unit, in US, dollars. Constant dollars give the most reliable measure of productivity. But there can be problems in converting current dollars into constant dollars. There are judgment calls in determining deflators or reflators used to adjust current dollars to a base year. There can be changes in mix that affect comparisons between years. When the inflation rate is low, to simplify the calculations current dollars can be used, assuming that both outputs and inputs are about equally affected by price changes. Constant dollar calculations should be more accurate. But with low inflation current dollar calculations are faster, and may also be about as useful for identifying productivity change and trends.

In addition to total productivity, partial productivity measures can be calculated for each of the inputs and charted over time to show trends and changes in trends:

- Productivity of labor: $\dfrac{O}{L}$

- Productivity of capital: $\dfrac{O}{K}$

- Productivity of materials: $\dfrac{O}{M}$

- Productivity of energy: $\dfrac{O}{E}$

- Productivity of programmed fixed costs: $\dfrac{O}{PFC}$

Measures can be physical units where this is practical, constant dollars, or current dollars. At the levels where work is done, measures are typically in physical units, such as X units of output/Y hours of labor, or X units of output/Y Kwh (or, if more than one kind of energy is used, Btu.)

At the operating level, for materials input where there is one material, or one major material used in making a part or a product, units also work well, such as for a punch press, X units/Y pounds (or ft^2) of sheet metal. At a higher level where there are many materials that go into the products or there are many materials and many products, the measures can be in dollars.

There is general agreement on the above formulas. But in defining output, and defining inputs there are options.

Output

Output measures on the manufacturing floor are clear. It is the output from a machine, from a production cell, from a process or a stage of a process, from a team. And the typical measure is units. In other areas, defining outputs is not so clear. In finance and accounting there are outputs that can be measured—monthly closings, quarterly financial reports, budget reports, variance analysis, and many more. But what is the output of the legal department? Human resources? Corporate planning? Marketing? Environmental relations? Research and development? The office of the CEO?

In service businesses, developing output measures for the people providing the services to customers is similar to developing the measures in manufacturing. For administration in service businesses, output measures—as in manufacturing administration—are not obvious.

As described in Chapter 1, a viable, very complex, probabilistic system such as a corporation has a built-in tendency to maintain itself in its present state. For stability, in system terms homeostasis, there is a system tendency to function today as it did yesterday. And there are many homeostats in the system to assure this. But also the system has another built-in tendency for change, learning, evolution, creativity, improvement—heterostasis. And there are heterostats in the system to assure this. In successful corporations, strong in heterostats, defining outputs at the level of management will be an opportunity for learning, creativity, and change to something better.

Productivity in everything the company does, the continuous improvement in outout/imputs, is essential for business success. Continuous improvement in everything we do means improvement in all functions in systems 5, 4, 3, 2, and 1. And to measure productivity requires the definition of outputs. Output is the expected result from the function. Not easy to define in measurable terms. The kinds of things that are easy to count or measure usually are not what matters. We can count meetings, customer calls, training sessions, reports, proposals, briefs, audits, and documents of all kinds. But what matters is some kind of performance that contributes to the company's success in creating and keeping customers in ways profitable for the company.

Defining outputs is a job for all functions. Creative thinking helps. A market researcher sitting in on a product R&D meeting offered a suggestion on how to accomplish a certain function in the product. The engineering director responded, "Good idea; you just made an invention!" Creative thinkers ask questions like, "Why . . . ?" "How can we . . . ?" "What if . . . ?" They also ask, "What is the output, or the outputs, needed from this function to help the company achieve its purpose and goals?"

Thinking creatively will find an output that is a tangible, measurable result from work done or action taken. To measure productivity change, this output can be measured in relation to the inputs that produced the output. For example, in R&D, an output might be contribution margin on new product sales first three (or five) years in relation to the cost of R&D new product research three (or five) years previous, moving 3-year totals. For R&D on process improvement, a similar measure can be used—process benefit (cost reduction, greater output, faster cycle time) in relation to R&D process improvement expense. There's great opportunity for creatively defining outputs and measures for productivity improvement in all functions. Good definitions and measures motivate desired performance.

Labor Inputs

For productivity measures at the level of the total profit-center business, labor inputs are measured in dollars, the total compensation cost for all company people.

For total productivity measures in operations, labor inputs and all other inputs are in dollars. But in operations, partial productivity measures are most useful, and these can usually be measured in units— output per labor hour, output per unit of raw material, etc. When the output measure is in units, the labor input measure must also be in units. And the most useful unit measure of labor is labor hours. For manufacturing productivity measures on the shop floor where the work is done, both output and labor input will be measured in units. Measures aim to achieve and maintain the current standard of performance, and over time continuously improve. Industrial engineering technologies, R&D, and the quality technology of Kaizen are helpful methods for continuous improvement in labor productivity. Labor productivity improvement comes from process improvement—improving the way the work is done.

In areas outside of the manufacturing floor there will be cases where both output and labor inputs can be measured in units. But in many cases that may not be possible, or practical. Then, measures in dollars can be used. The human resources function has many outputs: employee benefits planning and administration, wage and salary planning and administration, recruiting, succession planning, separations, training, labor relations, contract negotiation and administration, community relations, and an important responsibility often neglected—developing organization capability and motivation.

To find useful measures of outputs and inputs requires creative thinking. Constant dollars with the base year periodically adjusted may be the most accurate measures. But in periods of low inflation, current dollars will provide useful measures. Productivity measures are neither right nor wrong. They are some degree of usefulness. They are useful when, measured consistently, they help us improve productivity.

In Human Resources we might begin with functions using the most person-hours of work. What is the output, or outputs? How can output be measured? In units? In dollars? How can person-hours or payroll costs be related to an output? Would an overall productivity measure of the function be more useful than productivity measures for individual outputs? Could there be a productivity measure for the entire group of HR functions, a productivity measure for the whole human resources group? HR may decide on "soft" productivity measures rather than quantified measures, a description of an output in relation to its cost. Working out productivity measures will lead to improvement in HR operations.

Capital Inputs

In manufacturing, at the level where the work is done, capital inputs can be expressed in units of machine hours. The capital productivity measure is number of parts or units per machine hour. At higher levels, output is more than a single item from a single machine, so we can not use measures in units. At the process, department, plant, or company level, capital inputs will be expressed in dollars. And in this calculation, there are choices. Data can be taken from the chart of accounts, but which accounts? And are the accounting numbers the best ones to use? For depreciation expense, for example, the original cost of a machine might be $100 K. We depreciate $100 K. But seven years later the replacement cost may be $170 K. What should the depreciation be? Figure 7.2 shows one recommended way to calculate capital inputs in dollars for an accounting period.

The method presented in Figure 7.2 includes an interest charge for capital employed. This interest rate is a bank type of interest rate, a normal cost of capital for the company. The rate should remain stable over time to avoid distorting the time series measures of capital costs. When it is appropriate to change the rate, the effect of this change should be noted in both the individual and the time series reports.

Item		How Measured
1. Working Capital:		
2. Cash	_____	Monthly average
3. Accounts Receivable	_____	Monthly average
4. Inventory	_____	Monthly average
5. Total Working Capital	_____	Total of lines 2, 3, and 4
6. Fixed Capital employed:	_____	All fixed capital employed, valued at replacement cost.
7. Total Capital:	_____	Total of lines 5 and 6
8. Normal Interest Charge on Total Capital	_____	A company-selected rate of return on capital X Total Capital (line 7)
9. Depreciation	_____	Straight-line depreciation of the replacement value (line 6)
10. Associated Capital Costs		
11. Property Taxes	_____	Property taxes paid or payable for the period
12. Insurance	_____	Property insurance costs paid or payable for the period
13. Maintenance	_____	Maintenance costs incurred for the period
14. Total Associated Capital Costs	_____	Total of lines 11, 12, and 13
15. Total Capital Costs	_____	Total of lines 8, 9, and 14

Figure 7.2   Management economics measures of capital costs

Figure 7.2 also includes higher valuations of fixed capital and depreciation than is reported in financial reports. The method calculates capital inputs using economics concepts rather than accounting concepts and is considered more realistic. This method is recommended for both total productivity measurement, and for the partial measure of capital productivity.

Materials Inputs

In manufacturing, at the level where work is done, unit measures are used wherever possible, always aiming for improvement in yield. At higher levels there will be some number of outputs, and some number also of materials used. So productivity measures will be in dollars. Constant dollars are best, using a recent base year updated every few years. Or in times of modest inflation, current dollar calculations can be useful. "Useful" means helpful in maintaining the highest level of productivity we have achieved, and not slipping back, and continuously improving from there.

Energy Inputs

Energy inputs are typically measured in units, kilowatt-hours for electricity, gallons or liters for oil or gasoline, cubic feet or Btu's for gas, Btu's for coal. For more than one kind of energy input, Btu's would be the measure. In operations that are major users of energy, such as chlorine production or aluminum production, unit measures in relation to units of output would be the productivity measure. For total productivity measures, the energy inputs would be converted into constant, or current, dollars.

Programmed Fixed Costs Inputs

Programmed fixed costs are the fixed cost inputs other than labor and capital. In the chart of accounts, programmed fixed costs are the line items in the expense accounts of sales, general, and administration functions except for employment costs and capital costs. Examples include advertising, purchased research, outside legal counsel, consulting fees, travel, entertainment, postage, telephone and telecommunications, vehicle expense, office supplies, dues and subscriptions, outside auditors, and contributions. Programmed fixed costs are classified as fixed cost because that is the way each of these costs is incurred. Each cost is incurred by someone's decision. They do not change in relation to level of output or level of sales revenue.

Monitoring Total Productivity

At the level where work is done the partial productivity measures of labor, capital, and materials are the most useful, using unit measures of output and input. Typically, measures of labor productivity, materials productivity, and capital productivity can be developed by work groups and their supervisors, and used within the group for productivity measurement and improvement. Within work groups, kaizen is a practical method for improvement. Kaizen involves everyone in finding better ways. Training in basic industrial engineering is also helpful.

At higher levels, with more outputs, and a greater number of inputs, total productivity measures and the partial productivity measures are calculated in monetary terms. Companies using productivity measures at these levels can check their measures against the above description. One common error is using a dollar term in the numerator for output and a unit term in the denominator for inputs, such as:

$$\text{Productivity} = \frac{\text{Sales revenue}}{\text{Number of employees}}$$

The same formula, with profit in the numerator, is another example. Management may like this kind of a measure because it has a natural bias toward improvement, resulting from inflation increases in the numerator. With inflation, even low inflation, sales revenue rises, and reported profit tends to increase. But the number of employees remains the same, unless changed by management decision. An improvement would be to change the denominator from "number of employees" to "total employee compensation." With this change we have the partial productivity measure for labor, in current dollars.

If your company does not use measures of total productivity, experiment. Prepare the measure for a profit-center business using annual figures. Prepare the measure for last year, and for two years ago. What is the difference? Make quarterly calculations over these two years and up to the present. What do you see? What useful information have you learned in preparing the measures? From this experience you can evaluate the usefulness of the total productivity measure for improving productivity. The aim is a productivity level equal to or better than the best competitors, and continuous improvement from there. Benchmarking is a good way to check productivity level.

TOTAL FACTOR PRODUCTIVITY

Total factor productivity uses "value added" as the output measure, instead of total output of goods and services, with labor and capital as the inputs. This is a useful productivity measure for a total profit-center business.

Value added is a measure of the value created by the company. The company's people using the company's capital resources create value for customers. The measure of value added is the difference between the cost paid to others for the materials, components, and supplies that go into the production of the company's products, and the sales revenue received from the sale of the products. Value added is a measure that management needs to pay attention to. But it's not required for financial reporting, so it typically goes unseen. The chart of accounts, however, does have the line items needed to calculate value added. The formula for Total Factor Productivity:

$$TFP = \frac{VA}{L+K}$$

TFP = Total factor productivity
VA = Value added
 L = Labor input
 K = Capital input

Labor input is calculated as total compensation paid to all employees, including the cost of benefits, social security contributions, worker comp, and any other employment costs. The estimated amounts of periodically paid incentive compensation and bonuses for the accounting period needs to be included in the labor input. Otherwise there is a distortion in the labor input for the period in which these amounts are paid.

Capital input can be calculated by the method shown in Figure 7.2, or by some variation of that method. The methods used for calculating VA, L, and K should be communicated along with the measures themselves. The point of productivity measures is to help all involved continuously improve productivity. So TFP like any productivity measure needs to be reported in a time series trend. Trend charts of VA, L, and K; and trend charts of total factor productivity and the partial measures VA/L and VA/K are more useful than tables of numbers. Both should be reported. The 3-month moving average is a practical and useful charting method.

The trends of VA, L, and K determine the trend of TFP, so improvement efforts concentrate on these three. How to improve? Here are some basic ways:

To increase VA: Increase sales with little or no increase in L and K
                 Improve mix
                 Reduce variable costs
                 Add high value-added components
                 Develop and market high value-added new products
                 Increase price
To reduce L: Eliminate error
                 Reduce rework
                 Reengineer work processes
                 Kaizen

To reduce K: Process reengineering
                 Improve capital productivity
                 Outsourcing (depending on effect on VA)

ECONOMIC PRODUCTIVITY

Economic productivity is a different and broadened kind of a total factor productivity measure. It measures the productivity of the profit-center business in creating economic success. It is an early-warning indicator of developing changes in profitability, before these changes show up in the P&L statement.

We are accustomed to "score card" kinds of measures used to evaluate performance. Developed originally at the corporate level for evaluating company performance, score card measures are often deployed to lower levels of the corporation. A job of management is to know and understand what happened. That's important. But the task of management is to create a desired future, next month, next quarter, next year, next many years. Measures can do more than evaluate past results. The right measures can help management, and everyone else, achieve desired results. Economic productivity, and the partial measures of the economic productivity of labor, capital, and programmed fixed costs, are these kinds of measures.

Requisite variety is essential for effective decisions. The variety in the controller (management) must equal the variety in what is being controlled and directed. Economic productivity and its partial measures help achieve requisite variety for managing the creation of value for customers.

The corporation, and each VSM profit-center business in the corporation, as specified in its Resource Bargain, is a structure of people and capital resources for the purpose of creating customers. Using purchased inputs, the company's people with the company's capital resources develop and produce the products and services sold to customers. The customer value produced by the company is the financial measure of value added (VA). Value added is the margin between sales revenue and the cost of the purchased inputs that went into those sales. Value added is a measure of what the company creates. How successfully the company, and each VSM profit-center business, creates value added is quantified in the measure of economic productivity (P$). Economic productivity can be measured monthly or quarterly. Monthly measures and 3-month moving averages of economic productivity measures help guide management decisions and actions toward the achievement of desired profitability.

Developing the Economic Productivity Measures

Each of the VSM businesses, coordinated and aligned with all others in support of company purpose through its Resource Bargain, can develop economic productivity measures to help them manage and direct their operations. Monitoring these measures enables and supports their self-control.

Economic productivity, P$, like all productivity measures, is a measure of output over input. The output measure is value added. The input measures are people costs (L), capital costs (K), and programmed fixed costs (PFC):

$$P\$ = \frac{VA}{L + K + PFC}$$

There are two methods for measuring value added:

Method 1. The conventional measure of value added includes all costs paid to outsiders as inputs to the production of the firm's products and services. So all of these costs—purchased materials, components, energy, supplies, and programmed fixed costs—are subtracted from sales revenue to calculate value added. This is the value added figure used in the total factor productivity measure described earlier in this chapter.

Method 2. This method includes programmed fixed costs as one of the firm's inputs in creating value added. This method includes all of the firm's fixed costs—L, K, and PFC—as the inputs that create the value added. This is the method used in calculating economic productivity. In measures of economic productivity, all fixed costs are constantly in the management spotlight, aiding in their control. Economic productivity also includes the partial measures:

Economic productivity of labor
Economic productivity of capital
Economic productivity of programmed fixed costs

The input measure for labor is the total compensation paid to all employees, including incentive compensation and bonuses, the cost of employee benefits, the cost of payroll taxes such as social security and workers' comp, and any other compensation costs.

Direct Labor, a Fixed Cost   Many textbooks, and much accounting practice, classifies direct labor as a variable cost. Management economics and economic productivity classify direct labor in almost all cases as a fixed cost. It's a fixed cost because it is changed by a management decision to increase or decrease the number of employees, or make changes in compensation. But direct labor can be a variable cost. For a landscape contractor who hires hourly labor for a particular job, that labor would be a variable cost for that job, increasing variable costs and reducing value added. The full compensation costs for the contractor and other employees would be a fixed labor cost.

Similarly, contract labor could be fixed or variable. Hired for the job, contract labor would best be classified as a variable cost of the job, increasing variable costs and reducing value added. Contract labor employed on a time basis makes it a fixed cost for that period increasing value added, but increasing also the input of labor cost.

Using accounting measure for decision support, management often outsources production to reduce labor costs and improve profitability. Labor costs can be reduced by management decision, but the effect on profitability is uncertain and can be anything from a plus to a minus. A very complex, probabilistic business does not run on cause and effect. It runs on interventions and consequences. Accounting is not a very reliable guide for evaluating very "iffy" consequences. Cost reduction of $X will not increase profit by $X, and may even reduce profit. In considering cost reductions it is unwise to think: Cost reduction = Profit improvement. Other metrics can be much more helpful, such as the measures of management economics (Chapter 11) and the productivity measure of economic productivity.

Outsourcing reduces labor cost, but how much will total labor cost be reduced? After outsourcing, for most companies most of the fixed labor cost still remains. Most companies will still have more than 90% of their fixed labor costs. The percentage will vary by company. The cost saving per labor hour may be significant, but there are other considerations. In today's lean, high-tech manufacturing plants, direct labor will likely be less than 5% of total labor costs. Total labor input includes all compensation and employment costs for all employees including top management, all managers, all professionals, everyone.

Among other considerations, outsourcing very likely will increase variable costs. The total cost of the outsourced product becomes a variable cost. Increasing variable costs reduces value added. When making outsourcing decisions it is wise to evaluate the probable consequences on value added, using the measures of economic productivity. Value added is where the dollars come from to pay fixed costs and earn operating income. In addition to evaluating the effect of outsourcing on value added, if the outsourcing is to another country there are other important considerations, the now and probable future:

- Relative shipping costs
- Relative delivery time
- Reliability
- Security
- Political situation in the supplier country
- Social situation in the supplier country

Capital Cost Inputs   Capital inputs can be calculated by the method illustrated in Figure 7.2, or some variation of that method. Whatever the method used, each calculation needs to be made in the same way. Economic productivity uses economic measures of capital costs that are different from the accounting measures, and more realistic.

Accounting treats capital as a stock. For productivity measures we need to consider capital as a flow, how much capital input went into the creation of the value added. See Figure 7.2.

Programmed Fixed Costs Inputs   Programmed fixed costs inputs can be selected from the company's chart of accounts. They will be the sales, general, and administrative costs other than those included in labor and capital inputs.

Partial Economic Productivity Measures

The partial measures of economic productivity are three:

1. Economic productivity of labor, P$(L)
2. Economic productivity of capital, P$(K)
3. Economic productivity of programmed fixed costs, P$(PFC)

The formulas are:

$$P\$(L) = \frac{VA}{L}$$

$$P\$(K) = \frac{VA}{K}$$

$$P\$(PFC) = \frac{VA}{PFC}$$

Economic productivity measures, and the partial measures, are calculated in current prices and costs. Company financial reports and company profitability are measured in current prices and costs. Companies work with current prices and costs, aiming toward specified objectives expressed in current dollars. Economic productivity also uses current prices and costs to help management and all decision-makers achieve targeted financial objectives. The company has to be productive in achieving these objectives whatever the changes toward inflation or deflation.

Economic productivity measures are easy to calculate for any profit-center business. Trends and changes in trends will show if the economic health of the enterprise is improving, weakening, or staying about the same. Problems developing will be seen long before they show up in financial reporting. When the trend measures show a developing profit problem, the measures of economic productivity, and the partial measures, provide information on the kinds of actions needed. Economic productivity measures are early warning indicators of changes in profitability, providing also information for decisions on corrective actions.

Economic productivity can be monitored monthly or quarterly. Figure 7.3 shows a format developed by a medium-size manufacturing company for monthly reporting.

Economic productivity and the partial measures of the economic productivity of labor, capital, and programmed fixed costs can be reported in data, and in 3- month moving averages time series charts showing trends and changes in trends. Best use of the measures and trends is in creative/dialog sessions of professionals and managers knowledgable about operations and environmental influences. Continuous monitoring and evaluation determines actions as needed to achieve desired performance.

How to Improve Economic Productivity

Economic productivity can be improved by increasing value added in relation to inputs, or by reducing the inputs of people costs, capital costs, and programmed fixed costs in relation to value added. Increasing value added in relation to inputs requires knowledge of product and transaction economics. "Standard" or "full-cost" data are not relevant. Operations and marketing people need to know the current variable costs for each product and transaction, and the selling price. The difference between variable cost and selling price is contribution margin (CM). Contribution margin can be measured in dollars (CM$)

	Jan	Feb	Mar	Apr	May	etc.
Sales Revenue						

Costs paid to outsiders
  Material
  Supplies
  Parts and sub-assemblies
  Goods purchased for resale
  Utilities						

Value added						
Value added percent						
People costs (L)						
P$(L)						
Capital Costs (K)						
P$(K)						
Programmed fixed costs (PFC)						
P$(PFC)						
Total of L, K, PFC						
P$						
Indexes (base year = 100) P$						
P$(L)						
P$(K)						
P$(PFC)						

Figure 7.3   Monthly reporting of economic productivity

and in percent of sales price (CM%). Contribution margin is value added.

Reducing the cost of inputs in relation to value added is less eliminating people and capital, and more using these resources wisely. An important part of the wise use of human resources is to rely on their capability for self-organization and self-control. With the VSM, system thinking, and the right management technologies for quality and productivity and the other key performance areas, the people themselves will resolve any problems with value added or cost of inputs. Useful improvement actions include the following:

Increasing value added in relation to inputs:
- Determine the target for average CM% needed to achieve profit objective
- Maintain data on CM% for products and transactions
- For low CM% products look for opportunities to reduce variable costs or raise price

- Find opportunities to sell more high CM% products to Improve mix to higher CM% transactions
- For product development set CM% targets for new products
- Include CM$ and CM% targets in budget objectives and incentive compensation plans

Reduce people costs in relation to value added:
- Reengineer business processes
- Use lean manufacturing and lean operations technologies

Reduce capital costs in relation to value added
- Use lean manufacturing and operations technologies
- Reduce working capital:
  > Reduce inventory by learning and applying just-in-time methods
  > Reduce accounts receivable by actions to reduce days sales outstanding
- Increase use of other companies' capital
- More "virtual" operations
- Develop strategic partnerships and alliances
- Increase sub-contracting (depending on effect on value added)

Reduce programmed fixed costs in relation to value added
- Use up-to-date project management technologies
- Establish performance measures for advertising and promotion
- Set targets for individual PFC accounts

Developing economic productivity measures for a profit-center business is not difficult and can be done quickly. All the data needed are in the chart of accounts. But the data are used in a new way, and the information provided can be a revelation! Typically, the measures will provide a view, unseen before, that will lead to decisions and actions of great benefit to the economic health of the enterprise. The information can help decision-makers keep the organization lean and responsive in times of prosperity, and effectively cope with changes in the economic landscape.

In any company, or any profit-center business in the company, the usefulness of economic productivity measures can be evaluated by making the calculations for the current year-to-date, for last year, and for two years ago. Where data are not available in the accounting record they can usually be approximated accurately enough. Calculate also the partial measures for the economic productivity of labor, capital, and programmed fixed costs for these same periods.

Usually the measures of economic productivity provide information about the business that is new and different from what was known before. Whatever that information is, it can help decision-makers strengthen the economic health of the enterprise. Used over time, the measures can help them improve both short-term and long-term profitability.

ONE COMPANY'S EXPERIENCE WITH ECONOMIC PRODUCTIVITY

Figure 7.4 shows economic productivity data for a capital-intensive division of a large corporation. The data summarized in Figure 7.4 are calculated as explained in the following paragraphs:

Output. Sales revenue received for products and services sold.

Purchases. These are the variable costs of production, paid to outside sources for the materials, components, subassemblies, supplies, resale items, and energy used in producing and distributing the products and services sold. Energy used for heating, lighting, and air conditioning or for any purpose other than an input to production is not a variable cost, but is included as a programmed fixed cost. Technically, purchases should be valued as of the time of sale (replenishment cost) since the proceeds from the sale of products and services must provide for their replenishment. However, unless inflation (or deflation) rates are high, or production cycles long, valuation as reported in the accounting record will provide

	Year 1		Year 3		Year 5	
	$	Index	$	Index	$	Index
Output	173,614	100	201,184	116	219,874	127
Purchases	88,761	100	106,668	120	118,620	134
Value Added (VA)	84,853	100	94,516	111	101,254	119
Labor Cost (L)	18,714	100	23,736	127	32,514	174
Capital Cost (K)	32,243	100	39,663	123	54,741	170
Programmed Fixed Cost (PFC)	9,550	100	11,308	118	14,380	151
L + K + PFC	60,507	100	74,707	123	101,635	168
Economic Profit	24,346		19,809		(381)	

Figure 7.4   Economic productivity data, Division M

adequately useful information, and will greatly simplify the calculation. LIFO valuation, being closer to replenishment cost, was used in this study.

Value added (VA). Value added is the difference between sales revenue and the variable costs of the products sold. This is the value that was created by the company. This amount must pay all fixed costs with the remainder, if any, being operating income. Or, if not enough to pay all fixed costs, the difference is an operating loss. With all fixed costs in the denominator, in monitoring the measures of economic productivity we see the level and the trend of:

· Contribution margin
· Fixed costs
· Operating income

Labor cost (L). Labor includes total people costs for all employees, including wages, salaries, incentive compensation, bonuses, benefits, and employment taxes. Data as reported in the accounting record, rather than replenishment cost, is usually the appropriate measure and was used in this study. Total people costs are the costs of the human talent that created the value added.

Capital cost (K). Capital cost is the cost of the capital inputs used in producing the value added. Various methods can be used in calculating the cost of capital inputs. From the view of economics, using only the data as reported in the chart of accounts undervalues the real capital input. For example, it is wise to adjust for inflation in calculating depreciation cost. If we don't revalue assets, we under-allow for depreciation and over time liquidate our fixed capital resources. This study used the method shown in Figure 7.2 to calculate capital input.

Programmed fixed costs (PFC). These are the costs incurred for sales, general, and administrative expenses such as advertising, promotion, travel, entertainment, telephone and telecommunications, office supplies, postage and delivery services, and professional services. All the sales, general, and administrative accounts that are not people costs or capital costs are included in programmed fixed costs. L, K, and PFC include all company fixed costs.

Examining the Data

Figure 7.4 summarizes economic productivity data. We see output rising more slowly than purchases, and value added therefore rising

	Year 1		Year 3		Year 5		Year 6	
	Ratio	Index	Ratio	Index	Ratio	Index	Ratio	Index
Economic productivity, P$	1.40	100	1.27	90	1.00	71	0.83	59
Economic productivity of labor, P$(L)	4.53	100	3.98	88	3.11	69	2.85	63
Economic productivity of capital, P$(K)	2.63	100	2.38	91	1.85	70	1.47	56
Economic productivity of programmed fixed costs P$(PFC)	8.89	100	8.36	94	7.04	79	6.31	71

Figure 7.5   Economic productivity measures, Division M

more slowly than output. While value added is rising slowly in relation to output, the inputs of people costs, capital costs, programmed fixed costs, and the total of all three, are rising rapidly in relation to output. Figure 7.5 summarizes the economic productivity measures calculated using the data shown in Figure 7.4.

In Figure 7.5 we see P$ declining from 100 in the base year to 90 in year 3 and to 71 in year 5. At the time this study was made, the budget for year 6 was being prepared, so P$ was calculated from the proposed budget figures. The result showed a further decline to 59.

Partial measures were also developed. The economic productivity of labor, P$(L), declined from 100 in the base year to 88 in year 3, to 69 in year 5, and to 63 in the proposed budget for year 6. The economic productivity of capital, P$(K), declined from 100 in the base year to 91 in year 3, to 70 in year 5, and to 56 in the proposed budget for year 6. The economic productivity of programmed fixed costs, P$(PFC), also showed a sharp declining trend.

Actions Taken, and Results

None of this information—this view of performance and trends—was previously known. The data were in the accounting records, but the information was not in the accounting records. The data in Figure 7.4 show Value Added in year 5 slightly less than the amount needed to pay all fixed costs (people costs, capital costs, and programmed fixed costs). However, financial reporting continued to show profit because of lower charges for capital in the accounting record. But profitability was not satisfactory, which motivated this special study. If economic productivity measures had been available from year 1, management would have had more than two years of reliable early warning that a profit problem was developing. If the division had relied on the conventional budget process in year 6, the profit problem would have grown worse.

From consideration of the measures of P$ and the partial measures, and with broad participation, strategies were changed and new and different objectives established. People recognized the profit problem and the reasons for it, and what they could do to improve performance. They analyzed product and transaction value added. For products, value added is contribution margin, the difference between product variable costs and selling price. Contribution margin can be measured in dollars (CM$), and as a percent of selling price (CM%). They successfully increased product CM% by finding opportunities to reduce variable cost, and opportunities to increase selling price. They found opportunities to increase sales of high CM% products. They set CM targets for new product development. They identified and concentrated on target customers and target prospects. They made CM$ a part of the company's incentive compensation plan for sales people. Within a few months the downward trends in economic productivity, and in profitability, began to improve.

OUTCOMES [1]

Asbestos, a mineral product used for more than a hundred years for insulation and fire protection was discovered to be a health problem for people exposed to airborne particles. Litigation, as of 2005, has led to the bankruptcy of 67 companies and taken $54 billion from asbestos companies in fines and awards. A leaking hazardous waste dump in Niagara Falls led to litigation and remediation costs for a major chemical company. The invention of nylon created a new and better material for women's hosiery, and led to a huge new business in textiles and high-performance plastics. Enron's aggressive accounting, bogus asset sales, and special entities that created wealth on paper and income for selected investors reported profit in the company's income statements that wasn't really there, and led to the company's collapse in bankruptcy.

Business management is not only the management of company operations to produce desired performance results for the next accounting period. Equally important is the management of company operations to increase the pluses and reduce the minuses in the longer-term outcomes from everything the company is and does. Actions today cause consequences tomorrow. We need to think ahead and act today on our responses to the following questions:

- What outcomes may result from company products and services over their life cycles?
- What could be longer-term outcomes from what the company is and what the company is doing?
- What might be outcomes from the actions of employees?
- How will the company's present activities gain or lose from changes in the external environment?

Outcomes can be plusses, from additional revenue to transformation, and they can be minuses, from additional costs to bankruptcy. Management must manage today for outcomes tomorrow, to increase the plusses, and minimize the minuses. In management we need to think of two O's in the numerator of the productivity formula:

$$\text{Productivity} = \frac{\text{Outputs} + \text{Outcomes}}{\text{Inputs}}$$

Outcomes Add to or Subtract from Company Success

A company that must clean up toxic waste or remediate a landscape is paying a cost for an outcome that could have been prevented if it had acting differently, earlier. If use of the company's products over their lifetimes proves dangerous or injurious to health, the consequences for the company are outcomes. The costs of writing off inventory and unneeded capital equipment are outcomes. Gains or losses on the sale of a company business or other asset is an outcome. Failure over time to continually adjust to or take advantage of changing conditions can result in "restructuring," a costly outcome. Hiding profit reality with fraudulent accounting can be fatal.

Currently, company income statements often report income "after items." The company might have really lost 60 cents a share last quarter, but reports a profit of 40 cents a share "after items." Checking the footnotes, it turns out these items were: (1) writing off an unneeded plant built earlier during a boom period, (2) legal costs incurred in several non-recurring lawsuits, (3) writing off goodwill associated with an acquired business that no longer fits with the company's strategy, and (4) several severance settlements with departing executives. Not including these "items" the company made 40 cents a share. All four of these non-recurring items are outcomes from previous management actions that the right actions then could have minimized or prevented. In their decisions and actions, managers at all levels of recursion as they focus on today's operations, need also to be aware of potential outcomes, to optimize the plusses and minimize or eliminate the minuses.

Outcomes that can be pluses include:

- Proliferation of new products from proprietary new technology. From GE's discovery of polycarbonate resins, the company launched Lexan, the first product in what became the world's number one business in engineering plastics.
- Proliferating a company's specialized technology into new products and markets. Corning specializes in glass technology, from dinnerware to optical fiber. When the boom in optical fiber collapsed, corning regained volume with the growing demand for flat screen TVs and computer monitors.
- New uses for company products and technology. DuPont discovered nylon, a new material replacing silk for women's hosiery. What began in the 1940s as a replacement for silk in hosiery, grew in many formulations for countless fabrics and textiles, and for plastic materials for engineering and specialty applications.
- Expanding the use of new, better, lower-cost processes. Nucor, beginning as a minimill using a new process to produce steel grew to become the largest steel producer in the United States.
- Proliferating from a key invention in what will become a major new industry. From the invention of the operating system for IBM's first personal computer, a tiny Microsoft grew to become the number one software company, making its founder the world's richest man.
- Recovery and recycling as a business opportunity. Waste Management, by recycling or properly disposing of other people's trash created a profitable business and improved the environmental consequences of waste disposal.
- Gains on spin-off of non-strategic subsidiaries to stronger hands.

Outcomes that can be minuses include:

- New technologies competing with the company's products or ways of doing business, such as the proliferation of plastics materials

tailored for packaging applications, a minus outcome for makers of paper and metal packaging; a plus outcome for plastics.
· The need to remediate environmental contamination caused by the use or disposal of company products.
· Litigation resulting from company actions or the use of company products, including: product liability, class actions, legal costs of government investigations of company practices and fines imposed, OSHA and EEOC charges and fines.
· Costs of writing off unsold products and unneeded capital equipment.
· Customer claims.
· Losses on the sale of company businesses or capital assets.
· Restructuring costs.
· Aggressive accounting and financial arrangements inflating sales and profit, and later leading to costly restatements.

Ethical violations are a special consideration. Large organizations strive to earn and maintain a reputation for ethical behavior. The consequences from any unethical actions can be much more than bad publicity and fines levied. There can be negative effects on customers, and on employees. VSM companies will have a corporate parameter on ethical behavior, with its communication channels and audit capability helping to assure company-wide acceptance and ethical behavior. The special communication channel will be very sensitive to any questionable transactions or directives when they first appear so that immediate corrective actions can be taken.

In addition to aggressive accounting, executive pay and perquisites is one of the areas of ethical grayness. Pay-for-performance plans, that reward performance that is real and better than the norm, can make this area more rational through wise selection of performance measures including measures of outcomes.

A Productivity Measure for Outcomes

For a productivity measure for outcomes, we modify the formula for economic productivity (P$) to cover a longer term, and to include the plusses and minuses from outcomes:

$$LGP\$ = \frac{LCVA + LCVAO}{LCL + LCK + LCPFC + LCCO}$$

LCP$ = Life cycle economic productivity

LCVA = Life cycle value added. The value added from the life cycle sales of the company's products and services (sales revenue minus the variable costs incurred to produce the products and services sold)

LCVAO = Life cycle value added from positive outcomes. The value added in revenue and other funds received from beneficial outcomes over the life cycle (total receipts minus variable costs incurred)

LCL = Life cycle labor costs. The life cycle compensation costs for all employees

LCK = Life cycle capital cost. Life cycle capital costs, calculated as shown in Figure 7.2 or some variation of this method

LCPFC = Life cycle programmed fixed costs

LCCO = Life cycle cost of negative outcomes. The life cycle costs of negative outcomes such as those listed above

For practical use of this formula for a productivity measure for outcomes, select a life-cycle time period that is a reasonable time frame for examining sales revenue, input costs, and outcomes. This will be a judgment call for the company. Three years would probably be a minimum, or maybe five years, or seven. For the time frame selected, calculate the measures and monitor trend. If a three-year time frame is selected, calculate the measures for the last four or five years. As of the end of the third year, begin plotting 3-year moving averages continuing the 3-year moving average with each annual calculation. For past years, data may not be available, but numbers can probably be approximated.

Making the calculations will focus interest on outcomes, and interest in outcomes will bring outcomes to the table whenever decisions are made. What we learn in making the calculations is probably what matters most. Trends in the slowly moving trend chart will not be as useful as the trend charts suggested in Chapters 5 and 11. But preparing the measures can be very useful. What is learned will add a new dimension to operating management—a continuous awareness and thinking ahead of possible outcomes. This awareness and thinking ahead can avoid or minimize harmful outcomes, and can perhaps also expand the favorable outcomes. Actions today can maximize the positive outcomes, and minimize or prevent the negative outcomes. From experience, continuously improve the measurement method, and the use of information learned.

Awareness of outcomes is increasing. The more egregious outcomes are reported in news reports. In thinking about measuring and managing outcomes, a good start is to review the outcomes the company has experienced recently. At the same time, survey the environment to learn about outcomes experienced by other companies. Begin measuring and monitoring outcomes. This process begins a continuous awareness of possible outcomes in all the company is and does. An awareness of possible outcomes will be on the table whenever decisions are made. And decision-makers will continually search for projects, programs, and actions desirable now, and also with potential for favorable outcomes.

A good way to think about outcomes, and act today to increase the favorable and minimize the unfavorable, is to make outcomes a part of key management processes, including:

- Developing the company's vision, mission, or business definition
- Developing plans and budgets
- Developing financial statements

Working in each of these processes, think about answers to four questions:

1. What outcomes may result that can benefit our company?
2. What outcomes may result that can make our company a leader?
3. What outcomes may result that can damage our company?
4. What outcomes may result that could kill our company?

Then make changes to emphasize the positive, minimize the negative, and eliminate any possibility of an outcome that can kill the company. Managing for outcomes is part of managing for success.

OVERVIEW: THE ESSENCE OF CHAPTER 7

With the evolution of quality measurement and improvement and the evolution of productivity measurement and improvement, both quality and productivity have evolved to the same end-result definition:

The production and delivery of company products and services to customers without error and without waste and satisfying customers' needs and expectations, and continuous improvement in this process.

While the end result is the same, the measures in operations are different. Quality measures focus on the attributes of products, services, and processes to assure they meet desired specifications. Productivity measures focus on the efficiency of producing a desired result. The end result of high quality and high productivity is the definition cited above.

Three of the system science principles embedded in the Viable System Model (VSM) help companies achieve high quality and high productivity:

1. Recursion. Every system is comprised of sub-systems and is itself part of a larger system. The corporation as a VSM is itself comprised of eight or fewer subsystems that are also modeled with the VSM. Each of these major subsystem VSMs is also comprised of subsystems modeled with the VSM. And so on through additional levels of recursion. All have the same system structure and system characteristics. In each, the different and better management principles from system science improve performance.

Instead of a hierarchy, the corporation is a web of VSM business units all with the same characteristics, the same functions, the same capabilities for their areas of operations. This structure empowers people throughout the company to do what needs to be done for the success of their business unit. High quality and high productivity are a part of that success.

2. Self-organization and self-control. All viable systems have a capability for self-organization and self-control. In the corporate network of business systems, each has the capability for self-organization and self-control for achieving desired performance in all seven key performance areas, including quality and productivity.

3. Requisite variety. The cybernetics in the VSM tells us that for effective control, the variety in the controller (management) must be equivalent to the variety in what is being controlled (operations and the consequences from environmental change). This challenging requirement can be achieved with the VSM structure of recursions and the self-organization and self-control at each level of recursion.

Quality measures and technologies are thoroughly reported in the literature and not included in this chapter. World-class quality today is the technologies, measures, and methods of "lean operations," all derived from total quality control and the Toyota production system.

In operations, at the plant level, many productivity measures are used, measuring a physical output in relation to a physical input. Examples include defect-free parts per worker-hour, assemblies per shift, parts per hundred pounds of raw material, labor hours per engine assembly. Whenever output and input can both be measured in physical terms, good productivity measures can be monitored for change and improvement.

Higher levels, however, can't construct such simple productivity measures. There are many different outputs and many different inputs. The only common measure is dollars. This chapter offers four productivity measures useful at the level of a profit center business.

1. Total productivity. The formula for total productivity measures all outputs and all inputs:

$$P = \frac{O}{L + K + M + E + PFC}$$

P = Productivity
O = Output satisfying customer expectations
L = Labor input, all company employment costs
K = Capital input that produced the output
M = Materials and parts input used to produce the output
E = Energy input used to produce the output
PFC = Programmed fixed costs for the period

Total productivity measures total output and the total of all inputs. Using this formula requires a unit of measure that can be applied to all the outputs, and to each of the inputs. The only common measure for all of them is the monitory unit; in the US, dollars. Constant dollars give the most reliable measure of productivity. But there can be problems in converting current dollars into constant dollars. There are judgment calls in determining deflators or inflators used to adjust current dollars to a base year. There can be changes in mix that affect comparisons between years. If inflation rate is low, measures in current dollars can be useful, and much easier to calculate. Very likely both outputs and inputs will be similarly affected by inflation. Constant dollar calculations should be more accurate. But current dollar calculations are faster, and may also be about as useful for identifying productivity change and trends.

2. Total factor productivity. Total factor productivity uses value added as the output measure, with labor and capital as the inputs. This is a useful productivity measure for a total profit-center business.

Value added is a measure of the value created by the company. Value added is sales revenue minus the cost of purchased materials, components, and supplies that went into the production of the products and services sold. The company's people using the company's capital resources create the value added, also called contribution margin. Value added is not in the chart of accounts or the accounting system, so it typically goes unseen. The formula for Total Factor Productivity:

$$TFP = \frac{VA}{L+K}$$

TFP = Total factor productivity
VA = Value added
 L = Labor input
 K = Capital input

Labor input is calculated as total compensation paid or payable for the period to all employees, including benefits, social security contributions, worker's comp, and any other employment costs.

Capital input can be calculated by the method shown in Figure 7.2, or some variation of that method. TFP like any productivity measure needs to be reported in a time series trend. 3-month moving averages for TFP, and for the partial measures, VA/L and VA/K, are more useful than a table of numbers. Both time series charts and numbers should be reported.

3. Economic productivity. Economic productivity measures the productivity of the profit-center business in creating economic success. The output measure is value added. The input measures are people costs (L), capital costs (K), and programmed fixed costs (PFC):

$$P\$ = \frac{VA}{L+K+PFC}$$

Economic productivity (P$) includes programmed fixed costs as an input. This puts all fixed cost—L, K, and PFC—in the spotlight and improves control of these costs. In almost all cases direct labor is included in labor cost as a fixed cost. Only when direct labor is hired for the job is it a variable cost.

The three partial measures of economic productivity should also be monitored:

Economic productivity of labor, P$(L)
Economic productivity of capital, P$(K)
Economic productivity of programmed fixed costs, P$(PFC)

The formulas are:

$$P\$(L) = \frac{VA}{L}$$

$$P\$(K) = \frac{VA}{K}$$

$$P\$(PFC) = \frac{VA}{PFC}$$

Economic productivity measures, and the partial measures, are calculated in current prices and costs.

Economic productivity measures are easy to calculate for any profit-center business. Trends and changes in trends will show if the economic health of the enterprise is improving, weakening, or staying about the same. Economic productivity measures are early warning indicators of changes in profitability, providing also information for decisions on any needed corrective actions. The chapter suggests ways to improve economic productivity, and profitability.

4. Outcomes. Asbestos, a mineral product used for more than a hundred years for insulation and fire protection was discovered to be a health problem for people exposed to airborne particles. Litigation, as of 2005, has led to the bankruptcy of 67 companies and taken $54 billion from asbestos companies in fines and awards. The invention of nylon created a new and better material for women's hosiery, and led to a huge new business in textiles and high-performance plastics.

Business management is not only the management of company operations to produce desired results for the next accounting period. Equally important is the management of company operations to increase the pluses and reduce the minuses in the longer-term outcomes from everything the company is and does. Actions today cause consequences tomorrow. We need to think ahead and act today on our responses to the following questions:

- What outcomes may result from company products and services over their life cycles?
- What could be longer-term outcomes from what the company is and what the company is doing?
- What might be outcomes from the actions of employees?
- How will the company's present activities gain or lose from changes in the external environment?

Outcomes can be plusses, from additional revenue to transformation, and they can be minuses, from additional costs to bankruptcy. Management must manage today for outcomes tomorrow, to increase the plusses, and minimize the minuses. In management we need to think of two O's in the numerator of the productivity formula:

$$\text{Productivity} = \frac{\text{Outputs} + \text{Outcomes}}{\text{Inputs}}$$

Outcomes add to or subtract from company success. With awareness today of possible outcomes, present actions can increase favorable outcomes and reduce or eliminate the negative. When decisions are made it is wise to consider possible outcomes in the decision process.

NOTE

[1] Some of the material in this section was first reported in the article by William F. Christopher and Carl G. Thor, titled "Outcomes: Cost Management for Success Today, and Tomorrow." *Cost Management,* November–December, 2004. Used with permission.

Chapter 8

The Viable System Model and Innovation

Innovations in technology and in commercial concepts create new companies, and in existing companies create new revenue; new successes. For all companies, new and old, continuing innovation creates the company's future. Innovation produces new, different, better products and services; and new, different, better operations and management methods that will be needed for continuing success in a changing world. Without innovation, the company will have no future.

GOOGLE

In 2005, Google, with 5,680 employees (up 88% from 2004), recorded sales revenue of $6.1 billion (up 92.5%) and net income of $1.5 billion (up 267%). In 2005 Google, with its stock over $400, had a market valuation of $120 billion.

Ten years earlier, in 1995, there was no Google. The future founders, Larry Page and Sergey Brin, met that year as students on the Stanford University campus. By the end of that year they were collaborating on a new search engine called BackRub, named for its unique ability to analyze the "back links" pointing to a given web site. As word got around the campus, BackRub's reputation spread. Larry and Sergey

Holistic Management, by William Christopher
Copyright © 2007 John Wiley & Sons, Inc., Publication

bought a terabyte of disks and created their first data center in Larry's dorm room. After being unable to license their technology to the major portals of the day, they decided to start their own company. In September, 1998, Google, Inc., with the two partners and one employee, opened its door in a garage in Menlo Park, California; the company mission to "organize the world's information and make it universally accessible and useful."

Still in beta testing, the new Google, Inc. was answering 10 thousand queries a day. Google's reputation as the best search engine grew rapidly, helped by favorable reporting in the press. In 1999, in larger office space and with eight employees, Google was answering 3 million queries a day, and the beta label came off the web site. In 2005, only seven years after start-up, Google was handling more than 200 million queries a day, with more than five thousand employees providing cost-effective advertising, and a wide range of revenue-generating search services producing more than $6 billion in revenue.

Over its first seven years of life, Google, Inc. could also be called, Innovation, Inc. The company began with a technology innovation—a new, different, better search engine. In seven years Google became a huge and profitable company by continuing technical innovation, and by innovations in applying the technology in marketable products and services. Innovation created the company. Continuing innovation is creating its future.

UNDERSTANDING INNOVATION

Innovation begins with a discovery, an invention, a new method, an idea. There are many discoveries, many inventions, many new methods, many new ideas. But very few of these become innovations. Only those that become products or services that are different, better, and a greater value for customers can become a successful innovation. In 1956 General Electric research chemist, Dan Fox, discovered polyarylcarbonate resin. That was an invention. The innovation was the commercialization of polycarbonate resin as a thermoplastics molding material for engineering applications—the first of the "engineering plastics," now a multi-billion dollar business for GE.

In a successful company, decision-makers at all levels know that there is always a better way. They aim to discover and apply the better ways that will create the future of their company. Better products and services. Better ways of working. Changes needed to survive and succeed in the company's changing environments—commercial, technological, economic, social, political, educational, and ecological. For alert companies, environmental changes bring opportunities for innovation in the different products and services newly needed.

Innovation is a key performance area for any company intending to continue as a viable, very complex, purposeful, probabilistic system over changing times. Over the times ahead, companies will not remain viable—capable of living in their environment—without successful innovations. Environments change. Customer needs and wants change. Competitors change. Technology changes. Change happens in all of the company's environments, and this change can threaten and replace existing products, services, and methods. Adjusting to environmental change is not enough. Successful companies find opportunities in environmental change and discover, develop, and innovate products, services, and methods to satisfy changing needs.

In the technological environment, research expands human knowledge in all directions, faster, and faster. Whatever the company's technologies, new threats to existing products and methods and new opportunities for new, different, better products and methods continuously appear. Alert companies deal with the threats by discovering the opportunities that are right for them and innovating the new, different better.

Whole new areas of science and technology appear that change everything. Digital technology is one of these. We have had more than a decade of experience with digital innovations. The manuscript for this book was not prepared on a typewriter for an output of typed pages. It was prepared on a computer whose output will produce printed page proofs and then a printed book. Digital technology controls machines on the factory floor, machines on the road and in the sky, and appliances in the home. Letters travel to any destination in the world, instantaneously, by internet. Information on everything is instantly available anywhere. We can carry our telephone in our pocket, and it takes and sends pictures, sends text messages, calculates, and connects to the internet, too. Digital technology is new, and already changes much of what we do, with the pace of change accelerating.

Other new areas of science and technology are appearing that will change many things, in different ways. Nanotechnology, creating structures on a nano scale. Biotechnology, working with the basic elements of life. And what other new technologies will appear?

There is another new science that is not an area of science, but a total of science—system science and cybernetics. This new science discovers how things work and how they relate and interrelate: in the sciences, in the natural world from the nano to the cosmological, and in human society. System science can help us structure and manage a business enterprise. Also, system science can be especially useful in helping us deal with the growing ecological threat confronting all humanity.

In a business enterprise, at all levels of recursion, the technological environment is part of the VSM, with information flowing to and from. Threats are seen, early. Opportunities discovered. Many eyes and many minds in all levels of recursion see and learn much more that can the eyes and minds in only a few.

Changes in the ecological environmental bring increasing threats, threatening companies, and threatening also all humanity. Companies individually, and in collective efforts, are working to reduce harmful effects on the ecological environment resulting from their operations. In the early stages, government regulation was the driver. Now conserving the environment has become good business, satisfying public demand beyond the requirements of government regulations. Many companies are finding conservation more a contribution to profitability than an added cost. Process engineering can reduce energy consumptions. Recycling gets more value from raw materials. Waste reduction increases yields and improves efficiency. Changes in the ecological environment are not only threats; they also offer opportunity.

General Electric may not be using the VSM and system thinking, but in their "ecomagination" initiative the company is applying some VSM principles. The ecomagination initiative, announced in 2004, doubles the corporate R&D budget for energy and environmental technologies to $1.5 billion, aiming for annual revenue of $20 billion by the year 2010. At the time of the announcement, ecomagination included 17 technologies, some in the early stages of development. In system terms, the ecomagination strategy became a corporate parameter extending to all levels of recursion.

All GE operations search for and develop ecomagination products and services in their areas of operation. In energy operations, that means wind turbines, improved photovoltaic panels for producing electricity from sunlight, "H System" gas turbines that use new technology to produce more electricity per thousand cubic feet of gas, and gasification of coal for generating electricity. In aircraft engines it means the engine for the new Boeing 787 that uses 20% less fuel per seat mile. With ecomagination technologies, the company's own energy efficiency is targeted to improve by 30% over the next seven years. Energy use, instead of increasing 40%, will actually decline. Ecomagination technologies will also reduce the company's carbon emissions. Ecomagination innovations at all levels of recursions will lighten the ecological footprint of the company and the ecological footprints of the company's customers.

For all companies, changes in all the company's environments—technological, commercial, economic, political, social, educational and ecological—bring threats and opportunities. The VSM and system thinking help companies see the threats, and discover the opportunities. For information on maintaining viability in the company's changing environments, see Chapter 10.

Because of its importance and popularity, we see and hear, and read a lot about innovation. But the word seems to have several meanings. As used in this book, innovation does not mean new ideas, or inventions, or discoveries, or creativity, or a new approach, or something different. All of these are important. Innovation can not happen without them. They are the starting point for innovation. Innovation is the process of applying a new discovery, a new invention, or a new idea in a process, product, or service that is new, different, better, and very likely lower in cost than anything available before, and creating customers and users for the new, different, better. Innovation is not something new. Innovation is making something that is new, different, better, successful in application and use in the marketplace. The market determines what will be an innovation.

CONTINUOUS IMPROVEMENT

Innovation comes in more than one size. Little innovations produce "continuous improvement," continuing to do what we are doing in simpler, better, lower cost ways. Many small improvements over time become big change. Successful companies involve all their people in finding and implementing small improvements in their workplace. Hundreds and thousands of small improvements, in total, become big improvement and lower cost.

Japanese manufacturers pioneered methods for involving employees at all levels in continuous improvement. They called their methods, kaizen tien. The kaizen name is well known for continuous improvement, and practiced in many forms by Western companies. A team may use a kaizen blitz to attack a specific problem, and not stop until they have a solution working. But few companies apply the kaizen tien methods for involving all employees all the time in continuous improvement. While the term kaizen is well known, the term kaizen tien and the methods for involving all employees in continuous improvement is not well known. However, some Western companies are now using these methods, and reporting improved productivity and significant cost reductions. Kaizen tien is one of the Japanese technologies brought to the West by Norman Bodek who gave it the English name, "quick and easy kaizen," in his publications.

Quick and Easy Kaizen

Quick and easy kaizen revolutionizes the employee suggestion system traditionally used in the West. In the traditional Western suggestion system, employees are invited to submit suggestions. Suggestions are then reviewed by others to find any that have merit and would be worth adopting. For ideas implemented, the employee who submitted the idea might receive an award related in amount to the value of the idea. In practice, few suggestions are offered, and few of these adopted.

Quick and easy kaizen revolutionizes this traditional suggestion system. The employees, not management, run the suggestion system. And it is no longer a suggestion system; it is an improvement system. All employees are asked to submit ideas for improving the way their work is done. Ideas for improvement are a part of doing their jobs. And improvement ideas aren't just occasional; they are every month, and more than once a month. Employees don't just think about ideas. They think also about benefits. And they themselves implement their ideas.

It takes only a few minutes to write down an improvement idea, probably a little longer to estimate the cost saving if it's a cost saving idea. A kaizen memo might be written on the shop floor, in the office, or at the breakfast table at home; anywhere. Employees know well the work they do, and where there are opportunities for improvement. They welcome quick and easy kaizen, and typically offer one improvement suggestion a month, or more. Figure 8.1 illustrates a typical quick and easy kaizen suggestion form, as filled in by an employee in a manufacturing company.

When employees write their ideas on the idea form, they give a copy of the form to their supervisor. The supervisor reviews all ideas the same day they are received, and discusses each of them with the employee who submitted the idea. Unless it is decided not to implement the idea, the idea will be implemented by the person who submitted it, with involvement of others, if appropriate. Idea forms are often posted

```
┌─────────────────────────────────────────────────────────────┐
│              QUICK AND EASY KAIZEN IDEA MEMO                  │
│  NAME: Tom Barrett                                           │
│                                                              │
│  TEAM: 116        SHIFT: 1st          DATE:   9/14/05        │
│                                                              │
│  IDEA: Replace drill and eliminate .75 diameter spot drill   │
│        from program. Replace with drill/chamfer              │
│        combination drill.                                    │
│        Savings, see attached sheet                           │
│        save $11.396 per year                                 │
│                                                              │
│                                                              │
│                                                              │
│   ☑ SELF–IMPLEMENTED    ☐ NEEDS REVIEW                       │
│  IDEA IMPROVES:                                              │
│    ☐ SAFETY ☑ QUALITY  ☑ THROUGH  ☐ CUSTOMER ☑ COST         │
│                          PUT        SERVICE     SAVING       │
└─────────────────────────────────────────────────────────────┘
```

Figure 8.1 Typical quick and easy kaizen idea (Source: Bunji Tozawa and Norman Bodek, *The Idea Generator: Quick and Easy Kaizen*, PCS Press, 2001)

for a time so that others may also benefit from the idea. Sharing is an important part of quick and easy kaizen. When an idea involves another department, the supervisor will see that the person suggesting the idea gets together with the appropriate person in the other department for acceptance and implementation.

Quick and easy kaizen works. In the early 1990s Woody Morcott, CEO of Dana Corporation, asked each of Dana's 80,000 employees to submit two creative ideas per month in writing, and to implement 80% of them. For over 10 years Dana's employees have been submitting some 2 million improvement ideas a year with about 80% of them implemented.

Technicolor used a conventional suggestion system. In 2001, 1,800 employees submitted 250 ideas with 113 implemented. Then the company learned about quick and easy kaizen, and began to use it. Three years later the company implemented more than 10,000 ideas from the same number of employees resulting in a much happier workplace and reducing costs by more than $10 million [1].

With quick and easy kaizen, management asks employees at all levels to offer their ideas for improving the way their work is done.

Ideas become a part of every job. And the ideas are implemented where the work is done, by those who submitted the ideas.

"Participation" and "involvement" and "empowerment" are just words, hard to make real in a top-down administrative hierarchy. It's hard to order participation, involvement, and empowerment. These words don't fit a structure of top-down control. But, sponsored by top management, quick and easy kaizen is a way to make participation, involvement, and empowerment work for continuous improvement.

In all recursions of the VSM, the VSM designs participation, involvement, and empowerment into the way work is done. People in operations work in "black boxes," unknown and not entered by higher level management. The black boxes, each a viable, very complex, purposeful, probabilistic system, controls itself. Self-organization and self-control *is* empowerment, and requires participation and involvement.

Quick and easy kaizen thrives in a VSM environment. Quick and easy kaizen involves everyone; all participate; all are empowered to implement their ideas. A corporate parameter can make quick and easy kaizen part of the way the company works. At all levels of recursion, the employees themselves run the system. Employees themselves implement their ideas.

Companies with conventional employee suggestion systems get employee suggestions by the dozens. When companies use the methods of quick and easy kaizen, within two years they can be getting suggestions by the hundreds and thousands, with three-quarters or more of these suggestions implemented, improving performance, reducing costs.

Value Analysis Tear-Down

Value analysis tear-down is a new technology for the continuous improvement of products, processes, and services. Yoshihiko Sato pioneered value analysis tear-down in Japan. The value analysis tear-down technology combines the conventional tear-down process with value analysis technology. Using this technology, work teams in manufacturing companies redesign and improve the company's products by examining needed functions and discovering better ways to provide those functions. Within a few years, value analysis tear-down was adopted by all 11 of Japan's automobile manufacturers, and by many other Japanese manufacturing companies. The value analysis tear-down technology is now used also in service and other industries wherever there are physical elements to be improved or invented.

The value analysis tear-down process begins with evaluation of the best of competitive products and also the company's products. The process examines functions performed and functions desired by customers and how the product and the individual components of the product provide these functions. The value analysis process then uses value analysis techniques in searching for different, better, lower cost ways for producing and delivering desired functions. To get a range of knowledge and experience involved in the process, value analysis tear-down teams are made up of individuals from different disciplines. The process also provides for review and inputs from others. Figure 8.2 shows how value analysis tear-down is used for product improvement and innovation.

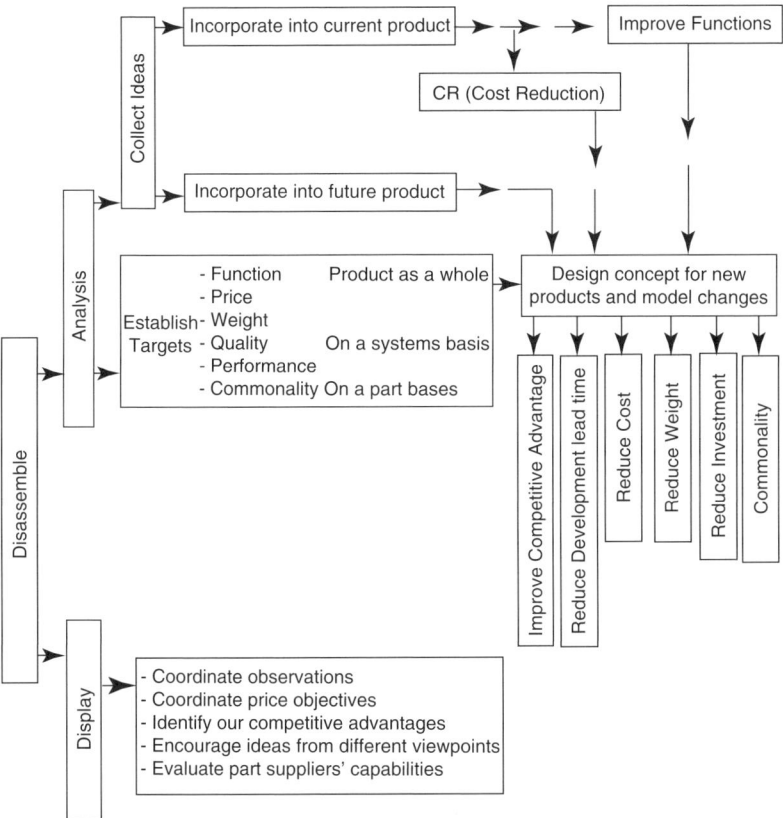

Figure 8.2   Value analysis tear-down process for product improvement and innovation (Source: Yoshihiko Sato and J. Jerry Kaufman, *Value Analysis Tear-Down: A New Value Analysis Process for Product Improvement and Innovation*, Industrial Press, 2004. Used with permission.)

Companies using value analysis tear-down have used it mostly for product and process improvement, to catch up with and go beyond what competitors are offering. Value analysis tear-down helps companies continuously improve their products and processes. Value analysis tear-down can also discover a different and better way to provide an important function. Designing this different and better way into a unique new product can be a successful product innovation for the company. Value analysis tear-down can be both continuous improvement and innovation.

Innovation comes in many sizes. Quick and easy kaizen releases the creative skills of all employees for finding and implementing small improvements; small innovations in the way they do their work. Quick and easy kaizen may find bigger improvements, too, bigger innovations. Value analysis tear-down discovers big improvements in products and processes, medium-size innovations. Value analysis tear-down can also discover new and different ways to provide a function, which can become a major product innovation.

THE VSM STRUCTURE FOR INNOVATION

Continuous improvement maintains the present. Innovation creates the future. In the VSM, system 4 is the center for innovation. System 4 includes R&D; strategic planning; and the futures work of marketing, human resources, finance and accounting, quality and productivity, and legal. System 4 also includes communication links with the seven environments described in this book—the commercial environment, the technical environment, the economic environment, the social environment, the political environment, the educational environment, and the ecological environment. Each system 4 function maintains a continuing relationship with its relevant environments to find and deal with threats, and to discover and exploit opportunities. Figure 8.3 illustrates system 4, its functions and relationships, and its communication channel with the environments. Figure 8.3 is the same as Figure 2.10 in Chapter 2, shown here to visualize the essential role of system 4 in innovation.

System 4 includes all the outside and future functions of the company:

- Planning. This book, in Chapter 5, proposes continuous planning, making changes whenever appropriate. Planning looks ahead for the longer term, typically five years or more. Twenty-five years

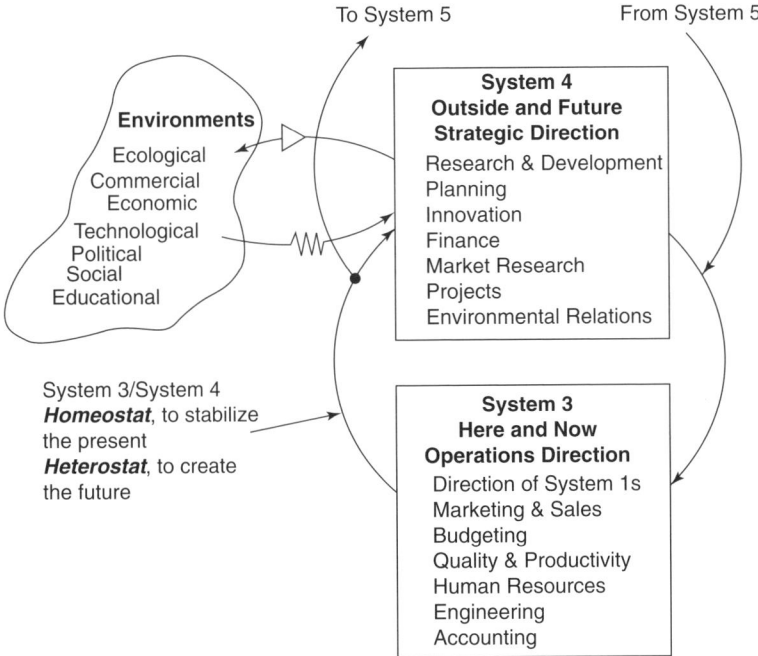

Figure 8.3   System 4, the VSM center for innovation

would be good. A long-term view of what the company anticipates and will aim for in 25 years and 50 years can help guide actions today.

· Research and Development (R&D). Typically, corporate R&D laboratories concentrate on the "R," research at the frontiers of science; to discover, to file patents, to find opportunity. Corporate R&D laboratories pretty much leave the "D," development, to the operations units that will commercialize their discoveries. In the VSM view, corporate R&D is looking for the innovations that will change the company. So corporate R&D executives might want to think about strengthening the development function with marketing, engineering, and finance experts. Note the 3M example later in this chapter.

· Innovation. Innovation is making something new, different, better, successful in the marketplace. System 4, in R&D, makes the first stages of corporate innovation happen. Later stages are directed through the system 3/4/5 linkages to change the corporation.

· Projects. Corporate projects are the organization structure for making corporate change happen.

- Corporate parameters. Corporate parameters guide the actions of all levels of recursion, from recursion 0 (the corporate VSM) to recursion X (however many recursions there are).
- Environmental Relations. System 4 monitors all the company's environments, contributing to, and learning from.

Note in Figure 8.3 the system 3/system 4 linkage, and the linkage of both with system 5. The system 3/4 linkage coordinates the here and now with the outside and future. This linkage is a major homeostat, maintaining stability. This linkage is also a major heterostat, encouraging and supporting innovation. The linkage of systems 3 and 4 with system 5 strengthens this heterostat. System 5 directs and balances the needs of system 3 here and now with the needs of system 4 outside and future.

We tend to think of innovation as a corporate function, and much of the literature on innovation deals with the direction and management of innovation by corporate R&D and corporate executive leadership. The VSM agrees with the importance of corporate innovation. The corporate VSM with its system 4 and system 3/4/5 linkages and environmental communications must discover the new and better and create the innovations that will create the corporation's future. But the corporate system 4 does not have the capability to do the same for other levels of recursion. They lack requisite variety.

Responsibility for innovation at each level of recursion is the responsibility of the system 4s at that level of recursion. They have the responsibility, and the capability, to discover the new and better and create the innovations that will create the future for their businesses. They may use corporate R&D on research projects, under whatever the company policy and terms may be. But at all levels of recursion, the responsibility for innovation is with each system 4 for their viable, very complex, purposeful, probabilistic system. Innovation happens throughout the company. Figure 8.4 illustrates system 4s at two levels of recursion from the Corporate VSM. In Figure 8.4, circles identify the system 4 centers for innovation through these two recursions.

The first level of recursion from the corporate VSM shows the VSMs for each of the four system 1s in the corporate VSM. Each of these four is identified with a number 1. In the first recursion from the corporate VSM there are four VSM business units, each with a system 4 innovation center, circled. The second level of recursion from the corporate VSM shows the 15 VSMs for the system 1s in the four VSMs in the first recursion. Each of these fifteen is identified with a number 2.

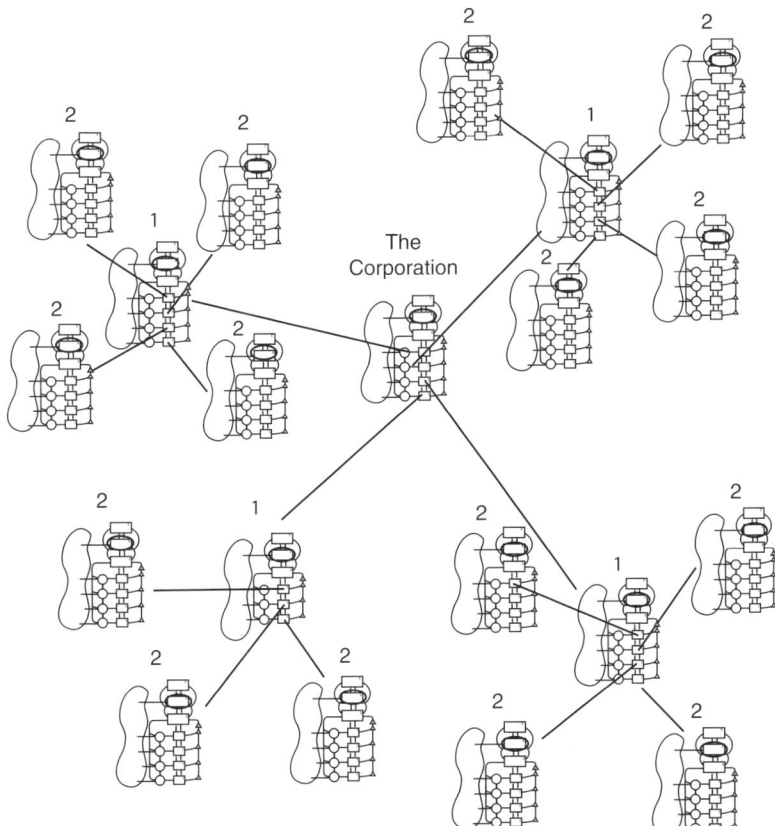

Figure 8.4 Corporate VSM with two recursions, all with system 4

All can be modeled with the VSM, each VSM with a system 4 center for innovation.

The third recursion would be the VSMs for each of the system 1s in the fifteen second recursion VSMs. Counting up the system 1s in the fifteen second recursion VSMs, we see that the total for the third recursion is 60. Each can be modeled with the VSM. Every VSM has a system 4. Each system 4 is responsible for innovation in that VSM business unit. The first recursion includes 5 system 4s, the corporate system 4 and the four system 4s in the corporate system 1s. The second recursion adds 15 system 4s. The third level of recursion adds 60 more. In this corporate VSM and its three recursions there are 80 system 4 centers for innovation. Innovation happens at all levels from corporate to work group.

Figure 8.4 can show only two recursions of the corporate VSM. To show three, or four, or five levels of recursion on one page would require a very large sheet of paper. Also, a sheet of paper shows only two dimensions. More realistically we should visualize recursions in all directions, as if in space. However, there is no value in showing all levels of recursion in a single figure.

In practice, we deal only with the VSM "in focus" and the next level of recursion. So we deal first with the corporate VSM and the recursion from that VSM. Then the VSM "in focus" becomes each of the VSMs at that recursion (the number 1s in Figure 8.4) and the recursion from that VSM. Then the VSM "in focus" becomes each of the VSMs at that recursion (the number 2s in Figure 8.4). In this way we can go through whatever number of recursions may be desired. Always we are dealing with a system in focus and a recursion from that system. And the "we" is not corporate headquarters, it is the people in those systems. They deal with one VSM as the system in focus, and the next recursion from that VSM. The one VSM can be anywhere in the corporation.

Always, throughout the company, each system is firmly connected to the next higher level of recursion. Appropriate coordination through-out the company is achieved through the Resource Bargains that define each system, and the communication channels. And always, for any one location in the company, the connection to the corporate VSM is linear, and easy to chart and understand.

In each of the VSMs in this network of VSMs there is a system 4 working to find discoveries, inventions, and new ideas to create innova-tions that will build the future of their business units. The system 4s in all recursions, from recursion 0 (the corporate VSM) to recursion X (however many recursions there are), creating their futures, collec-tively creates the future of the corporation.

SOME INNOVATION STORIES

Innovations start with a new idea, a discovery, an invention, new knowl-edge. A software idea launched the internet, a very significant innova-tion. Software ideas launched Google, Yahoo, eBay, and many other businesses.

General Electric

A scientific invention or discovery in any of the sciences can launch a significant innovation. Thomas Edison invented the electric light bulb in 1879. Then, to provide power for light bulbs, he invented a steam dynamo (generator), safety fuses, sockets, switches, a distribution system, and electric meters to measure the electricity used. All this came together in 1882 with the start-up of the Pearl Street station in lower Manhattan. The six jumbo dynamos in the Pearl Street station produced 600 kilowatts, enough to power 7,200 light bulbs. The Pearl Street station was the beginning of the successful innovation of electric lighting, replacing gas lighting. The Pearl Street station also launched the innovation that evolved into the country's present electricity grid providing a new, different, better, and lower cost energy source for lighting and power. Innovation is everything that's needed to make the invention successful and widely used.

The invention of polycarbonate polymers, the invention of a process for manufacturing the polymer, and a strategy for commercialization, launched General Electric into the innovation of engineering plastics. An invention or discovery, with whatever else may be needed, creates successful innovation. Discovery is essential before there can be innovation. Then innovation can apply the discovery in processes, products, and services to create new and needed values for customers.

3M

For years innovation has been 3M's basic business strategy. The company was organized and managed for innovation, and sales revenue expanded with 30% or more of sales revenue each year from products new in the previous four years. Freedom was an important part of the 3M innovation climate. A 3M parameter was that all technical employees may spend 15% of their time on projects of their own choosing, provided only that the project have potential commercial value for 3M. A 3M chairman, Lewis Lehr, frequently emphasized his view, "If you build fences around people, you get sheep, and you can't keep growing with sheep" [2].

By 2003, 3M had 12 research centers with 6,500 employees in the corporate R&D Center. Most were working on innovation within the technologies of the company's existing businesses. Few were working on the new-and-future technologies that could create a sustainable future for the company. To strengthen the here-and-now company operations, most of the scientists in the corporate R&D Center were transferred into the business groups using the technologies in their areas of research and expertise. Corporate R&D was left with scientists working in the new-and-future technologies that could change the company.

The new corporate R&D also included marketing experts to help plan and direct the early stages of innovation. Corporate R&D became both discovery and innovation. Corporate R&D for years had been working on projects in nanotechnology materials, but with few results. The new R&D structure—here-and-now in operations, and new-and-future in corporate R&D—put additional resources into the nanotechnology projects, added marketing talent, and by 2005 3M reached annual sales of $500 million, and 33% market share in nanotechnology materials. The company offered 14 nanotechnology products, including nano-enhanced films for ultra-bright displays in laptops, cell phones, air traffic control systems, and other products; natural-looking dental fillings; and super-conductive power cable.

3M may not know the VSM and system thinking, but their recent moves in their structure of R & D matches the natural order of things in a VSM structure.

Studebaker

In the early 1800s three families of Studebakers emigrated from Germany for a freer life in America. Several went into blacksmithing and wagon making, developing the design that became the famous Conestoga wagon that carried settlers into the West. When settlement in Ohio began to open up they found a ready market for their sturdy wagons. John Studebaker then settled in south-western Ohio, where he opened a blacksmith shop and raised five sons. One of the sons, John, traveled to California in 1853 to make his fortune in the gold rush. He quickly saw that he could make more money by selling to the miners than by panning for gold, and set up a business making wheelbarrows. Applying his wagon-making skills to making wheelbarrows he was very successful, and "Wheelbarrow Johnny" returned to Ohio with $8,000 in cash.

With this nest egg the five brothers formed the Studebaker Wagon Corporation and began building wagons on a large scale. Because their wagons were extremely durable, the company was awarded contracts for building wagons for the Civil War. During the Civil War the reliability and ruggedness of Studebaker wagons became legendary, and after the war the company prospered as their Conestoga wagons carried settlers to the western frontier.

In 1902 the company began making electric automobiles, then in 1904 gasoline-powered automobiles, again earning a reputation for reliability and ruggedness. During World War I Studebaker produced thousands of trucks, ambulances, gun carriages and other ordnance for the war effort. Automobile production resumed again after World War I and in the 1920s Studebaker's award-winning Big Six was the country's leading touring car. Studebaker's reputation for reliability and durability continued. During World War II, all production switched again to war production.

Still innovative, after World War II Studebaker was "First by far with a post-war car." But then Studebaker faded when the company fell behind in its manufacturing methods in it's multi-story plant in South Bend, Indiana. Quality and productivity declined, their cars losing their reputation for reliability and durability. Costs were not competitive. Its cars were still design winners with the Avanti and the Spectre, but sales slumped. After three mergers, Studebaker ended up in Cooper Industries, no longer making automobiles.

Innovation created and recreated success for Studebaker for more than a century. But there's always a future and only continuing successful innovations can create the company's future success. Good answers don't last forever. And on-going company success also requires on-going success in all seven of the key performance areas described in this book. Studebaker, in the end, was still innovative in the designs for their cars, but fell short in the key performance areas of organization capability, quality and productivity, creating and keeping customers, and profitability.

With continuous improvement, Studebaker could have made the best wagons at the lowest cost, but that would not be enough for success in the twentieth century. In the twentieth century Studebaker still provided their customers with transportation, but with a new technology, different, and better products. Innovations of new technology, new concepts, or new ways of working can bring break-through change and improvement, fast. The future is created by innovation. But business success requires high achievement in the other key performance areas, too.

Amgen

In 1980, George Rathmann resigned from his position as Vice President of R&D for a major drug firm to co-found a biotechnology start-up, Applied Molecular Genetics, Inc. The new company, later renamed Amgen, aimed to develop new, better medical treatments from the discoveries of university research in splicing DNA from one organism into the genome of another. In 1984, an Amgen scientist cloned the gene to make Epogen, an engineered form of a human protein that stimulates the production of red blood cells. Rathman formed a partnership arrangement to develop a manufacturing process. Having the product and a process for reliably producing the product, Amgen made Epogen a biotech success for treatment of anemia in cancer and kidney disease patients, with annual sales over $1 billion. Cloning the gene to make Epogen was an invention. Making Epogen a new and successful treatment was an innovation.

General Electric's Lexan Business

In 1956, Daniel W. Fox headed a research project in the General Electric Research Laboratory in Schenectady, New York, seeking new and different thermally stable, hydrolysis-resistant, thermosetting insulating resins. Fox's desire to capture some of the outstanding properties of polyethylene terephthalate led to his discovery of polyarylcarbonates. When he chose bisphenol-A as the monomer the result was an unexpected, high-melting point, dimensionally stable, transparent, tough thermoplastic polymer. It wasn't a good insulating resin. But it was an interesting polymer, with unique properties. It became the basis for the polyarylcarbonates commercialized by GE as Lexan polycarbonate plastics. H. Schnell, working for Bayer in Germany, made the same discovery at about the same time.

Both General Electric and Farbenfabriken Bayer independently announced the discovery of, and plans to produce, polyarylcarbonate plastics. GE would not be the only producer. There would be both product and marketing competition. GE transferred the polyarylcarbonate project from the GE Research Center in Schenectady, New York, to the Chemical Development Department (CDD) in Pittsfield, Massachusetts, for development and initial marketing. Fox moved to Pittsfield to continue his work in the CDD laboratory. Polyarylcarbonate was not one polymer, it was a family of polymers. Decisions had to be made on the product to commercialize and for what applications. From the CDD knowledge of the new polymer's properties, and knowledge of plastics applications, CDD named the new plastic, Lexan, and decided to offer it as a new thermoplastic, injection molding material for engineering applications.

CDD announced the new Lexan to an overflow audience at the annual technical conference of plastics engineers at the Sheraton Cadillac hotel in Detroit, Michigan, in January 1958. At that time, CDD had only limited supplies of the resin from pilot plant production. CDD marketing sought customer evaluations for commercial applications, emphasizing Lexan's unique properties: high strength, heat resistance, dimensional stability, unusually high impact resistance, and transparency, making the resin suitable for engineering applications well beyond the limits of other plastics. These properties required that Lexan had to be well-dried before molding, and molded at higher temperatures and pressures than used for other injection molding materials. To emphasize these requirements, pilot plant production was packaged in sealed, white, metal containers, with clear instructions on the label.

A market study by a major research firm had identified 15 potential large-volume applications for Lexan. CDD marketing was instructed to "shoot with a rifle, not with a shotgun" aiming for these 15 applications. The marketing director did not disagree, but did otherwise. He had experience fishing for catfish in Indiana. Not knowing where the catfish are, the best way to catch them was to put out several long lines with a number of baited hooks on each line. When there was a bite on one of the lines, that's the one to pull in.

To find commercial applications for Lexan, marketing used this catfish strategy. They used publicity and presentations at engineering society meetings to find prospective customers. They knew Lexan's strengths and limitations. When a company proposed a Lexan application, CDD marketing evaluated and advised on the application and the customer's molds and molding equipment. Where the evaluation looked promising, a molding test was scheduled. A CDD marketing person traveled to the site and supervised each test, instructing on proper handling of Lexan and the best molding machine settings, and answering questions and resolving problems. Also attending was the phenolics salesperson in that area, from the GE Division that would later be running the Lexan business. At the demo, the customer's people ran the process and ran the molding machine. The CDD goal was to help the customer learn how to make good Lexan molded parts. It was best for them to do it, not watch it. For molding demos at that time the big plastics companies would send in a team dressed in their company's shop-floor attire. The company team would take over and run the demo while customer people watched.

The CDD catfish strategy and marketing's evaluation and supervision of every application worked. There were no Lexan failures. No misapplications. Innovation is heuristic. The way to success has to be learned day by day. And innovators learn the most and the fastest from customers and their applications. By the time CDD was preparing their appropriation request for the first commercial plant, they had

more sales, more customers, and far more applications than were originally projected. And none of the 15 "shoot with a rifle" applications
had yet been commercialized. Innovation is a search; we have to learn
our way.

Lexan was the first thermoplastic material offered as an engineering
plastic. Sales grew rapidly to exceed a billion dollars, establishing GE
as a leader in the new class of engineering plastics. Polyarylcarbonates
was a discovery. Lexan and a customer-focused marketing program
created a new class of materials and a new engineering plastics industry, a major innovation.

INNOVATION OPPORTUNITIES

From discoveries in bioscience, computer and software science, nano-
science, materials science, and all other areas of research and discovery,
successful companies will develop the new, different, and better products and services that will create their futures. Innovation begins with
discovery. But innovation is not the discovery. Innovation is turning
the discovery into new, different, better products and services and
making these products and services successful in the marketplace.

Companies can organize to encourage and support creativity and the
innovations that will create the company's future. The VSM and system
thinking structures the whole company for the innovations needed to
create the company's future. Conventional management organizes for
innovation by setting up project teams for an identified innovation, and
by organizing innovation groups separate from the company structure
and controls. Examples of separate structures include Lockheed's
Skunk Works, Xerox's PARC, the US army's Defense Advanced
Research Projects Agency (DARPA), GE's Chemical Development
Department, Procter & Gamble's "The Gym," Motorola's Metro City,
and Samsung's Value Innovation Program (VIP) Center.

The typical corporate R&D center concentrates on invention; the
specification of a new, different, better product applying the technology; and a process for making the product. During this R&D process,
the project becomes more and more shared with the company unit that
will commercialize the product. At some point the project is transferred
to Division X which develops marketing strategy, a marketing plan,
and initial commercial testing and sales, and then full-scale commercialization. This transfer is often a point of contention, with
R&D feeling that operations do not effectively commercialize their

inventions, and operations feeling that R&D does not give them the new products they need. But overall, the system works well enough to create many successful innovations. Traditional management does produce innovations.

In the VSM, at the corporate level, system 4 includes corporate R&D, corporate planning, and the futures functions of marketing, human resources, finance, and legal. All of these functions use the system 4 communication channel with the company's environments, and the system 3/4/5 linkages to focus on innovations that will change the company, including:

- Discovery of technology that can become a new company business, such as we are seeing now in nanotechnology, in the biosciences, and in information technology
- Basic research in technologies that will bring new business opportunities to all or many of the company businesses at other levels of recursion, such as GE's 17 technologies in the company's "ecomagination" strategy
- Research in technologies that will improve quality and productivity in all levels of recursion, such as Toyota's development of the Toyota production system (TPS), now generalized into "lean operations"
- Research in system science and its possible application in R&D, and its application in company structure and management

We can innovate in social areas and the way we organize and manage our companies as well as in technical areas. We have made some progress: from straw boss to supervisor, to coach, to teams; from authoritative to participative; from manual and directed to skilled and collaborative, from centralized to decentralized. We continuously improve our conventional management processes in the seven key performance areas described in this book: creating and keeping customers, quality and productivity, innovation, organization capability, physical and financial resources, public and environmental responsibility, and profitability. But in management methods and processes, discovery and innovation lag. We prefer to improve the conventional rather than to discover and innovate the new, different, better.

We need the best in management technologies and management methods from system science. There is need also for excellence in what we manage—the management technologies for the company's key performance areas, including innovation, and the other key performance areas described in this book. There is always a better way in both how we manage and what we manage.

At the level of each recursion throughout the company, in each of the company's viable systems, system 4 with its linkages with the environments, and the system 3/4/5 linkages focus on innovations that will change and strengthen their business. A business at any level of recursion, by mutual agreement may bring a research project to corporate R&D. Making the project a collaboration from the beginning avoids the traditional problem of transfer. The decision-makers at that recursion level can have the requisite variety needed to make wise innovation decisions for that business. The purpose of business is to create and keep customers. The closer innovators are to the customer, the more successful the innovation can be.

Traditional management, with participation and empowerment, can achieve continuous improvement. And traditional management, with organization structures operating separately from company procedures and practices can achieve successful innovations. Management using the VSM and its system thinking and cybernetics, achieves innovations from the small continuous improvements to major, company-changing, innovations. The structure of innovation centers in the system 4s at all levels of recursion, and each system 4 with its knowledge of its business and its knowledge of its environments, make innovation happen throughout the company.

Innovation can be evolutionary or revolutionary. The toaster-oven was an evolutionary innovation, a better toaster with more functions. The microwave was a revolutionary innovation, new, different, better, faster. The fax was a revolutionary innovation, a faster way to deliver letters and documents. Then the computer and the internet became a further revolutionary innovation, a new, different, faster, better, lower cost way to deliver letters and documents, and much more. New technology creates new ways of providing value; different ways, better ways, faster ways, lower cost ways. In all of science, the frontiers of knowledge are expanding fast, creating great opportunity for revolutionary innovation in the company's products and services. The VSM with its linkages with the technological environment, the commercial environment, and the other company environments can find the innovations right for the company's businesses at each level of recursion, including innovations in management.

For innovations in management consider best practices derived from system science and cybernetics as these are presented in viable system model (VSM) and the on-going experience of companies using this model or other learning from system science. Also, continuously consider the evolving best practices in the seven key performance areas described in this book. The right innovations in the practice of management will be essential for continuing company success.

For innovations in management consider best practices derived from system science and cybernetics as these are presented in the viable system model (VSM) and the on-going experience of companies using this model or other learning from system science. Also, continuously consider the evolving best practices in the seven key performance areas described in this book. The right innovations in the practice of management will be essential for continuing company success.

Experience with the technologies of quality measurement and improvement demonstrates that there is always a better way. This is a good idea to keep in mind in confronting problems and opportunities. Search for the innovations in all functions; the new and better ways that will create the company's future. Discover the better ways and make them happen. The system 4s and the system 3/4/5 linkages at all levels of recursion have the responsibility for discovery and innovation in each of the VSM businesses. Discoveries may be found in-house, in R&D, in operations, or in any of the company's environments. After discovery and development by system 4, the work of people in systems 5, 4, 3, and 2 will be needed to make the innovation happen.

TECHNOLOGY FORECASTING

Technology forecasting is risky, but less risky than not looking ahead. A discipline of technology forecasting developed after World War II, led by James R. Bright and Milton E. F. Schoeman, professors at the University of Texas, and Joseph P. Martino, Theodore J. Gordon, Marvin J. Cetron, and others. By the 1960s technology forecasting became an important part of strategic planning. In addition to their annual budgeting, large companies extended their view five and ten years ahead in their strategic plans, which included their forecasts of the technologies important to their success. Planning grew more and more complex, and by the 1970s, companies were beginning their planning and budgeting cycle mid-year and ending often after the beginning of the budget year.

With system science, key performance areas, and the VSM, it is now possible for even large companies to greatly simplify their long-range planning and budgeting, as described in Chapter 5. Long-range planning, including technology forecasting and innovation, also can be continuous, always with a current map for the years ahead.

The system 4s at all levels of recursion, not only the corporate level system 4, will be centers for technology forecasting and innovation. From both internal and external resources, each system 4 will aim to discover and bring into their business the technology discoveries and changes that can build the future for their business. The corporate level system 4 will be concerned with technology discoveries and changes that will change the corporation. The changes 3M made in the structure of R&D in 2003, described earlier in this chapter, were in agreement with this concept, whether or not 3M was aware of the VSM and system thinking. R&D for divisional technologies was placed in the Divisions. Corporate R&D concentrated on technologies that would change the company, such as their nanotechnology research and innovation.

In all the system 4s' technology forecasting, methods used will include the traditional, and also the new and different. Innovation happens in all disciplines, including technology forecasting.

Parameters

Traditional technology forecasting quite successfully forecasts performance parameters, such as efficiency of illumination sources, maximum thrust from liquid propellant rocket engines, energy use per ton-mile of cargo in rail transport, and efficiency of external combustion engines.

But forecasting of parameters has nothing to say about how the improvement will be achieved. Broadly described was an "envelope curve" or a trend line projection of the parameter, with the inventions needed to make it happen yet to appear. See Figure 8.5.

Owners of sports stadiums will be interested in the increasing efficiency of illumination sources, but manufacturers of lighting will be interested in discovering the new technology that will provide the more efficient illumination. Invention cannot be forecast, but it can be observed, which may be good enough for innovative companies. Observation of what's happening in the technologies that can build the future of their business is a responsibility of each system 4.

Substitution Theory

As companies continuously improve and further develop their technologies, they need also to be alert for any new and better technology

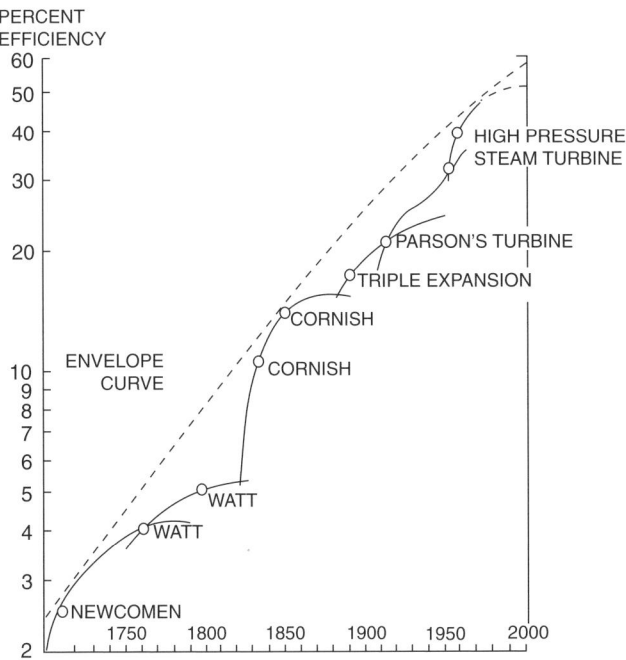

Figure 8.5 Envelope curve for efficiency of external combustion engines

that could become a replacement for what they are doing now. One of the ideas from technology forecasting states that if a new technology can replace an existing technology, it will. So, in developing and continuously improving Technology A, look for, and scan the environments for a technology B that can replace the Technology A. IBM made better and better electric and then electronic typewriters. But as desktop computers and word processing software appeared, IBM spun off their typewriter business into Lexmark, and concentrated on desktop and notebook computers. Years later the company spun off desktop and notebook computers into Lenova as a business less desirable for the company's future.

As shown in Figure 8.6, at time T1 technology B is invisible to those developing and promoting technology A, or technology B is seen but dismissed as no threat. After time T2, only technology B satisfies customer expectations. Technology B companies prosper, and the wise ones are searching for technology C. Wise leaders expect continuing improvement in parameters important to customers. They aim to be first with the new and better technology that offers the improvement.

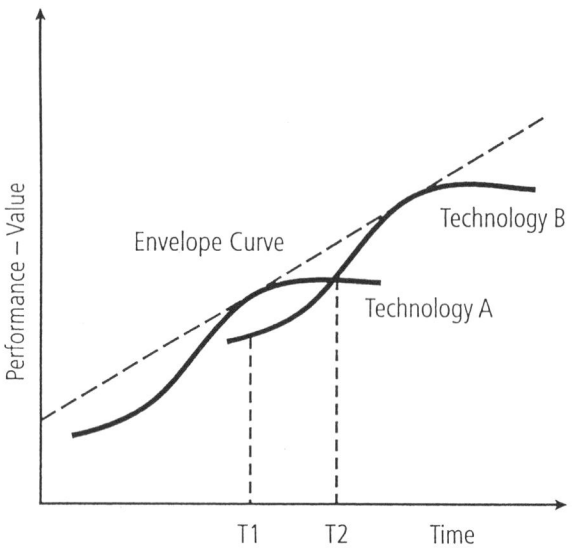

Figure 8.6 New technology will replace old technology

Diesel locomotives were already on the rails in 1935 when the chairman of Baldwin Locomotive assured stockholders, "Steam has powered America's railroads for a hundred years and will continue to do so." Typically, technology B is invisible to decision-makers in companies using technology A until it's too late to be a part of the new innovation. The Baldwin chairman may have been following the parameter of efficiency of steam engines. He should have been following a parameter of customer value such as cost per ton-mile.

New technologies will change business methods as well as products, processes, and services. Toyota's production system (TPS), now evolved into "lean," revolutionized manufacturing. New technology may come from internal research and development. More likely the new technology will come from outside sources—other companies, academia, government research, university research technology centers, special purpose associations, individual experts, and wherever else research is being done. In everything we do there is always a better way, a different way, sometimes a revolutionary way. Creativity will find such ways. Innovation will make them happen. The VSM and system science are new discoveries of the last fifty years. They are now in the early stages of innovation in the management of enterprise.

INNOVATION METHODS

For finding and creating the new and different, traditional management uses such methods as:

1. Procedures for authorizing research projects
2. Project and venture criteria
3. Check lists; rating scales
4. Review groups
5. Prescribed procedures
6. Market studies
7. Financial analysis
8. Project management with check points and deliverables
9. And to escape from the above, sometimes
   Skunk works
   Independent R&D groups, such as PARC
   Development groups separate from operations
   Venture groups

Successful companies will use separate innovation groups like those listed under number 9 above. They may also use some of the other methods listed above, but later in the innovation process as the project moves toward commercialization. A company using the VSM will have innovation centers in the system 4s, the company's outside and future functions, and the system 3/4/5 linkages at all levels of recursion. For finding and developing innovations they will use more effective methods than methods 1 to 8 listed above, including:

1. Concept development, finding what can be
2. Searching, searching, searching for the new, different better
3. Matching technology and market opportunity
4. Discovering a superior customer value
5. Relating to company purpose
6. Using a continuously evolving project plan as team members learn their way
7. Operating separately from "the company way," like the innovation groups listed in #9 above.

At all levels of recursion, innovation projects will:

- Make change happen, continuously building the future of the business with:
    New technology
    New, different, better products
    New, different, better services
    New, different, better processes
    New business ventures
    New, different, better business practices
- Define the innovation in terms of the customer:
    Who is the customer?
    What are customer needs, values?
    What new, different, better values will be offered?
- Have a specific goal to be achieved by a target date
- Have clearly defined project boundaries and relationships that are within the unit's Resource Bargain (the unit's definition, boundaries, purpose, resources, and goals)
- Be led by an entrepreneurial project champion committed to making the project succeed
- Use project management methods that are separate and different from project management in operations:
    Heuristic, learning the way toward the goal
    Constantly evolving
    Informal, qualitative
    Self-managed
    Fast acting. Do it! Fix it!
    Barriers? Go over, under, around, through. Keep going.
    Problems? Resolve. Ignore. Go around.
    Opportunities? Exploit.

Innovation projects change each VSM business, and collectively change the company. Working on innovation projects also changes and develops people. Innovation team members experience all business functions—planning, research, engineering, manufacturing, marketing, finance, human relations, logistics, legal. All skills combine to match technology and commercial opportunity to make innovation happen.

Innovative organizations set goals for innovation. 3M aimed for and achieved 30% of sales from products less that four years old. Innovation goals might be set in terms of:

- New product sales
- New product contribution margins, percent and dollars
- Production cycle time reduction—units per hour, labor hour, machine hour; worker hours per unit, such as X hours per car; process cycle time; set-up or change-over time
- Management cycle time reduction, such as time to market, budget preparation time from months to days, performance reporting from periodic to continuous
- Output/Input
- Sustainability

TRIZ [3]

TRIZ (pronounced "Treez") is the Russian acronym for Theory of Inventive Problem Solving. In 1946, Genrich Altshuller, a patent agent in the Soviet Navy, began studying both foreign and domestic patents searching for a structure or method by which inventions were made. He studied some 200,000 patents and identified about 40,000 that embodied innovations. Further study of these patents revealed 40 patterns of invention. These patterns are themes or abstractions that recur many times. Altshuller believed that these patterns could be the basis for a structured method for innovation.

After "perestroika" and the fall of the Soviet Union, Altshuller's work became recognized throughout the world. In 1992 the leading TRIZ scientists in the world relocated to the United States. TRIZ now has over 50 years of research and development and has been used to solve thousands of inventive problems in a wide variety of disciplines.

There are four fundamental concepts in TRIZ:

(1) Paradox. Altshuller observed that most technical problems contain a paradox, such as: make it stronger but make it lighter; make it more powerful but make it smaller and more fuel efficient; increase capacity (of a process) and reduce cycle time. An engineering solution seeks to compromise or optimize by finding an acceptable balance of useful and harmful effects. An inventive solution, by contrast, resolves the paradox by discovering a new and different way to provide the function.

(2) Ideality. Research of the worldwide patent library and other sources of inventive achievements revealed that technological systems tend to evolve in the direction of increasing ideality. Systems became smaller, less costly, more energy efficient, pollute less, and so on. TRIZ defines ideality as the ratio of a system's useful functions to its harmful functions. Useful functions include: the purpose for which the system was designed, functions that support or contribute to the system's purpose, and other useful outputs provided by the system.

A system's harmful functions include the cost to design the product, the space it occupies, the noise it emits, the energy it consumes, the resources needed to maintain it, manufacturing costs, etc. The best solution to a problem advances a system on its evolutionary path toward ideality.

(3) Resources. There are six classifications of resources.
- Functional—the capability of the system to perform additional functions
- Fields—any available energy, action, or force
- Information
- Substances—materials
- Space—existing unoccupied space
- Time—time intervals before, during, or after the process

TRIZ scientists look very hard for available resources that can be employed to improve useful functions, reduce or eliminate harmful functions, or resolve paradoxes.

(4) Inventive principles. In Altshuller's original work he identified 40 inventive participles. The inventive principles are themes or abstractions found in inventions that are repeated over and over. Altshuller determined that the inventive principles could be applied to solve a broad spectrum of inventive problems and he developed an innovation algorithm, a step-by-step procedure to generate inventive problem solutions. Today, the TRIZ community has identified over a hundred patterns of invention.

For more information on TRIZ, refer to: *Simplified TRIZ: New Problem-solving Applications for Engineers and Manufacturing Professionals*, Rantanen, Kalevi with Domb, Ellen; CRC Press, Boca Raton, FL; 2002.

FAST

Another structured approach to innovation developed from value analysis technology. Value analysis aims to identify the relative importance to customers of product and service features and benefits, and to then discover better, different, lower cost ways of providing those features and benefits. Speed? Accuracy? Reliability? Weight? Cost? Size? Design? Brightness? Taste? Heat resistance? Whatever the features and benefits most important to customers there is always a better way to provide it. Function analysis system technique (FAST) provides a value analysis technology for innovation by discovering better ways to provide a desired function [4].

Both TRIZ and FAST are structured approaches for discovery and innovation. Both have produced important innovations. Both demonstrate that an engineering approach can produce innovations.

CREATIVITY [5]

Throughout history, great thinkers and great leaders have esteemed creativity [5]:

Heraclitus, "The only thing permanent is change."

Benjamin Franklin, "To cease to think creatively is to cease to live."

Napoleon, "Imagination rules the world."

Woodrow Wilson, "Originality is simply a fresh pair of eyes."

William James, "Genius, in truth, is little more that the faculty of perceiving in an unhabitual way."

Arnold Toynbee, "To give a fair chance to potential creativity is a matter of life and death for any society."

Winston Churchill, "No idea is so outlandish that it should not be considered with a searching but at the same time with a steady eye."

Einstein, "Imagination is more important than knowledge."

H. G. Wells, "Human history is in essence a history of ideas."

METHODS FOR CREATIVE THINKING

Creativity is the starting point for innovation. Every innovation begins with a new idea, a discovery, an invention. These may come from a structured approach like value analysis tear-down, TRIZ, or FAST. Or they may come from creative thinking seeking the new, different, better. How do we think creatively to find, discover, invent the new, different, better? There are many techniques for creative thinking to generate ideas.

Brainstorming

Linus Pauling wisely observed, "The best way to have a good idea is to have lots of ideas." Brainstorming is a quick way to get lots of ideas. To resolve a problem, to respond to a situation, to conceptualize a new product, to improve performance in any of the key performance areas discussed in this book, brainstorming can generate lots of ideas. The procedure:

1. Clearly state the question: "How can we _____?
2. Assemble a small group of people involved or knowledgeable about the situation, and one or two or three experts in completely different areas.
3. Use an intelligent, creative moderator knowledgeable in the subject area.
4. Assemble informally in a conference room usually with chairs for participants, but no conference or work tables (chairs can be omitted, too).
5. Facilitator presents the question and leads a short discussion to assure that the question is understood along with relevant information about it (5 to 10 minutes).
6. Have a large easel pad at the front of the room and a person well-informed in the subject area to write down the ideas. Better is two easels and two writers, to alternate.
7. Moderator asks that all ideas be short, just a few words, no elaboration. Then run a 20-minute intense idea session with participants calling out ideas as fast as the ideas come to them. Logical ideas, far-out ideas, dumb ideas, wild ideas, conventional ideas, imaginative ideas, anything. Writers, alternating, write down the ideas using a black marker. Moderator inspires the flow of ideas, maybe contributes one or two, may suggest building on a submitted idea, and sees that all ideas are captured by the writers. Moderator calls "time" at the end of about 20 minutes. There will likely be more than 50 ideas.

8. Post the ideas on the wall and number them from 1 to X. Conduct a short discussion to determine if there is now any general agreement on the best solution. Often, the people owning the problem will be participating in the brainstorm. And sometimes this evaluation process will arrive at a decision on the action to be taken.

9. If there is no agreement, give each participant a piece of paper with numbers 1 to 5, and asks each to select the five best ideas, ranking them by their numbers from first choice to fifth choice.

10. Tabulate the votes. Do this in whatever way is most convenient. One way is simply to mark up the listing of ideas posted on the wall as the ballots are counted, marking 1 for a first choice, 2 for a second choice, 3 for a third choice, 4 for a fourth choice, and 5 for a fifth choice. Use a red marker. Then add up the "scores" by counting 5 for each number 1, 4 for each number 2, 3 for each number 3, 2 for each number 4, and 1 for each number 5. Mark the total scores with a blue marker.

11. Give the complete list of all ideas with the voting and the scores to the people who will be dealing with the question, which will likely be some number of the people in the brainstorm group. A good way to give the results to each person is to transcribe the questions, the voting, and the scores in rank order from highest score to lowest, and including also the zero scores, and make copies.

The summary above is a conventional style of brainstorming that has been used successfully ever since Alex Osborne, an advertising executive, invented brainstorming in 1939. Variations in this procedure will also be effective. Digital technology can also be used in structuring a brainstorm session, even with participants in distant locations. Any digital brainstorm, however, will follow the same general outline.

Brainstorming will be one input of several to the resolution of the question posed. While brainstorming is usually a group activity, individual brainstorms can come up with good ideas, too. Anyone can sit at her/his computer, type the question on a blank screen, then start listing ideas. Typically, with an "anything goes" guideline, ideas will come as fast as they can be written down. After 10 or 15 minutes, stop, and appraise the list. Use, or develop further, whatever appears useful.

Paradoxical Thinking

TRIZ gives us a structured way to resolve a technical paradox creatively. In all areas, paradoxical thinking can deal with opposites to discover new, different, and better ways. Paradoxical thinking is a technique for creative thinking, and there are three methods for doing it: the contrarian method, the Hegelian method, and the Janusan method.

The Contrarian Method   This method is credited to Humphrey Neill, a New England investment advisor who found that investors can do better by doing the opposite of prevailing opinion. He invented the word, "contrarian," and developed a discipline for contrarian investing. Contrarians question the obvious, and prevailing ideas, and look for ideas in the opposites. They ask "What if the opposite is really true, then what?" They examine opposites in relation to changing conditions in the marketplace and in the general environment, and often find opportunity in opposites. His 1951 book, *The Art of Contrary Thinking*, was written for investors, but his methods apply in other areas as well.

The Hegelian Method   In the early nineteenth century Georg Wilhelm Friedrich Hegel taught dialectical logic, contrasting a statement, or thesis, with its opposite, or antithesis and searching for a synthesis, something different that combines both. Thesis, antithesis, synthesis. A safety match will light and it also won't light. A pocketknife will cut when open, but won't cut when closed. Most companies have employees and managers. In the 1960s Texas Instruments thought about that paradox. Managers work for the company. Employees work for the company. Texas Instruments came up with a new idea—make all employees managers. Everyone manages their part of the company. How this idea works was explained in Scott Peterson's classic, *Every Employee a Manager* [6].

Today, using the VSM accomplishes what TI was seeking then. By the principles of recursion, black boxes, and self-organization and self-control everyone manages their part of the company.

The Janusian Method   This method is credited to Albert Rothenberg who titled it Janusian after the Roman god of gates and beginnings, who looks in opposite directions at the same time. Janusian thinking is bringing two opposites together in your mind, considering all aspects and dimensions of both, similarities, conflict, interplay, and from all this creating something new and different. Rothenberg reported that all the major discoveries he had studied in the fields of art and science resulted from Janusian thinking. As an example, in his book, *The Emerging Goddess: The Creative Process in Art, Science, and Other Fields,* he describes the Watson and Crick discovery of DNA—two identical strands of molecules connected in opposing spirals; two opposites existing together.

Etienne Klein, author of *Conversations with the Sphinx: Paradoxes in Physics,* contends that all advances in physics have come from the struggle with paradox. Paradoxical thinking has been a major source of innovation. For more information on paradoxical thinking, see *The Paradox Process,* by F. D. Barrett [7].

Divergent Thinking

We have learned convergent thinking through all of our schooling, and much of our experience. We learn our "tables," $3 \times 4 = 12$, $2 + 4 = 6$. Albany is the capital of New York State. Columbus discovered America in 1492, a kilogram is a thousand grams, the atomic number for hydrogen is 1. Convergent thinking has only one right answer. Any other answer is wrong. All our education is learning the right answers, convergent thinking. We are not taught how to think, when the questions don't have right answers, when questions have many possible answers, or when "right" answers, later, turn out to be wrong.

Divergent thinking seeks alternatives. Asking, "What is a frying pan for?" convergent thinking will say, "For frying food." Divergent thinking would produce many different answers: a weapon to use against intruders, a percussion instrument, a container for picking berries, a tool for drawing large circles, a paperweight that will also hold things, a pan for baking large pies, and more. Divergent thinking can produce more than one right answer. Maybe there is an attribute of a frying pan that can inspire a new design for a completely different kind of product. Divergent thinking can produce discoveries and inventions that can become successful innovations.

At the beginning of any project, plan, or proposal, divergent thinking can often find a new and better approach. To achieve the desired result, what alternatives might work better. Brainstorming can encourage divergent thinking. Convergent thinking will recognize any good ideas.

Bioheuristics

Bioheuristics, earlier referred to as "bionics," finds creative ideas from nature. System science describes natural systems as well as human systems. And we can often find in natural systems a source for creative ideas. Alexander Graham Bell got his idea for the telephone from the way tiny bones of the inner ear function. The idea for the flexible, hydraulic landing gear on navy fighter aircraft that take the punishment from landing on aircraft carriers at sea came from observing the legs of a grasshopper. The very popular Velcro fastener copies the tiny barbs which cause burrs to cling to clothing.

The following steps will discover new ideas using bioheuristics [8]:

1. State the problem to be resolved.
2. Search the world of living creatures to discover some animal, bird, insect, plant, reptile, or amphibian that has an attribute or attributes related to the kind of problem you are dealing with.
3. Study the creature selected. Make notes. Get a lot of information about habits, characteristics, attributes, behaviors. It's important to be very familiar with the creature before beginning work on the problem.
4. When you know the creature well, go back to the problem. Chances are good that there is something about the creature that will suggest new solutions to the problem. For example, suggesting a horse to solve a communication problem might suggest movement. Movement might suggest a rotating bulletin board that will attract more attention than the stationary bulletin board that employees walk right by without even a glance.

Concept Displacement

Concept displacement, a method credited to Donald A. Schon, takes an idea or a method used in one area and applies it in a different area. What is old, or not very new, in one area can be a brilliant new idea in a different area. Many internet shoppers, or potential shoppers, are concerned about security. Some internet marketers now solve that problem with an old idea: Buy now, and we'll bill you. How can they do that? How could the seller check credit ratings instantaneously, during the transaction? This offer required an invention. The solution was software that can check the buyer's credit rating with all three credit-rating services in two seconds. Creditworthy buyers immediately get the offer, Buy now; we'll bill you.

A good way to use displacement is to be aware of good ideas in many fields. Toyota became the world's most successful automobile company by developing a new, different, better way to build cars, the Toyota production system. The Toyota production system, now referred to as lean manufacturing, is the goal of all automobile companies today, and now also the goal of all other kinds of manufacturing companies. Other industries are discovering lean, too. The healthcare industry, with very different kinds of companies, is now beginning to use the methods of lean to improve their operations.

Random Word Play

We can get creative ideas from random words. Random word play forces us to think outside the box. First, select a random word. With eyes closed, open a dictionary, and touch one of the pages. Then, with eyes open, select the word touched. Or, do the same with any print material. Or, spread out a newspaper on the floor and flip a dime on it. Select the word under the dime. There may be more than one. Choose the word most under the center of the dime. Or, use any other method to get a random word.

Then, in a small group, play around with the random word relating whatever comes up about the word to the problem. This is a technique that teaches creativity, thinking in very unrestrained ways, trying to make connections. And there will be connections, and maybe just the idea needed. Summing up:

1. Write down the problem.
2. Find a random word.
3. Play with the word in relation to the problem, get ideas.
4. Test each idea as a possible solution to the problem.
5. Keep at it for 15 minutes to a half hour.
6. Write down the best ideas produced.
7. Agree on next steps. Take action.

Deliberate Dreaming

It's not uncommon for people to wake up with a solution to a problem they were worried about, or the answer to a question they had been searching for. Brains don't sleep. They work all the time. Brains dream during the night, and they can dream also during the day. Dreams can provide solutions and answers. Creative intelligence may be particularly high during sleep and dreaming. Robert Louis Stevenson described how he used deliberate dreaming for his imaginative stories, "Treasure Island," "Kidnapped," and other stories. Elias Howe discovered his design for sewing machine needles from a dream in which he saw Zulu warriors with spears having an eye-shaped hole in the pointed ends.

Deliberate dreaming can be learned. Here's one recommended method [9]:

1. Choose a goal or problem you feel strongly about.
2. Work on the goal or problem persistently for a day or two before the dream.
3. Discuss the goal or problem with one or more people.
4. Have a passive, relaxed evening.
5. Go to bed thinking about the goal or problem.
6. Drift into sleep with the intention to dream about it.
7. When you wake up in the morning, keep eyes closed.
8. Recall the dream.
9. Go over and over it several times.
10. Open your eyes.
11. Write down or dictate the dream immediately.

CREATING A CLIMATE FOR INNOVATION

Innovation is a function of system 4 and the system 3/4/5 linkages. Reread the Chapter 2 discussion of system 4. Think of your company in the VSM structure. There will be a corporate VSM with a system 4 and its linkages, and some number of system 1s. Each of these system 1s is a viable, very complex, purposeful, probabilistic system that can also be mapped with a VSM having a system 4 and its linkages, and its own system 1s. And each of these system 1s is also a viable, very complex, purposeful, probabilistic system having a system 4 and its linkages, and its own system 1s. And so on for however many recursions there may be in the systems structure of the company. System 4 is at many locations, and in the work of many people throughout the corporation. Every system 4 at all levels of recursion throughout the company deals with the outside and future for that unit. Each of these system 4s and their linkages is a center for innovation.

In the larger organization systems, such as a corporation, system 4 will include many people, in corporate research, corporate planning, and the futures work of marketing and sales, finance and accounting, human resources, and others. In small organizations system 4 will include these functions but few people and the part-time work of people working primarily in system 3, the here and now of operations. A company mapped using the VSM will see system 4 functions performed at many locations throughout the company. The key point, for innovation, is that innovation is a responsibility of people working at the many system 4s throughout the company. Innovation happens at the corporate level. Innovation happens also at all levels of recursion. Successful companies innovate at all levels of recursion. Information on successful innovations travels on the system 1s information channel to other operations, and on the special channel to higher-level management.

The corporate system 4 seeks innovations in new technologies, new methods, and major new products and service areas that will change, even transform, the corporation. At all levels of recursion the system 4s in the business units seek the same for their units. Discovery is the starting point for innovation, and many eyes and many talents are needed to discover the new, different, better, lower cost processes, products, services, and methods needed throughout the company. Corporate R&D and the other functions in the corporate system 4 can discover the new, different, better, lower cost changes needed at the corporate level. But they lack the requisite variety to do the same for other levels of recursion. Discovery and innovation are responsibilities of the system 4s at each level of recursion. Only at each level of recursion can there be requisite variety for the discoveries and innovations needed at that level of recursion. Innovation is an important part of the self-organization and self-control at each level of recursion. The system 4s in the VSMs at all levels of recursion instill and strengthen the climate for innovation throughout the company.

For success today and also tomorrow, companies concentrate on both continuous improvement and innovation.

CONTINUOUS IMPROVEMENT + INNOVATION

Continuous improvement strengthens. Innovation creates the future. The VSM and system thinking helps companies do both.

Company success depends on constant and continuing improvement in everything the company does. But continuous improvement is not enough to create the company's future. In addition to continuous improvement, success requires finding and using the right new technologies and methods in products, services, production methods, and business practices. Successful companies continuously improve the old, and continuously innovate the new, different, better. Continuing company success requires both continuous improvement and innovation.

Everyone finding and implementing improvements in the way they do their work brings continuing improvement for the company. With everyone involved, little changes by the hundreds and thousands add up to big change for the company; improved productivity, cost reductions. Continuous improvement helps maintain and improve competitiveness. But more is needed for continuing company success. That something more is innovation: new, different, better products, services, processes, and business practices.

At all levels of recursion, successful companies involve their employees in continuous improvement (kaizen). They also include the heterostats in their structure to achieve innovations that are right for creating the organization's future (Eureka!). Companies using the VSM and system thinking achieve both continuous improvement, kaizen, and innovation, Eureka!, more effectively than can be achieved by conventional management. The VSM:

- Includes all the company's environments in the model of the company, and in the models, also, for units at all levels of recursion
- Includes change and improvement elements (heterostats) in the model, in the system 4 and the system 3/4/5 linkages
- Structures the company through recursions, with each business unit modeled with the VSM:
  Defining the business and its goals
  Each with its system 4 heterostats for change and improvement

The VSM structures the company as a machine for continuous improvement and innovation. Figure 8.7 illustrates the effects of continuous improvement (Kaizen) and innovation (Eureka!) on company performance.

Innovation requires flexibility, qualitative perceptions more than quantitative measures, quick learning about the technology and quick learning from customers, fast response, and entrepreneurial leadership

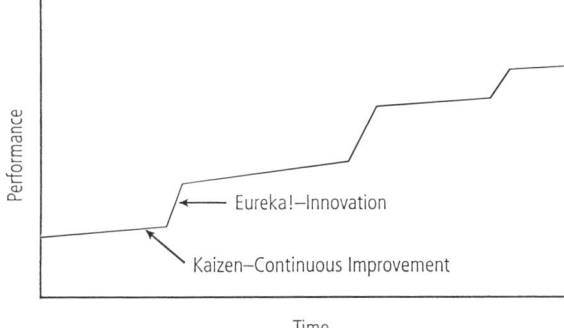

Figure 8.7 Continuous improvement and innovation

Requirements for Success	Continuous Improvement	Innovation	
		Evolutionary	Revolutionary
• Technology	Improved	Extension	Replacement
• Market event	Global competition	Changing needs	New needs
• Resources:			
People	Refocused skills	Improved skills	New skills
Capital	Some additional	Equipment and tooling change	New kinds of facilities, equipment, and tooling
Materials	Little change	Some change	Substantial change
Information	New	New	New, different
• Structure	Existing, some project management	Project management	Innovation teams or venture unit
• Feedback	Formal, quantitative	Quantitative and qualitative	Informal, qualitative
• Leadership	Business manager	Project manager	Entrepreneur
• Profitability:			
Contribution margin	Improved	Improved	High
Cash flow:			
Short-term	+	–	– – – –
long-term	+	+ + +	+ + + + + + +

Figure 8.8 Continuous improvement and innovation requirements for success

that makes results happen. Innovation is different in its nature from normal operations, and needs a different nurture. Figure 8.8 lists the characteristics of successful continuous improvement, and successful innovation.

Innovation brings big change and improvement. With the VSM and system thinking, innovation happens throughout the company. At the corporate level there may be an R & D center in system 4. The "R," research, seeks discoveries in the areas of technology important for the company. The "D," development, is the first phase of innovation. Development applies the invention in a marketable process, product, or service that is new, different, better, and very likely lower in cost. Development also includes the development of a process to produce the product. And development includes marketing strategy, a marketing plan, and commercial sales. The marketing plan may include conventional beta testing, market research, and market tests. And for significant innovations the marketing plan will likely include innovative methods in communications, promotion, and distribution. In all areas of development those involved will seek new, different, better, more effective methods. Innovation changes and improves methods as well as products.

Continuous improvement helps the company remain competitive and achieve today's profitability goals. Continuous improvement is essential for success today. But it is not enough for success tomorrow. Creating a future demands more. Creating a future requires innovation. Innovation performs a function or satisfies a need not just better, but in a different, higher quality, more useful, and usually lower-cost way.

The typewriter was an innovation, replacing the pen for the production of business documents. And the typewriter continuously improved, from manual to electric, to electronic. New features were added: changeable type, correction ribbons, justification, memory. But continuous improvement was not enough. The desktop computer with word processing software replaced the typewriter. The innovation of the computer and word processing software produced the needed output better and faster, and made possible additional outputs, at higher quality and lower cost.

The accelerating discoveries of science and engineering accelerate also innovation. New, different, better. There is always a better way. Successful companies continually convert the discoveries of science into products and services that satisfy customer needs in new, different, and better ways.

Another area of discovery and innovation for the corporate system 4 will be the new, different, better, lower cost discoveries and innovations in the company's key performance areas: creating and keeping customers, quality and productivity, innovation, organization capability, financial and capital resources, public and environmental responsibility, and profitability. Corporate system 4 people will search for and bring into the company best practices in each of the key performance areas, and search for discoveries and innovations in each of these key performance areas.

As managers and others at all levels of recursion participate in the mapping of their businesses with the VSM and understanding the model's system science, they are participating in innovations in company structure and management. They will find what best fits their company, and add their experience and discoveries to the knowledge base on VSM applications. Their experience will strengthen the climate for innovation throughout their company—in processes, products, and services, and in all the company's key performance areas, too. At all levels of recursion, the system 4s design discovery and innovation into corporate structure, with goals and performance measures in each business unit at all levels of recursion.

Conventional management creates discovery by imposing guidelines, and criteria for approving research projects, and creates innovation by prescribing procedures. Top-down works well in the view of those doing the directing, and top-down management has found successful methods.

At Lockheed, Kelly Johnson created the company's famous Skunk Works separate and away from company operations and constraints to develop the XP-80. Today the Lockheed-Martin Skunk Works is the company's center for innovation of advanced aircraft. In 1970, Xerox opened the Palo Alto Research Center (PARC) with a team of world-class scientists and gave them the mission to create the architecture of information. PARC scientists were very successful, but their early discoveries in computer technologies were commercialized by other companies. Today PARC operates as a Xerox subsidiary pioneering interdisciplinary research in physical, computational, and social sciences for commercialization by Xerox and other strategic partners.

Innovation can happen, whatever the company's management philosophy. But with the VSM and system thinking, innovation becomes a part of every business. Many self-organizing, self-controlling centers for discovery and innovation at all levels of recursion throughout the company can keep the company among the leaders in its areas of operations. Recursions are neither centralization nor decentralization. Recursions are a different way of structuring and managing the company. With recursions there is no loss of control; there is strengthened control. Discovery and innovation are guided by the Resource Bargains serially coordinated from the corporate VSM through all levels of recursion, and by communication in the business channel. Leadership for innovation comes from the system 5/4/3 linkage at each level of recursion, from recursion 0, the corporate level, to recursion X.

With the VSM, a corporate parameter can require innovation goals and performance measures in plans and budgets at all levels of recursion. With the VSM, involvement and self-control are not issues; they are part of the VSM. The VSM structures recursion after recursion, each business unit with its innovation center, each self-organizing and self-controlling. The involvement and empowerment we seek to authorize in the conventional business model (usually unsuccessfully) is inherent in the VSM. The VSM and system thinking is a management innovation that inspires innovation throughout the company.

OVERVIEW: THE ESSENCE OF CHAPTER 8

Innovation resolves problems, drives growth, and creates the new, different, better products, services, and ways of working that will build the company's future. Everything we see, or touch, or use is today's result from past innovations. Past innovations created what we see today and accept as "the way things are." And today's inventions, discoveries, and innovations will be our future. For our companies, it's wise to concentrate on what those innovations will be. The VSM can help.

The VSM organizes heterostats, centers for innovation in the system 4s in all business units at all levels of recursion. The system 4s monitor the external environments—commercial, technical, economic, social, political, educational, and the ecological. This monitoring keeps the company informed on environmental change, finding and dealing with threats, and discovering opportunities for innovation.

Innovations can be small, a part of the company's continuing drive for continuous improvement in products and services, and in all the company does. Quick and easy kaizen and value analysis tear-down are useful methods.

Innovations can be big, and very big, changing the company, and business units within the company. For these innovations, technology forecasting, substitution theory, TRIZ, FAST, and creative thinking are useful methods for discovering the new and better that can become major innovations. Innovation begins with a new idea, a discovery, an invention. In technical areas, these may come for structured approaches like TRIZ and FAST. In all areas these may come from creative thinking, including: brainstorming, paradoxical thinking, divergent thinking, bioheuristics, random word play, and deliberate dreaming, as described in this chapter.

The VSM structure, with heterostats in all business units at all levels of recursion, creates a climate for innovation. The organizational conditions for continuous improvement, evolutionary innovation, and revolutionary innovation are summarized in Figure 8.8.

NOTES

[1] Norman Bodek and Chuck Yorke, *All You Gotta Do Is Ask,* PCS Press, Vancouver, WA, 2005.

[2] David P. Sorensen, *Innovations: Key to Business Success,* Crisp Publications, 1997.

[3] Much of this information comes from *TRIZ,* a September 2006 essay by Peter P. Hanik, P.E., Managing Director, Pretium Consulting Services, LLC.

[4] J. Jerry Kaufman and Roy Woodhead, *Stimulating Innovation in Products and Services: With Function Analysis and Function Mapping,* Wiley-Interscience, New York, 2006.

[5] For more information on creativity see the publications of Management Concepts, Ltd., Kingston, Ontario, Canada, F. D. Barrett, President, and books by the authorities mentioned in this chapter.

[6] Scott Peterson, *Every Employee a Manager,* McGraw-Hill, New York, 1970.

[7] F. D. Barrett, *The Paradox Process,* Amacom, New York, 1997.

[8] F. D. Barrett, *The Management of Change,* Newsletter, Management Concepts, Ltd., Vol. 17, No. 6, 1987, p. 16.

[9] F. D. Barrett, *The Management of Change,* Newsletter, Management Concepts, Ltd., Vol. 17, No. 3, 1987, p. 8.

Chapter 9

The Viable System Model and Organization Capability

The human resources department (HR) deals with many "people" kinds of functions—wage and salary administration, incentive plans, benefits, labor negotiations and administration, recruiting, orientation of new employees, safety, compliance with employee-related regulations, terminations, training, performance appraisal, contributions to charities and non-profit institutions, and more. But another, and different kind of function needs to be number 1 among HR functions—continuously improving the capability of the organization to achieve its purpose.

A company is a viable, very complex, purposeful, probabilistic system:

Viable, capable of surviving in its environment

Very complex, with all this complexity needing to be coordinated toward the achievement of company goals

Purposeful, structured and managed to achieve its purpose

Probabilistic, with company performance and external change uncertain and varying

The company's people must maintain company viability, manage the complexity, and guide the probabilistic company performance to the

Holistic Management, by William Christopher
Copyright © 2007 John Wiley & Sons, Inc., Publication

achievement of company purpose. How well this is done depends on organization capability. Organization capability needs to be the major focus of the HR function. The viable system model and its system science and cybernetics can help.

THE COMPANY'S GREATEST RESOURCE—ITS PEOPLE

A system—any system—is what it does. The viable, very complex, purposeful, probabilistic system that is a company *is* what it *does*. What every business does is create and keep customers. Without customers there is no business. Creating and keeping customers requires every part of every business to do its job superbly well to accomplish the goals in all the key performance areas that are needed to create and keep customers. It is the whole company system that creates and keeps customers. What the company needs to accomplish in all its areas of operations is spelled out in detail in the company's continuous plans and budgets (see Chapter 5). Continuous plans and budgets guide operations to the achievement of desired goals in each of the company's key performance areas:

1. Creating and keeping customers
2. Quality and productivity
3. Innovation
4. Organization capability
5. Physical and financial resources
6. Public and environmental responsibility
7. Profitability

In each of these areas, the continuous budget does not measure variances for response from operations. The continuous budget measures progress toward goals and provides information for actions as needed to keep progress on track toward the goals, and modifying the goals when appropriate. Each business unit at all recursions throughout the company is a viable, very complex, purposeful, probabilistic system. Each defines its purpose and maps the times ahead in its continuous plans and budgets. Each measures and manages its performance in the seven key performance areas. At the corporate level, and in each of the units at all recursions, the achievement of their desired objectives depends on the capability of everyone in those organizations.

Continuous improvement in the capability of the organization to achieve desired goals is the key performance area that makes success in all the other key performance areas happen.

The capability of the organization is what all the company people can do using all of the company's tools and technology resources. What the company's tools and technology resources are, and how they are used, is determined by company people. The company is its people, a boundless resource that can continuously improve company capability. People as individuals, in teams, in shifts, in departments, in groups and units of all kinds throughout the company need an environment that encourages and supports and motivates high achievement. The VSM and its system science principles provide this kind of environment. In this chapter we look at motivation, design of jobs, viability, theory Y, collective IQ, and the VSM structure and methods that create high-performance organizations.

A clear understanding of recursion is important in using the VSM and system thinking for continuously improving organization capability (see Recursion Chapter 1). Management's task at all levels of recursion is to accomplish what's intended. How? By enlisting, encouraging, supporting, developing, and fully using the company's one boundless resource—its people. With the viable system model and system thinking, this happens.

Frederick Herzberg, in his 1966 seminal book, *Work and the Nature of Man* [1], pointed out that all the administrative responsibilities of the HR department, which he called *hygiene, or maintenance, factors*, can satisfy or dissatisfy employees. These administrative responsibilities are, for the most part, what HR departments do—wage and salary administration; labor negotiations and contract administration; health insurance, pension plans, vacation plans, and other benefits; performance review policies and administration; recruitment; training programs; community relations; and maintaining the appropriate records on all of these. These can satisfy or dissatisfy employees, but they have little or no effect on motivating job performance. The motivating factors, Herzberg found, are achievement, recognition, the work itself, responsibility, and advancement.

Herzberg proposed an additional role for HR: finding ways to meet the motivator needs of employees. He proposed a new "motivator department" as a part of HR. The motivator department would have three tasks: (1) re-education of workers and management on the motivator factors, (2) job enlargement, and (3) remedial work to deal with technological change, poor performance, and administrative failure.

Herzberg advocated designing broader-horizon jobs, in a supportive environment. That was before the principles of system science were clearly defined and widely communicated. Herzberg was improving hierarchical management. He was trying to make happen in that environment what happens naturally in a VSM environment. The concepts of recursion, black boxes, self-organization and self-control, and requisite variety at all levels of recursion is the best thing that could happen for the motivator department of HR and for the company. Teaching and extending the VSM and system thinking throughout the company, HR can make Herzberg's vision a reality. Recursion, black boxes, self-organization and self-control, and requisite variety at all levels of recursion are not only the way systems work, they motivate company people, and expand company capability.

MOTIVATIONS

People are different in what motivates their behavior and their performance: Some motivations:

Achievement	The need for success as measured against some internalized standard of excellence
Power	The need for control or influence either directly over others or over the means of influencing others, and control over resources
Change	The need for new, different, better; discovery; innovation
Endurance	The need to complete tasks, achieve goals
Affiliation	The need for close interpersonal relationships and friendships with other people
Order	The need for neatness, clarity, predictability
Autonomy	The need for self-sufficiency, independence, nonconformance
Deference	The need to work cooperatively with others; avoid conflict
Exhibitionism	The need to be the center of attention
Nurturance	The need to help other people
Commendation	The need for approval from others, recognition
Assertiveness	The need to express and advocate views and positions

The above are all patterns of behavior that influence performance. But individuals are complex. They are not, characteristically, motivated by one of the above motivations. Instead they are motivated by some combination of all, or most, of these. On a scale of 1 (low) to 10 (high), an individual might be 9 on achievement, 6 on power, 5 on order, 8 on autonomy, 9 on change, 7 on endurance, 6 on affiliation, 1 on deference, 7 on exhibitionism, 3 on nurturance, 3 on commendation, and 4 on assertiveness.

All of these motivations are useful in business organizations. Successful management and executive people at all levels of recursion will likely be high in two of these motivations—achievement motivation and power motivation. They may also be high in change motivation and endurance motivation, with varying levels of other motivations. Commenting further on achievement and power motivations:

Achievement Motivation

High achievement motivation is desirable in all areas of business. The purpose of a business is to create and keep customers and achieve its goals in all the key performance areas. The business system is purposeful; its aim is to achieve its goals. David C. McClelland, at Harvard University, pioneered in the study of achievement motivation. In studying people with high achievement motivation he found no relationship with education, social position, intelligence, or race. High achievers had only one thing in common: they all learned in their earliest years the satisfaction in doing things for themselves and accomplishing a result. Feeding themselves. Tying their shoes. Hitting a baseball. Riding a bike. Painting a picture. Baking a cake. Building a model airplane that flies. Getting an "A." As they grew in years, they continued achieving, and enjoying the satisfaction from achieving desired goals. They became self-motivated achievers.

McClelland found that self-motivated achievers have three common characteristics in the way they work:

1. They set their own goals.
2. Goals are achievable, but not easy.
3. They seek prompt, reliable feedback on progress toward goal achievement, less from other people or reports and more from the work itself.

In his book, *The Achieving Society* [2], McClelland reported on his studies of the motivations demonstrated in children's books in countries and cultures over the last three thousand years. He coded the books for the motivations demonstrated by the characters in the books. He then compared the motivations demonstrated in the books with the success of the country or culture as measured by economic growth. In countries where the children's books were most of all on the theme of achievement, he found a positive and significant correlation with the success of the country. An environment for achievement helps people learn achievement motivation.

We can't relive our childhood to learn achievement motivation. But McClelland found that achievement motivation can be learned by adults. He worked extensively in India, teaching achievement motivation. At that time India was a very bureaucratic, socialist economy. Bureaucracy smothers the achievement motivation. McClelland found that his students could learn achievement motivation with exercises that gave them the satisfaction of accomplishing a desired result. Some of his students went on to form their own businesses. India today is an entrepreneurial economy, achieving great successes. McClelland's work perhaps helped make this change happen.

From McClelland's work and other experience, six steps seem to be key to increasing on-the-job achievement motivation:

1. Design jobs with acceptable risk in the form of attainable, but meaningful objectives
2. Through participation and dialog, establish objectives
3. Structure work to provide feedback from the work itself on progress toward the achievement of the objectives
4. Recognize achievement
5. Assure that the achievement is meaningful and important to the individual(s) and to the team or group
6. Relate the achievement to group and company goals

Item 3, feedback, is essential for high-performance organizations. For all company people, feedback from the work itself controls their performance. All of the six steps listed above are needed at the levels where the work is done, and stay at the levels where the work is done. Self-organization and self-control unleashes powerful motivations.

Power Motivation

People with high power motivation may benefit a business, or harm it. McClelland also studied power motivation and found two levels, which he termed immature power motivation and mature power motivation. People with immature power motivation use power for their own personal desires and interests, using and even abusing people rather than supporting them. People with a mature power motivation use power for constructive social and economic purposes, supporting, encouraging, and rewarding others. Instead of two clear levels of power motivation, the reality is a range from very immature to very mature. A person with a mature power motivation may at times use power in an immature way. We see this when executives award to themselves unreasonable executive perks and bonuses. We see this immature power motivation in many dictatorial country leaders who enrich themselves and maintain their position at high cost to their countries' citizens. We see immature power motivation not just at the top, but in all areas of society where individuals having the power and the opportunity take advantage of others, or their situation, for their own benefit. Power can corrupt, a little, or a lot.

Company people high in power motivation will perform best if they have a mature power motivation, and also a high achievement motivation. McClelland's research suggested that in our American society there may be a declining achievement motivation and a rising power motivation. Whatever the reality, good corporate practice is to encourage and develop achievement motivation, and limit misuse of power through a corporate parameter on values that really becomes "the way things are done in this company."

Other Motivations

Two other motivations are especially helpful in business organizations—change motivation and endurance motivation. Creating the company's future requires change. People are needed who will discover the changes that are right for the company and make them happen. For both the stability of the present (homeostasis) and the creation of the future (heterostasis), there is always much to be done. At all levels of recursion the company needs people with the endurance motivation who get the work done and achieve goals. And at all levels of recursion the company needs people with the change motivation to be part of creating the future.

The assertiveness motivation is usually a plus. But in the extreme, assertiveness becomes aggressiveness or even hostility. So assertiveness can be a plus or a minus depending on how it is expressed. All the other motivations can be helpful, or at least not hurtful, in the company's pursuit of its purpose.

Drake-Beam-Morin, the large HR consulting firm, in their assessment work of Fortune 500 executives, discovered three critical characteristics of those who made it to the VP level and beyond. While many characteristics were found, only these three characterized almost all executive officers:

1. Above-average intelligence; not necessarily high, but above the average of college-educated people
2. High need for achievement
3. High energy level; ability to work long hours without tiring

These three characteristics—intelligence, achievement motivation, and endurance motivation—will also be found in many people in positions throughout the company. These people produce desired results. From these people come future executive officers.

We can think of motivations as a kind of need, something in us that we need to satisfy. When we satisfy the need, we feel good. When we cannot satisfy the need, we feel frustration and discontent. Performance improves when the design of jobs provides environments and circumstances in which these needs, these motivators, can be fulfilled. Then we have self-motivated people, happy with their company and with the work they do.

An understanding of motivation is useful in the design of jobs, and in recruiting for specific jobs. A general perception of motivations is revealed in each person's job history and personal history. But few people are very aware of their own pattern of motivation. There are simple written tests that measure motivations. Some companies have offered these tests to management and professional people. When this is done, it's best for the person taking the test to also score the test using the scoring guide provided with the test. Only the individual taking the test knows the result.

MOTIVATIONS AND THE VSM

People are different. Each of us has a combination of motivations inspiring our actions. Each of us has unique knowledge, skills, capabilities. Each of us has unique limitations. This is all part of the huge variety—the complexity—in business operations as defined in system science and the VSM. System science and the VSM gives us the structure and the management principles for coordinating the great variety in this probabilistic behavior to achieve company goals.

Black Boxes

As described in Chapter 2, each operations system, at each level of recursion, is a black box to higher level management. Higher level management lacks the capability, the requisite variety, to intervene inside the black box to fix things or to make changes to improve performance. But higher level management does know what goes into the black box—information and resources—and what comes out—performance results. Higher-level management also knows the Resource Bargain that defines what the black box operations system is, its boundaries, its purpose, its resources, and its goals. And higher level management has the requisite variety to change the Resource Bargain when appropriate, to change performance results. The black box, however, remains a black box to higher level management.

Within the black box we see a self-organizing and self-controlling system that can be described with the VSM. The black box includes management systems 5, 4, 3, and 2; and some number of viable system 1s. The five systems:

- System 5: Executive direction
- System 4: Outside and future, strategic direction
- System 3: Here and now operations direction
- System 2: Regulatory direction
- System 1s, The operating units. There will be from 2 or 3 to as many as 8 in each VSM; each of these a viable business unit also with systems 5, 4, 3, 2, and 1s.

What these systems are and what they do is described in Chapter 2. The people in the management systems 5, 4, 3, and 2 can have the requisite variety to manage and control those management systems— their performance and their cost. And the people in the viable system 1s—black boxes to the higher-level management in systems 5, 4, 3, and 2—can have the requisite variety for the self-organization and self-control to manage and control their systems.

The VSM and system thinking puts the responsibility for the work where the work is done. That encourages and develops achievement motivation. Self-control provides better control than would be possible by imposed control from higher-level authority, which lacks requisite variety. Indirect control works better than imposed control. Indirect control lets control happen where the work is done. The VSM provides the structure and the management methods that motivates and coordinates control where the work is done more effectively than imposed control from above. Indirect control improves performance. Indirect control allows decisions to be made where there can be requisite variety.

Designing Jobs

Work, of course, is done at all levels, in all systems through all recursions. In every business system there is system 5 work, system 4 work, system 3 work, system 2 work, and system 1 work. Each system 1 also can be modeled with the VSM with its systems 5, 4, 3, 2, and 1s; and those system 1s can also be modeled with the VSM each with its systems 5, 4, 3, 2, and 1, . . . and on through all recursions.

The traditional company organization chart is a hierarchy of people and units: CEO; vice president, finance; group president, Group A; general manager, business X; etc. Viewing the company as a viable, very complex, purposeful, probabilistic system, the VSM shows functions and their relationships, not people. The VSM and system thinking provides a model of what needs to be done, and where it can be done. So, in all recursions the VSM is very helpful in the design of jobs and defining job responsibilities and relationships.

The VSM and system thinking can improve the design of all jobs—executive, management, professional, supervisory, operator, and all others. People in their jobs perform the functions that create company success. The VSM and system thinking give us six valuable assists in the design of jobs:

1. The idea of functions—where they are, and how they interrelate
2. The idea of recursion
3. The idea of business definition, boundaries, purpose, resources, and goals—the Resource Bargain
4. The idea of black boxes
5. The idea of self-organization and self-control
6. The idea of requisite variety

All of these ideas are presented in Chapters 1 and 2, and are commented on throughout this book.

For the design of jobs at all levels, and in all recursions, the VSM and system thinking improves the design of jobs:

- Every job exists in some level of recursion, and will be primarily in one of the VSM's systems at that level of recursion:

  System 5, executive leadership

  System 4, direction, outside and future

  System 3, direction of here and now operations

  System 2, coordination of here and now operations

  System 1, operations
- At each level of recursion, the system 1s become the next level of recursion, each modeled with the VSM. Recursions continue to the level of process and work group.
- At all levels of recursion, all the functions needed for the success of that unit fall into one or another of the five systems listed above.
- At each recursion level, jobs are designed to perform functions in one of the systems 5, 4, 3, or 2. A position in system 3, here and now operations, may at times work in system 4, the outside and future. A system 3 executive will at times work in system 5, executive direction, and at times in system 4. Whatever their "home" system, it's important for people to recognize at all times the system level where they are working, and those functions and responsibilities.
- System 1 people will have jobs in the next level of recursion in system 5, 4, 3, 2, or 1.
- Jobs are designed around functions and will include goals and performance measures for those functions.
- Performance measures are not for performance appraisal; the measures are designed to help the person and the group or team achieve the goals.
- The measures stay where the work is done.
- Self-organization and self-control works!

THE VSM AND COMPANY PERFORMANCE

The VSM and system thinking give us a new framework for designing, leading, and managing the organization. And using the VSM and system thinking greatly increases the ability to implement best practices in the seven key performance areas throughout the company.

As companies gain experience with the VSM, and with best practices in the seven key performance areas, lessons learned can be shared. Useful information will flow in the system 1s communication channel to the other system 1s, and through the special communication channel to other parts of the company. Lessons learned in one place can be useful elsewhere, too.

Some CEOs are well known and recognized for implementing change and creating success through new and better management practices. Their work often benefits from system principles at work in their companies, whether or not they have awareness of these principles. Apples fell to the ground even before we knew about gravity. The idea of the VSM and system science is that our viable, very complex, purposeful, probabilistic system that is our company works the way the VSM and system science says it works whether or not we know anything about system science.

An Example: General Electric

Consider the recent history of the General Electric Company, viewed through the eyes of the VSM. Jack Welch, the former chairman of the General Electric Company inspired company growth and success primarily by his skill in handling the most important responsibility of system 5: defining the company and determining the company's purpose and goals and then structuring the company to achieve its purpose and goals.

This responsibility is more than a one-person job. All who work in system 5 are involved. Others, too, will be consulted. But in GE, Welch was the leader in defining what the company should be and its goals. He, with the rest of system 5, then established a corporate structure that could be that kind of company, and run itself in achieving intended goals. He defined the corporate VSM, and the recursions from the corporate VSM, although his design was not described in those terms.

And there was more than structure. There were also the key performance areas that determine company success. For GE, Mr. Welch emphasized four:

1. Quality and productivity. GE implemented six sigma to assure quality, improve productivity, and reduce cost. Training programs taught the technologies and methods of six sigma. All company units used six sigma methods. Everyone was involved. Six sigma

became part of the way GE did its work. With its successes, GE became a model for six sigma excellence.

2. Creating and keeping customers. In the 1950s, GE emphasized what the company then called "market orientation" in all business units' plans and budgets. What the company does in the marketplace determines company success. Market orientation of the business creates market position, a key measures of business success. And this success comes from creating and keeping customers, one by one, and doing this better than competitors. As long as anyone can remember, and in the company's documented history longer still, GE has been driven to serve, satisfy, and delight customers. Jack Welch expressed the company's traditional focus on this key performance area in a challenging way. He asked all GE businesses to be number 1 or number 2 in the markets they serve. The measure of market position depends of course on how the market is defined (see the Telechron case, in Chapter 5). So for the number 1 or number 2 standard to be effective there needs to be agreement on market definition between the business unit and higher management; in system terms, the higher level system 3.

3. Organization capability. GE has long emphasized the continuing education of its people. The company's center in Crotonville, New York, is a business school for GE people, teaching seminars and short courses on best practices. Jack Welch was a frequent lecturer at Crotonville. At Crotonville, and at many locations throughout the company there is ongoing education for engineers, sales and marketing people, finance and accounting people, managers, supervisors, and all others. Continuing learning is a part of a GE job. Jack Welch added a new dimension in organization development by asking management people to continuously improve performance by pruning their organizations' poorest performers and recruiting high-talent people.

4. Profitability. GE has always considered the achievement of targeted profitability an absolute requirement. Jack Welch's GE accomplished this by the design of the company—the first responsibility of system 5 executive leadership—and by the concentrated efforts in these four key performance areas.

To many, it was Jack Welch's dominating and persuasive personality that made GE's success happen. His personality certainly helped, and his intellect, too. These qualities helped the GE management team design the company for success, the number one responsibility of system 5. In the expanding economy of the 1990s GE success was impressive. But in the earlier years, while the Welch leadership was designing the company, success was not at all assured. What was then called "restructuring," but in systems terms was "designing the company," resulted in plant closings and divestitures. Mr. Welch was referred to as "Neutron Jack," comparing his actions to the effects of the neutron bomb that kills the people, but leaves the buildings standing. But there were not only shutdowns and divestitures; there were acquisitions and additions, too. The company was being designed for the years ahead. And in the years ahead, the company thrived. And the viable, very complex, purposeful, probabilistic system that was the new GE could only thrive through the self-organizing and self-control capabilities of all the viable, very complex, purposeful, probabilistic systems at all levels of recursion, and the communications channels that drive all systems, whatever the IT department installs. Designing the company continued, throughout the Welch years.

For Jack Welch's successor, the Board elected Jeff Immelt as the company's new CEO. As president and CEO of GE Medical Systems, among Immelt's achievements was his impressive success in creating and keeping customers and in growing revenue through innovation.

Jack Welch had created a great company. What would be the company's future in the changing times of the new century? First of all, retain the company's strengths. Then focus those strengths on the needs ahead. Discover the technologies that will create future businesses. Grow less from acquisition; more from internal growth. Expand the technological and marketing resources to make internal growth happen. GE's corporate research center in Schenectady, New York, the "House of Magic," added scientists to discover and develop tomorrow's technologies. Top marketing officers were appointed for corporate and for each of the company's major business groups, and five thousand additional salespeople were hired.

Jack Welch designed the General Electric Company for his time. For the times ahead, Chairman Immelt sees the company being continuously reinvented for internal growth through innovation. A major theme for innovation will be sustainability. The world around us is changing in many ways unfriendly, even threatening, to humanity. Looking ahead to create the GE for the future, Immelt launched an ecomagination/innovation strategy to create new, different products, services, and processes that are better for customers and users, and friendly for the environment. GE doubled its research budget for energy and environmental technologies to $1.5 billion aiming to double sales revenue in this area to $20 billion by 2010. Initially the company's ecomagination initiative concentrates on 17 technologies. GE intends to be an industry leader in creating a sustainable future.

Another Example: Google

After developing and testing their unique new search engine, Stanford students Sergey Brin and Larry Page launched Google, Inc. in a garage in Menlo Park, California, in September, 1998. The company, two partners, one employee, and the Google search engine, was answering 10 thousand search queries a day. In 2005 just seven years later, the company had 5,680 employees, and the Google search engine, with many additional features and products. The company was operating globally and answering some 200 million search queries a day, more than 50% outside the United States. The company was growing fast in number of employees, sales revenue, and profit. Google attracts high-talent people who want to work for the company:

- In Google they would be doing important work.
- They would be working with very talented people.
- There is opportunity for growth and advancement.
- They want to be a part of achieving the company's mission: "Organize the world's information and make it universally accessible and useful."
- The company's ethics policy is appealing: "Do no evil."
- They like to be a part of something that really matters.

Google has built its business on continuous innovation, including— Google Toolbar, wireless search, Google Zeitgeist, Google Image Search, Google Catalog Search, "Google in a Box" for inside the corporate firewall, Google AdWords, Google News, Froogle, Google Desktop, Google SMS using text messaging, Google Print, Goggle Maps, Google Personalized Homepage, Google Sitemaps, Google Blog Search, and a continuing stream of search aids, languages, media searched, and targeted advertising technologies. Google is the technology leader in organizing the world's information. People want to be a part of making something new, different, better, happen.

The Googleplex headquarters in Mountain View, California, is a happy place to work—a collegial environment, interaction with others, on-site doctor and dentist, massage and yoga, professional develop-ment opportunities, on-site day care, running trails, plenty of snacks and a free chef-prepared lunch, with work and play not mutually exclu-sive. Other Google sites are similar.

Googlers range from former neurosurgeons, CEOs, and US puzzle champions to alligator wrestlers and former Marines. Whatever their backgrounds, Googlers make interesting colleagues.

People in every country and every language use Google. Googlers think, act, and work globally to make the world a better place. For Googlers, there are hundreds of challenges to solve, creative ideas to explore, important new products to develop, innovations that millions of people will find useful.

Larry Page, Sergey Brin, and the Google Board may not be thinking about general system theory, the VSM, and system thinking, although they would likely be familiar with cybernetics. They designed a company to accomplish a purpose: to "organize the world's information and make it universally accessible and useful." The company could readily be diagrammed using the VSM and its recursions. Executive leadership steers the company. The company runs itself to accomplish its purpose. This kind of company environment attracts talented people.

PERFORMANCE APPRAISAL [3]

Corporations today have big investments in software and systems for performance appraisal, standardized and followed throughout the company. However, while the process is standardized, the standards are followed in a variety of ways by the hundreds, or thousands, involved in the process. The whole process tends to fall into one of Herzberg's "hygiene or maintenance" factors that can satisfy or dissatisfy partici-pants, but contribute little or nothing to motivation and performance improvement.

Companies want documentation for wage and salary administration, for decisions on promotions, and for support in legal issues relating to discrimination and affirmative action, and more. The performance appraisal system can provide this documentation. The following list of performance improvement goals is taken from a Fortune 500 compa-ny's Performance Appraisal Manual:

1. Improve employee performance
2. Advise employees as to how their performance is viewed

3. Encourage employee feedback (upward communication to supervisor)
4. Provide legal protection (in event of termination, or claims)
5. Determine salary awards
6. Assist in succession planning
7. Justify promotions

These are all important goals for the company. But years of experience with a variety of performance appraisal methods shows little success in achieving these goals through performance appraisal systems.

Performance appraisal methods include:

1. Global impressions. This method uses summary ratings like, "outstanding" or "moderately satisfactory." Sometimes the global impression is stated in a paragraph describing the employee's overall performance.
2. Trait-rating scales. Traits are lists of personal qualities. The rater checks on a numerical scale the extent to which the employee possesses such qualities as dependability, initiative, and diligence.
3. Behavior-rating scales. Employees are rated on the extent to which they display behavior thought to be related to successful performance.
4. Performance outcomes. Employees are appraised by their achievement of their goals or objectives.
5. Hybrid systems. Employees are rated by some combination of the above.

Of the above, performance outcomes, evaluating employees by their achievement of their goals or objectives, is the most widely used, and generally thought to be the most effective. But that general impression is little reward for the huge time and cost investment in performance appraisal that shows little return—if any—in improving performance, the most important of the seven goals listed above.

Is there a better way? Some possibilities:

1. Maybe put the whole matter in a more positive light. Instead of "performance appraisal," maybe "performance recognition," or "achievement process." Employees don't like to be "appraised." Appraisers don't like to "appraise." Neither the employees nor the appraisers like all the paperwork. Both are either satisfied or

dissatisfied with the appraisal method. But few are motivated or empowered for improvement.

2. Make performance appraisal a continuous process, ongoing, focusing on goals and objectives, and best ways to reach those goals. Instead of an annual cycle, goals at the beginning of the year and appraisal near the end of the year, make the process continuous. Employee goals typically are not annual goals. Have the current goals always in view and in mind, with frequent contact collaborating on goal achievement. Performance is a continuous process, like the continuous planning and budgeting discussed in Chapter 5. Continuous is better than annual. And continuous will be more a "performance dialog" than a "performance appraisal."

3. Think of performance appraisal through the lens of the VSM and the principles of system science and cybernetics. Systems 5, 4, 3, and 2 would do performance appraisals or continuous performance dialogs with people in those functions. In the system 1 businesses people in each function would, similarly, have their performance appraisals or continuous dialogs. A continuous performance dialog could be a productive way to organize a performance improvement process at each level of recursion.

4. There would be no corporate mandated performance appraisal system. There could be a corporate parameter requiring a performance improvement process, and model processes could be provided. At each level of recursion the "how to do it" would be decided at that level. And any documentation would remain at the level of origin; no submission to higher management levels. However, information on successful experience could flow in the special communication channel to higher management and to other parts of the company. With many business units developing their own methods, new and better ways will be found continually, and communicated. For company-wide promotions, jobs can be posted on the company web.

5. Wage and salary administration and individual salary awards could be handled separately from the performance improvement process, as could documentation for evidence in defending equal employee opportunity claims and other employee claims.

Companies using the VSM will find many ways to very much simplify and very much improve their performance appraisal practices.

VIABILITY

A business is a viable system. It can live, and continue to live, in its environment. When the business is no longer viable, when it can no longer live in its environment, it dies.

The VSM, as presented in this book, includes seven environments. The first six of these environments are human environments, part of our culture. We can call these six, "cultural environments." Our company is part of, embedded in, and related in many ways to these six cultural environments. The six cultural environments and the company are all embedded in, and dependant on, the seventh environment, the ecological environment. The seven environments:

1. The commercial environment
2. The technical environment
3. The economic environment
4. The political environment
5. The social environment
6. The educational environment
7. The ecological environment

All companies live in all of these environments. Some companies might prefer a somewhat different listing of their environments. But whatever the listing, all but one of the environments will be environments that are part of our culture. The one that is not part of our culture is the ecological environment which sustains all the others.

Companies are more-or-less comfortable living in their cultural environments. A part of their life is adjusting to the threats and finding the opportunities presented by changes in these cultural environments. High-performance organizations develop the capabilities needed to deal with the threats and discover and develop the opportunities resulting from changes in the six cultural environments.

The six cultural environments, however, vary in their importance to the company and to each of the business units at all levels of recursion. Probably most companies and their business units consider the order of importance about as listed above. Customers, competitors, and suppliers are in the commercial environment. That's number 1. Changes in the technical environment can be threatening, and also opportunity for innovation. R&D searches for technology innovations. A big part of the company's future depends on relationships with the technical environment. Opportunities for innovation, as well as threats, arise from changes in the other environments as well.

For most of our economic history, development of organization capability focused on the skills needed to live in the changing world of these six cultural environments. As populations grew, and economies expanded into globalization, change in these six environments accelerated. The later years of the twentieth century and the dawning of a new millennium opened our eyes to a new world. Now, the environment that matters most is number 7, the ecological environment.

All the six cultural environments live in the ecological environment. All the world's six billion people live and work in the ecological environment. And the ecological environment is changing, presenting threats, and demanding human innovation as world population continues to expand to a projected stabilization at 9 to 10 billion people by midcentury. That's not just a statement with a number in it. The road to midcentury confronts us with the greatest threats ever confronted by humanity in all its 100 thousand years on this planet.

More and more, companies recognize the threats in environmental change. But change offers opportunity as well as threats. How will we achieve sustainability in a world of huge and rapidly growing populations, and a huge and even faster growing global industrial economy. For a sustainable world, all the goods and services of today's economy are obsolete. New and different products, new and different services, new and different ways of working, new and different ways of living, new and different almost everything will be needed. Industry serves needs. There is great opportunity in the new and different.

The new focus for success is growing the company capability to innovate the new and different products, services, and ways of working and ways of living now needed for sustainability in a finite and threatened ecosphere. Conserving the environment is conserving the human race. For more information on company sustainability in our changing environments, see Chapter 10.

VSM, THEORY Y, AND THE HR MOTIVATOR DEPARTMENT

Reading what the experts say about the new generation's attitudes toward their jobs, their careers, and their employers confirms the common saying, "The more things change, the more things stay the same." What changes in people is some of the fads, the add-ons, the music, the fringes. The values, the fundamentals live on, though the environment we live and work in changes.

The Greatest Generation, the Boomer generation, Gen X, now Gen Y, and the arriving Gen @; each seems very different. Each new generation has different experiences. Their environments are different. But look below the surface, and you find a common core. The news reports and literature describing the attitude of young people today toward work and career share a theme in common with those in earlier generations. For Gen Y and it seems also for Gen @ers, from reports on their attitudes and behaviors, what matters is the vision and strategy of the company; the caliber of management; doing good, not harm; the opportunity to make a contribution that matters. They want to find positive values in their company, and meaning in their work. In 2005, Google was hiring ten people a day. These young people see Google as a company that is working to change the world, a company that is doing exciting things, a company where they would have room to do great things. Engineers at Google could use twenty percent of their time to pursue their own projects. Young people want to contribute; they want to be a part of something that matters. Sounds like Gen X, Boomers, and the Greatest Generation, too!

New? Different? Contemporary writers today contrast these attitudes to their own descriptions of generations past when, they say, employment meant a good day's pay for a good day's work, and tenure in exchange for loyalty. These writers weren't there generations ago. They are looking for differences, not threads of continuity. They misrepresent the past to contrast with their view of the present. Today's young people they are writing about are professionals; knowledge workers. Generations ago there were also knowledge workers, but fewer of them.

Generations ago, a factory was a few supervisors and managers, and a lot of hourly employees doing routine work. Today a factory is very sophisticated equipment and processes, programmed and operated by professionals; knowledge workers. Other kinds of work have been similarly transformed. The people doing the knowledge work generations ago had much in common in their attitudes with the young people of today.

In 1960, Douglas McGregor, a pioneer in behavioral science, published his seminal book, *The Human Side of Enterprise.* In this book he presented his "theory Y," derived from behavioral science. His research confirmed that theory Y is a more realistic assumption about people than the assumptions that seemed to underlie much management practice. He labeled those conventional assumptions about human behavior as "theory X." Conventional, authoritarian management seemed to assume:

1. People dislike work and will avoid it if they can.
2. People avoid challenge and responsibility.
3. Most of all, people look for security in their jobs.
4. Because people dislike work and won't accept responsibility, they must be directed, controlled, coerced, or threatened to get them to do what they should do.

This set of assumptions McGregor called Theory X. They seemed to underlie much management practice. From these assumptions could come different management types, from hard or strong on the one extreme, to soft or permissive on the other. Hard management means tight controls, close supervision, and use of coercion and threat of punishment to get the work done. Soft management tries to satisfy people's demands to keep harmony in the organization. Hard management is authoritarian and results in poorer performance, antagonism, militancy, and uncooperative attitudes. Soft management in its concern for personal relations produces harmony but ineffectiveness, and a lazy workforce that continually produces less but expects more. McGregor described both hard and soft management not so much as being wrong, but as being irrelevant. From the work of behavioral science he described another list of behaviors, which he called theory Y:

1. Work is as natural for people as play or rest. Depending upon what it is, work can be satisfying or frustrating, and it will accordingly be done willingly or unwillingly.
2. People will work toward objectives to which they are committed.
3. Commitment to objectives relates to need satisfaction.
4. Under appropriate conditions, people not only accept responsibility but seek it.
5. Typically, people have more ability than they utilize in their job.

McGregor pointed out that theories X and Y are assumptions about human behavior. But theory Y is supported by the findings of behavioral science. He felt that theory X had become unrealistic for business enterprise. Theory X assumptions were self-fulfilling. When management acted on the basis of these assumptions, people did behave that way. And theory X assumptions were very limiting. They permitted certain possible ways of organizing and directing human effort, *but not others.* On the other hand, theory Y opens up a broad new range of possibilities.

The VSM and system thinking is one of those possibilities. The VSM and the principles of theory science *requires* theory Y kinds of assumptions. We can say that system science and the VSM also discovered the theory Y assumptions, coming from a science different from behavioral science. Douglas McGregor would be very happy with the principles of system science and the VSM! As he noted: "If, however, we accept assumptions like those of Theory Y, we will be challenged to innovate, to discover new ways of organizing and directing human effort." McGregor was thinking of theory Y in the hierarchical structure we see in the typical company organization chart, and hoping to discover new ways of organizing and directing human effort. System science and the VSM is a new and different way of organizing and directing human effort, the kind of way that McGregor was hoping for. Theory Y was a valid statement of reality in 1960. And it still is, for the greatest generation, for the boomers, for Gen X, for Gen Y, and for Gen@.

Hertzberg, in proposing a "motivator department" in the HR function was thinking also of a hierarchical organization structure, managed and controlled by higher-level authority. For the hierarchy, HR would be the place for a motivator department. Could a motivator department work anywhere in a hierarchy? Could motivators come from above? Probably, yes, if HR could create work environments favorable to theory Y assumptions. Motivations are part of what each person brings to the job. Motivations flourish throughout the company depending on the work environment. Motivators can't be installed.

System science and the VSM offer a valid view of what the company is and how it works. And when we understand system science and the VSM we discover the better ways of organizing and directing human effort that McGregor was looking for. System science and the VSM provide the motivators that Hertzberg thought might be nurtured in the corporate hierarchy by an HR motivator department. HR will find system science and the VSM a long-sought key to effective organization, management, and development.

The VSM and Theory Y

Theory Y works, of course, in any kind of management structure, wherever there is room for it to work. But when we understand our company as described in the VSM, and we structure and manage the company as described in the VSM, we see that theory Y is an essential part of the system. Without theory Y assumptions, executive management could not see and understand black boxes, requisite variety, self-organization, and self-control.

Consider the VSM structure. The corporate VSM describes a viable, very complex, purposeful, probabilistic system as described in Chapter 2. The VSM models functions, not titles. The VSM includes the environments the company lives in. The VSM includes communication channels. The VSM includes the principles that describe how systems work and communicate to accomplish their purpose. Among these principles:

- Recursion. At each level of recursion each viable, very complex, purposeful, probabilistic system can be modeled with the VSM.
- Requisite variety. Amplifying the voice of management and attenuating variety in operations and in the environments, decisions are made throughout the company where requisite variety can exist to make decisions wisely.
- Black boxes. Each VSM is a black box to higher-level management. Higher-level management lacks requisite variety to intervene intelligently within a black box.
- Self-organization. Every system has a capability for self-organization. Systems aren't "organized by." Systems organize themselves.
- Self-control. Through feedback from the work itself the system itself controls its performance to achieve desired purpose.

Think about the corporate VSM showing functions and relationships; everything that's needed to make the corporation successful. Jobs and units can be designed to produce the results needed from each function. How could these jobs be done without the reality of theory Y assumptions? The corporate VSM also defines the system 1s, which become recursion 1 from the corporate VSM. Each system 1 is a VSM like the corporate VSM with the same system characteristics and the same theory Y assumptions about people.

Continue on with recursions to the level of plants, departments, processes, work groups. All can be modeled with the VSM. All have the same system characteristics. All require theory Y assumptions. That's the way people, in general, are. The VSM and system thinking is what Douglas McGregor was looking for—a new way of organizing and directing human effort.

The VSM and the Motivator Department

Herzberg, of course, was thinking of how to bring a motivating structure of work into a hierarchical enterprise structure. How better than to put a motivator department into the hands of the HR function. HR was concerned with people. HR stood at the executive level. HR could install and administer functions, like performance appraisal. An HR department could install motivators. But HR did not welcome Herzberg's idea. Motivator Departments did not appear. No response was probably the right response. Motivators can't be installed. Motivators have to happen within people according to how human effort is organized and directed.

The VSM and system thinking is a different way to "see" the company and how the company works. Great discoveries come from seeing old things in new ways. If we change the way we look at things, the things we look at change. When we look at our company through the lens of the VSM, the company we're looking at changes. Or, rather, our understanding of what the company is and how it works changes. The VSM leads us to new discoveries about our company. There's no big restructuring that might win applause from Wall Street. But important changes begin.

Changes begin with mapping the company into the VSM model and understanding the system science and cybernetics embedded in the model. This requires us to put all the boxes on the present organization chart into the VSM. What belongs in system 5, executive leadership? What belongs in system 4, the outside and future? In system 3, the here and now? In system 2, the coordinating homeostat? What are the system 1 business units? Stafford Beer would lead a management group through this exercise to a first draft VSM in a half-day dialog session, explaining the system science and the cybernetics. And those participating would begin to see their company in a new way. They would begin to see their own responsibilities in a different way. They would begin to see new possibilities for the company.

A first draft VSM is very preliminary. Still needed:

1. Clear understanding of the system science principles embedded in the VSM
2. A clear and inspiring definition of the company and its purpose

3. Additional work on the VSM
4. Clear understanding of the communication channels
5. Key metrics of performance
6. Clear assignment of responsibilities for the VSM functions to individuals
7. Assigning relationships with the seven environments
8. Definition, boundaries, purpose, resources, and goals for each system 1; their Resource Bargains.

Each of the above needs to be worked out in collaboration among those involved. And the final VSM worked out through this process is not the final. The VSM, continuously monitored by system 4, continues to evolve.

The process summarized above produces a VSM for the corporation. The same process would be followed to develop a VSM for each system 1 at each level of recursion. Learning and applying the VSM has been a highly motivating experience for members of the Greatest Generation, the Boomers, Gen X, Gen Y, and for all we know about Gen @ will be for them, too. For all perceived differences, achievement motivation, power motivation, change motivation, endurance motivation, and theory Y assumptions needed for company success, seem to continue through all generations.

The VSM way of organizing and directing human effort:

- Recursion
- Black boxes
- Requisite variety
- Self-organization
- Self-control

provide the climate for motivation. The VSM relies on McGregor's theory Y, and is the motivator Hertzberg hoped could happen.

COLLECTIVE IQ [4]

Douglas Engelbart has been called the patron saint of the computer industry. He pioneered the hardware and software that converted computers from data machines into information machines. Engelbart made the computer the essential tool for knowledge workers. He invented the mouse, videoconferencing, multiple-window screens, and hypertext. He visualizes how the new powerful tools of digital technology can raise the collective IQ of organizations.

Companies, he says, depend on their "capability infrastructure" for their success. That capability infrastructure is the combination of the company's human system and its tool system. The tool system includes facilities, media, machinery, computers and all manifestations of digital technology, and other technologies used by the company. Human-based capabilities combining with tool-based capabilities have created a very high-level capability infrastructure. A company capability infrastructure can:

- Design and manufacture multi-gigabyte computer chips
- Deliver a package across the country tomorrow morning
- Build a space station
- Deliver a pizza in 30 minutes
- Each year build a car that is better than the car built the year before
- Manufacture to six sigma quality
- Produce a blockbuster movie

Englebart contends that the development of tool systems has progressed far faster and further than has the development of companies' human systems. The capabilities of today's tool systems are far beyond the capabilities of the companies' human systems to employ them fully. So the company's capability infrastructure lags behind what is possible. How to improve the human system? Dr. Englebart's solution is to increase the organization's collective IQ (CIQ).

Collective IQ can be the focus for improving organization capability, and increasing the organization's capability infrastructure. The new digital technology makes possible the concurrent development, integration, and application of knowledge that continuously adds to the company's collective IQ. Figure 9.1 illustrates the knowledge domains of a manufacturing company. The company's knowledge resources include all company functions: management, marketing, finance, legal, procurement, quality, manufacturing, and engineering; plus subcontractors, suppliers, customers, and joint-venture partners.

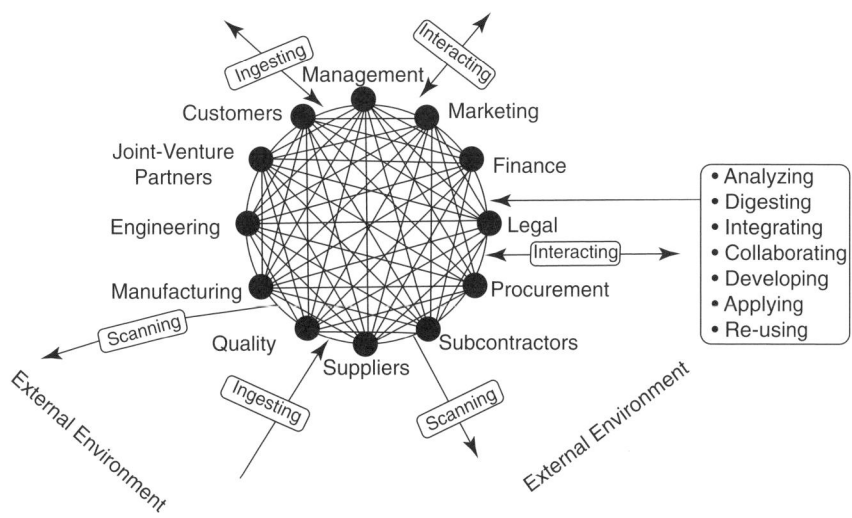

Source: Douglas Engelbart, *Collective IQ*, unpublished
Essay, 1995. Used with permission.

Figure 9.1 Knowledge domains of a manufacturing company (Source: Douglas C. Engelbart, *Collective IQ*, unpublished essay, 1995. Used with permission.)

All the functions of the company system continuously scan the relevant environments. Information from the environments is continuously ingested into the company system. Inside the company system, continuous analyzing, digesting, integrating, collaborating, developing, applying, and re-using this information increases collective IQ. The capabilities of the tool system are more wisely employed. The company's capability infrastructure grows.

Figure 9.1 looks very much like the VSM with its linkages into the environments. The VSM and system thinking offers a structure and direction of work that can continuously improve the company's collective IQ and the company's capability infrastructure.

OVERVIEW: THE ESSENCE OF CHAPTER 9

Any system—including the viable, very complex, purposeful, probabilistic system that is a corporation—is what it does. What companies do is create and keep customers. And everything the company does in creating value for customers and creating and keeping customers is done by people. The company's greatest resource is its people. Or, stated more meaningfully, the company is its people and their capabilities.

Of seven key performance areas that determine company success:

1. Creating and keeping customers
2. Quality and productivity
3. Innovation
4. Profitability
5. Organization capability
6. Physical and financial resources
7. Public and environment responsibility

organization capability is the performance area that determines success in all the others.

There are many motivations influencing behavior. Individuals are typically motivated in varying degrees by several motivators. Important motivators needed in company people include achievement motivation and endurance motivation. Achievement motivation is typically learned beginning with childhood experience. But achievement motivation among company people can be learned and strengthened from the way jobs are designed. The way jobs are designed in the VSM structure and methods of management teach and improve achievement motivation. In leadership positions throughout the company, a mature power motivation and change motivation also help strengthen organization capability.

The company organization chart shows a hierarchy of organization units, each reporting upward to the next higher level of authority, to the CEO and the Board of Directors, the highest authority. The Viable System Model (VSM) is not a hierarchy. It does not show people. It shows the functions needed for the company to achieve its purpose, and the relationships and communications among these functions. And it identifies and defines the operating units of the company that produce the products and services that define what the company is. A system, and a company, is what it does. The VSM also includes information channels, and the links with the company's outside environments—commercial, technical, economic, political, social, educational, and ecological.

The company VSM, and the recursion of this model throughout the company, provide a framework for the design of jobs that will motivate performance, and help assure continuing improvement in company capability. In this chapter some General Electric experiences and some Google experiences are related to the VSM to describe how VSM structure and management principles improve organization capability.

A short section on performance appraisal describes how the VSM structure and management principles offer new approaches for performance appraisal. Like the VSM, performance appraisal would begin with a purpose—to improve performance where the work is done, continuously improving company capability. Wage and salary awards would not be an outcome from, or tied to, performance appraisal. Wages and salaries satisfy or dissatisfy. The job itself is the motivator. Instead of an annual performance appraisal, a continuous performance achievement dialog can be a motivating experience, improving performance.

In the last 50 years, two seminal books very much informed, but perhaps little affected, the management of people in business organizations: *The Human Side of Enterprise*, by Douglas McGregor (1960), and *Work and the Nature of Man*, by Frederick Hertzberg (1966). Both books were based on extensive research. What both books advocated required change in traditional management. But hierarchical organization structures could not easily accommodate Hertzberg's "motivator department" or McGregor's "theory Y." The VSM network structure and management principles rely on theory Y, and do what Hertzberg proposed for a motivator department.

McGregor and Hertzberg were working during the time when scientists were conducting the research that led to general system theory, system science, and the VSM. The connection was not made at that time. But it can be made now. The VSM way of organizing and directing human effort—recursion, black boxes, requisite variety, self-organization, and self-control—provide the climate for motivation. The VSM depends on McGregor's Theory Y, and is the motivator Hertzberg hoped could happen.

Douglas Engelbart, the patron saint of the computer industry, advocates continuously increasing "collective IQ" to expand the company's "capability infrastructure." The VSM and system thinking offers a structure and direction of work than can increase collective IQ.

NOTES

[1] Frederick Herzberg, *Work and the Nature of Man*, World Publishing Company, Cleveland and New York, 1966.

[2] David C. McClelland, *The Achieving Society*, Van Nostrand, New York, 1961.

[3] Much of the information in this section is reported in John D. Drake, *Performance Appraisal—One More Time*, Crisp Publications, Menlo Park, California, 1997. Used with permission.

[4] Douglas C. Engelbart, *Collective IQ*, unpublished essay, 1995.

Chapter **10**

The Viable System Model and Public and Environmental Responsibility

This book defines a company as a viable, very complex, purposeful, probabilistic system. As a system, a company has the attributes that system science describes as characteristic of all systems. These system characteristics give management at all levels:

- A new way to see and understand how the company works
- A new way to structure the company and its businesses at all levels of recursion
- New ways to lead all efforts toward the achievement of company purpose and goals
- A capability for greater achievement

VIABILITY IN FAST-CHANGING ENVIRONMENTS

"Viable," the ability to live in its environment, is in the definition of a company as a system. Any existing company is viable, for now. But the company lives in the seven environments described in this book, and these environments continuously change, evolve. Will the company be viable tomorrow? This chapter deals with the important question of sustainability—how the company can continue to be viable and successful in its continually changing environments.

Holistic Management, by William Christopher
Copyright © 2007 John Wiley & Sons, Inc., Publication

Why should we be concerned about sustainability? Companies have lived successfully in these changing environments all their lives and expect to continue to do so. What is different now? What is different now is environmental change that rapidly obsoletes past practices and threatens viability like never before.

A company launched in 1950 came into a world of 2.5 billion people. After 100,000 years of human life on earth, in the year 1950 world population reached 2.5 billion. Now world population is over 6 billion, heading for 9 to 10 billion by mid-century! Our technical environment has enabled agriculture to expand to feed these ballooning numbers, and has supported a standard of living for many beyond the dreams of earlier generations. To meet the needs and wants of expanding populations, since 1950 global economic output, in 2001 dollars, grew from 7 trillion dollars to 46 trillion dollars, converting the world's resources into products and services for people. And all this huge growth and expansion has happened on our finite earth, which we now can see from outer space; a small, green, water planet alone in space, orbiting around a minor star, our sun.

On the road to 2050 as world population grows toward 9 to 10 billion, and industrial output grows even faster, the company's environments will change faster than ever before. Expect never before seen change in each of the environments—commercial, technical, economic, social, political, educational, and ecological. Huge threats. Urgent opportunities. These seven environments in the year 2005 were very different from what they were in 1975. With the much, much greater changes happening now, what will they be by 2035? This chapter summarizes some of what's happening.

Sustainability is possible, but not assured. Note in the definition of viable the words, "capable of continuing to exist." Companies have the capability now. Will they have it next year? Five years from now? Twenty-five years from now? We are comfortable with the idea of the half-life of an engineer's training being maybe five to seven years. What is the half-life of company sustainability? Probably less. Sustainability will require continuing learning, changing, acting, transforming.

Today most companies are viable, capable of continuing to exist in their environments. But do they have the capability of continuing to exist in the seven continuously changing, evolving, transforming environments they relate to? If they wait for the unfolding of history to answer that question, the answer will be "no." Instead of waiting, companies need to continuously learn, change, adapt; deal with threats, find new opportunities in the environmental change around them. Environmental change in each of these seven environments is threatening, and full of great opportunity.

Of the seven environments companies relates to, six are environments created by our civilization, our culture: the commercial environment, the technical environment, the economic environment, the political environment, the social environment, and the educational environment. The seventh is the ecosphere, the thin layer of earth, water, and atmosphere surrounding our planet that is the home for all life on earth, the earth's biosphere. The company and the six cultural environments interact, each with all the others, and all are embedded in and interact with the ecological environment. See Figure 10.1, which is a repeat of Figure 2.3 in Chapter 2. The ecosphere changes for

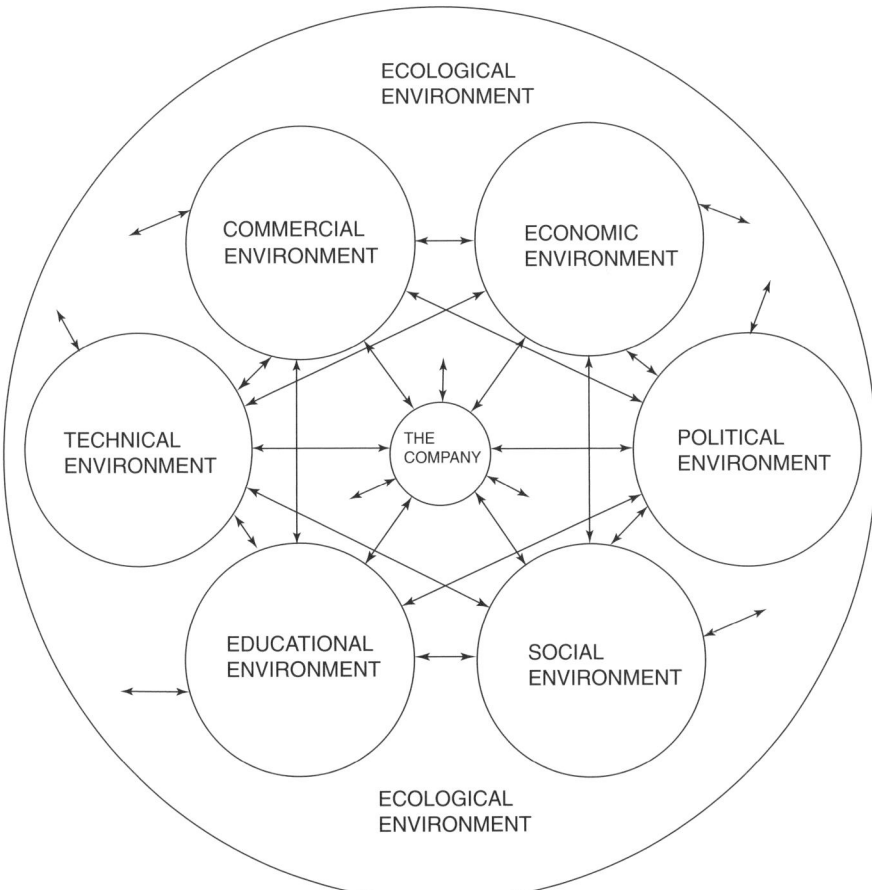

Figure 10.1 The company interacting with its environments

natural reasons. But the actions of six plus billions of people now on earth, and billions more yet to come, change it, too.

SIX CULTURE-MADE ENVIRONMENTS

First, let's consider the six culture-created environments that our company must continue to relate to successfully. We can understand and relate to these environments because they have been a part of our learning and experience. We know them well. And we have continued to know them well as they have changed and evolved. Companies have created great successes at the leading edge of change in the first three of these environments: commercial, technical, and economic. Companies, less innovational, less adaptive, can be hurt or killed by changes in these environments. Changes in the three other culture-created environments, political, social, and educational can be opportunities, or threats, too.

The pace of change in these six cultural environments is speeding up as a result of their complex interrelationships and the growing numbers in everything. How well do we know these environments for the years ahead? How will we keep our company viable—able to continue living in its changing environments?

The Commercial Environment

A system is what it does. The viable, very complex, purposeful, probabilistic system that is a corporation produces products and services and creates and keeps customers. To achieve sustainability, it must successfully and continuously deal with all six of the cultural environments. Among these, first of all a company must successfully and continuously deal with the environment where the customers are; the commercial environment. In this environment are all the customers and prospects, and their customers and prospects; all the company's competitors and prospective competitors; all the participants in the company's supply chain and prospective and possible alternatives; and all those who supply services to all of these. And everything in the commercial environment is continually changing. The commercial environment also interacts with the other cultural environments; more change.

But is change threat, or opportunity? All six of the cultural environments described in this book have been with us since the times of early civilizations, some five thousand years ago. All have continuously changed. In the commercial environment there was trade, goods for goods; then goods for money. As populations grew, the commercial environment grew and changed. Considering where we were, and where we are today, change in the commercial environment has certainly meant more opportunity than threat. Until now. Throughout human history the size, complexity, and rate of change in the commercial environment parallels the curve of economic growth.

Almost certainly that rate of growth, complexity, and change—and opportunity—will continue, unless a destructive intervention from a higher level of recursion happens. Where could such a destructive intervention come from? Most likely: The ecosphere. The biosphere. Or the social order.

Whatever may happen, the company must first remain viable in the commercial environment in whatever ways that environment grows and changes. Viability will depend on company performance in the key performance areas described in this book. For viability over the years ahead in all these performance areas, the company will have to be among the better; more likely among the best. To help achieve that goal, performance objectives in all of the key performance areas including social and environmental responsibility need to be included in the company's plans and budgets, along with and even more important than the financial objectives. Performance in all the key performance areas needs to improve continuously to assure viability in the commercial environment.

Companies are well-tuned to their commercial environment. Marketing and sales are in continuous contacts with customers and prospective customers, and with distributors, agents, and other intermediaries and service providers. They are also keenly intent on learning from their contacts all they can about customer needs and competitive actions, products, and capabilities. Purchasing is continuously in contact with suppliers, prospective suppliers, and all others in their supply chain to learn what is new and what is changing. All this monitoring helps companies discover and respond to threats and opportunities.

Not all knowledge about the commercial environment is known at corporate headquarters. It is known throughout the company. Businesses at all levels of recursion work in, know, and continuously monitor their commercial environments. The communications channels with the commercial environment are working. As Stafford Beer points out, companies behave the way the VSM says they behave whether or not they are aware of the VSM and system science. Companies deal successfully in their relations with their commercial environment, but they can do better. The VSM and the capabilities in the several levels of recursion help the company interact effectively in the commercial environment. The VSM can also help companies interact effectively in their other environments too. Ignoring what is happening in any of them can be harmful, even fatal.

A big change in the commercial environment is . . . globalization. For businesses today, customers, prospective customers, competitors, suppliers, and enablers are everywhere in the world. Country, area, and cultural differences bring new opportunities, and new threats. Intensely involved in their commercial environments, companies are increasingly aware of the opportunities and threats in globalization. Change is happening. Success will depend on how each business performs in its key performance areas to meet the requirements of the increasingly global commercial environment.

Sustainability in the commercial environment requires performance among the best in the key performance areas. Sustainability also requires dealing successfully with the opportunities and the threats in globalization and other changes in the commercial environment. Using the VSM and its structured communications with the commercial environment at all levels of recursion will help.

The Technical Environment

The technical environment is an environment companies interact with to assure that they use the best technologies to achieve their goals. New technology creates different, better, lower cost products and services. Technology also creates different, better, and lower cost processes and alternatives to what the company is doing now. And new technologies will be needed to find sustainability in a world of swelling populations.

The scientist, Edwin Land created Polaroid Corporation in 1937 and achieved a dominant position in polarized sunglasses, a new and different kind of sunglasses. Later he invented and developed the instant film Polaroid camera, with first commercial sales in 1948. The instant Polaroid camera created a big market for a new and different kind of photography—instant pictures. Polaroid was built on invention and innovation. But Polaroid was late in entering the market for digital cameras, and offered no significant innovations. By that time Polaroid was managing what it had created more than inventing and innovating the new, different, better. The company filed for bankruptcy in 2001, its greatest value its well-known trademark earned from the company's success in instant cameras.

The Haloid Company, a manufacturer of photographic paper and equipment, developed and in 1959 commercialized the world's first plain paper photocopier. The photocopier used the process of xerography. The company changed its name to Xerox, and expanded rapidly through the 1960s. Then, during the 1970s, with basic patents expired, the company was threatened by high-quality, lower-cost copiers from Japanese competitors. In the 1980s and on, Xerox responded, employed new, low-cost, high quality, design and manufacturing methods. The company discovered digital printing methods and other technology that greatly expanded their product line and the services the company offers. Technology created new customer benefits and made Xerox a leader in lean manufacturing. The company met the competitive threat and recovered to become the world's largest document management company. Continuing success requires the discovery and innovation of the new, different, better.

Breakthroughs replacing earlier technology soon face the next breakthrough. Leaders need to be early with whatever comes next. Whatever comes next will be discovered by the company, or, more likely, found in the technical environment. Successful companies closely monitor the technical environment for both threats and opportunities, and act on what they find.

Technology change changes the ways we live. The steam engine powered the industrial revolution. Steam gave us the railroads. Trains could carry more people faster, farther, and more comfortably than horses; and freight much more efficiently than horse-drawn wagons. Steam could power ships more efficiently than wind. Then came oil and the internal combustion engine to put the nation and the world on wheels and in the air; and the telephone and radio to revolutionize communications. All the new technologies rapidly improved in continuous evolution and revolution. Our parents and grandparents saw huge changes over their lifetimes. Now we see those kinds of changes in a decade. What will we see by 2035? Even more amazing advancements. And even much more serious threats.

Technology forecasting is risky, but less risky than not looking ahead. A discipline of technology forecasting developed after World War II, led by James R. Bright and Milton E. F. Schoeman at the University of Texas, and Joseph P. Martino, Theodore J. Gordon, Marvin J. Cetron, and others. Technology forecasting became an important part of strategic planning, a discipline that was becoming a part of annual planning and budgeting at that time. Large companies were heavily involved in their annual planning and budgeting cycles, including strategic planning and technology forecasting. In the 1940s plans and budgets were prepared in December for the following year. Typically, the plan was to continue doing what the company was doing. The budget was X% more. By the 1970s, with strategic plans, technology forecasting, and complex budgets, companies were beginning their planning and budgeting cycle mid-year and ending often after the beginning of the budget year.

Traditional technology forecasting quite successfully forecasts performance parameters such as passenger-miles per hour of civilian aircraft, efficiency of illumination sources, and maximum thrust from liquid propellant rocket engines. But forecasting of parameters had nothing to say about how the improvement would be achieved. While parameters could be forecast, the inventions needed to make it happen were unknown. Invention cannot be forecast, but it can be observed, which may be good enough for innovative companies. See Chapter 8.

Technology forecasting helps us see ahead. In recent years new technologies have appeared to help product engineers discover the new technology and the new higher-performing products, among these technologies, TRIZ. Analyzing hundreds of thousands of invention descriptions in world patent databases, Genrikh Altschuller and his associates discovered logic paths for technological innovation. These methods help users of TRIZ discover next-generation new products. See Chapter 8.

The VSM and system thinking help companies find the changes in the technical environment that matter to them. At the corporate level, system 4 continually communicates with the technical environment, and the other environments too, for information on anything that matters to the achievement of company purpose. In each of these environments there is huge complexity, however much attenuated far beyond the match of whatever complexity, however amplified, could exist in corporate system 4. No requisite variety there. But corporate system 4 does not need to know everything out there in the technical environment, or any other environment. They only need to know what needs to be known at the corporate level for the achievement of company purpose. So they select out that narrow slice from the technical environment—or any other environment—and leave the rest, some of which will be picked up by the system 4s in other parts of the company as important for them.

The corporate system 4 is not alone. All viable systems at all levels of recursion also have working communication channels between their system 4s and the environments that relate to their businesses. For the technical environment, each of these tens or hundreds of system 4s select the parts of the technical environment that matter to their business, and these they monitor. Each system 4 attenuates the complexity in the technical environment to their specific interests and concerns. A corporate system 4 cannot attenuate enough the complexity in the technical environment, or any other, to achieve requisite variety for all company interests. But all system 4s, collectively, can. Nor can the corporate system 4 amplify the variety in management enough for requisite variety for all company interests. But all the system 4s, collectively, can.

With the company's large network of system 4s, and large network of management people involved, there can be requisite variety where decisions are made. The company knows what it needs to know and acts where it needs to act. What the company needs to know is not aggregated in the corporate system 4 planning department. What the company needs to know exists throughout the company, where it is needed.

Whatever a company has seen and learned in the technical environment, and what the company knows today, is history. New, different, better, lower-cost technologies appear faster than ever. In 2006 at the "Singularity Summit" at Stanford University, leading scientists and futurists, presented what they know now about what technology will be in the very near future. Among their views:

- Moore's law on exponential growth for transistors on a chip may apply now in all of human progress and innovation. Gordon Moore, co-founder of Intel, in 1965 stated that the number of transistors on a chip doubles about every two years. Moore's Law, proved accurate. In 2006 the number reached 1 billion with the exponential growth rate expected to continue for the foreseeable future.
- Within a few decades, machine intelligence will surpass human intelligence.
- The 100 years of this new century will produce more than 20 thousand times the technological progress of the previous century.
- Nanotechnology will create any physical product using low-cost information processes.
- Reliable urban robot driving will be available by 2010. Just get in the car, key in your destination, and the car will take you there, following all the traffic rules.
- By 2030 most of the miles driven will be robot driven.

- Nanotech will take over manufacturing in the 2020s.
- By the 2020s we will be able to upload our brains into computer storage.
- Human aging will be reversed; illness prevented.

This is only a short list in what will become, in reality, a long list of technical advances that is changing everything in this new century. Now think of this surging technology progress in a world of 6+ billion people increasing to 9 to 10 billion by mid-century. Technology advances in a micro-scale and nano-scale world. But 6 and 10 billion people live in a human-scale world. A 50-year-old in 2050 will be the same as a 50-year-old was in 1950; possibly more intelligent, possibly healthier. But present trends add doubt on those two possibilities. In any case, the 50-year-old in 2050—and the other 9 to 10 billion inhabitants of planet earth—will need human-scale housing, human-scale clothing, a human-scale diet, human-scale transport, human-scale occupations, human-scale entertainment, human-scale everything.

Perhaps the singularity will occur when the 20 thousand times speed-up in technological change confronts the sustenance needs of 9 to 10 billion people on a finite earth scaled to the sustenance needs of perhaps 2 to 3 billion people. In every company, the system 4s have a lot of work to do in the technical environment to keep their company or business unit viable.

The Economic Environment

In both the commercial environment and the technical environment, the company is an active participant. Those environments, like the company, are affected by cycles in the economic environment. For all our knowledge and fine-tuning, we still have periods of strong economic conditions followed at some point by slow-down or recession, followed at some point by strong economic conditions again.

In today's complex world it is not everything moving the same way at the same time. The economic environment in some areas, some industries, some countries, some technologies, may be moving differently from others. Successfully relating to the economic environment is a matter of observation; knowing what's happening that can affect the company and the individual business.

For big picture projections of the economic environment for the country and world-wide, corporate planning can retain services providing this information and send the information on to operations at all levels of recursion through the routine communication channel. All relate to the big picture. Specific information by industry and market can be left to the system 4s at each level of recursion. What relates to the specific business at each level of recursion needs to be known in that business.

For the economic environment, as for the other cultural environments, the VSM and system thinking structures a way to interact with each of them successfully. The corporate level deals with corporate needs. At each level of recursion the businesses at that level deal with their specific needs. The corporation has a huge amount of knowledge, but not all at one place. The knowledge is where it's needed. By many attenuations of environmental complexity, and many amplifications of the voice of management, requisite variety can be achieved where decisions are made.

The company's commercial environment relates to the economic environment. The total economic environment includes much more than we see in the commercial environment. The total economic environment includes inflation/deflation, interest rates, taxes, exchange rates, comparative advantage/disadvantage, and all else in the national and global economy that affects the company. Like the commercial and technical environments, the economic environment brings threats and opportunities on a global scale. And, as in the commercial and technical environments, the company strategy for sustainability in the economic environment is performance among the best in the key performance areas described in this book . . . with a keen eye always on what's happening in the natural and global economic environment.

The Political Environment

Institutions in the political environment impose taxes, and create legislation and regulations in the public interest that all must comply with. Institutions in the political environment may also be customers.

Taxes, legislation, and regulations have consequences for companies. So companies, individually and through business organizations, present these consequences and their position to legislators and regulating agencies. Others, with supporting or conflicting interests do the same. Where, in all this information, is the public interest? That will be decided by the legislators, and the regulators, who also have their own experience and research to guide them. Amid all the conflicting influences, their responsibility is to find the public interest.

For all who have their specific interests and concerns there is the separate matter of campaign contributions. A continuing legislative drive to regulate large campaign contributions seems always to fall short of its goals. Whatever happens with legislative controls on campaign contributions, technology and the internet are changing campaign fund-raising, and campaigns themselves. Organized efforts, and also unorganized popular efforts, can attract huge numbers of small contributions and raise huge sums. And candidates using the internet as a communications medium can reach large numbers of voters at low cost, also helping to democratize elections.

New ways of communicating will also change how business and industry, and other interests, communicate their messages, and receive messages, in the political environment. Companies need to find, and use, the most effective; as will others.

Companies, in presenting their interests will do well to present their interest supportive of the public interest. Finding and keeping the public interest in mind in developing their positions, companies and industries can strive for a position that will also further the public interest. Well-run companies are good citizens. Well-run government considers the interests of all its citizens. A position good for the company or industry but bad for the public interest will hardly be persuasive.

At the corporate level, top management will have the main responsibility for relationships with the federal government and may maintain a Washington office and retain professional lobbyists to assist in these relationships. Companies may also collaborate through trade and professional organizations in their representations to government on specific issues. In addition to relationships with the federal government, top management will have responsibility for relations with multi-government collaborations such as the United Nations and the World Trade Organization.

What is represented to government and how are important. In the United States the federal government is of the people, by the people, and for the people. Individual constituencies have their specific interests. All need appropriate consideration. Government needs to understand the interests of business and industry. And business and industry needs to relate to what's wise for the country.

The political environment is more than the federal government in Washington. It is also the regional offices and activities of government agencies throughout the country. It is also state and local governments and their agencies. Responsibility for relating to these becomes the responsibility of the top managements at the levels of recursion operating in those states and localities. As with other environments, the VSM and system thinking structures a network of relationships between the company and the political environment.

The above paragraphs describe business relationships with the political environments in the United States. But today's business world is global. So the company's political relationships need to be structured similarly at all levels of government in the countries where the company operates or sells its products. The network of relationships in the political environment is global. Sustainability for the company requires constructive relationships in all the relevant political environments.

The Social Environment

In the company and at all levels of recursion it is the HR function in system 3—the here and now of operations—that has the responsibility for dealing with the social environment. But HR also has functions in system 4, the outside and future. In addition to the here and now, HR has a responsibility to find in the social environment any changes developing that may be threats or opportunities for the company. HR responsibility includes today's community relations, and also the identification of changes and trends in the society that may have consequences for the company.

Community relations includes supporting the arts, local charities, and other activities important to the communities where the company has operations. Community relations also includes encouraging and supporting employee participation in community service work. At all levels of recursion, in all communities where the company operates, community relations is a part of good company citizenship.

Identification of changes and trends in the society that may have consequences for the company is an area of uncertainty; but important. Population growth increases congestion, lengthens commutes, fills open spaces around plant locations with residential and commercial development. Growing immigration makes the English language one of several. Congestion, declining education levels, and changing values and conventions increase social ills—poverty, crime, corruption. Increasing knowledge about digital technologies among young job seekers may create opportunities. Increasing diversity and market segmentation may offer new opportunities, and new problems. In any area or country, with changing populations and immigration is it one society, or several? Whatever is happening, what does it mean for the company?

Companies cannot much influence the social environment out there in the world around them. Some elements out there are threatening: crime, and the much more threatening, terrorism. Companies need a level of security that can defeat both of these. Other negative characteristics in the society, companies can deal with in their hiring practices: poor literacy, dishonesty, poor work habits, bad health habits, self-centeredness, carelessness, and other negative characteristics that seem to be increasing in our rapidly growing, less educated, and diverse society. Also, in their supplier certifications companies need to consider the character of the people and organizations they deal with.

A social environment important to the company and where the company is a molding influence, is the social environment within the company. Here, the guiding principle is organization capability. See Chapter 9.

While companies cannot much influence the social environment around them, that social environment can much affect the company. The social environment is full of customers. Some may be direct customers, others customers of the company's customers, or their customers. The wants and needs of people out there in the social environment need to be perceived and understood by people in the company's VSM system 3, the here and now operations, and in system 4, the outside and future. This understanding feeds into product and service design, and into all the company does in creating customers.

Whatever the social environment, that is the world we work in. As the social environment changes and evolves, the HR communication links need to discover the opportunities, and assemble the information that will enable the company to deal with the threats. This activity going on at all levels of recursion enables all parts of the company to live successfully in its social environment. Sustainability in the social environment means monitoring and understanding the changes that can affect the company, and acting in ways that will help the company achieve its purpose.

The Educational Environment

In the United States from its early years, public education has been an important part of growing up, for the children, and for the country, too. Through grade eight, students got a rigorous education in reading, writing, arithmetic, civics, American history, and more. Those continuing through high school learned at an advanced level, and in additional subject areas. At the high school level there were also choices for training in the trades. In 1862 the Morrill Act granted federal lands to the states for establishing colleges that would offer education in "agriculture and the mechanic arts," extending the then-prevailing classical curriculum of American and European colleges and universities. Under the Morrill Act, states rushed to establish "land grant" colleges that have evolved to become the state university systems we have today. For children growing up, public education was free, and required through high school. The country's literate, educated citizenry created a great country. Over the twentieth century college attendance ballooned, increasing the numbers of well-educated citizens.

Education Goals   In the later years of the twentieth century education at the elementary and high school levels was working less well. School systems in other countries were graduating students with higher levels of achievement, especially in math and science. By the 1980s many states, and the federal government, were working on ways to improve public education. In 1990 the National Education Goals Panel was established as an independent agency in the executive branch to assess and report on state and national progress toward achieving eight National Education Goals. These eight goals were [1]:

1. By the year 2000, all children in America will start school ready to learn.
2. By the year 2000, the high school graduation rate will increase to at least 90 percent.
3. By the year 2000, all students will leave grades 4, 8, and 12 having demonstrated competency over challenging subject matter including English, mathematics, science, foreign languages, civics and government, economics, arts, history, and geography, and every school in America will ensure that all students learn to use their minds well, so they may be prepared for responsible citizenship, further learning, and productive employment in our Nation's modern economy.
4. By the year 2000, the Nation's teaching force will have access to programs for the continued improvement of their professional skills and the opportunity to acquire the knowledge and skills needed to instruct and prepare all American students for the next century.
5. By the year 2000, United States students will be first in the world in mathematics and science achievement.

6. By the year 2000, every adult American will be literate and will possess the knowledge and skills necessary to compete in a global economy and exercise the rights and responsibilities of citizenship.

7. By the year 2000, every school in the United States will be free of drugs, violence, and the unauthorized presence of firearms and alcohol and will offer a disciplined environment conducive to learning.

8. By the year 2000, every school will promote partnerships that will increase parental involvement and participation in promoting the social, emotional, and academic growth of children.

The National Education Goals also specified specific objectives under each of these goals.

Look again at each of the eight goals. In each of them we are still a long way from achieving the goal. The high school graduation rate would seem to be an achievable goal. But in 2005, one-third of the students who had entered high school dropped out before graduation.

We are now years into the new century, and our national education goals for the year 2000 remain a very distant dream. ACT produces one of the United States' leading college admissions tests. Comparing past ACT scores with students' grades their freshman year, ACT determined "benchmark" scores for English, reading, math, and science. Benchmarks indicate the skill level needed for a 70 percent chance of earning a C or better, and a 50 percent chance of earning a B or better in the student's freshman year in college. In 2005, about 40 percent of the nation's high school graduates took the ACT. Of these, 68 percent achieved the benchmark in English, 51 percent achieved the benchmark in reading, 41 percent achieved the benchmark in math, and 26 percent achieved the benchmark in science. Only 21 percent achieved the benchmark in all four. We are a long, long way from our education goals.

Over recent decades a lot of work has been done in the United States to improve public education. There are many examples of high-achieving schools. But progress toward national goals is modest, if any. It seems that for the most part trends are taking us further away from our National Education Goals instead of toward them.

Consider the VSM We seem more ready to set high-achievement goals than we are to do what needs to be done to achieve these goals. The country's education system is a huge viable, very complex, purposeful, probabilistic system. In what it does, it functions like all other systems, as described in this book. The country's education system can be modeled with the VSM as can the systems in each of its many levels of recursion to the level of the individual school, and departments within the school. Seeing the education system in the light of system science, it is apparent that in the highest level metasystem, the US Department of Education, there can be no panel or commission or any combination of talent that can design and achieve change in educational achievement many recursions away at the level of the individual school. They lack requisite variety.

The higher level system can set parameters that apply throughout all levels of recursion, and these need to be as limited as possible, and set wisely. But at each level of recursion the "what" and "how" of achievement needs to be worked out in each of the operations at that level for that operation, but not for operations at further levels of recursion. With a systems view, thousands and tens of thousands and probably hundreds of thousands of people would do what needs to be done at their system level to improve the performance of their operations. The end result at the school level can then be well-educated graduates.

Examining the education system through the eyes of system science and the VSM would likely result in some restructuring in the total system, and would certainly result in changes in management practices. But the capability for graduating well-educated students at all levels could be significantly improved.

Improving education achievement levels throughout the country cannot be accomplished through algorithms designed in a metasystem, several recursions away. We are dealing with heuristics and the requirement is requisite variety. Each level of recursion can control performance at that level of recursion, but that capability does not extend to other recursions. To deal with the huge complexity we will need to involve all levels of recursion and establish requisite variety and control at each level of recursion for that level of recursion. In total, many, many people will be involved, not in following an algorithm from a higher level, but in finding better ways for their level of recursion. There will be experiments. Many good ways will be found. There will be communication among operations at each level of recursion, and between levels of recursion. Everyone in the education system can accomplish much more at their level of recursion for their level of recursion than can be accomplished by interventions from a higher level.

The comments above sketch only briefly the value of the VSM and system thinking in education. Visualizing education in the light of the VSM, corporations using the VSM can see where and how they can interrelate with the education environment in ways beneficial to both.

This book describes how the VSM and system thinking can improve performance in a corporation. Similarly, the VSM and system thinking can improve performance in any viable, very complex, purposeful, probabilistic system such as:

- an education system
- each recursion of an education system to the level of the individual school
- any department of government
- a government—national, regional, or local
- a political party
- a charity
- a non-government organization (NGO)
- and other organization established for a purpose

The Company Role   How does the company relate to the educational environment? At the corporate level, and at each level of recursion, communication and liaison might be assigned to one or more people in system 4. Or, because of its importance, this responsibility might be assigned to an executive officer in system 5, system 4, or system 3. Companies are affected by the quality of public education. High school graduates, and high school dropouts too, become their employees and their customers. And in the United States the capability of these young people is less than it needs to be.

In the United States, the swelling numbers of students and their diversity in languages, cultures, race, family backgrounds, and physical and mental abilities is overwhelming an education system that has not evolved fast enough to educate today's students to their needed levels of achievement. Continuing innovations will be needed. Companies, with their heterostats that produce successful innovations may be able to contribute to innovations needed in public education. The companies come from a good perspective—the employers of public education's graduates, and the suppliers of the products and services they will need.

Innovations will be needed in all aspects of the public education system: curriculum, facilities, funding, teaching and learning methods, and more. Like a company, a school system is a viable, very complex, purposeful, probabilistic system. The VSM and system thinking could help in mapping where change and improvement is needed. And where there is need, innovation skills can find answers.

Today, we don't have before us a blank slate. There is much research, many experiments, many school successes, and many teacher/student learning successes. By continuing to work and innovate at many levels—US Department of Education, state departments of education, school districts, high schools, middle schools, elementary schools, individual class rooms—we can find our way to goals like those aimed for by the year 2000. Companies with their several levels of recursion can pair with the levels of the education system in their liaison and communication with the educational environment.

There is value, too, in liaison and communication with colleges and universities. Among university professors are authorities in all the environments the company relates to, and these authorities want and need the perspective of successful companies. American colleges and universities are among the best in the world. They don't have the catch-up problems of public education. But they do have the problem of continuing to be among the best, to control the cost of a college and university education, to find new ways to educate, to be more involved in adult continuing education. In liaison and communication with colleges and universities, "learning corporations" may contribute also to a "learning society."

Historically, company relations with the educational environment have been mostly for the employment of high school, college, and university graduates. With education goals for the year 2000 still a distant dream, companies can do more. At the local level, where improvement in achievement levels and decreasing the high school drop-out rate are especially needed, companies can help. They can support experiments to find and apply better methods in teaching and learning. They can encourage employees to participate in volunteer work. Monitoring the educational environment will find special ways the company can help.

At the college and university level, companies can both contribute to, and draw from the research and the specialized knowledge of talented professors. Company involvement with universities can find practical ways to learn from and to help each other.

Company sustainability in relation to the educational environment means supporting change and improvement in primary and secondary education, and collaborating in the appropriate ways at the university level.

ECOLOGICAL ENVIRONMENT

Our ecological environment includes two levels of systems:

1. The higher-level system is our ecosphere, the thin layer of earth, water, and atmosphere surrounding our planet that is the home for all life on earth
2. In the first recursion from the ecosphere is the biosphere, all the flora, all the fauna, all the life on earth, including ours

The six cultural environments discussed briefly above exist within the earth's biosphere. Our cultures, our cultural environments, our governments, our economy, our institutions, our companies, and all of us and our standard of living have all evolved in a sustaining biosphere; our biosphere continuing to be viable within a sustaining ecosphere. For humanity and our cultures and institutions, how sustainable is our biosphere? Our ecosphere? What will be the situation in ten years? In fifty years?

The ecosphere includes geologic systems, ocean systems, river systems, weather systems, climate systems, and more; all that is needed to support life on earth. And life appeared on earth and evolved to become today's very complex biosphere. The biosphere includes all life forms, all the flora, all the fauna. The biosphere depends on all the systems of the ecosphere for its sustainability. Individual species within the biosphere depend also on the sustainability of its interrelationships with the rest of the biosphere. The human population of the earth exists within a complex web of relationships with the rest of the biosphere. Because of our numbers and our expanding economies we are causing changes in the biosphere which we depend on for our existence. And we are causing changes in the ecosphere which all the biosphere depends on for its existence.

The Situation Today

We can trace our human history and pre-history over some ten thousand years. And if we are perceptive in what we learn, we will see that our world today is fast growing into crises more threatening, more intractable, than anything confronted by humankind in our ten thousand years of history. Few people living today have experienced an uncrowded world. One long lifetime ago most people lived in that kind of world. People one long lifetime ago could not even imagine what we now read every day in the news and experience every day in our lives.

Many are good things: 69% of American families owning their own homes. Homes heated and cooled automatically. The families in the 107 million American homes owning an average of 1.9 cars. Tires that run tens of thousands of miles without need of repair, instead of tens of miles, then repair it yourself. Heaters and air conditioners in cars— just set the temperature you want. People living in suburbs instead of in town near their jobs or on the farm. People commuting to work in their own cars instead of by streetcar. Air transportation for everyone in airplanes carrying more than three hundred people at speeds of 500 miles an hour. Vacations in Europe or Asia, not just at the near-by lake. Life expectancy almost eighty years. Retirement for everyone. Social security and medicare. Health insurance. Surgery that repairs or transplants human organs. Automatic washing machines, and driers too. Telephones you can carry with you in your pocket, and they take and send pictures, too. College education available for all. Interstate highways and freeways. Streets and highways plowed after snow storms. One long lifetime ago all these and many others were futuristic dreams, if dreamed at all.

Nor could people living one long lifetime ago even imagine the threats confronting us today: Nuclear threats. Mercury in fish. Illegal immigrants. Terrorists. 9/11. Global warming. Weather changes. Water shortages. Pollution. Safety for ourselves and our children. Weapons of mass destruction. Identity theft. Rising sea levels. One long lifetime ago, none of these threats and many others could not even be imagined.

We confront two groups of accumulating threats: (1) changes in the biosphere and in the ecosphere making our environment less livable and less provident for people, and (2) social ills.

One long lifetime ago life and news and interests centered on work, family, schools, church, community. National boundaries and a little bit into neighboring countries was about as far as we could stretch our minds and interests. Even as recently as 1939, when Germany sent its army into Poland at the start of what became World War II, the prevailing view was, "Those Europeans. Fighting again." What happened over there was no concern of ours. What a change—from then to now, the beginning of century 21!

Look at Figure 10.2. It looks simple, a sort of backward "L" on a chart. But think what that backward L is telling us. That line is a chart of the earth's human population over the last 10 thousand years. Over 10 thousand years human population rose slowly, then in the last

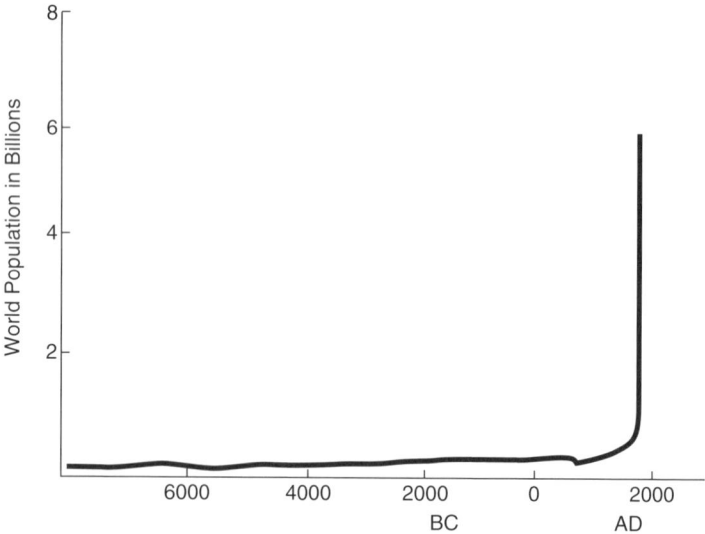

Figure 10.2   World population, 8000 BC to 2000 AD [2]

300 years began to turn upward. In 1800, the world's human population reached almost one billion. By 1920, after World War I, world population reached a total of two billion. Then in only eighty years more, from 1920 to the year 2000, world population tripled to 6.0 billion, heading toward 10. Over ten thousand years the world's human population grew slowly. Then in one lifetime, the population curve went straight up and two billion tripled to six! If Figure 10.2 had a sound track, sirens would be screening, and alarm bells would be deafening. Humanity in a finite biosphere in a finite ecosphere on a finite earth, alone in space orbiting around a minor star, now confronts uncharted territory.

The consequences from what this figures tells us will be dramatic changes completely unexpected. Unexpected and dramatic changes will result from growing social ills as populations surge, and as the impacts of these populations and their growing economies on the biosphere and on the ecosphere accumulate. At this time many people are aware of the threat from global warming and are beginning to act to reduce the threat. But few are even aware of additional consequences from ballooning world populations, equally threatening. These threats, and ideas for dealing with them, are discussed in this chapter. Revolutionary change will need to happen in our companies, in governments, and in all human institutions.

In the revolutionary change now beginning, all today's "things" become obsolete: automobiles and their infrastructure, houses, buildings, appliances, transportation, manufacturing plants and products made, food production and foods produced, health services, education, everything. The earth is not large enough for 9 to 10 billion people to live the way people in the developed countries live today. Getting to 1950 and avoiding tragedy on the way will be the greatest achievement of humankind. From science and technology must come great innovations. From the world's people must come a new unity in purpose. Present trends must change. Continuing viability and success will come to those companies helping to make happen the transformation to a livable and sustainable world for 9 to 10 billion people.

Now look at Figure 10.3. This picture is not moonrise viewed from the Earth. Figure 10.3 is a picture never before seen by humans— Earthrise, photographed from the moon. That's the earth out there in space, the surface of the moon in the foreground, photographed by Lunar Obiter 1 while orbiting the moon in 1966. One long lifetime ago the earth, vast in expanse as perceived by our human senses, was our reality. "Out there" was the moon, the solar system, and beyond that, many stars. But what mattered was the earth. And on the earth what mattered was our part of the earth, our work, family, schools, church, community. But over the last half of the twentieth century everything changed. With space exploration "out there," and

Figure 10.3 Earthrise, seen from the moon

globalization here on Earth, our awareness has become global, and cosmic.

Five hundred years ago we learned the Earth is round. Now we understand our vast earth as a small planet orbiting a minor star in the outer regions of one of billions of galaxies, each with billions of stars. Over the last fifty years we learned our place in the universe. We learned that our earth is a very special planet, and very well placed in its orbit around its star, our sun. It's a water planet, with earth, an atmosphere, and the right amount of warmth from the sun to support a huge variety of flora and fauna that is all life on earth. Dominant among all life on earth is humankind.

One long lifetime ago we were two billion people inhabiting the Earth. The bounty of the earth could well provide for our numbers. An optimum human population for planet earth, for an adequate standard of living for all, is typically estimated somewhere in the range of two to three billion people. But today, experts assert that for today's six billion people, poverty can be eliminated with a basic standard of living achievable for all. Considering the living condition of so many of today's six billion people and today's accumulating social ills and ecological ills, other experts see this assertion as a dream. If we resolve the social ills and the ecological ills, there remains the problem of resources. Edward O. Wilson, Harvard Professor and Pulitzer prize-winning author, in this book, *Consilience*, states that to raise the standard of living of all the world's six billion people to the US level with existing technology would require two more planet earths [3]! What lies ahead for our one planet earth and the coming nine to ten billion people within the next 50 years?

Future 1: Crash and Chaos

Look again at Figure 10.1, with world population now six billion, and heading almost straight up. Population experts expect this growth line to follow a sigmoid curve, leveling off at nine to ten billion some time around mid-century. Look again at Figure 10.2, earthrise as seen from the moon. There's the earth in the void of space. No expanding earth, no expanding ecosphere and no expanding biosphere to accommodate growing numbers of people.

We face the greatest challenge ever confronted by humankind: sustaining our human culture and our human values in a world of six billion people heading fast toward nine or ten billion, all dependent on a finite biosphere and a finite ecosphere that are already degrading.

Figure 10.4 presents one forecast for the future of humankind on earth. This forecast presents humanity with a doomsday, rapidly approaching. Within the next few decades world populations and countries and cultures may crash in chaos, from some combination of biosphere and ecosphere degradation, severe social ills, civil strife, economic collapse, or some combination of catastrophic events resulting from a stressed population inhabiting a stressed planet. Huge and growing numbers of people stress the planet. Industrial expansion growing even more rapidly than populations stresses the planet. Huge numbers of people uneducated, unemployed, and poor stress the social order. Fast-growing social ills and civil strife increasingly stress the social order. A stressed social order increasingly stresses the planet. This human footprint on planet earth increasingly stresses and degrades the biosphere, and the ecosphere. Crash and chaos could happen.

Figure 10.4 is not a happy future. But it's a very possible future, even the most likely future from present trends. Yet few people today are at all aware of the situations ahead that could make this future a reality. And probably fewer still would be willing to undertake today what needs to be done to lessen the threat of this future. Most people think "green" means saving the environment. Few realize that "green" means saving humanity.

The road toward crash and chaos gives few clues or warning signs of what lies not far ahead. As we travel along we see more and better

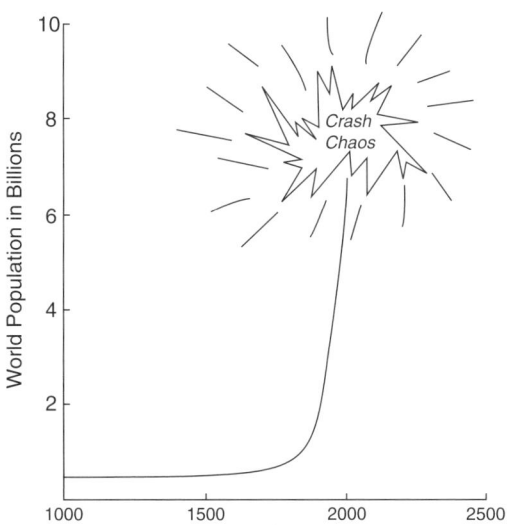

Figure 10.4   Future 1. Crash and chaos

products and services, more choices, more options, more opportunities, rising expectations, more growth. People see the Parable of the Twenty-Ninth Day as just a story; not about them.

Parable of the Twenty-ninth Day

A large pond in a nature preserve on the edge of town was a pleasant place to visit. No boats, no fishing, no swimming, no houses or construction; just nature, a few trails, woodlands, and pond; a small, self-maintaining natural system. One morning a ranger noted, along a secluded shoreline, a lily pad topped with a glistening white lily with golden, radiant tones. That water lily was something new. The next day, she checked to see if the lily was still there. It was, and a second one was there also. The following day there were four lilies, all in fragrant bloom.

The ranger was busy on other matters for a few days. Then, five days later she checked again. Now there was a small area filled with brilliant lilies, a delightful perfume in the air. She counted the blooms. There were one hundred and twenty-eight. She realized that from day one, these beautiful lilies had been doubling in number each day. She reported the lilies to the chief ranger who went to the site, saw the lilies, and then called the editor of the town's weekly newspaper. The editor sent a photographer to the pond the following day to take a picture. There were 256 beautiful blooms, and a delightful aroma.

The following Monday, the weekly newspaper appeared with the picture and story about these beautiful lilies. People went to the pond to see for themselves. By now, the lilies were putting on a spectacular show, filling a small area of the pond. Each day the crowds of visitors grew. Each day the lilies expanded, their display more brilliant than the day before. The ranger had seen the first lily on May 1. It was now May 28, and the pond was half filled with gorgeous lilies, the fragrant aroma reaching into the town itself.

Everyone was excited about May 29, and all the town rushed to see the lilies. There they were, filling the entire pond, each lily a treasure, all together a spectacular display. Brilliant. Glowing.

After seeing that display, excitement intensified for the following day. The townspeople awoke that morning to find a pungent aroma in the air. They rushed to the pond. All was death and decay. No blooms. Only dead petals and lily pads floating in polluted water. And the 29th day was so beautiful.

Future 2: Stabilize and Maintain

Remember the twenty-ninth day. Chaos can quickly follow great success. Society may not face complete collapse and chaos. A more likely future, perhaps 60/40, would be some chaos, some collapse, and then revival with world population stabilizing at some number well below 10 billion.

Future 2 stabilizes world population in the range of 9 to 10 billion people some time around mid-century. Population may then stabilize at that level over the following years, or gradually decline, following a typical sigmoid growth curve. Or, if we are wise enough, world population will stabilize at 9 to 10 billion, then rapidly decline to more sustainable numbers in the range of perhaps 4 billion people, or less, as shown in Figure 10.5. For this future to happen, we will need to reduce the human impact on the environment as world population grows to stabilize at 9 to 10 billion. That's a huge task, and we don't yet know all that needs to be done, and how. We will have to discover the way. And how will we deal with the increasing social ills within and among rapidly growing populations?

Future 2 could be our goal. We are on the population track. But we are not on the sustainability track. A transformation from where we're headed now to a light enough human footprint on the environment to sustain the coming world population will be the greatest and the most important task ever undertaken by humankind. We need to discover

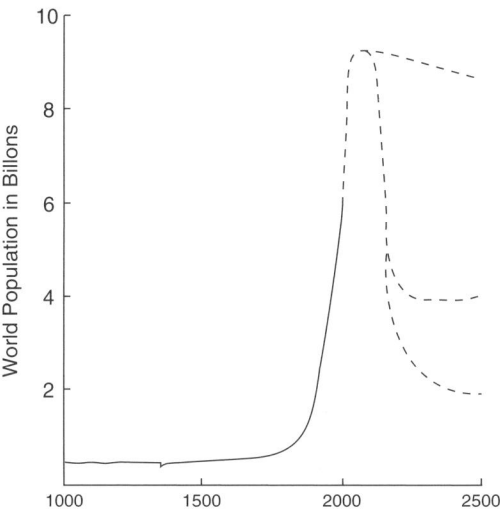

Figure 10.5 Future 2. Stabilize and maintain, or decline

how, and then we will need to do what needs to be done. Whatever that is, we will be much different and live much differently than we do today. Instead of conspicuous consumption, conspicuous conservation. Emphasis on quality instead of quantity. If we succeed only partly, we'll see some combination of both Future 1 and Future 2, or Future 1 and no Future 2. The tipping point is now, or more likely, it was yesterday.

In his book, *Our Final Hour*, Sir Martin Rees, Cambridge University professor and England's Astronomer Royal, reviews the many threats to the future of humankind. He offers a scientist's appraisal of threats, including population growth, a degrading ecosphere and biosphere, violent events of nature, and plagues. And now, new in human experience, we face threats from the discoveries of science, as well as benefits. Accidental events causing mass destruction can result from these discoveries. Or small groups or individuals aiming to destroy now have the capability to make use of these discoveries for mass destruction. Overall, Rees estimates the odds for civilization reaching the year 2100 at 50/50 [4].

However, Rees seems to expect that civilization will come out on the plus side of those 50/50 odds. He notes that most things that have had a long life, like human civilization and cultures, will continue to live longer still. The environments they depended on endured. Now our environment—the biosphere and the ecosphere—are threatened and already changing, fast. Many observers who see no future ahead for human civilization in view of the accumulating threats, still have a conviction that we will, ultimately, be wise enough to find our way to sustainability.

Long life does not assure a future. Our cultural history goes back some 5 thousand years. And we *homo sapiens* have been living on this earth for some 100 thousand years with a recorded history over the last 5 thousand years. That seems a very long time. But the *Cro-Magnon*, who we think primitive but who were very similar to us *homo sapiens*, lived on this earth more than three times as long. Will we be wise enough to endure as long?

After 75 million years of dominating the earth, dinosaurs disappeared in an instant of geologic time. After some seven hundred years, in the late seventeenth century Easter Island's complex Polynesian society collapsed, it seems, in civil war. Their depleted environment could no longer support their numbers. Evidence suggests that other civilizations that collapsed, such as the Maya in Mexico and Guatemala and the Anasazi in southwestern United States, collapsed largely from changes in the environment they depended on and the resulting civil strife. Their environment was local. Our environment is the worldwide biosphere and ecosphere.

Where We Are

Our civilization is a metasystem, several recursions up from the system that is our business. Both our civilization and our company, and all the system recursions in between and beyond are viable, very complex, purposeful, probabilistic systems. Both and all the systems in between and beyond can be modeled with the VSM. The recursions from human civilization to the company might go something like this: recursion 0, human civilization; recursion 1, our culture; recursion 2, country group; recursion 3, our country; recursion 4, the national economy; recursion 5, the industry; recursion 6, our company. In this book we deal with the company as the system in focus, recursion 0, and further recursions 1, 2, 3, and onward through the structure of the company. All recursions are viable systems. All viable systems can be modeled with the VSM.

We can also think of recursions upward from human civilization which might go something like this: human civilization, the earth's biosphere, the earth's ecosphere, the earth, the solar system, the Milky Way galaxy, the known universe, whatever is beyond the known universe. Cosmologists might define more than one recursion from our solar system to the Milky Way galaxy, and more than one recursion from the Milky Way galaxy to the known universe.

The concept of recursion, the understanding of system science, and the representations of the VSM can help us map our way to sustainability. In all the recursions listed above, "viable" is in the definition of the system. Viable: capable of continuing to live in its environment. The biosphere and the ecosphere are vital parts of our company's environment. They are equally vital environments for each of the recursions between our company and the ecosphere. All depend on the ecosphere to remain viable, to continue living.

No business on its own can remediate a degrading biosphere or ecosphere. Nor can any one corporation, one industry, one economy, one country, one country group, or one culture. All of human civilization, plus the chance occurrences of what happens in the recursions beyond, will determine what happens in the earth's ecosphere. Chance occurrences from higher levels of recursion, such as a large asteroid striking the earth, or a change in the polarity of the earth, may or may not happen. Most likely, such changes will not happen. But we know that human civilization with all its levels of recursion to where we live and work is changing the biosphere and the ecosphere in threatening ways. For its sustainability on this earth, human civilization and all its levels of recursion to where we live and work can and will need to be taking massive remedial, corrective actions between now and 2025. The year 2025 will likely be beyond the tipping point if we don't take action now. Our goals:

· Do no harm.
· Help restore what has been harmed.

Individuals can do their part in where and how they live. Companies can do their part by eliminating harmful waste discharged to air, land, or sea, and remediating damage already done. Industry is moving in this direction. Reengineering production processes, recycling, closed cycles producing no discharge, and other discoveries and methods have rapidly reduced harmful discharges. And many companies can point to successful remediations. But much greater effort and much greater urgency is needed to get to the end result, fast. Do no harm. Restore what has been harmed.

For our company that means working for a lighter and lighter impact on the biosphere and the ecosphere in all that we do, aiming for zero harm in less than 10 years. By communicating what we do in our business, we can influence other businesses at our level of recursion, and we can influence actions at higher-levels of recursion; the corporation, the industry, the economy, our country, our world. And listening and learning from other levels of recursion in both directions we can continuously improve. Success in maintaining a healthy and provident biosphere and ecosphere depends on all of us in what we do in lightening our footprint, continuously and fast.

Lightening the human footprint on the biosphere and the ecosphere will depend on the number of people making the footprints and how they live. Ten thousand years ago world population was probably less than 10 million; by the time of the Roman empire, some 300 million. In the nineteenth century world population reached a billion, and 2 billion in the early twentieth century. By the end of the twentieth century, and mostly in the last half of the century, world population had grown from 2 billion to 6 billion and was still rising sharply. In the 50 years, from 1950 to 2000, world population exploded from 2.5 billion to 6 billion, up 140%. Over those same 50 years, to meet growing needs and wants, global economic output grew from 7 trillion dollars to 46 trillion dollars (both figures valued in 2001 dollars), up 557% [5].

Our human footprint has grown enormously, and we are now seeing the consequences. Six billion people in their daily lives affect both biosphere and ecosphere. And population still rises, with growth expected to follow a sigmoid curve and stabilize at 9 to 10 billion at some time about mid-century. A huge world economy also affects both biosphere and ecosphere. And the world economy still expands and may relate to population growth and stabilize at half again the present level, or more if people continue to increase their consumption of goods and services.

Threatening Trends

Our world of 6 billion people with our 46 trillion dollar global economy lives in the biosphere. The biosphere, including us, lives in the ecosphere. We now see threatening trends in both the ecosphere and the biosphere.

Global warming. Temperature and climate changes affecting agriculture and livability, changing weather patterns, destructive storms, melting glaciers and polar ice, sea levels rising

Water shortages. Falling water tables world-wide from the Ogallala to the deep aquifer under the North China Plain that is already reducing grain harvests, lack of potable water in many areas, rivers running dry from overuse of the water, demands of agriculture and cities in conflict

Loss of arable land. Erosion, desertification, water shortages, farmland diverted to "development"

Pollution. Air, land, lakes and rivers, oceans; worldwide

Extinction of species. Species disappearing from our earth with extinctions now hundreds of times the normal rate. Geologic history records six periods of great extinctions, claiming from 60 to 95 percent of existing species. From what we now know, what humans are doing on earth is the major cause of a seventh great extinction, happening now on a scale like the earlier six.

Social ills. Poverty, hunger, illiteracy, crime, unemployment, oppression, intolerance, civil wars, HIV and threats of pandemics, nuclear proliferation, terrorism, and the capability of small groups and individuals to cause mass destruction. Rapidly growing human populations to huge numbers degrades both our civilization, and the earth's biosphere and ecosphere.

Awareness of these threats grows rapidly. All media—television, the internet, radio, newspapers, magazines, books—broaden this awareness with both factual, and doomsday reporting. Fortunately, doomsday is not yet factual, although a likely outcome. The threats are real, overwhelming, and already appearing in our lives. Awareness is growing, but not fast enough. We have much to learn, and much to do. The threats we know about, the sustainability we must find, and the new ways we must live demand a collective effort on a scale greater than the mobilization of people and resources that won World War II. But we'll be winning a different victory—sustainability.

More needs to be said about extinctions of species. We *homo sapiens* are one of the species, and the dominant species on earth. Our impact on the biosphere and the ecosphere seem to be a major cause of the current seventh extinction. During the sixth extinction, at the boundary of the Cretaceous and Tertiary periods 65 million years ago 95% of all species on earth disappeared. All the other extinctions lost more than 60%. In this seventh extinction, what will determine the survivors? Good luck? Or, the collective wisdom of the human population, the only life on earth endowed with a highly developed intellect?

Stafford Beer, a pioneer in system science and its application in business enterprise, and developer of the VSM, in 1975 wrote [6]:

> The laws of ecosystem are not answerable to a criterion of success which necessarily includes the survival of man. The most likely systemic outcome of the things we are up to is a sudden, catastrophic, population decline. So whereas the catastrophic population collapse typically cuts back the species to about a third of its peak strength, homeostasis sometimes overdoes it. Thus whole species become extinct.

> What we have to say to our educated cybernetician-in-the-street is that if this fate were to overtake our species, nature betrays no cybernetic law. Nature can afford to shrug off the incident. She has been up evolutionary blind alleys before. Man seeks to impose his own objective function on the natural homeostat; his failure is his own failure; his extinction is his own affair.

ENERGY

We are not without knowledge on where to look to begin finding solutions to our energy problems. "Different" is a bigger part of the solution than simply more of what we are doing now.

Buckminster Fuller's Analysis

R. Buckminster Fuller, world-renowned inventor, professor, and phi-losopher, writing in *ReVISION*, in 1983 wrote:

> The total energy used daily by all humans aboard Spaceship Earth—albeit at only five percent overall efficiency—amounts to less than one four-millionth of one percent of spaceship Earth's daily income of expendable energy imported from the universe around and generated within it.
>
> It's now technically feasible, with presently proven technology, to impound and distribute to humanity this vast overabundance of cosmic energy income. Through foresight and design, it is possible to phase out all further use of fossil fuels and atomic energy which comprise nature's cosmic energy savings account.

The earth's daily income of energy, Fuller points out, includes solar-generated windpower, wavepower, and hydroelectric power; and especially vegetation-produced alcohols, the "grand central reservoir of cosmic-radiation-and-gravity-produced energy" readily available for human use.

Fuller was wary of atomic energy, and the plan to ". . . safely bury atomic radiation wastes within the constantly-changing structure of our planet's minisculely thick, ever-altering crust-surface. Whoever is responsible for such statements is hiding information critical to the con-tinuation of human life aboard our planet. . . . Nature, inhabiting planet Earth with biological organisms, did so deliberately because it was clearly evident that biological protoplasm could not prosper and endure safely any closer to atomic energy radiation generators than 91 million miles. With all the Universe to work in, nature selected planet Earth at this optimum, safe distance from the 'atomic energy plant' Sun."

Fuller thought our survival on planet earth depends on how wisely we use the extraordinary capabilities of our human minds. "The present worldwide crisis powerfully suggests that we all are undergoing a final examination as to whether to bomb ourselves into oblivion, overcrowd a despoiled planet or let our minds take command, exercise our design science option, and turn the human occupation of planet Earth into a physical success."

Nuclear

There are two dimensions of nuclear energy: (1) the peaceful use of nuclear energy to generate power, and (2) the wartime use, or terrorist use, for mass destruction. Both need to be carefully controlled.

Nuclear Power   The world's first commercial nuclear power plant opened in UK in 1956, with a capacity of 45 MW. Installed nuclear capacity rose quickly to reach 1 Gigawatt in 1960. By 2005 installed nuclear capacity worldwide reached 366 GW. In the United States, the country that produces the most nuclear power, in 2006 there were 104 commercial nuclear generating units producing a total of 101 GW, about 20% of the country's electrical energy. Construction of nuclear power plants declined after the 1979 Three Mile Island accident in the United States, which was contained within the containment building, and the 1986 Chernobyl disaster, which spread deadly radioactive fallout over a large area. Now, with energy demand outpacing supply there is renewed interest in nuclear power. In the United States the Energy Policy Act of 2005 enables future development of nuclear power.

Proponents of nuclear power emphasize the safety record of nuclear plants, and the environmental benefit—no harmful emissions to the atmosphere, a big advantage in comparison with coal plants. The cost of permitting and building the plants remains a problem. And there are potential safety problems:

1. The possibility of disastrous radioactive contamination by accident, by sabotage, or by terrorists.
2. The possibility that in some countries their peaceful nuclear power plants would be used for the production of nuclear weapons.
3. The continuing problem of storing radioactive wastes for long periods of time, up to 10,000 years.

At the present time spent nuclear fuel rods and other radioactive wastes accumulate at each power plant location, temporarily. By 2003 the United States had accumulated about 49,000 metric tons of spent nuclear fuel, temporarily stored on site, mostly in spent fuel pools requiring constant maintenance. In the US the plan is to transport and store these wastes permanently in a stable structure deep in the earth's crust in Nevada, the storage structure nearing completion. Nevada objects. So do many scientists who contend there is no such structure reliably stable for 10,000 years. And is 10,000 years long enough? Then there's the commonsense view that it is very presumptive of us humans with a recorded history of only 5,000 years, however "expert" we may be, to confidently store for 10,000 years nuclear wastes that are hazardous to life on earth. But what then will we do with all those spent fuel rods accumulating at the plant sites?

Nuclear Weapons More needs to be thought about the threat of nuclear weapons. Today that threat is even greater than it was in 1955 when Bertrand Russell, Albert Einstein, and nine other prominent nuclear scientists joined in signing the Russell-Einstein Manifesto. The Manifesto, written after the testing of the H-bomb, and at the height of the Cold War noted that "... a bomb can now be manufactured which will be 2,500 times as powerful as that which destroyed Hiroshima." The Manifesto also stated that "... the best authorities are unanimous in saying that a war with H-bombs might possibly put an end to the human race. It is feared that if many H-bombs are used there will be universal death, sudden only for a minority, but for the majority a slow torture of disease and disintegration."

The Manifesto concluded with a resolution inviting "... this Congress, and through it the scientists of the world and the general public, to subscribe to the following resolution:

> In view of the fact that in any future world war nuclear weapons will certainly be employed, and that such weapons threaten the continued existence of mankind, we urge the governments of the world to realize, and to acknowledge publicly, that their purpose cannot be furthered by a world war, and we urge them, consequently, to find peaceful means for the settlement of all matters of dispute between them.

This Manifesto was Einstein's final public act. He died shortly after signing it.

In 2005, on the 60th anniversary of the Hiroshima bomb, Joseph Rotblat, the only living signatory to the Manifesto, wrote an op-ed letter published in *The New York Times*. Dr. Rotblat had conducted studies on the fallout from the hydrogen bomb test in Bikini Atoll in 1954. Over the years he has been a leading authority on the biological effects of radiation. In his *New York Times* letter, Rotblat referred to the Manifesto and stated, "Now, two generations later, as the representatives of nearly 190 nations meet in New York to discuss how to advance the Nuclear Nonproliferation Treaty, we face the same perils and new ones as well. Today we confront the possibilities of nuclear terrorism and of the development of yet more new nuclear warheads in the United States. The two former superpowers still hold enormous nuclear arsenals. North Korea and Iran are advancing their capability to build nuclear weapons. Other nations are increasingly likely to acquire nuclear arsenals ..." Days after writing his *New York Times* letter, Joseph Rotblat, in his 97th year, died.

If we fail to control the nuclear threat, the human race could become one of the species lost in the seventh great extinction now happening.

Oil

As Buckminster Fuller pointed out, oil is part of the world's cosmic energy savings account, deposited within the crust of the earth over thousands and millions of years by heat and pressure. Oil has driven our economy for only one century, with the world now using oil at the rate of about 83 million barrels a day. How long can we withdraw oil at this rate and higher from nature's energy savings account? Most likely we can be withdrawing oil for a long time. But not at today's withdrawal rate and higher, according to Hubbert's peak.

M. King Hubbert was a highly-regarded oil geologist working in the Shell Research Laboratory in Houston, Texas. In 1956 Hubbert predicted that US oil production would peak in the early 1970s and then decline. His prediction was based on analysis of oil discoveries, oil production, and oil usage from the earliest days of the oil industry. Hubbert saw that oil production followed the typical bell-shaped curve, rising to a peak and then, he expected, declining. He discovered from his analysis that while new discoveries and advances in drilling technologies can be impressive, there comes a time when demand outpaces all possible advances in supply, and supply begins to decline. Experts dismissed Hubbert's prediction and pro-Hubbert and anti-Hubbert factions argued their positions until the mid 1970s, when Hubbert's Peak did happen, and US oil production began to decline.

In 1969 Hubbert published the results of his study of world oil production, which he found also to be following the typical bell-shaped curve. He predicted world oil reserves would reach 2.1 trillion barrels, with peak production reached about the year 2000. Kenneth S. Deffeyes grew up in the oil patch, and after graduating from the Colorado School of Mines and Princeton as a petroleum geologist, began work in the Shell Lab in Houston. Hubbert was working there at the time and was regarded by all as a superstar. Deffeyes learned from Hubbert, and carried on Hubbert's work. He was enough convinced of the reality of Hubbert's Peak that he left Shell early for a career in teaching and further research at Princeton.

Deffeyes published his latest book in 2005, *Beyond Oil: The View From Hubbert's Peak* [8]. Deffeyes calculates world oil reserves reaching 2.013 trillion barrels with Hubbert's Peak happening on or about 2005. The world's oil reserves are not easy to measure. They are 90%

owned by countries, not companies. In the late 1980s, OPEC countries announced increases in their reserves. How real were these claims? What was real was that, with higher reserves, under their quota system they could pump more oil. And Hubbert's Peak came closer.

Even if both Hubbert and Deffeyes are wrong in their prediction, Deffeyes is confident that they are not very wrong. Deffeyes' conclusion is that in view of the validity of Hubbert's Peak, the oil industry, other industries, and governments should have been developing alternatives over the last 15 years to avoid the energy crisis of severe oil shortages beginning now.

All Fossil Fuels Are Finite

The solution to the oil problem, many think, will be nuclear energy, or coal. Professor David Goodstein, Professor of Physics at California Institute of Technology, and author of *Out of Gas—The End of the Age of Oil*, points out that neither nuclear nor coal can be the solution. Goodstein is confident we confront an oil crisis; that Hubbert's Peak is real. An oil crisis may happen this year, or in 10 years, or in 20 years. In the scale of human history 10 or 20 years is insignificant. We confront an oil crisis. What happens then?

Nuclear? If we mean conventional nuclear power like we use in the United States, Goodstein notes that means uranium 235, which presents two problems: (1) We would have to build 10,000 of the largest plants possible to generate the 10 terrawatts of fossil fuel we're burning, and (2) with all these plants operating, the known reserves of uranium would last for 10 to 20 years. To increase the amount of fuel we could use some uranium to breed plutonium 239. But then we're making plutonium, a huge danger in this troubled world. Could nuclear fusion be the answer? Professor Goodstein notes that for 50 years nuclear fusion has been 25 years away, and it's still 25 years away. Our response to Hubbert's Peak has to happen now.

Clean coal technology, including the liquefaction of coal, has been proposed as part of the solution. The world has huge reserves of coal. For the huge amount of energy needed, with whatever the coal technology, there will be unpredictable amount of damage to the environment and we would soon encounter a Hubbert's Peak for coal.

All fossil fuels, oil, natural gas, coal, and nuclear are finite. We are left with the realization that a meaningful response to Hubbert's Peak must have two dimenions: (1) Relying on Fuller's "grand central reservoir" of cosmic radiation and gravity-produced energy as our continuing source of energy, including biomass, solar, wind, tides, waves, and geothermal, and (2) Using much less energy.

CRASH AND CHAOS?

Hubbert's Peak is a huge problem, until we find a sustainable way to deal with it. That sustainable way, when we discover it, will likely include both Fuller's "grand central reservoir," and finding ways to use much less energy. Discovering our response to Hubbert's Peak is only part of the bigger problem of conserving the earth's biosphere in which we live, and the earth's ecosphere in which all the biosphere lives. Without resolution of our energy problem and our biosphere/ecosphere threat, crash and chaos, even extinction, are likely.

Crash and chaos could come from nuclear bombs or radiation or spreading civil threats resulting from cultural conflict or growing numbers of people lacking food, shelter, education, and other basic needs. Random acts of nature such as a large comet or asteroid colliding with earth, or a season of violent volcanic eruptions could be threats. Or crash and chaos could come from an increasingly degrading ecosphere leaving the biosphere unable to support increasing numbers of people. Pulitzer Prize winning author Professor Jared Diamond in his book, *How Societies Choose to Fail or Succeed,* writes, ". . . the world's environment problems will get resolved, in one way or another, within the lifetimes of the children and young adults alive today. The only question is whether they will become resolved in pleasant ways of our own choice, or in unpleasant ways not of our choice, such as warfare, genocide, starvation, disease epidemics, and collapse of society."

What might be the pleasant ways of our own choice? We are well aware of the threats described above. As recently as 1950, none of today's major threats confronted us or were even imagined. In 1950 the earth we inhabited was huge, stable, unchanging, providing our needs. In 1950 we were 2.5 billion people on the earth; our world economy about one-seventh the size it is today.

We have traveled a long way toward crisis since 1950. It wasn't planned that way; it just happened. And it happened as we resolved the great problems of the Great Depression and World War II. In 1950 the world was recovering from worldwide depression, and the destruction of the war. People needed jobs, income, recovery from frugality. And recover we did. "The Greatest Generation" of the depression and World War II years, over their careers created and enjoyed the highest standard of living the world has ever seen, far beyond what we could have dreamed of in the dark days of the Great Depression and World War II.

During the Great Depression the dream was "a chicken in every pot." By 1950 the dream was "two chickens in every pot, and a car in every garage." And we grew far beyond that. We solved the problems of the Great Depression, and organized to solve the problems of relations among countries by creating the United Nations.

But solving the great problems of our times has led to different and even greater problems. To reverse present trends toward crash and chaos, we will need an even greater "Greatest Generation" in the young people living today. The problems we confront in the years 2005 to 2025 are far greater, far less understood, and far more threatening than were the problems of the 1930s and 40s confronting depression and World War II. During the war we thought that our civilization hung in the balance. Civilization endured. Over the first decades of this new century we will see what happens to present trends toward crash and chaos, and if or how our civilization will endure. By 2025 the world's first generation of the century in what they do, will determine whether our civilization is heading toward crash and chaos, or will continue to endure, and how.

ALTERNATIVES TO CRASH AND CHAOS

There is a way. One dimension that needs to change is world population. Look at Figure 10.2 showing world population growth over the last 10 thousand years. There was no threatening growth rate until very recent years. Over 10 thousand years, world population reached one billion in the nineteenth century, and two billion in the early part of the twentieth century. Then, following the depression and World War II, in just three generations, world population exploded to populate the earth with more than six billion people. Today, experts project that declining fertility rates will slow world population growth to stabilize at 9 to 10 billion sometime around mid-century. Will that be our future?

With the empowerment and greater education of women, and their participation in all aspects of the economy and all aspects of public life, fertility rates are falling. In many developed countries the fertility rate is already below the replacement rate of 2.1. Fifty-eight countries now have fertility rates below 2.1. Spain is one of the lowest at 1.2. But seventy-eight countries have fertility rates above 4.0. Nigeria, with Africa's largest population, 109 million people, has a fertility fate of 6.2.

World population will continue to grow. Even in countries with fertility rates below the replacement rate, populations continue growing because of longer life spans, immigration, and the last part of the population explosion after World War II at childbearing age as are many of the children of that population explosion. China, in 1980, had a population of slightly less than one billion and an enforced population-control policy of one child per family. Twenty-five years later, in 2005, the population was 1.3 billion. In twenty-five years China's population, under a rigid population control policy, grew by more than the total 2005 population of the United States. The UN predicts world population in 2050 will be somewhere in a range between 8 and 11 billion, most likely 9.1 billion. But what then?

If fertility rates and populations ballooned in the twentieth century, can they equally fall in the twenty-first century? Population growth is generally predicted in a sigmoid curve. Sigmoid curves, or growth curves, are characteristic for yeast cells in a petri dish, new products in a marketplace, population growth, and other growth processes. From the starting point, sigmoid curves show slow growth then growth accelerating at an increasing rate until it reaches an inflection point where an accelerating rate of growth changes to a decelerating rate of growth to level off at a maximum level that can be supported in the subject's environment. The leveling off may then be followed by decline. See Figure 10.6.

If the growth of world population follows a sigmoid curve, it will be a very condensed one. After 10 thousand years of slow growth, in only 100 years population growth accelerated at an increasing rate until now

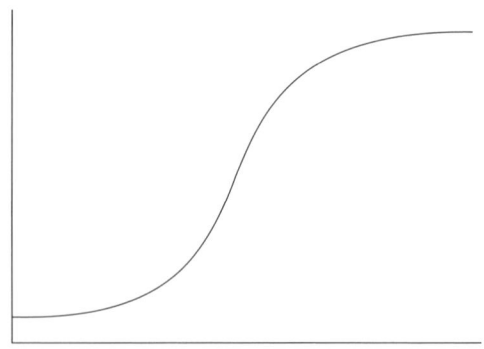

Figure 10.6   Sigmoid curve

it seems to be at an inflection point, changing to a decelerating rate of growth, but at year 2000 still growing fast. With fertility rates falling, the rate of growth should continue to slow, to stabilize world population at zero growth sometime around the middle of this 21st century. If the world reaches zero population growth and stabilizes by 2050, that would mean a world population, according to UN projections, of some 9 to 10 billion people. Reaching zero growth later would mean a higher world population; earlier, a lower population.

Could 9 to 10 billion people, with the economy they would need, live on earth with a standard of living like that in Europe and America today? Not likely. The European and American standard of living for that many people would probably need four earths instead of one. But, if we are wise enough to find the way, 9 to 10 billion people could exist on the earth with a low-consumption (compared with today) but civilized and even happy lifestyle.

All in a span of 150 years, from about 1900 to about 2050, world population will have grown from less than 2 billion people to stabilize at a level of some 9 to 10 billion. Could population growth then reverse the process and begin to decrease at an accelerating rate, then at a decelerating rate until stabilizing at zero growth in an additional 150 years? Could that decline stabilize at an optimal level of some 2 to 4 billion people? We are not yeast cells in a Petri dish, stabilizing at a maximum. We are a huge network of viable, very complex, purposeful, probabilistic systems. We have an amazingly powerful collective intellect. We, by what we do, will determine what happens.

World population will crash in chaos during the first half of this century, or we will learn how to achieve sustainability in a world of some 9 to 10 billion people. With that many people, we will be living very differently from the way we live in the developed countries today. But it could be a good life, and happier. Success will be more what we are rather than what we own. And for the developing countries life could be a far better than now. We confront three challenges in achieving sustainability for our biosphere and our civilization:

1. How to speed up the decline in fertility rates
2. How to find the technologies and learn the behaviors that will reduce and eliminate the growing social ills, and the strife among countries and cultures
3. How to discover the technologies we will need, and the actions we must take to assure a sustainable biosphere and ecosphere providing a good living for 9 to 10 billion people

Present trends point toward crash and chaos. These trends can change, and we are beginning to see some positive developments. Governments establish regulations protecting the environment, and are beginning to collaborate multi-nationally on actions needed to control pollution. Corporations now have senior level executives responsible for the company's environmental relationships, and business organizations are advocating conservation actions. Universities are establishing research centers for the environment and offering degree programs in environmental science. An increasing number of NGOs work in the various areas of the three challenges listed above. Change is happening, but still too slowly. We need to accelerate the rate of change in our sigmoid curve toward sustainability. We have to find our way, and live our way to sustainability in a world of 9 to 10 billion people by mid-century. We'll have to be measurably on track toward that goal by 2025.

There will be many surprises along the way; some happy, some tragic. If we avoid crash and chaos, by mid-century we will be living sustainably in a world of 9 to 10 billion people. Sigmoid curves tend to stabilize at or slowly decline from their maximum. But in our population sigmoid curve we are unique. We were 10 thousand years in slow growth. Then, unless we crash on the way, in only 150 years, population growth has accelerated, appears now to have passed an inflection point, and is beginning to decelerate to stabilize at 9 to 10 billion people around 2050, if projections prove reasonably accurate. Will population then remain at or about this level, or slowly decline, over the following centuries? That's typical of sigmoid curves.

But we are unique. We are a vast network of viable, very complex, purposeful, probabilistic systems. And humanity is an influence in all of these systems from the lowest up to and including the ecosphere that is the home of all life on earth. That influence and our collective intellect can achieve sustainability, even in a world of 9 to 10 billion people. And after world population achieves zero growth, that influence and our collective intellect can, and let us hope will, achieve declines in world population the equal of the 150 years of ballooning growth.

Spain and Italy, now have fertility rates of 1.2, 43% below the zero growth rate. Fertility rates world-wide are falling. Could they fall fast enough to stabilize world population by mid-century, then move down the back side of our sigmoid curve to stabilize at an optimum world population perhaps in the range of two to four billion people?

If we can achieve sustainability in a world of 9 to 10 billion people by about 2050, or earlier at a lower level, and in the following years achieve increasingly rapid declines in population, we will see the greatest flowering of human civilization in all of time. This projection, of course, is not realistic. Not practical. Blue sky. Just a dream. But today's collective intellect can make it happen! We have incentive—escape from crash and chaos. Always realistic and always practical will always continue present trends toward crash and chaos. We can do better.

We will need to learn how to ask the right questions. We tend to ask questions about solving problems that when solved only bring us bigger problems. Repeating our experience of the last half of the twentieth century will carry us to crash and chaos. We solved the problems of the Great Depression by producing more and more goods and services for more and more people. We improved our standard of living. But growing social ills, and a degrading environment now threaten the future of living.

WHAT COMPANIES ARE DOING

We have an energy problem. What are the right questions for leading us toward solution? The chairman of a major oil company, in a magazine ad in 2005, stated the "tough questions" this way: (1) "How do we meet the energy needs of the developing world and those of industrial nations? (2) What role will renewables and alternative energies play? (3) What is the best way to protect our environment?" These seem practical and environmentally aware questions. But are these the right questions? The answer to the first question is more energy. Is more energy the answer to the energy problem? Can a sustainable ecosphere survive 50% more energy consumption than now?

The right first question would be the third question stated differently: *In the next 50 years, how do we conserve the environment and repair what has already degraded while world population grows from six billion people to 9 to 10 billion people?* How to restore and conserve the biosphere and the ecosphere is the first question. Conserving the environment is conserving the human race. Answering this question wisely will mean that 9 to 10 billion people will be living with less energy, probably much less, than today's six billion. We will have to learn very quickly how to ask the right questions.

DuPont has been a leader in responding to environmental challenges. The company set a goal to reduce the emission of greenhouse gasses by 65% below 1990 levels by 2010 and achieved that goal by 2005. As the company's global production increased 36%, global energy use was reduced by 7%, amounting to a saving of $2 billion. The company is tapping into Fuller's "grand central reservoir" by aiming for 10% of its global energy needs to come from renewable resources, and teaming with the Energy Department to develop bio-based materials and biofuels. Environmental change brings opportunity as well as threats.

General Electric in 2005 announced its new ecomagination strategy involving all company businesses in developing products and services good for the environment, and offering superior value for customers. With ecomagination, what's good for the environment can also be good for GE, and for GE's customers. GE also established a new division to commercialize products and services developed from the company's expanded research in new environmental technologies.

Most major companies are now much involved in reducing emissions, reducing energy use, and reducing their impact on the environment. They see what is happening in countries implementing the Kyoto Protocol, and are making their own judgments on what lies ahead. They aim to stay ahead of the curve. While there may be costs, there are also significant cost reductions and new product and new service opportunities.

Companies are acting collectively, too. The United Nations Global Compact asks companies to embrace, support and enact, within their sphere of influence, a set of 10 principles in the areas of human rights, labor standards, the environment, and anti-corruption. The ten principles include three on the environment, stating that businesses should:

Principle 7. Support a precautionary approach to environmental challenges

Principle 8. Undertake initiatives to promote greater environmental responsibility

Principle 9. Encourage the development and diffusion of environmentally friendly technologies

Years in development, the Global Compact went into effect on 30 June 2005, with 977 companies that had been participants in the Compact for at least two years. By 2006 the Global Compact included nearly 2,200 companies from more than 80 countries. By the end of two years, corporate participants are required to disclose to their stakeholders on a regular basis their progress in implementing the Global Compact's ten principles. But the three environment principles are far short of what companies need to do. They are more attitude than action. And we need great actions.

These three environment principles are more awareness than action and would have been appropriate 25 years earlier. But now, in the early years of global warming, water shortages, loss of arable land, pollution, and the current extinction of species actions are needed. Our environmental principles need to be: (1) Do no harm. (2) Help restore what has been harmed.

In September, 2005, the Business Roundtable announced their S.E.E. Change sustainable growth initiative, Social responsibility, improve the Environment, grow the Economy. In its announcement, the Business Roundtable notes that ". . . the business community possesses a set of skills, resources and incentives that are uniquely valuable in enhancing long-term environmental and social well-being. . . . And by investing in technological innovation, new product development and responsible stewardship, these companies can both reduce their own environmental footprints and lower the costs that businesses and consumers incur for energy, water, vital raw materials and products." Companies report to the Business Roundtable on their measures of progress. Company reports are available on the internet at <www.businessroundtable.org.>.

Most business organizations throughout the world now include environmental conservation in their business plans and actions. But the focus is still primarily on growth, on development, but each with an adjective in front: sustainable growth, sustainable development. Adjectives seldom prevail over, or even along with, the nouns they modify. We have not yet got to the point where sustainability is the noun, with growth and development the adjective, subordinate to what's needed for sustainability. Our ideas on growth may change. Our ideas on development may change. Gross Domestic Well-being (if we can find such a measure) may be more a measure of success than Gross Domestic Product.

"DEVELOPMENT"

Consider today's (2006) view of growth in the United States. One headline proclaims, "In the coming 25 years the biggest wave of development since World War II will turn America's major metro areas into giant "megapolitans" Consider Buckeye, a crossroads town on Interstate 10 west of Phoenix, population 15 thousand. With developments already planned, within 20 years Buckeye is expected to become a metropolis nearly as large as Phoenix. And Phoenix will be expanding east and south, too, creating a Phoenix/Tucson megapolitan. A total of 10 such megapolitans with urban and residential construction linking today's central cities into new, huge megapolitans:

Boston/New York City/Washington
Atlanta/Raleigh/Durham
Miami/Tampa
Pittsburgh/Detroit/Chicago
Houston/New Orleans
Phoenix/Tucson
Las Vegas/Los Angeles
San Francisco/Sacramento
Seattle/Portland

This surge in "development" is driven by population growth and developers hungry for the millions and billions in real estate profits that such development will bring. They see "development." Are they aware of the constraining adjective, "sustainable?" Sustainable development. Would they ever think that "sustainability" is really the first consideration? Without inventions not yet discovered, sustainability can not see "megapolitans" in the United States southwest desert. Or maybe anywhere. Today's concepts of development become obsolete for a world population much greater than now. "More" is not the answer. Some kind of "different" is needed. We need to find the development that will be right for a world of 9 to 10 billion people, a US double its present population.

We need to change our perspective. The environment isn't something out there that we should take care of. The environment is the ecosphere we live in: the air we breathe, the water we need, and the soil where we live and work and grow our food. The environment is also the biosphere, one recursion from the ecosphere; a part of the ecosphere and dependent on it. We are a part of and depend on the biosphere for our food and sustenance. And the biosphere is a part of and dependant on the ecosphere. In a time of degrading ecosphere and degrading biosphere, "a precautionary approach," "initiatives to promote responsibility," and "diffusion of environmentally friendly technologies" are hardly enough. We need: (1) Do no harm. (2) Help restore what has been harmed.

Whatever we do, nature will adjust. But will nature's adjustments include us? The answer to that question will be determined by what we do over the next 50 years. And the direction toward what we do over the next 50 years will be determined by our actions over the next 20 years from 2005 to 2025. We don't have to worry about "saving the earth." The earth has already gone through six periods of great extinctions. Most species perished. But life on earth continued, and evolved anew. And will again, after this seventh great extinction, whether or not we are among the survivors. We are not challenged to save the earth. We are challenged to save ourselves.

THE TWENTY YEARS FROM 2005 TO 2025

People and countries and cultures today seem unready and unwilling to really undertake a transformation to sustainability. What we see is today. Our home. Our job. Our city. Our Country. We see today. Today we may be at day twenty-something in the Parable of the Twenty-ninth Day. Today looks beautiful. We don't see 2050. Will 2050 be our day 30? More and more people are beginning to see the accumulating threats. More and more people are beginning to think about the next 50 years. And as degradation in our natural environment hurts more and more, as the pain and danger of social ills increases, and as strife among nations and cultures grows, people may begin to see the need for change enough to empower a transformation to sustainability.

Change is beginning to happen, but not fast enough. Companies are actively reducing harmful emissions, reducing energy usage, increasing renewable sources for energy and raw materials. Expecting Kyoto-type requirements in the near-term future, companies in the United States are urging regulatory action by the federal government to establish standards for all. And in the US, local governments are taking actions. While the federal government has not signed the Kyoto Protocol, 12 state governments and more than 200 cities have enacted laws to reduce greenhouse gas emissions. And in the Congress, "cap and trade" legislation is being considered for controlling greenhouse gases. But there is not yet support for a more effective control—a tax on emissions.

No person or group or institution or government can map the plan to a sustainable society of 9 to 10 billion people. That map is not an algorithm. It's an heuristic. We'll have to find our way. The way has to be found, and lived, as we go. Programmers write algorithms. Millions of people and thousands of institutions will be needed to discover the heuristics on our way to sustainability.

We'll need new technologies. We'll need new processes and methods. We'll need new behaviors. And we'll have to discover all of these, and use them wisely. And if we are to find our way to sustainability in a world of 9 to 10 billion people by 2050, we will need to discover many of those technologies, processes, methods, and behaviors and have them working for sustainability by 2025. By 2025 we will need to be clearly on our way to sustainability. In 2005, we were clearly not yet on our way. By 2025 we will have to be well into accelerating growth in all that will be needed to achieve sustainability.

No person, no commission, no UN secretariat can lead the transformation to sustainability. Any of these, and all of these together, lack requisite variety. Thousands and tens of thousands of initiatives will be needed, with real time communication among them. Universities with Institutes or Centers for environmental research, individually, will make important contributions. They may also form global networks of such Centers to expand their capabilities, increase their contributions, and expand their influence. NGOs working on social problems, or on environmental issues can do the same. Industries and governments will have to be involved. And the United Nations. There will be thousands of leaders, tens of thousands of institutions, hundreds of millions of people involved in a transformation to sustainability. The greatest effort of all humanity will be needed to deal successfully with the greatest threat ever confronted by all humanity.

The VSM and system thinking gives us a conceptual framework. A transformation to sustainability will be a vast network of systems extending to include all the earth's institutions and people. The highest level metasystem does not yet exist. It would not be a huge structure with many experts. The metasystem would be small. It would not be sitting at the top, running the transformation. It will be embedded somewhere in the middle of things. And there would likely be many other high-level systems between that metasystem and today's institutions that will be working on the transformation. A transformation to sustainability will create and run itself, like the internet creates itself and runs itself. The transformation metasystem would assure that the transformation can create itself and run itself. Question: Will that metasystem be a human system . . . or a nature system?

Systems have the capability of self-organization and self-control. The biosphere organizes itself and controls itself. The ecosphere organizes itself and controls itself. Both now do this with influences imposed by humankind. The result is change not favorable for humankind. The biosphere has no concern for how its changes may affect one of its species. The ecosphere has no concern for how its changes may affect the biosphere. But we humans have a great concern. Will we be wise enough to form among us a self-organizing, self-controlling transformation to sustainability?

OVERVIEW: THE ESSENCE OF CHAPTER 10

When we see the company in the light of the VSM and system science, we understand the definition of the company as a viable, very complex, purposeful, probabilistic system. This chapter deals with the "viable" part of that definition: Viable: Able to continue to exist in its environment.

This chapter discusses seven environments the company lives in. Six of the environments were developed over time by our culture: the commercial environment, the technical environment, the economic environment, the social environment, the political environment, and the educational environment. All of these environments, our company, and all of us live within the seventh environment, the ecological environment. In all of these environments, and most of all in the ecological environment, we see rapid and disruptive change. Viability becomes a growing problem. This chapter discusses actions needed to resolve the growing problem of viability.

The Commercial Environment. A system is what it does. A business system creates and keeps customers. First of all a company must successfully and continuously deal with the environment where the customers are, the commercial environment. In this environment are all the customers and prospects and their customers and prospects, all the company's competitors and prospective competitors, all the participants in the company's supply chain and prospective and possible alternatives, and all those who supply services to all of these. And everything in the commercial environment is continually changing.

A big change in the commercial environment is . . . globalization. Customers, prospective customers, competitors, suppliers, and enablers are everywhere in the world. Country, area, and cultural differences bring new opportunities, and new threats. Intensely involved in their commercial environments, companies are increasingly aware of the opportunities and threats in globalization. Change is happening. For each company, and each business, success will depend on how they perform in the key performance areas described in this book. Goals and performance measures in these areas will be the key part of all plans and budgets, and a key requirement for maintaining viability in the commercial environment.

The Technical Environment. In the VSM structure all business units at all levels of recursion maintain contacts with the technical environment to assure that their business uses the best of the technologies needed to achieve their purpose. New technology creates different, better, lower cost products and services. Technology also creates different, better, and lower cost processes and alternatives to what the company is doing now. New technology resolves problems.

The VSM with its structured communications to and from the technical environment helps assure each business can discover and apply the technologies that will maintain viability and assure success in creating and keeping customers. The pace of technological change will be hundreds, even thousands of times faster than it was over the last 50 years of the twentieth century. Technology change was fast then. The speed of technological change continues accelerating and we can expect an exponential rate of change over the years ahead. New kinds of technology—nanotech, biotech, and digital tech among them—will continuously change almost everything. At the corporate level, and at all levels of recursion, the system 4 innovation centers now have a huge responsibility in their monitoring of the technical environment to find the ways to keep the company viable.

The Economic Environment. The economic environment includes inflation/deflation, interest rates, taxes, exchange rates, comparative advantage/disadvantage, and all else in the national and global economy that affects the company. "National" and "global," both together, must be considered the economic environment. Like the commercial and technical environments, the economic environment brings threats and opportunities. And, as in the commercial and technical environments, the company strategy for sustainability in the economic environment is performance among the best in the key performance areas described in this book.

With the VSM structure, each business is in close touch with all that matters to that business in the economic environment. Conditions in the economic environment can be an important consideration in the timing of major decisions.

The Political Environment. Finding and keeping the public interest in mind in developing their positions, companies and businesses and their industry associations can strive for positions that will also further the public interest. Well-run companies are good citizens. Well-run government considers the interests of all its citizens. A position good for the public interest can also be good for the company.

At the corporate level, top management will have the main responsibility for relationships with the federal government and may maintain a Washington office to assist in these relationships. Companies may also collaborate through trade and professional organizations in their representations to government on specific issues. Government needs to understand the interests of business and industry. And business and industry needs to relate to what's wise for the country.

The political environment is also the regional offices and activities of government agencies throughout the country. And the political environment is also state and local governments and their agencies. Responsibility for relating to these becomes the responsibility of the top managements at the levels of recursion operating in those states and localities. As with other environments, with the VSM and system thinking companies structure a network of relationships between the company and the political environment.

The company's political relationships need to be structured similarly at all levels of government in the countries where the company operates or sells its products. The network of relationships in the political environment is global. At all levels the key to success is superior performance in the key performance areas described in this book.

The Social Environment. In the company and at all levels of recursion it is the HR function in system 3—the here and now of operations —that has the responsibility for dealing with the social environment. HR also has a responsibility to find in the social environment any changes developing that may be threats or opportunities for the company. HR responsibility includes today's community relations, and also the identification of changes and trends in the society that may have consequences for the company. The VSM's network of communications with the social environment discovers these changes and trends. System 3 HR at each level of recursion sees that their business acts appropriately.

Sustainability in the social environment means monitoring and understanding the changes that can affect the company, and acting in ways that will help the company achieve its purpose.

The Educational Environment. The US federal government set eight goals for education by the year 2000, including:

Goal 2. By 2000 high school graduation rate will be 90%. Actual was about 67%.

Goal 5. By the year 2000 US students will be first in mathematics and science achievement. In tests administered by the Program for International Student Assessment (PISA), in the year 2000 US students were about average among the 30 OECD member countries.

We set high goals, and then depart further from them. The VSM structure and system principles applied in the education system could very much improve education achievement. Companies can help. The companies come from a good perspective—the employers of public education's graduates, and the suppliers of the products and services they will need. Companies when experienced with the VSM, in all their levels of recursion will be operating where the schools and the school systems are, federal, state, and local. Companies, with their heterostats that produce successful innovations may also be able to contribute to the change and innovation needed in public education.

Ecological Environment. After 10 thousand years of slow growth, between the year 1950 and the year 2000, the human population of planet earth ballooned from 2.5 billion to 6 billion. The standard of living for many grew rapidly and world economic output in constant dollars grew from 7 trillion to 46 trillion in those same 50 years. On a grand scale we solved the problems of the great depression and World War II, expanding from poverty to plenty. But the road to plenty has created the greatest crisis ever confronted by humanity: how the projected world population of 9 to 10 billion people by mid-century will exist on our finite earth.

The "Parable of the Twenty-ninth Day" shows us how growth and glory can turn suddenly into chaos and collapse. Are we near our 29th day? Or will our collective intellect lead us to stabilization, a decline in numbers, and a culture even better than now?

Our world of 6 billion people with our 46 trillion dollar global economy lives in the biosphere. The biosphere, including us, lives in the ecosphere. We now see threatening trends in both the ecosphere and the biosphere:

Global warming. Temperature and climate changes affecting agriculture and livability, changing weather patterns, destructive storms, melting glaciers and polar ice, sea levels rising

Water shortages. Falling water tables world-wide from the Ogallala to the deep aquifer under the North China Plain that is already reducing grain harvests, lack of potable water in many areas, rivers running dry from overuse of the water, demands of agriculture and cities in conflict

Loss of Arable Land. Erosion, desertification, water shortages, farmland diverted to "development"

Pollution. Air, land, lakes and rivers, oceans; world-wide

Extinction of Species. Species disappearing from the Earth with extinctions now hundreds of times the normal rate. Geologic history records six periods of great extinctions, claiming from 60% to 95% of existing species. From what we now know, what humans are doing on earth is the major cause of a seventh great extinction, happening on a scale like the earlier six.

Social Ills. Poverty, hunger, illiteracy, crime, unemployment, oppression, intolerance, civil strife and civil wars, HIV and threats from pandemics, nuclear proliferation, terrorism, and the capability of small groups and individuals to cause mass destruction; rapidly growing human populations to huge numbers degrades both our civilization, and the earth's biosphere and ecosphere.

We are beginning to see approaches to sustainability. We have known for 30 years that the oil industry has reached "Hubbert's Peak," and production will be slowing in a world of rising demand. Future energy sources will be at or close to zero environmental impact, and different from oil, coal, and nuclear. Apart from environmental impact, coal and nuclear would reach their own Hubbert's Peak within a quarter century.

The solution to the energy crisis will not be found in some combination of oil, nuclear, and coal technologies. More likely success will result from incoming and renewable energy sources, plus sharp reductions in energy usage. Conventional thinking can prove that this likely success is not practical, unrealistic. But innovation thrives in making the not practical and the unrealistic the most practical and the most realistic.

A transformation to sustainability will be a vast network of systems extending to include all the earth's institutions and people. A transformation to sustainability will create and run itself, like the internet creates itself and runs itself. All of us and all our institutions in everything we do will be part of the transformation.

Systems have the capability of self-organization and self-control. The biosphere organizes itself and controls itself. The ecosphere organizes itself and controls itself. Both now do this with too many influences imposed by humankind. The result is change not favorable for humankind. The biosphere has no concern for how its changes may affect one of its species. The ecosphere has no concern for how its changes may affect the biosphere. But we humans have a great concern. Will we be wise enough to form among us a self-organizing, self-controlling transformation to sustainability?

NOTES

[1] United States Code, Title 20, Chapter 68, Subchapter 1, National Education Goals.

[2] Jonas Salk and Jonathan Salk, *World Population and Human Values,* Harper & Row, New York, 1981.

[3] Edward O. Wilson, *Consilience,* Vintage Books, New York, 1999, p. 308.

[4] Martin Rees, *Our Final Hour,* Basic Books, New York, 2003.

[5] Lester R. Brown, *Plan B: Rescuing a Planet under Stress and a Civilization in Trouble*, W. W. Norton & Company, New York, 2003.

[6] Stafford Beer, *Platform for Change,* John Wiley & Sons, New York, 1975, p. 310.

[7] R. Buckminster Fuller, "Experiment in Individual Initiative," *ReVISION,* Vol. 6, No. 2, Fall, 1983.

[8] Kenneth S. Deffeyes, *Beyond Oil: The View from Hubbert's Peak,* Farrar, Straus and Giroux, New York, 2005.

[9] Jared Diamond, *How Societies Choose to Fail or Succeed,* Viking, Penguin Group, New York, 2005.

Chapter 11

The Viable System Model and Profitability

Of all the performance numbers important to top management, the profit numbers are number 1. Quarterly profit compared with the previous quarter and year ago. Earnings per share, this quarter, last quarter, and year ago. ROI. ROS. ROE. In recent years reporting has emphasized value for shareholders—earnings per share and stock price.

IS PROFIT AND SHAREHOLDER VALUE THE COMPANY PURPOSE?

Many business people today state that the purpose of their company is to create value for shareholders. This book, guided by Stafford Beer's VSM and its system science and cybernetics and Peter Drucker's key performance areas, states purpose differently.

Shareholder value derives from company profitability and investor views on the company's future. Profitability and the company's future derive from successful performance in all the key performance areas. Purpose is what the company aims to do. A system is what it does. In 1908, the purpose of the Ford Motor Company was to make a car that everyone could buy. The Model T put America on wheels and investors prospered. In 1998, the purpose of Google, Inc. was to organize the world's information and make it universally accessible and useful. Google and its investors prospered.

This book states that the purpose of every company is to create and keep customers. That is what successful companies do. Each company in its purpose will state the unique value it will offer to customers; to create customers, and to keep customers. Ford offered a low cost car. Google offered a new, different, better search engine. Both created and kept customers. Both created value for shareholders. For how long depends on success in the key performance areas, especially creating and keeping customers. Ford dominated the market for some two decades until the 1920s when with poor performance in key performance areas, especially in organization capability, the company lost its dominant position to General Motors. Google after seven years is still the market leader, and still creating value for shareowners.

In his book, *The Practice of Management*, Peter Drucker wrote, "If we want to know what a business is we have to start with its *purpose*. And its purpose must lie outside of the business itself. In fact it must lie in society since a business enterprise is an organ of society. There is only one valid definition of business purpose: *to create a customer.*"

Theodore Levitt, the renowned professor of business administration at Harvard University, speaking at a meeting of a chemical company's management group, advised, "Don't think of your company as manufacturing chemicals. Think of your company as manufacturing customers."

Creating customers creates business success. As in the examples of Ford and Google, the company purpose gives direction to how the customers will be created.

TWO METRICS: ACCOUNTING AND ECONOMICS

In the VSM, corporate top management includes the leaders of system 5, system 4, system 3, and system 2. Then, at each level of recursion there are the additional top managements—the leaders of system 5, 4, 3, and 2—of those businesses. At each level of recursion, top management at each of the businesses aims to achieve targeted profit numbers. At corporate and all recursion levels top management aims for profit objectives this month, this quarter, this year. But top management needs to think also about profitability not only for 4 quarters, but also for 20 quarters and 40 quarters ahead, and more. For 4 quarters and for 40 quarters, profitability depends on successful achievement in all the key performance areas.

Profit numbers begin with operating income, the income from what the business does. The business is what it does. It creates and keeps customers by developing, producing, and marketing products and services offering values and satisfaction for customers. The operating income statement summarizes the financial results from what the business does. But top management doesn't manage operating income. Top management, and everyone else, manages all the key performance areas that produce operating income.

The operating income statement measures each business unit's contribution to company profitability. This chapter discusses operating income in the language of economics, specifically the economics of the firm, which this book calls "management economics," and is also referred to as "managerial economics." An operating income statement in management economics terms provides information useful to all involved for making the decisions and taking the actions needed in the key performance areas to produce desired profitability.

Profit numbers and profitability trends affect stock prices, which determine market value, and the value of stock options. Profit numbers also affect incentive compensation. So there are many reasons for reporting good numbers. The drive for good numbers can lead to the creation of reported profit by actions in the finance department. But real profit can only result from success in company operations, measured in operating income. And useful measures of operating income require economics measures. Accounting measures are not enough; they can be misleading, as an increasing amount of the current literature on cost and profit measurement are pointing out. However, the chart of accounts can usually provide management economics measures as well as accounting measures. So companies have the needed data. They just don't have the needed information.

On the day this author was beginning to write this chapter, July 13, 2005, Bernard Evers, WorldCom's former chairman and CEO, was sentenced to 25 years in prison for fraudulent accounting that led to bankruptcy for WorldCom, wiped out billions of dollars for WorldCom investors, cost thousands of employees their jobs, cost retirees their pensions, and led to billions of dollars in "settlements" paid by the company's financial advisors and enablers. The management, and the accountants, at WorldCom had good data, but they produced unreal profit measures.

The losses from fraudulent accounting at WorldCom, Enron, Adelphia, Tyco, Parmalat, HealthSouth, and others, and the trials and "settlements" that resulted, focused the attention of management on what's real. Public policy, expressed through Sarbanes-Oxley, and the public interest, expressed through the investigations and trials, demand an end to financial transactions and accounting that reports profitability that is not really there. The numbers in profit reporting need to be real. The rule book has changed for business and industry, and for their auditors, legal advisors, and investment bankers.

Profit measures by generally accepted accounting principles (GAAP) measure profit reliably, as profit is defined in the accounting rules. But executives, motivated to report "good numbers" and assisted by their financial advisors, can interpret those rules to allow practices that create unreal profit. When the numbers hide a reality of bad numbers, at some point there's a crash. Executive management, their financial advisors, GAAP, and the Sarbanes-Oxley safeguards all have to work together to assure reliable profit reporting.

The rules of accounting are designed to apply in all companies and all situations to assure reliable financial reporting. So everyone learns accounting rules and measures. And accounting measures became management measures, too. They show when things are going well. But they don't show why things are going well so those involved can do more of whatever that is. They show when things are not going well. But they don't show why, to help those involved take appropriate actions. Management needs metrics different from, and in addition to, financial accounting. Management economics offers those metrics.

Finance and accounting and GAAP are needed for profit reporting. Economics and management economics are needed for managing operations and the seven key performance areas to result in desired profitability.

In recent years the accounting profession has recognized the need for new and different measures for management. From this recognition came the development of "management accounting" and the "balanced scorecard;" significant advances, but not adequate. There is another approach. Instead of starting from accounting and finding ways to provide better information for management, why not start with economics, specifically, the economics of the firm-management economics. The new structure and management principles described in the VSM and system thinking provides an overall framework for effective management. The principles of management economics, and best practices in the seven key performance areas described in this book, give us new tools for performance improvement in all the key performance areas, including profitability.

The economics of the firm, management economics, uses economic measures, which in some cases may be similar to the accounting measures; in other cases very different. Some of the differences:

- Instead of standard costs we use current cost. And the best current cost is replenishment cost.
- We don't calculate profit figures for individual products. It is the total profit center business that creates profit or loss. Products contribute to profitability, and we measure and manage those contributions.
- We don't use the terms "overhead" or "burden." With the VSM and management economics there is no overhead. There is no burden. All fixed costs are essential and measurable contributors to business success. Who wants to be a part of overhead or burden?
- We manage fixed costs where and when incurred.
- We measure and manage total fixed costs by its major categories—people costs, capital costs, and programmed fixed costs.
- We solve the problem of how to allocate by eliminating allocations.
- We don't measure success by monthly comparisons of actual with budget. We measure success by progress toward goals in all the key performance areas.
- We don't measure and explain variances from budget. We measure progress toward goals and continuously act to achieve the goals.
- We value assets at replacement cost, and continue to depreciate all assets in use.
- We don't use the terms or the measures "cost of goods sold" and "gross margins." Neither of these measures is helpful in understanding what's happening, or for decision making. We use more informative terms and measures in a management economics operating income statement explained later in this chapter.

We commonly think of profitability as a reward for investors through dividends and stock appreciation. Profitability also rewards company people through incentive compensation plans. But the real need for profitability is an economic need—providing the funds for creating the future of the company. Maintaining present operations requires investment. The innovations and new business programs and ventures that create the future require investment. However financed, this investment comes from company profitability. Without profitability the company has no future. And profitability comes from operations, what the company does.

The VSM and system thinking helps the company do better what it does. In the VSM, finance and accounting functions are in both system 3, the here and now of business operations, and system 4, the outside and future. Accounting is primarily in system 3, accounting for operations in the here and now. Finance is in both system 3 for financing today's operations, and in system 4 for financing the future of the company. The VSM models functions. An individual can work in more than one of the five VSM systems.

The VSM and system thinking puts a sharp focus on operations, through all levels of recursion. A system is what it does. What the system does is done in operations. A corporation, at all levels of recursion, may have dozens, or hundreds, of VSM business units, each producing operating income or (loss). The managers, professionals, and operators in each of those business units produce operating income by successfully achieving their objectives in seven key performance areas: creating and keeping customers, quality and productivity, innovation, organization capability, physical and financial resources, public and environmental responsibility, and profitability. The importance of each of these seven will vary from one company to another, depending on circumstances. For some companies there may be other key performance areas especially relevant to that business. Often, though, any additional key performance area will fit comfortably within one of these seven.

Profitability, of course, results from performance in all the key performance areas. But there's a discipline in profitability measurement that helps us identify where there is needed change and improvement in any of the other six areas as explained later in this chapter and illustrated in some of the examples.

At all levels of recursion operating income, the source of company profitability, depends on and derives from success in all of the key performance areas. The VSM and system science gives us the understanding of how systems work so that system capabilities can be used at all levels of recursion to achieve desired results. The VSM gives us a more realistic view of how the company works. It changes the task of top management from running the company to structuring the company so that the company can run itself. At each level of recursion the first task of top management in each of those businesses is to structure that business so that the business can run itself. The VSM and system thinking give us the principles for designing a structure that produces desired results through self-organization and self-control. The system itself, at all levels of recursion, monitors performance and environmental change for any actions needed to achieve desired goals. The system's homeostats and heterostats always need to be working.

The system structure in the VSM is different from the traditional organization chart. It models functions. It models recursions. It describes how the company works. It includes information as a part of structure. It includes the environments outside the company that the company relates to, and establishes communication channels to and from these environments. The VSM teaches us the principles of system science that give us better ways to lead and to manage. It gives us a framework for successfully applying best business practices in all the key performance areas, including the key performance area of profitability.

WHERE DOES PROFITABILITY COME FROM?

Convention says that profitability comes from the products and services sold by the company. And convention has established accounting rules for calculating the full cost of each product and service. Comparing this full cost with the sales revenue received for the product or service gives us the profitability of the product. This process gives us precise numbers, and a high comfort level for making decisions. But these decisions will not likely be wise decisions, for two reasons:

1. The premise that making products profitable as measured by prescribed accounting measures will make the company profitable is not confirmed by experience.
2. The prescribed accounting procedures for measuring product profitability is very misleading.

There is a better way and it comes from economics, specifically the economics of the business, management economics. Management economics says that profitability is a function of the total business, not the sum of the profit of individual products. We need to understand the economics of the total business. And we need to understand the economics of individual products, which contribute to the profitability of the business. Management economics gives us the methods, and the measures, for both. And these methods and measures that give us this understanding are much simpler than the conventional accounting measures.

The VSM and system science sees the company as a viable, very complex, purposeful, probabilistic system as described in chapters 1 and 2. The system is what it does. What the system that is a business does is create and keep customers by producing products and services satisfying customer expectations. There is more to the system than producing and delivering products and services. The system needs all the functions described in the VSM to do what it does. The total system, all parts of it, are needed to succeed in all the key performance areas and produce profitability. The system itself is what makes a profit, or (loss). And the economics of the system are much simpler than full-cost accounting; an order of magnitude simpler!

MANAGEMENT ECONOMICS

Management economics derives from the pioneering work of Joel Dean at Columbia University more than half a century ago. He researched and taught what he called "managerial economics," and published his seminal work under that title in 1951 [1]. Managerial economics was prominent in business school courses for decades, but recently, when it is most needed, seems to have faded from university curricula and from use in business. Everything measured in dollars has become what finance and accounting says it is. We need to open our eyes to the economics of the individual business.

Universities concentrate on the study of economic systems, and markets; the "big picture," the company's economic environment. Even "microeconomics" dealing with industries, markets, competition, trade, and smaller pieces of "macroeconomics" is a big step above the economics of the transactions in the individual firm. There is a huge need today for an understanding of the economics of the individual firm. Dean called this economics "managerial economics." This book calls it "management economics," because of the values it offers for management decision-making at all levels where decisions are made involving costs, revenue, and profitability.

Management economics begins with the same basic concept as the VSM. The VSM says that all the functions of the system are essential for the system to do what it does and accomplish its purpose. Management economics says that all the functions of the company—a viable, very complex, purposeful, probabilistic system—are essential for achieving profitability objectives. The total business makes a profit, or (loss). As noted above, conventional accounting methods for calculating the profitability of individual products produces numbers, but these numbers don't lead to wise decisions. Management economics offers a different, and valid methodology for understanding the variables that determine company profitability.

At all levels of recursion, management economics helps decision-makers evaluate the probable economic consequences from decisions and actions taken. Management economics is a discipline that can be understood and used by everyone for making decisions and acting in ways that will contribute to the achievement of profitability objectives. Management economics uses data from the accounting chart of accounts, but uses this data in different ways and brings in additional information to provide the understanding needed for wise decisions for managing costs, revenue, and profitability.

Accounting measures were not designed for decision-making. They were designed for use by all companies to assure comparable monthly, quarterly, and annual financial reporting. They report past performance for both financial reporting and for tax accounting. All this is a big, complex procedure, which must be done right. So everyone learns accounting. But accounting does not deal with all the key performance areas. And the information needed for management decisions is different from what is needed for taxes and financial reporting. Decisions are about the future, and measures are needed that help decision-makers understand the present situation, and the likely future consequences of decisions. Decision-makers throughout the company, at all levels of recursion, need management economics.

As we begin using management economics we will find many opportunities for simplification; for getting more information with less data. We no longer need full-cost data on products. We don't report and analyze variances from monthly, quarterly, and annual budgets. We leave cost of goods sold and gross margins to the accountants. We don't agonize over the best way to allocate fixed costs. There is no best way. And with management economics we don't allocate. We lose control of fixed costs when we allocate them to products or other units, however we do it. We can only control fixed costs where and when they are incurred. Using management economics requires less data, but gives us much more useful information for decisions and actions.

Management economics helps us understand the likely consequences of present actions, and helps us act in ways most likely to make these consequences favorable and consistent with business purpose and goals.

Management Economics Principles

System science gives us a new way to structure and manage the company. The VSM gives us a systems model for our company and for all the business units at all recursions from the company VSM. All are viable, very complex, purposeful, probabilistic systems. All the functions of the system are essential for what the system does. Management economics takes the system view. All the functions of the business, whether or not the business is modeled with the VSM, are needed to produce profit or loss. Individual products contribute to profitability. And so do all the other functions in the VSM model. All are essential. There is no overhead. Management economics looks at:

- Revenues, by product, product group, markets, customers, channels, and whatever other sources of revenue the business has
- Costs, by kinds of costs and where, why, how, and when incurred
- Cost and revenue relationships, changes over time, and how these changes can be managed
- Key measures and trends in relation to goals
- Opportunities for improving profitability

With management economics we see more clearly how costs and revenue relate and interact. Management economics creates measures that quantify these relationships. Monitoring these relationships and changes in them tracks progress toward operating income goals. Most of the data needed is already in the company's information system, but with management economics, the data are used in new ways. Management economics deals with transactions, and is easy to learn and use. It is a language for operations that everyone can understand and use.

Management economics begins with five new, different, and important principles:

1. We don't calculate profit figures for individual products, services, customers, or contracts. But we do keep a very close eye on the variable costs incurred for each product. The total profit-center business produces profit or loss. There is no useful profit figure

for a product. Accounting can construct such figures, but for decision-making these figures should carry a warning label: "This figure should not be used for making decisions." Products, services, and transactions incur costs and contribute to profitability, and management economics measures, and manages, these costs and contributions. The business, a viable, very complex, purposeful, probabilistic system, is what makes a profit. This principle together with principle 2b resolves the problem of how to allocate fixed costs by eliminating the need to allocate.

2. Costs are managed according to how they behave:

   a. Variable costs are assigned to the products for which they were incurred.

   b. Fixed costs are assigned to the organizational units that incur them. Total fixed costs are managed by their major categories: people costs, capital costs, and programmed fixed costs.

3. Revenue is managed according to market demand and opportunity for the products and services offered by the profit-center business for:

   a. Markets and market segments, and

   b. Individual customers and transactions.

4. Profitability is managed according to the interacting relationships between costs and revenue, which can be expressed in an income model. The income model identifies and quantifies all variables and displays the present situation for each accounting period. The key variables in the model include: sales revenue, fixed costs, contribution margin percent, break-even, and operating income. Time series charts of each of these interacting variables can be monitored for information that will signal any needed actions to achieve desired operating income.

5. Evaluation of what is important is determined by the business unit's definition of its purpose; in the language of the VSM, as stated in its Resource Bargain. This is an important point to keep in mind in evaluating new investment opportunities. Management is inclined to look first at financial measures such as discounted cash flow rate of return, or payback. It is wiser to think first about the purpose of the business, and how essential the investment is to the achievement of that purpose.

For many people, this may look like a new set of principles. For many who see products as the source of profit it is hard to see that really it is the total profit-center business that makes a profit or (loss). To calculate product profitability requires the allocation of fixed costs. People involved in allocating these costs have developed more and more sophisticated methods for allocating fixed costs "more accurately," aiming at improving control of costs. Working with management economics we find that there is no right way to allocate. However done, allocation loses control of fixed costs. In management economics we control fixed costs, not by allocating them out, but by controlling them where and when incurred. And working with principle 1, the word overhead disappears. There are fixed costs. But none of these are overhead. In a well-designed systems structure all jobs and all costs are needed for the system to do what it does, and earn a profit. Overhead is not a helpful concept. So management economics does not include the word overhead in its vocabulary.

The president of a company beginning to use management economics was concerned about not allocating some fixed costs. The company was planning a major promotion on one of its products. The promotion would include an advertising and promotion expense of $XX. Management economics says that advertising and promotion is a fixed cost. Shouldn't this fixed cost be allocated to that product?

Management economics would measure the success of the promotion in a different way. Of course the company wants to know if the promotion is successful; and as the promotion proceeds, should it be changed, increased, reduced, dropped. Management economics would manage the promotion not as an activity, but as a project with specific objectives in sales revenue and contribution margin by target dates. The targeted dollar contribution margin objective would be the expected "normal" plus more than enough to pay for the advertising and promotion fixed cost. Project success can then be measured in comparison with project objectives on a continuing basis, making continuous adjustments along the way—more of this, less of that, expand the program, shut it down, whatever is interpreted from the feedback.

At all levels of recursion there are the normal, on-going operations. Any significant changes in the on-going, such as a major promotion, are accomplished through projects, each managed by best practices in project management. In today's fast-changing economy, projects are an important part of company management. Management economics enables us to set financial goals for projects and gives us the measures for monitoring progress toward those goals and taking actions as appropriate.

While management economics offers more useful information for decision-making, business people have learned accounting principles and practices and apply these also for management purposes; in their view, successfully. So it's hard to recognize that, for management purposes, other metrics from economics can be more useful, and can help them make better decisions. They will find that working with the five principles of management economics provides more reliable information, is much simpler, and empowers all decision-makers to improve results. Management economics is a discipline that everyone can understand and use in their daily decisions.

With a systems view we see the company as a viable, very complex, purposeful, probabilistic system with an increasing number of profit-center business units at each further level of recursion, as visualized in Figure 11.1. The five principles of management economics apply at the

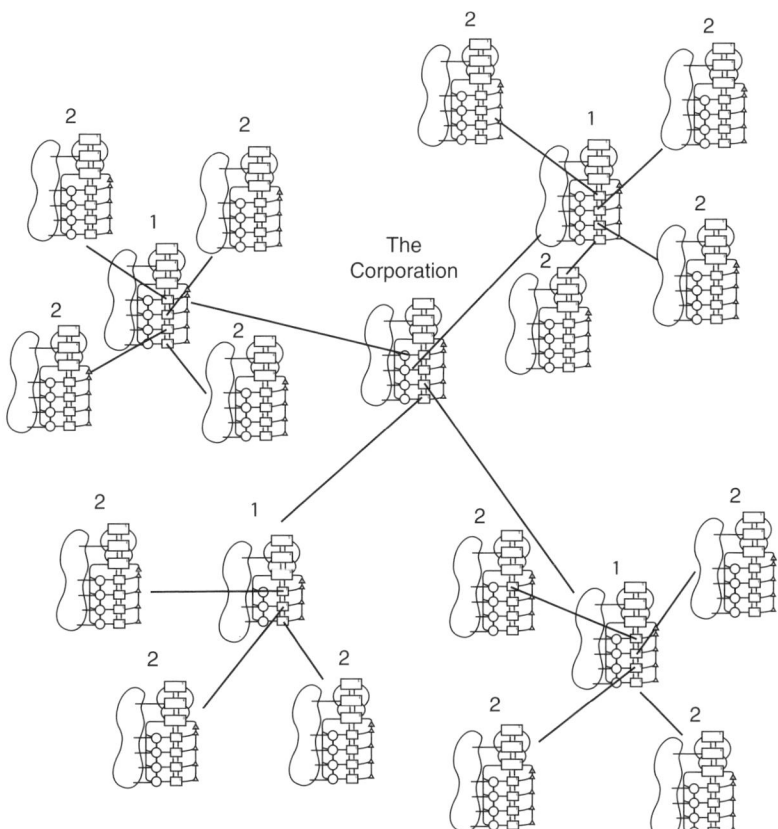

Figure 11.1   Corporate VSM with two levels of recursion

corporate level and at each of these dozens, or hundreds, of profit-center businesses.

Figure 11.1 shows the corporate VSM with four system 1s. The corporate VSM is recursion 0. Each of the four corporate system 1s is also a viable, very complex, purposeful, probabilistic system that can also be modeled with the VSM. Figure 11.1 shows these four VSMs in recursion 1, each identified with the number 1. The second level of recursion shows the VSMs for each of the system 1s in each of the four VSMs in recursion 1. The second recursion VSMs are identified with the number 2. In each of the 20 VSM businesses shown in Figure 11.1, and in the additional VSM businesses in further recursion, management economics methods and measures will help management people achieve profitability objectives.

The five management economics principles provide a systems concept that profit is a function of the total business unit, that there are many interacting elements within the business, and between these elements and the external environments that must be managed if the business unit is to earn a desired profit. These relationships can be organized for the business unit in a very practical management economics operating income statement. The income statement begins with a classification of costs.

Costs

In management economics all costs are classified into one or the other of two kinds of costs: variable costs, or fixed costs. The definitions come from economics rules, not from accounting rules. In product costing, accounting uses the term, "direct costs." Variable costs as defined by management economics would be included in the accounting classification of direct costs. But the accounting definition of direct costs, depending on decisions made by the accountants, will likely include costs that management accounting will include in fixed costs. It is important to understand the management economics definitions of variable and fixed costs. Management economics defines costs according to how the cost behaves.

Variable Costs Variable costs are the costs of the purchased materials, parts, components, and energy used in the production of the company's products. These costs are incurred as needed for producing the product. The costs vary with production; they are variable costs. Typically materials, parts, and components are purchased in lots, and used continuously, so there is some degree of lag between purchase and use. The closer manufacturing operations are to stockless production (just-in-time), the closer variable costs are incurred as the materials, parts, and components are used. Whatever this relationship, it is an easy matter to classify these variable costs for each product. What to buy and who to buy it from are management decisions. But purchases are made and costs incurred as needed for production. Examples of variable costs include:

- Materials, valued at replenishment cost
- Purchased components, valued at replenishment cost
- Energy, valued at replenishment cost
- Packaging materials
- Freight
- Royalty payments
- Sales commissions
- Duty and other border-crossing costs

Management economics deals with today and the future, so the relevant cost is the present cost; the cost to replenish the variable cost item. The accounting record knows past costs and can choose to use FIFO or LIFO for accounting purposes. Of these two, LIFO is closer to replenishment cost, and LIFO is usually used in management economics. Purchasing, however, knows replenishment cost which is the best cost to use.

Fixed Costs   Fixed costs are not incurred as needed for production. Fixed costs are incurred by management decision. Some fixed costs, accountants refer to as "period costs" because they are time-related, rather than related to production. Property taxes are paid every year, unrelated to production. Salaries and wages are paid every month, the rate unchanged until changed by management decision or contract agreement. Sales, general, and administrative expenses (SGA) are fixed costs. They are incurred because decisions are made to incur them. Advertising, an SGA expense, is a fixed cost; it's a cost incurred by management decision. Management decision to spend 4% of sales on advertising varies advertising cost with sales, but it's still a fixed cost because it was incurred by management decision. For the next budget period, the management decision might be to spend a different percentage of sales, or perhaps a dollar amount. Costs incurred by management decision are fixed costs, even if the decision is to spend X% of sales revenue.

Fixed costs are essential for the production of products and for creating and keeping customers. In system thinking there is no "overhead." The VSM and its system science and cybernetics describe a structure and management principles for all companies, and organizations of all kinds. The model identifies the functions needed for a viable, very complex, purposeful, probabilistic business to achieve its goals. All functions are needed; all are important. None can be called "overhead." Management economics classifies fixed costs into three major groups:

1. People costs. People costs include all wage, salary, incentive, and bonus compensation payments; the costs of all employee benefits; payroll taxes; workman's compensation expense; and any other employment costs. For almost all companies, direct labor is a fixed cost. Direct labor cost continues until there is a management decision or a negotiated agreement to change it. Labor costs can be changed by changing pay rates, changing the amount of overtime or other special pay arrangements, by laying off employees, or by hiring additional employees. Production labor cost is a direct cost but not a variable cost. For most companies direct labor behaves like a fixed cost and is managed as a fixed cost. Direct labor cost varies only when management decision varies it. Direct labor cost does not vary with production like materials, parts, and components. For most businesses, all people costs are fixed costs, including direct labor.

However, in some businesses, direct labor is a variable cost. A landscape firm may hire from a labor pool as work is available. That labor would be a variable cost. A construction contractor hires subcontractors for parts of the construction job. These subcontractor costs, like materials costs, are variable costs.

2. Capital costs. These are the costs for owning and using the company's capital facilities. Using economics principles rather than accounting rules, many of these costs will be different, and higher, than when measured by accounting rules. Figure 11.2 illustrates a management economics view of capital costs.

Figure 11.2 is the same measurement of capital costs as used in Chapter 7 for measuring economic productivity. Economic productivity is one of the applications of management economics. Management economics converts capital investment costs from a "stock," to a "flow" over the use-life of the asset.

Item		How Measured
1. Working Capital:		
2. Cash	_____	Monthly average
3. Accounts Receivable	_____	Monthly average
4. Inventory	_____	Monthly average
5. Total Working Capital	_____	Total of lines 2, 3, and 4
6. Fixed Capital employed:	_____	All fixed capital employed, valued at replacement cost.
7. Total Capital:	_____	Total of lines 5 and 6
8. Normal Interest Charge on Total Capital	_____	A company-selected rate of return on capital X Total Capital (line 7)
9. Depreciation	_____	Straight-line depreciation of the replacement value (line 6)
10. Associated Capital Costs		
11. Property Taxes	_____	Property taxes paid or payable for the period
12. Insurance	_____	Property insurance costs paid or payable for the period
13. Maintenance	_____	Maintenance costs incurred for the period
14. Total Associated Capital Costs	_____	Total of lines 11, 12, and 13
15. Total Capital Costs	_____	Total of lines 8, 9, and 14

Figure 11.2   Management economics capital costs and measures

People costs and capital costs, together, are the "constant fixed costs" of the business. They are long-term costs, and continue until changed by management decision. Whatever the production level, whatever the sales revenue, whatever the operating income, whatever the company profit, these costs continue until changed by management decision.

3. Programmed fixed costs. All fixed costs that are not people costs or capital costs fall into programmed fixed costs. SGA expenses other than people costs and capital costs are programmed fixed costs, including advertising, promotion, travel, entertainment, telephone, professional services, contract research, dues and subscriptions, contributions, and the other SGA expenses. Programmed fixed costs are incurred by the decisions of many people in many functions. Differing from constant fixed costs, programmed fixed costs are short term, and can be changed more quickly in response to current circumstances.

Identifying costs as fixed costs does not mean that these costs don't change. It only means that they don't change until changed by management decision. The major part of these fixed costs, the constant fixed costs—people costs and capital costs—are the costs of the organization and structure needed to be in business. When the business does what it does—makes products, creates customers—it incurs programmed fixed costs and variable costs. And it creates revenue that pays all these costs, plus, if the business is successful, earns profit. The concepts and measures of management economics help all involved manage this whole process.

As discussed in Chapter 5 in the section on budgeting, few companies manage fixed costs well. Accounting practices don't even require companies to measure and know what their fixed costs are. Pieces of fixed costs are scattered throughout the chart of accounts and throughout the typical budget. In the individual profit-center businesses and for the total company the total of fixed costs is not known. The trend of fixed costs is not known.

Conventional budget practice assures that fixed costs will not be controlled; exactly the opposite of what is intended. Each year, managers propose additional funding for fixed cost items in their budgets. The proposals seem desirable and as funds appear to be available, increases are made. So fixed cost items, and the unseen total of fixed costs, tend to ratchet up year by year related to perceived need, but unrelated to affordability. Over time, fixed costs can grow to the point where a major "restructuring" may be needed.

Two management economics measures can add the dimension of affordability to decisions on fixed costs:

1. Monitoring total fixed costs and each of its three parts, people costs, capital costs, and programmed fixed costs will show trends and changes in trends. For each of these, a 3-month moving average is a reliable and simple measure of trend and changes in trend.

2. Monitoring contribution margin dollars (12-month moving total) and contribution margin percent (3-month moving average) will show trends and changes in trends. For managing contribution margin dollars, a 12-month moving total is used to compensate for any seasonality in sales revenue. Contribution margin percent is unchanged by seasonality (unless there is a significant seasonal change in mix), so the 3-month moving average is more useful. An important management responsibility is to manage the relationship between total fixed costs and contribution margin dollars. This relationship determines operating income; it needs to be known, measured, and monitored. But accounting doesn't measure total fixed costs, doesn't calculate contribution margin. Management is left with the crude measures of gross margins and fully-

costed products, and their own intuition to deal with profit problems. Management economics gives management sharper tools; managers make wiser decisions.

Management economics measures of costs and contribution margin provide the information needed to identify when total fixed costs are growing out of line with contribution margin earned. Management in businesses that use these measures considerably improved their control of fixed costs. See Chapter 5.

A Management Economics Statement of Operating Income

After we have defined and classified costs as described above, we can prepare a management economics statement of operating income. This statement will likely show a different and lower operating income than the accounting statement for two reasons:

1. Using management economics capital costs are calculated by the procedure summarized in Figure 11.2 will be higher than these costs as measured by generally accepted accounting practices. The management economics method is closer to reality.

A few years ago a whole philosophy of management, "Economic Value Added (EVA)" was developed to value and manage the company's capital assets more realistically. EVA calculates the weighted average cost of capital (equity plus debt), applies this cost to total capital and subtracts this capital cost from after-tax profit. The result is the company's EVA. If the EVA is positive, the company is adding value for shareholders; if negative the company is destroying value for shareholders. Consulting firms promoting EVA developed training programs to inform people throughout the company on the management of capital assets and to motivate actions for improvement. In the late 1990s there were many very successful EVA companies, and EVA became a popular management strategy. A few years later many of these successes faded, and EVA has pretty much disappeared. EVA did help companies manage their capital assets better, but in a complex way, oriented to shareholder value. Management economics helps companies manage their capital assets better and in a much simpler way, oriented to producing operating income.

EVA is all about getting more value from capital employed than the cost to the company of that capital. But the management of capital assets is only one of seven key performance areas described in this book. Companies need to perform well in all seven for company success. Management economics can help in all seven, and relate each to profitability. But each must be managed by best practices in those performance areas.

2. Using management economics the sales revenue number is the actual sales revenue for the period. For most companies the accounting number is also a good management economics number. A sale is made; revenue is earned. All sales made in an accounting period = sales revenue for the period. But those who want to report good numbers sometimes adjust sales revenue figures, too. Sales reported in the current period might really belong in a future period. A transaction might be reported as a sale that is not a sale, such as some kind of a sale/buyback arrangement. A sale that is not a sale of the company's products and services might be reported as sales revenue instead of some kind of a financial transaction. People can create sophisticated and complex financial transactions to improve the numbers, but not the reality. Sales revenue, of course, should mean sales revenue for the accounting period, in both the accounting numbers and the management economics numbers.

Conventional Operating Income Statement   Figure 11.3 shows an operating income statement for a manufacturing company in a conventional accounting format. All company costs for calculating operating income, as these costs are measured by GAAP, are included in this statement. And we can rely on the sales revenue figure, unless someone is distorting some numbers. "Cost of goods sold" is a mixture of variable and fixed costs, and useless for management purposes, whatever value it may have for financial reporting. Gross profit, the difference between sales revenue and cost of goods sold, needs to be higher than SGA expenses to earn operating income, but gives management no

Sales Revenue		$ 38,724,000
Cost of Goods Sold		35,578,000
Gross Profit		3,146,000
SGA Expenses:		5,574,000
Selling	$ 2,274,000	
Distribution	1,750,000	
Development	474,000	
Administration	1,076,000	
Operating Income		(2,428,000)

Figure 11.3   Company A: Conventional operating income statement

useful information. All we know from this statement is that the business is not operating profitably.

Management Economics Operating Income Statement   We can restate the conventional operating income statement in management economics terms and get much more useful management information. Figure 11.4 is Figure 11.3 expressed in terms of management economics. It shows the same sales revenue figure, $38,724,000. But capital costs are $708 K higher calculated by the management economics method shown in Figure 11.2, which increases the reported loss by that amount.

Figure 11.4 gives management new, different, and more useful information, previously unknown:

- Contribution margin dollars (sales revenue minus variable costs of those sales)
- Average contribution margin percent (contribution margin divided by sales revenue)
- Total fixed costs, and the totals for the three major categories of fixed costs
- Breakeven (fixed cost, divided by contribution margin percent)
- A more realistic figure for operating income

The sales revenue of $38,724,000 required $24,764,000 in variable costs, so the company earned a contribution margin of $13,960,000, or 36.05% of sales. Every dollar of sales brought the company 36.05 cents of contribution margin to pay fixed costs and provide operating income. But in this case, the contribution margin is not enough to pay the fixed costs of $17,096,000 so there is an operating loss ($3,136,000).

Sales Revenue (S)		$ 38,724,000
Variable Costs (VC)		24,764,000
Contribution Margin $ (CM$)		13,960,000
Contribution Margin % (CM%)		36.05%
Fixed Costs (FC)		17,096,000
People Costs	$ 9,018,000	
Capital Costs	5,326,000	
Programmed Fixed Costs	2,752,000	
Breakeven (BE)		47,423,000
Sales Revenue Above (Below) BE		(8,699,000)
Operating Income		(3,136,000)

Figure 11.4   Company A: Management economics operating income statement

What actions can make this business profitable? There are three possibilities: increase sales revenue, increase average contribution margin percent, reduce fixed costs.

1. Increase sales revenue. We see that breakeven is $47,423,000. Once breakeven is reached, on sales above breakeven 36.05 cents of every sales dollar is operating income. If the company's short-term objective is $2 million in operating income, that could be accomplished, all else staying the same, by increasing sales $5,548,000 above breakeven to a total of $52,971,000. That number is easy to calculate, but increasing sales revenue 36.8% would be difficult or impossible to achieve in the short term. But with a target account sales campaign as described in Chapter 6, and a well-planned new product program, sales can be increased. That could be part of the management response.

2. Increase average contribution margin percent. Using the process described in Chapter 6, a product line audit will calculate contribution margin for each product. There usually will be a big range. In this case, the contribution margins ranged from less than zero for one product, to 78% for the highest; the average, 36.05% as shown in the income statement. There are four approaches to improving average contribution margin percent:

   - Increase sales effort on products with higher contribution margin percents to increase sales and average contribution margin percent.
   - Fix products with low contribution margin percents by reducing variable costs or increasing price.
   - In working on each of the above, concentrate first on higher volume products.
   - Plan new products for a specified higher than average contribution margin percent. In company A their new product goal for contribution margin percent was set at 50%.

People in most companies have never seen variable costs by product. They have never seen contribution margins by product. They have never seen a total of fixed costs. They have never before seen the relationship of contribution margin and fixed costs to operating income. Now they do. And with this information they will find ways for improving contribution margins. In Company A, management set a short-term goal of increasing average contribution margin percent to 43%, which would achieve the profit objective.

3. Reduce fixed costs. Any fixed cost reductions will lower the breakeven point beyond which the business will earn operating income.

The people in Company A considered very carefully all this new information shown in Figures 11.3 and 11.4, to find a combination of actions that could make their business profitable. The company was a subsidiary of a large corporation and had shown losses for three years. Corporate headquarters had sent in cost accountants, and ordered cost reduction programs. But there was no improvement in profitability.

Now the people in Company A began to see opportunities for change and improvement. Fixed cost reduction could not be a major part of their action. Major cuts would be needed for any significant improvement in profitability. But major cuts in the present people, capital, and programmed fixed costs would constrain the company's ability to do what needed to be done to improve profitability. They developed a 5-part action plan:

1. Increase average contribution margin percent to 43%, as noted above. They audited their product lines as explained in Chapter 6, found ways to fix many of the low contribution margin products, and worked to sell more of the high contribution margin products. They looked at contribution margins by customer, and found ways to improve some of the low ones. This work was done in Q2. By the end of the year, average contribution margin percent was over 40%.

2. Increase total sales revenue. Recognizing the Pareto principle of concentration, sales people identified their key target customers and prospects, and concentrated on increasing sales to this group while maintaining all other customers, too. In this process significant opportunities were found for additional business.

3. Set contribution targets for product development. Every new product development plan would include a projected contribution margin percent. The desired target was a contribution margin of 50% or more. The company custom-developed calendered film and coated fabrics for large customers, so was continuously developing new products. Including contribution margin goals in new product development helped significantly in improving mix.

4. Improve productivity in manufacturing operations. With success in the above actions, improvement in manufacturing productivity would be needed to increase output with no major new capital

investment. The company used lean manufacturing methods and quality/productivity methods and measures to improve productivity.

5. Monitor people costs, capital costs, programmed fixed costs, and total fixed costs to control these costs and make acceptable reductions.

Previous to this work with management economics to improve operating income, sales budgets and sales quotas were specified in pounds and dollars. But now, marketing and sales people saw that there is an additional and very important dimension to sales volume—contribution margin. Company sales and service people were already working to assure customer satisfaction in all sales transactions. And in customer satisfaction they were equal to or better than their competitors. Everyone in the company—sales, technical service, manufacturing, finance, accounting, product development, everyone—did their part in assuring customer satisfaction.

Including contribution margin in goals for sales and marketing was a new and different idea. Sales and marketing people now knew the economics of the products they were selling. They became business people. They brought sales revenue dollars to the company. They also brought contribution margin dollars to the company. They were marketing and selling to create and keep customers and satisfy their expectations. They were also marketing and selling to create business success for their company. Their goals and their performance measures were $X sales revenue and 43% of $X in contribution margin.

Marketing and sales people, with help from purchasing and accounting, audited all product lines to measure the present contribution margin for each product. They also looked at contribution margins for key customers. They set new and higher sales goals for high contribution margin products. They initiated a sales campaign to increase sales with key target customers. They worked with purchasing and product development to improve contribution margins in high-volume, low contribution margin products. They worked with product development people on high-opportunity new products aiming for 50% or more contribution margin. Collaborating with marketing and sales, product engineering expanded new product development, targeting high volume, high contribution margin products.

Manufacturing set goals for improving productivity to increase capacity from existing facilities. Manufacturing output was defined as product meeting specifications, produced without error or waste, delivered to customers and satisfying their expectations. Programs were developed for:

- Reducing setup time
- Reducing scrap and rework
- Automating in-process testing and control
- Increasing throughput rates

Lean manufacturing was the goal. Within two years, capacity was increased more than 50% without major capital investment.

All worked together to reduce variable costs in some of the high-volume, low-contribution margin products, and to increase price and/or reduce variable costs for the very low contribution margin products. Marketing and sales were successful in increasing sales volume and contribution margin dollars. Product engineering was successful in their product development projects. And the increased manufacturing capacity produced the increased output needed.

Within a year the business was profitable and meeting profitability goals. Average contribution margin increased from 36% to 43%, almost enough to reach breakeven without increased sales revenue. But sales revenue increased more than 10% to create operating income of almost $2 million. The same people who had been producing error and waste and three years of losses were now producing successful results. The change to profitability came not from restructuring, cutting people, replacing the general manager, and cutting costs. The change came from the same people using different and better methods.

After three years of unsuccessful, imposed cost reduction programs, they found better ways in management economics, target account selling, new product development, and manufacturing. Many company people were involved in the change to profitability: top management, marketing, sales, manufacturing, new product development, and finance and accounting. Using the new methods they realized that they could create a successful business. They became an effective organization. And their business became profitable.

The experience of Company A illustrates an important point. In most situations, when there is a compelling need for profit improvement, cost reduction may not be an important part of the solution. Companies exist to create value for customers. A measure of value created is value added. When companies need to improve profitability why not look for opportunities for the existing organization to create additional value? There's much more leverage for profit improvement in creating value than in cutting costs.

Company A added value by increasing contribution margins, by including contribution margin goals in new product development objectives, by improving mix, and by increasing sales revenue through best practices in creating and keeping customers. They had tried cost reduction for three years, the result: no improvement in profitability, low morale at all levels. With all involved in creating value, profit improved and morale soared.

But profit improvement is not a one-time thing. Good answers don't last forever. Technology changes. Competition changes. Best practices change. There are changes in the seven environments in the VSM model that the business relates to. Continuing success requires:

- Continuous monitoring of key management economics measures
- Using best practices and measuring progress toward objectives in the key performance areas
- Continuous monitoring of environmental change to discover threats and opportunities
- Using the information learned from the above for continuing innovation and continuing renewal

The continuous planning and continuous budgeting described in Chapter 5 uses all four of the above, in all levels of recursion, to guide the company to continuing success.

An Income Model

With the information in the management economics operating income statement we can prepare a model of the way the company produces operating income. See Figure 11.5. The income model measures sales revenue on the X axis, and operating income on the Y axis. Draw a horizontal line at 0 on the operating income scale. Above this point the business is earning operating income; below, operating loss. Plot the sales revenue for the period on the sales revenue scale, and draw a vertical line to the horizontal 0 line. Plot total fixed costs on the minus side of the operating income scale, in this case $17,096,000. At zero sales, operating income is a loss of $17,096,000, the total of fixed costs. For company A, for this reporting period, as sales are made, 36.05 cents

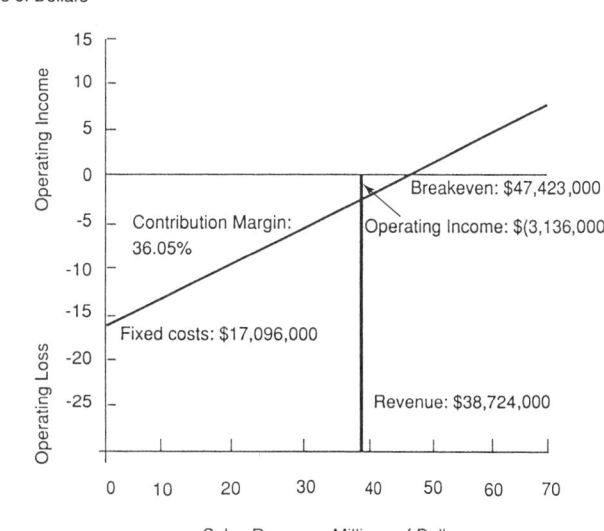

Millions of Dollars

Figure 11.5 Company A: Operating income model

of every sales dollar contribute to the payment of fixed costs to the point of breakeven. Above breakeven, 36.05 cents of each sales dollar is operating income. For this reporting period, breakeven was $47,423,000 (fixed costs of $17,096,000 divided by contribution margin percent, 36.05%).

As noted, Company A was a subsidiary of a large corporation, two recursions from corporate. For three years the company had reported significant losses, with no improvement from traditional cost reduction/ profit improvement programs. Then the management group used the VSM structure and management principles, and the concepts and the measures of management economics and key performance areas. They prepared management economics operating income statements. They prepared the income model for each accounting period. They began monitoring trends and changes in the key measures: sales revenue, fixed costs, contribution margin percent, breakeven, and operating income.

They assessed their options for improving operating income:

· Reduce fixed costs
· Increase sales revenue
· Increase average contribution margin percent

They determined that for their business the best way to become profitable and achieve profit objectives would be to find ways to increase average contribution margin percent, increase sales revenue through more targeted sales methods, and improve manufacturing plant productivity. They undertook the five-point initiative described above, using:

- The cost technologies of management economics, from the key performance area, profitability
- The management economics operating income statement and income model, also from the key performance area, profitability
- The marketing and sales technologies from the key performance area, creating and keeping customers
- Better methods for new product development from the key performance area, innovation
- Lean methods for manufacturing from the key performance area, quality and productivity

Within a year's time company A became profitable and achieved operating income goals.

Manufacturing companies have significant variable costs. But there are many service businesses with few or no variable costs. A consulting business will have very high people costs, some capital costs, and fairly high programmed fixed costs, but negligible variable costs. An airline will have high fixed costs—people, capital, and programmed fixed costs—and will also have significant variable costs—fuel and costs incurred for each passenger flight. A doctor's office or clinic will have fixed costs, but negligible variable costs. What would an income model for a service business look like? For a service business with zero variable costs, the customer value created is sales revenue. Figure 11.6 shows an income model for a service business with zero variable costs and fixed costs of $17,096,000, the same as for the manufacturing company.

In Figure 11.6, contribution margin is 100% of sales revenue. So breakeven = fixed costs, and above that point each dollar of sales revenue is a dollar of operating income. Businesses can have a range of contribution margin percent, from 17–20% (a distribution business) to 95–100% (a service business).

Whatever the business, operating income depends on the management of each of the key variables—sales revenue, variable costs, and

Millions of Dollars

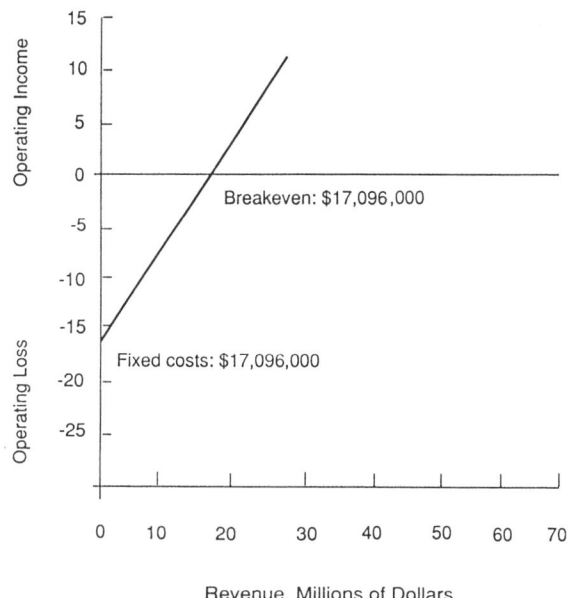

Revenue, Millions of Dollars

Figure 11.6   Operating income model, service business, zero variable costs

fixed costs. Management economics gives us the information we need to keep on course for achieving operating income goals, and when there are problems, to identify where change is needed in the key performance areas.

In the key performance area of profitability, management economics provides measures of the variables that matter—sales revenue, contribution margin, variable costs, and fixed costs. Improvement will require actions and performance in the other key performance areas: creating and keeping customers, quality and productivity, innovation, organization capability, physical and financial resources, and public and environmental responsibility.

In Company A the situation revealed by management economics measures required change and improvement in manufacturing productivity, creating and keeping customers, and innovation. Discovering the new and better ways and making them happen strengthened the organization and improved the performance of the company's physical assets. The management economics key measures for managing and improving operating income:

What to Measure	A Useful Measure
Sales revenue	12-month moving total, with monthly variance from year ago
Contribution margin dollars	12-month moving total, with monthly variance from year ago
Contribution margin percent	3-month moving average
Breakeven	3-month moving average
Total fixed costs:	3-month moving average
People costs	3-month moving average
Capital costs	3-month moving average
Programmed fixed costs	3-month moving average
Operating income	12-month moving total, with monthly variance from year ago

For examples of these measures see Chapter 5, Budgeting. The measures listed are easy to prepare, easy to understand, and very useful in helping to decide on appropriate actions. The important point is that we don't measure variances from a monthly budget and analyze the variances. The conventional budget is an algorithm, a specification of the future that we know will be different from whatever will be the reality. Life is not an algorithm. Life is an heuristic. We find our way, hour by hour, day by day, week by week. Wise companies budget continuously (see Chapter 5) and continuously measure and monitor trends toward desired annual and longer-term goals. Business can not be understood in a "snapshot" report for an accounting period. Business is a moving picture toward where the business is going. The measures listed above show us where we are going. The appropriate actions in the key performance areas help us get there.

Fixed costs and other measures that don't vary seasonally can be measured monthly, or, better, to smooth the numbers a bit, by 3-month moving averages. When there is seasonal variation it's necessary to use a 12-month moving total. Each month, the figure is for the 12-month period ending that month. In charting the numbers to show trend, it's best to plot at the midpoint. The 12 months from January 1 to December 31 are plotted at June 30. The 12 months ending August 31 are plotted at the end of February. 3-month moving averages are plotted at the middle month.

The word, "purposeful," is in the systems definition of a business—a viable, very complex, purposeful, probabilistic system. Purpose includes profitability, net income of $XX this year; $XXX in five years. Continuous budgeting and planning will use these numbers until there's a reason, at any time, to make a change. Purpose will also include objectives for the other measures in the income model—sales revenue, fixed costs, and contribution margin percent. Using management economies, for each of these, companies measure each month the trend toward budget and long-term objectives; not variances from a monthly budget.

We can use the operating income statement and the measures listed above to maintain and improve the operating income of a profit-center business. Like the people in Company A, we can find in the management economics income model and the management economics measures the leverages in the current situation, and decide on actions needed to improve operating income.

For improving operating income there are three opportunities:

1. Increase sales revenue
2. Reduce fixed costs
3. Increase the average contribution margin percent by:
   Reducing variable costs
   Increasing some prices
   Improving mix, by:
   > Working to increase sales revenue on higher contribution margin transactions
   > Finding ways to improve low contribution margin products and transactions
   > Developing new products with higher contribution margin percent

When the operating income of a profit-center business has declined, the decline resulted from some combination of:

Sales revenue decrease
Fixed cost increase
Contribution margin percent decrease caused by:
> Lower prices
> Variable cost increases
> Poorer mix

Dialog on all the income model measures can develop successful approaches for improving operating income. There's much more to profit improvement than cost reduction. In 18 businesses undertaking profit improvement projects using management economics principles and measures:

- Ten operating near breakeven or losing money became profitable.
- Eight with low profitability improved to satisfactory levels.
- In only 2 of the 18 businesses was cost reduction a major part of the profit improvement project.

For most businesses, profitability can be improved much more and much faster by creating value than by cutting costs.

The procedure followed by Company A, Figure 11.4 and 11.5, is typical:

1. Learn, prepare, and dialog the management economics measures.
2. Find the leverages.
3. Set targets.
4. Use best management practices in the key performance areas where change is needed.

Management economics can help us maintain and improve operating income. Management economics can also help us estimate the probable consequences from a company action, or the consequences from an impact from any of the environments in the VSM model. We put the changes on the income model, and estimate the consequences on all the variables. The process enables us to set measurable goals for decisions, monitor progress toward those goals, and take any appropriate corrective actions along the way.

When the management group of a profit-center business uses management economics, an operating income statement and an income model will be prepared at the close of each accounting period. Trends will be updated on the key measures—sales revenue, contribution margin dollars and percent, fixed costs, and breakeven. There will also be trends toward objectives in the key measures of performance in the other key performance areas discussed in Chapters 6 to 10. Group dialog will develop understanding of the current state, and how the business is progressing toward its goals. The group will agree on and support needed actions. Continuous monitoring. Continuously modifying plans and actions. Always aiming for the achievement of plan objectives, and changing these objectives when appropriate. That's the idea of continuous planning and budgeting.

In dialoging alternative actions it's important to keep in mind that each variable in the income model is connected with all the others. Changes in one will affect others, too. Everything relates to and affects everything else. The income model can help us understand these relationships and the consequences of a change. An increase in price increases contribution margin, but can also affect sales volume. An investment in facilities, a fixed cost, may support increased sales and contribution margin dollars. The income model and its measures give us a way of estimating the effect of changes on operating income.

Another Version of the Income Model

A manufacturing company in Brazil, a subsidiary of a US corporation, used the income model and the methods described above to improve profitability. In VSM terms, this company was three recursions from the corporate VSM. While the company was not using the VSM at that time, in their profit improvement program they used some of the VSM principles, and the idea of the seven key performance areas, with profitability one of the seven.

The company produced five product lines sold into seven market areas. Two product lines were each sold into a single market, one product line was sold into three markets, and two product lines were sold into five markets. The company was marginally profitable, and needed to improve profitability.

The company management group began their improvement process with an audit of product lines and markets served. For each product line in each market served they looked at: (1) sales revenue, (2) contribution margin, (3) market growth rate, and (4) the company's position in relation to competitors, which ranged from high (number 1 of 5, number 2 of 15) to low (number 3 of 3). They prepared a management economics income statement, and income model. From this information, company people gained an understanding of the relationships among sales revenue, contribution margin, fixed costs, and operating income. Understanding these relationships they quickly found opportunities for: (1) improving contribution margin percents for some products, (2) developing new, high contribution margin products, and (3) increasing sales revenue.

As work progressed, the company decided to manage its businesses by markets served instead of by product lines. In VSM terms this would mean, Recursion 0, the company; recursion 1, markets; recursion 2, product lines; recursion 3, plants.

The company strategy for improving profitability became:

- Improve average contribution margin through improvement in mix, improving the contribution margins in some individual products, and now, with information on contribution margins, better management of sales transactions
- Increase sales revenue through concentration on high-opportunity markets and products
- Develop new, high contribution margin products for identified market opportunities

Many company people were involved in the improvement process. Progress was monitored by monthly income statements and income models as described above. Figure 11.7 illustrates an abbreviated form of the company's management economics income statement for the first year of the improvement program, and the second year.

The improvement program did improve profitability; more importantly the program gradually changed to "the way we do things around here." In year 2, sales revenue was up $9.2 million, contribution margin was up a little more than three percentage points, and operating income was up 179%. An increase in contribution margin percent of three percentage points was a significant achievement, and a major part of the profit improvement.

Later, the managing director of the company, Gabriel Hevesi, developed an alternative form for the income model. Figure 11.8 shows this

	Year 1	Year 2
Sales Revenue (S)	$ 83,880,000	$ 93,096,000
Variable Costs (VC)	53,096,000	55,951,000
Contribution Margin $ (CM$)	30,783,000	37,145,000
Contribution Margin % (CM%)	36.7%	39.9%
Fixed Costs (FC)	29,304,000	33,012,000
Breakeven (BE)	79,847,000	82,737,000
Sales Revenue Above BE	4,033,000	10,359,000
Operating Income	1,480,000	4,133,000

Figure 11.7   Two-year management economics operating income statement, manufacturing company, Brazil

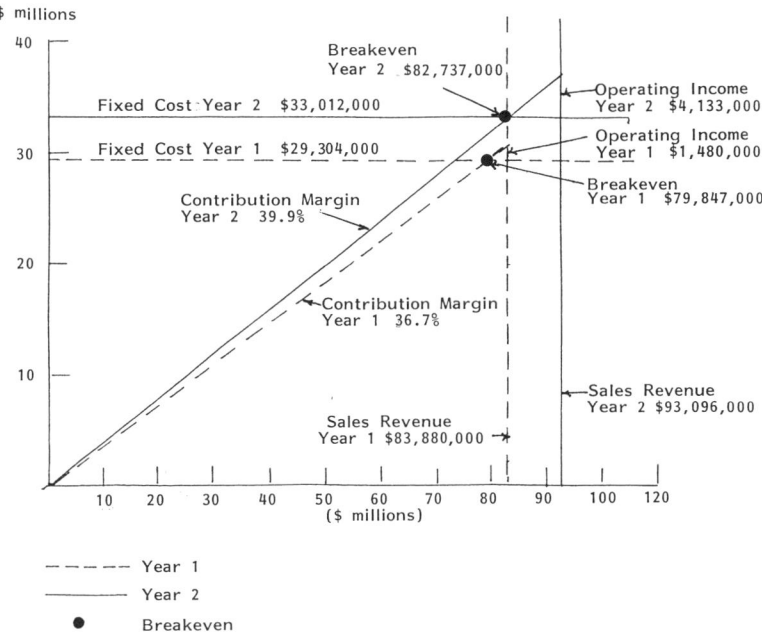

Figure 11.8 Two-year management economics operating income model alternate format, manufacturing company, Brazil

alternative form of the income model for the income statements shown in Figure 11.7. Figure 11.8 clearly shows that when contribution margin brings in enough cash to pay fixed costs, the company has reached the breakeven point where it begins to generate operating income. This chart shows both year 1 and year 2, visualizing the changes. Operating income is up due to increased sales revenue and a significant increase in contribution margin percent. The profit improvement would have been even better if the company had done better in control of fixed costs. With increases in sales revenue and income, fixed costs tend to increase because cash is available, and there are always perceived needs. Well-managed, a manufacturing company can typically support a sales increase of some 20% with little or no increase in fixed costs.

Using the income model it is easy to calculate the effects of changes in sales revenue, contribution margin, and fixed costs on operating income. In Figure 11.8, in year 2 if fixed costs had been the same as in year 1, breakeven would have been $73,445,000; sales over breakeven, $19,651,000; and operating income, $7,841,000. Similarly we can easily see the consequences of any changes in sales revenue, fixed costs, and average contribution margin percent. Monitoring these measures identifies developing problems. And monitoring these measures, especially the measures of product, customer, and market sales, may signal developing opportunity.

In service businesses revenue increases typically do require increases in fixed costs. In both manufacturing and services, monitoring fixed costs (3-month moving average) and controlling these costs in relation to sales revenue (12-month moving total) and contribution margin percent (3-month moving average) results in much better control of fixed costs. Total fixed costs are not totaled in financial reporting; they remain hidden in numerous account numbers in many parts of the organization, and poorly controlled. Management economics makes information on fixed costs an important input for management decisions.

Optimizing Concepts

For almost all businesses, the optimizing concept to work with is contribution margin and the relationships of contribution margin to fixed costs and sales volume. That's the concept advocated in this book. But there are two situations that bring up additional considerations:

1. Limited capacity. If production is constrained by process equipment, such as a reactor that is used to produce several products, contribution margin dollars per hour optimizes operating income. In the case of the reactor, the products producing the most contribution margin dollars per hour of reactor time contribute the most to operating income. However, the purpose of the company is to create and keep customers, so the first consideration has to be to produce the products needed by customers. So the real business problem is to eliminate the constraint. But there may be instances where contribution margin dollars per hour will be a consideration.

2. Limited raw material. If production is constrained by limited availability of a raw material used for producing several products, operating income will be optimized by producing products with the most contribution margin dollars per ton or unit of the material. Again, the first consideration is the production of products needed to create and maintain customers. Still, there may be occasions where dollars per unit of raw material will be a consideration.

Understanding the Income Model

When a management group first prepares a management economics operating income statement, and an income model of the business, they begin to understand the relationships among fixed costs, contribution margin, breakeven, sales revenue, and operating income. If operating income is not satisfactory they can consider possible changes that would produce the desired income. Increasing average contribution margin percent is a good place to start.

All involved need to understand the economics of each product and each transaction. Product economics are much simpler and much more real than the full-cost product costs calculated by cost accounting methods. Accounting is concerned with financial and tax reporting according to prescribed accounting rules. Here we are concerned with managing operations to achieve desired operating income. And for this purpose what we need is five easy-to-understand numbers for each product: (1) sales revenue, (2) sales price, (3) variable cost, (4) contribution margin dollars, and (5) contribution margin percent.

All of this information is in, or can be calculated from, the chart of accounts and supporting data. Figure 11.9 illustrates a product audit format. Figure 11.9 is a repeat of Figure 6.3. For more information, refer to Chapter 6. This kind of a product audit will produce surprises. A big surprise will be the range of contribution margin percents. It's not unusual to find a product where the contribution margin is less than zero—it's selling price less than its variable costs. A typical range of product contribution margin percents might be from about 10% to about 80%. Look at the products with high dollar sales. What is the contribution margin percent? For products with low contribution margin percents, how can contribution margin percent be increased? Where are there opportunities for increasing sales of high contribution margin percent products? Sales people, marketing people, and others knowing customers and markets can find the leverages. Product engineers, product managers, value engineers, and purchasing people can find opportunities for reducing variable costs. Working with the sales revenue and contribution margin information from the product line audit, a team of those involved will find opportunities for improvement.

Company A described earlier in this chapter experienced three years of losses and no improvement from conventional cost reduction programs. Then top management and others involved opened their minds to management economics, to new and different best practices

		Sales (add 000)						
Prepared by _____		Units	$	CM$	CM%	AV SP/Unit	Current SP/Unit	Action
Date _____								
Period:_____		___	___	___	___	___	___	___
Product Line _____								
Market Growth Rate (1) _____								
Competitive Position (2) _____								
P1:		___	___	___	___	___	___	_____
P2:		___	___	___	___	___	___	_____
P3:		___	___	___	___	___	___	_____
P4:		___	___	___	___	___	___	_____
P5:		___	___	___	___	___	___	_____
P6:		___	___	___	___	___	___	_____
P7:		___	___	___	___	___	___	_____
P8:		___	___	___	___	___	___	_____
P9:		___	___	___	___	___	___	_____
P10:		___	___	___	___	___	___	_____
P11:		___	___	___	___	___	___	_____
P12:		___	___	___	___	___	___	_____
P13:		___	___	___	___	___	___	_____
P14:		___	___	___	___	___	___	_____

(1) Indicate: High–growth over 8% per year   Low–growth less than 3% per year
                Medium–growth of 3% to 8% per year   Neg. –negative growth rate
     Note: all growth rates are in real terms–units or deflated dollars.
(2) Indicate Company position among all competitors.   Example: 2/10 = Company is number
     2 of 10 competitors in sales volume for this product line.
Key: CM - Contribution Margin
         SP - Selling Price

Figure 11.9   Product line audit

in creating and keeping customers, and best practices in improving manufacturing productivity. They audited their product lines for revenue and contribution margin information, and took appropriate actions. Average contribution margin increased from 36.05% to 43% and the business became profitable. Working with contribution margin information, and understanding the variables in the company income model, the people involved found ways to improve operating income.

The experience of Company A relates to the VSM and system thinking. The company and the corporation had not been using the VSM. But whether they knew it or not, their company works the way the VSM says all systems work, including the viable, very complex, purposeful, probabilistic system that is Company A. The solution to the company's profit problem applied the management principles of the VSM and system thinking:

1. The manufacturing company was two recursions away from the corporate VSM.
2. The profit problem could not be solved by executive action from corporate headquarters. Any executive from the higher level lacks requisite variety. Sending in cost accountants and ordering cost reduction programs did not work.
3. To higher-level executives, the manufacturing company is a black box.
4. The problem has to be resolved by many people in the manufacturing company. They could deploy requisite variety.
5. Every system has heterostats for change and improvement.
6. People in sales, product engineering, accounting, and manufacturing—working in the system function—became heterostats, seeking new and better methods, and applying these better methods to change and improve:

   Sales operations (key performance area 1, creating and keeping customers)

   New product development (key performance area 3, innovation)

   Manufacturing (key performance area 2, quality and productivity)

   Cost and contribution margin management (key performance area 7, profitability)

Actions in four key performance areas changed losses into profit, and also strengthed key performance area 5, organization capability.

Leverage

Some businesses are typically low contribution margin rate businesses; a distributor, for example. Some business are typically high contribution margin rate businesses; cosmetics or consumer luxury products, many service businesses, for example. Both can be profitable—or unprofitable—depending on the other variables in the income model. In low contribution margin rate businesses, businesses with 15% to 25% contribution margins, one leverage for improving operating income is cost reduction, especially productivity improvement that reduces fixed costs. In high contribution margin businesses, businesses with over 50% contribution margin rate, the greater leverage for improving operating income is increasing sales volume, and additional cost can be profitably incurred to achieve higher sales volume. For both low and high contribution margin rate businesses product line audits, and actions to improve the low ones and increase sales of the high ones, will improve the average contribution margin rate. In all businesses, creating value (additional contribution margin) is usually the fastest track to profit improvement.

The following are some ways to improve operating income in a low contribution margin rate business:

- Quality and productivity initiatives that reduce waste and get more work done with less use of resources (fixed costs)
- Use best practices in creating and keeping customers (see Chapter 6)
- Control inventory closely; aim for just-in-time (JIT)
- Challenge all fixed costs to find opportunities for reductions
- Tighten credit terms, and other sales terms
- Find ways to reduce cost of purchased items
- Find ways to reduce the length of time purchased items are owned by the company
- Investigate small order premiums, large order incentives
- Reduce freight in, cost of deliveries to customers, handling costs
- Reduce scrap, waste, rework
- Improve mix

The following are some ways to improve operating income in a high contribution margin rate business:

- Add salespeople
- Find additional ways to create customer value
- Use best practices in creating and keeping customers (see Chapter 6)
- Increase advertising and promotion
- Offer sales contests and incentives
- Offer consumer incentives
- Develop and introduce new, high contribution margin products
- Expand into additional geographic areas
- Expand into new markets
- Increase service and other areas of non-price competition
- Improve mix

Managers in most companies, in their profit improvement programs, act as if their company is a low contribution margin rate business. They seek cost reduction, and often take actions that limit opportunity for profit improvement. They assume that $XX cost reduction = $XX profit increase. That never happens. Cost reduction for profit improvement seldom succeeds, except when the income model says it will. The variables in the income model determine what happens. Understanding the income model, the trends of the variables, and the interrelationships among the variables will give those involved—but not higher level managers who lack requisite variety—the information they need to make wise decisions on profit improvement. Only those involved really understand the interrelationships, and know the important details that make up the numbers.

When decision-makers understand the management economics income model, they will find uses for it even when they don't have the numbers. Without the numbers they can estimate the probable consequences, plus or minus, from a proposed action. For example, sales people can use ideas from the income model in sales proposals to business and industrial customers. Every sales transaction has an effect on the customer's income model, as well as on the company's income model. While sales people don't know the customer's income model numbers, they have a general idea whether the customer operates with a high contribution margin rate, or low. They can then frame their proposal on how it will favorably affect the customer's income model. Everyone understands the relationships in the model whether or not they have ever seen these relationships in the form of an income model. So, using words, but not the actual model, the salesperson can present the beneficial effects of the offer, and then work with the customer to assure that these beneficial effects happen.

In our own company operations, where we do have the numbers, the income model is especially useful. For any project or initiative, we can put the initiative or project on the model, and using the best judgment of those involved, see what happens. The model gives us a method for appraising the consequences of any new undertaking. More that that, for initiatives that are agreed on, the model can be used for setting the objectives to be achieved. Measures can then be selected for monitoring progress toward the objectives.

A company, for example, might consider a significant expansion of its sales force to increase sales. They put the added fixed costs on the income model. Breakeven goes up, operating income goes down. They set targets for sales revenue and average contribution margin percent, targets that will achieve desired operating income. Fixed costs, contribution margins, and sales revenue can then be monitored, tracking progress toward the objective and taking any actions needed to reach the objective, or more. A major change of this kind will involve many considerations—recruitment, sales training, new product programs, production capacity, goals, performance measures, and more. Whatever the elements, agreement on the changes in the income model can set the goals for success, and the performance measures can then help achieve that success.

The management economics income model is useful in all areas of business operations, and in relations with customers and vendors. Knowing the numbers and understanding the variables will help company people at all levels make decisions and take actions benefiting the company.

In addition to income model information, the appropriate environmental and competitive information must be considered in the decision process. As discussed in Chapter 2, the VSM has communications links with what matters in all the company's environments: commercial, technical, economic, social, political, educational, and ecological. By the assigned responsibilities for monitoring these environments, the relevant information is provided where and when needed.

Monitoring the environments to detect what needs to be known is an important and very large subject area. The responsible functions in the VSM at all levels of recursion first identify what in all the great variety in each of the environments really matters to the achievement of the business unit's purpose. This first step makes a huge attenuation of variety. What matters in the environment is then monitored to detect what the decision-makers in the business need to know. This process attenuates the complexity in each of the environments, and amplifies the voice of management through the involvement of many people at all levels of recursion. With decisions made where the work is done, requisite variety can be achieved.

Adjusting for Inflation/Deflation

Management economics measures will calculate profitability lower than the accounting measures for two reasons: (1) management economics uses methods that result in higher costs of capital, and (2) management economics uses replenishment costs instead of either FIFO or LIFO. When there is even low inflation, profit figures and profit improvement will be overstated in the accounting record because of the effects of inflation. A management economics statement will be closer to reality.

In the United States, during the high-inflation rates in the 1970s, the effect of inflation on reported profit became an issue. Large companies were required to supply information in their annual reports on their profit figures adjusted for inflation. But with options in the methods for making these adjustments, companies tended to underreport the real effects.

In 1972 the manager of corporate planning in a manufacturing company became very concerned about the effects of inflation on his company's income statement. The company was in the midst of a profit improvement program, and was pleased that the current statement showed an increase in net income to $3.6 million. The planning manager talked with the VP, Finance, about adjusting the income statement to show the effects of inflation. The VP talked to his people and the collective judgment was that there would be too much work involved in making the adjustments, and the result would not be worth the effort. Doing the work as accountants would do it could be a lot of work for a group already struggling to meet deadlines. So the planner decided to make the adjustments himself. Instead of accounting detail, he used relevant price and cost indexes, and came up with an approximate income statement pretty much along the lines of management economics. Instead of an increase in net income, the inflation adjusted statement showed a decrease to a small loss. Top management preferred the accounting report, and took no interest in inflation adjustment.

To correct the accounting income statement for the effects of inflation (or deflation) important adjustments include:

1. Depreciation. Use straight-line depreciation of the current value of assets employed rather than the historical cost of only the assets still on the books. An appropriate concept of present value would be the present cost of an equivalent asset. A more practical method would be the historical cost of the asset adjusted by an appropriate cost index, including an allowance for productivity improvement. At time of replacement, the new asset will be different and better than the original. For success over time it is important to think about depreciation in real terms. The long-term consequences of under-reporting depreciation is the gradual liquidation of the company's capital resources.
2. Variable costs. Use replenishment costs rather than FIFO or LIFO or any other historical cost.

The principles of management economics, including the two mentioned above, adjust for inflation on a continuing basis.

Using the Income Model

From the income model for the business, management can develop a desirable level of fixed costs. Management can also set an objective for the needed average contribution margin percent to achieve targeted operating income at the projected level of sales revenue. Objectives for sales revenue, contribution margin, fixed costs, and operating income are important parts of the continuous budgeting and performance measures described in Chapter 5.

Looking for ways to improve operating income, those involved examine contribution margins (% and $) by product, by customer, and by transaction to identify which contribution margins are above the desired average rate, and which are below, and current trends. With this information, they can then work on ways for change and improvement: (1) sales plans and actions to increase the higher contribution margin transactions, (2) engineering and purchasing plans and actions to improve the contribution margin of low contribution margin products, by reducing variable costs, and (3) sales evaluation of where prices on low contribution margin products can be increased.

Variable costs can be reduced by reformulation or redesign of the product, by negotiating lower purchase prices, or in some cases by product substitution. Product substitution works when the customer can be offered a higher contribution margin product that the customer sees as a greater value. Figure 11.10 summarizes the variables in the income model that determine what the operating income will be.

The measures listed in the discussion of Figures 11.5 monitor each of the variables, and signal when all is on track toward goals, or when change is needed or desirable. The changes:

Sales revenue. Up increases operating income; down reduces

Fixed costs. Up reduces operating income; down improves

Average contribution margin rate. Up improves operating income; down reduces

Breakeven. Up reduces operating income; down improves

Sales revenue can be increased by the methods described in Chapter 6. Fixed costs can be managed by the continuous budgeting described in Chapter 5. In budgeting, however done, in addition to the line items

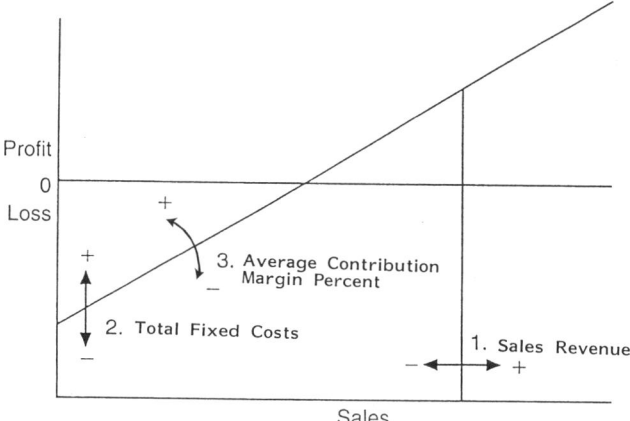

Figure 11.10 Income model variables

in the chart of accounts, it's important to budget also, and monitor the totals for:

· People Costs
· Capital Costs
· Programmed Fixed Costs
· Total Fixed costs

All fixed costs fit into these categories. None should be allocated. Allocation loses control and imposes meaningless burdens on the receivers of the allocations. It is a top management responsibility to establish the fixed costs needed for the business. These costs can only be controlled where and when they are incurred. People costs, capital costs, programmed fixed costs, and total fixed costs will be information unknown in most companies today. Monitoring the totals for each of the three categories and for total fixed costs in comparison with contribution margin signals when fixed costs are appropriately controlled, and when change may be needed, or desirable.

Contribution margin can be managed by product audits and by continuously evaluating the 3-month moving average of contribution margin percent. Increasing the average contribution margin percent is one of the most important leverages for improving operating income. Monitoring this measure will indicate "operations normal" or when change is needed.

Breakeven is arithmetic, fixed costs divided by contribution margin percent. Breakeven is managed by how we manage fixed costs and average contribution margin percent.

In any business the work of many people affects these variables. All need the measures in the management economics operating income statement and the income model, and the trend of these measures toward business goals. And all need to be involved in the plans and actions to keep the trends on track toward the goals. The plans and actions will be the changes needed in the key performance areas to achieve objectives in those areas, and the objectives also for operating income.

In terms of the VSM and system thinking, the measures described above, and what people do with them, are part of the system 3/system 4 homeostat that keeps the system operating toward its goals. These measures and what people do with them can also be part of the system 4 heterostat that creates the company's future by developing new and different products and services that offer new or greater customer values.

SOME THOUGHTS ON INCOME STATEMENTS

A system is what it does. A company is a viable, very complex, purposeful, probabilistic system. The company is what it does. What the company does is create and keep customers. The company develops, produces, and sells products and services to create and keep customers. So the principle financial measure for company performance is operating income. Operating income is what the company earns from what it does. Operating income is the source of profitability.

Operating Income by Management Economics Accounts

In the corporate VSM and in the VSMs at all levels of recursion, there is a top management comprised of system 5, system 4, system 3, and system 2. None of these are part of operations. Nor are they overhead. Their fixed costs pay for functions needed to achieve the purpose of the business. Their fixed costs are essential costs, incurred and controlled by the top managements at all levels of recursion. In management economics none of these costs are allocated to operations.

At the corporate level and at all levels of recursion, the first step in control of fixed costs is the budget for total fixed costs and each of the three kinds of fixed costs, people costs, capital costs, and pro-grammed fixed costs. A continuous budget, as proposed in Chapter 5, is the most effective budget. Then trend measures of the income model variables will enable effective control, with changes made as appropriate.

Total corporate operating income will be the totals from the operat-ing income statements of the business units at the first level of recursion from the corporate VSM. These are the major businesses, or business groups, of the corporation. These businesses or business groups in their operating income statements include the operating results from all company operations. So the corporate operating income statement simply consolidates these recursion 1 operating income statements, in the same format. To provide the most useful information for manage-ment, these operating income statements will be prepared using man-agement economics measures, as described in this book.

Income statements in management economics terms, income models, and trend measures of the key performance measures provide manage-ment direction throughout the corporation, all coordinated toward the achievement of company purpose. Corporate system 3 will want to review the income statements, income models, and trend charts with business and business group top managements in each of the first recursion businesses. They provide information that is helpful in dis-cussing the state of each of their businesses, and plans ahead. Similarly, system 3 in each of these first recursion businesses or business groups will want to review the income statement, income model, and trend measures with the top management of each of the business units in the next level of recursion. And so on, through all levels of recursion in the corporation.

For each of the first recursion businesses or business groups there can be an addition at the end of the operations income statement listing the fixed costs for systems 2, 3, 4, and 5, the top management functions of the business group. These fixed costs are a part of producing the operating income of the business group. The report format could be along the lines of:

Income from operations		XX
Group fixed costs		X
People costs	X	X
Capital costs	X	X
Programmed fixed costs	X	X
Group operating income		XX

The corporate operating income statement will be the total of the recursion 1 group or business operating income statements. The final item on the corporate operating income statement will be a listing of all corporate fixed costs, in a format like the above.

A Useful Addition?

Appropriate procedures can be specified in corporate parameters for management economics measures. Management economics measures are used in managing operations. Accounting measures are used for financial reporting. Both use the chart of accounts. But they use the chart of accounts differently.

Measuring operating income in terms of management economics is not proposed as a change in accounting and financial reporting. Accounting and financial reporting will be done as required by FASB. Management economics serves a different purpose. Using management economics, operating income statements, income models, and trend measures of the key variables become a part of the company's "management information system." They help decision-makers throughout the company make wise decisions.

Operations people throughout the company make many decisions daily using the information available, including management economics measures. Major decisions are best made through dialog among those involved, using all the information available, importantly including the management economics measures. In each operating unit, top management can dialog on the implications of the monthly management economics operating income statement, income model, and trend measures for any appropriate actions that may be needed.

The management economics operating income statement, income model, and trend charts of the key measures are simple to prepare from data in the company's chart of accounts. Unlike financial accounting, precision—the exact, right numbers—are not a requirement. Management economics needs only numbers approximate enough to provide reliable measures of the economic state of the firm, and the key trends. Someone knowledgeable in management economics, working with an accountant, in one afternoon can prepare an operating income statement and income model for the most recent accounting period. And management will have information unknown before.

Preparing financial statements is a function of system 3, where there are all the functions for the here and now, including the here and now functions of finance and accounting. System 3 can also be the center for preparing management economics measures. The management economics operating income statement and income model we have been discussing give us information and understanding on the primary source of company profit—operating income. The management economics operating income statement is most useful at the level of the individual profit center business.

Operating income is what the corporation earned from what it does—create and keep customers by producing, delivering, and servicing products that satisfy customer expectations. All fixed costs are included in the calculation of operating income. But there are additional transactions that need to be accounted for. The corporate income statement could be made up of the corporate operating income statement as described above. Then, in addition, these other transactions could be reported in a second part of a corporate income statement.

Each of these other transactions adds to or subtracts from profit. A management economics income statement could add these additional elements to the operations income statement, as illustrated in Figure 11.11.

To be successful, a company needs to earn the operating income needed to achieve desired company profitability. The operating income statement reports that measure of success. But companies can not manage operating income. Companies manage the key performance areas using best practices that can produce the desired operating income.

Company success in what the company does is measured by the operating income statement. To arrive at a profit figure for the company, operating income is adjusted by the plusses and minuses from the company's financial transactions. Figure 11.11 illustrates one way for including these transactions.

MANAGEMENT ECONOMICS INCOME STATEMENT

The first part of the company's management economics income statement presents the operating income statement described in this chapter. For the corporation, this would be the totals from the recursion 1 operating income statements. The next part of the corporate statement would be the listing of corporate costs. These costs could be listed by functions, as in Figure 11.11. Or they could be listed by the three classifications of fixed costs: people costs, capital costs, and programmed

Management Economics Income Statement
(add 000)

Sales Revenue (S)		$XXX,XXX
Variable Costs (VC)		XX,XXX
Contribution Margin $ (CM$)		XX,XXX
Contribution Margin % (CM%)		XX%
Fixed Costs (FC)		XX,XXX
People Costs	$ X,XXX	
Capital Costs	XXX	
Programmed Fixed Costs	XXX	
Breakeven (BE)		XX,XXX
Sales Revenue Above (Below) BE		XXX
Operating Income from Operations		**XX**
Corporate Costs		X
Corporate Headquarters	X	
Research & Development	X	
(List any other major groups)	X	
Corporate Operating Income		**XX**
Financial Transactions + or −:	$	**XX**
List, including such items as:		
Revaluation of Assets		X
Changes in Reserves		X
Pension Funding		X
Interest Paid		X
Interest Received		X
Restructuring Costs		XX
M & A		XX
Divestitures		XX
Etc.		
Income Before Income Tax		**XX**
Income Tax		X
Net Income	$	**XX**

Figure 11.11   Management Economics Income Statement

fixed costs. At the corporate level listing by functions is probably best. These corporate costs subtracted from operating income produces an operating income figure for the total corporation.

Then comes everything else: all the financial transactions affecting profitability like those listed in Figure 11.11. This management economics income statement includes in the statement everything the company does that results in the net income earned by the company. The figures will be different from the financial reports because of the management economics differences in cost calculations, especially the capital costs. But as discussed earlier, at the level of the profit-center business, the management economics operating income statement and income model provide different and much more useful management information.

Aggregations at the group and corporate levels loses usefulness for operations, but offers a higher-level usefulness. It shows what the group and what the corporation earned from what it does. A system **is** what it **does**. What the corporate system does is create and keep customers. A company must earn enough from what it does so that after all the other plusses and minuses, it earns desired profitability. A statement like Figure 11.11 shows the total picture—what the corporation earns from what it does, and all the plusses and minuses.

A statement along the lines of Figure 11.11 is not a financial statement. It is in no way related to financial reporting. Like all management economics measures, it is designed to provide information useful to company decision-makers. For business operations, the management economics income model helps decision-makers improve operating performance. A statement like Figure 11.11, along with monitoring change in the key measures, might be useful to corporate top management (recursion 0), for corporate decisions.

With all the post-Enron accounting scandals, many ideas have been presented for improving the company income statement. Standard & Poor's Core Earnings statement is a helpful example. The income statement shown in Figure 11.11 is a different kind of improvement, and for a different audience and a different purpose. It is not a statement for shareholders. It's a statement summarizing information for management. Its purpose is to help all decision-makers act in ways to keep the company on track toward its goals. It comes more from economics than from accounting. A management economics income statement presents, in one summary, all that matters in the economic success of the business. And economics success/failure = financial success/failure.

Management economics helps decision-makers improve operating income. Management economics can also produce a useful company income statement. In management economics there is no incentive to "make the numbers." In management economics the incentive is to understand current performance and to evaluate the probable consequences of proposed actions.

An important word of caution. As this book points out, recursions are black boxes to corporate management. Higher level management lacks requisite variety to deal with problems inside the black boxes. Those problems can only be handled successfully within the black boxes, coordinating with the next higher level system 3. Corporate system 5, executive leadership, has a major responsibility—defining the company and the company purpose, designing the structure needed to achieve that purpose, and making changes as appropriate in the structure needed to achieve that purpose. System science and the VSM is a useful model. With that job well done, the system's self-organizing and self-control capabilities will conduct operations to achieve company purpose. At the level of the corporate system 5, a corporate income statement in management economics terms is useful only as an aid for decisions on definition, purpose, and design of the total company system, and the management of corporate costs and financial transactions.

In addition to defining the company and company purpose, and designing the structure, the corporate system 5 also has the responsibility for controlling corporate fixed costs, but only the corporate fixed costs. Executive management can't control fixed costs within the black boxes, or any other aspect of those operations. They can arbitrarily cut the fixed costs and order other changes. They have the authority. But they lack requisite variety, and their intervention most likely will make matters worse.

SOME MANAGEMENT ECONOMICS EXAMPLES

Using management economics, understanding product and transaction costs and contribution margins, setting objectives for the key measures in the income model, and monitoring the measures toward those objectives can create remarkable achievement:

1. A specialty plastics start-up business determined actions needed, and achieved sales and income objectives for the start-up period.
2. Putting together two specialty products companies resulted in loss of market share and below breakeven performance. Using the management economics operating income statement and income model, the management group found the leverages for improvement, and using some of the best practices discussed in this book controlled fixed costs, improved contribution margins and mix, increased sales revenue, and achieved income goals.

3. A manufacturing company controlled fixed costs, found mix opportunities, and improved profitability.
4. A chemical manufacturer changed pricing strategy, increased margins, maintained market share, and improved profitability.
5. A manufacturer of plating equipment and chemicals established clear definitions (Resource Bargains) for its system 1 businesses. Using ideas discovered in the management economics operating income statement and income model, the businesses and the company controlled fixed costs, increased sales revenue by using best practices in creating and keeping customers, and improved profitability.
6. Using management economics information, a division general manager, on the tenth day of the month, was able to forecast reliably what the revenue and operating income would be for the month.
7. A machinery manufacturer in Spain identified changes needed in procurement that changed losses into profits, with no increase in sales revenue.
8. The management team in an equipment manufacturer in England made pricing decisions that ended losses and made the company profitable.
9. The management team of an Australian company, reviewing their income model, found their biggest leverage for profit improvement was sales revenue. Using best practices in creating and keeping customers they were able to increase sales revenue, and improve profitability.
10. In a specialty materials manufacturing business in Brazil, the management team determined their response to new cut-price competition. With plant productivity improvement, increased marketing expenses, and target account sales programs, the company maintained market share and maintained contribution margins.
11. A machinery and supplies manufacturer and reseller in Argentina operated profitably through a hyper-inflation period.
12. A distributor in France reduced fixed costs and increased profitability.
13. A producer of decorative laminates limited fixed cost increases and improved mix to increase contribution margin from 38% to 44%, improving profitability.

The principles and methods of management economics can help decision-makers improve operating income. The methods are simple, practical, easy to understand and use. At all levels of recursion, management economics gives those doing the work and making the decisions hands-on control of the economic consequences of their decisions and actions, and helps them maximize their contributions to achieving desired company profitability.

OVERVIEW: THE ESSENCE OF CHAPTER 11

Of all the company performance measures, profit measures are number 1 for top management and shareholders. They want to see growing profit, rising stock price. But profit results from good performance in seven key performance areas described in this book—creating and keeping customers, quality and productivity, innovation, physical and financial resources, organization capability, social and environmental responsibility, and profitability. Profitability results from the company's performance in all of these key performance areas. The key performance areas are what we manage to achieve profitability. Management economics gives us measures described in this chapter that help manage these performance areas effectively.

Many top management people assert that creating shareholder value is the company purpose. A theme of this book is that the purpose of a business is to create and keep customers. The purpose of Ford Motor Company in 1908 was to build a car that everyone could buy. And the Model T put America on wheels. In 1998 the purpose of Google, Inc. was to organize the world's information and make it universally accessible and useful. Both created customers. Both created value for shareholders. Both focused on creating value for customers. There are no right and wrong ways to define the purpose of a business enterprise. There are only different ways, some better than others.

Operating income is the source of company profitability. For operating income, and for all financial measures, the standard measures are accounting measures. Management is responsible for financial reporting. But management is also responsible for managing the company. Accounting measures designed for financial reporting are less than satisfactory for managing the company. Different metrics are needed: performance measures for each of the seven key performance areas described in this book. For the key performance area of profitability, the most useful performance measures are economics measures, management economics.

Five principles guide management economics:

1. There is no useful profit figure for a product. The total profit-center business produces profit or loss. Products, services, and transactions incur costs and contribute to profitability, and the measures of management economics monitor these costs and contributions to guide appropriate actions.
2. Costs are managed according to how they behave. Variable costs vary directly with production and are managed by product. Fixed costs change only by management decision and are managed where and when incurred; no allocations.
3. Revenue is managed according to market demand and opportunity.
4. Profitability is managed according to the interacting relationships between costs and revenue.
5. Evaluation of what is important is determined by the company's definition of its purpose.

Accounting practice and conventional budgeting leave fixed costs poorly controlled in many companies. Accounting has many line items in the chart of accounts for fixed costs, with no focus on total fixed costs. In the accounting record, company and profit-center business managers don't see total fixed costs, and the trend of these costs. Managers at budget time typically ask for increases in their fixed cost line item budgets. When money appears to be available, many of these increases go into the budget. Over time fixed costs ratchet upward, unrelated to sales revenue and contribution margin. Management economics measures, monitors, and controls total fixed costs by three major categories: people costs, capital costs, and programmed fixed costs.

Operating income statements prepared using management economics measures, and monitoring the trends of the key measures, give managers very useful information for managing the business. The measures in the management economics income statement can be charted in an income model that helps managers find opportunities for improving operating income. See Figures 11.3, 11.4, and 11.5 and the descriptions of these figures. Useful measures:

Key Measures	How to Measure
Sales revenue	12-month moving total, with monthly variance from year-ago
Contribution margin dollars	12-month moving total, with monthly variance from year-ago
Contribution margin percent	3-month moving average
Breakeven	3-month moving average
Total fixed costs:	3-month moving average
People costs	3-month moving average
Capital costs	3-month moving average
Programmed fixed costs	3-month moving average
Operating income	12-month moving total, with monthly variance from year ago

See chapter 5, Budgeting, for examples of these measures.

Management economics does not construct full costs for individual products. What matters for profit measurement is variable cost and contribution margin. Figure 11.9 offers a method for auditing products to determine these measures.

A management economics operating income statement and income model and their measures helps decision-makers improve operating income. Management economics can also produce a useful company income statement including everything the company does that results in the net income earned by the company (Figure 11.11). In management economics there is no incentive to "make the numbers." In management economics the incentive is to understand the current situation, to take appropriate actions to achieve company goals, and to evaluate the probable consequences of proposed actions.

NOTE

[1] Joel Dean, *Managerial Economics*, Prentice-Hall, New York, 1951.

Index